Reappraisals

Also by Peter Uwe Hohendahl

Building a National Literature: The Case of Germany, 1830–1870
(translated by Renate Baron Franciscono)

The Institution of Criticism

Reappraisals

Shifting Alignments in Postwar Critical Theory

Peter Uwe Hohendahl

Cornell University Press
Ithaca and London

First published 1991 by Cornell University Press.

International Standard Book Number 0-8014-2455-0 (cloth)
International Standard Book Number 0-8014-9706-X (paper)
Library of Congress Catalog Card Number 91-10217

Printed in the United States of America

Librarians: Library of Congress cataloging information appears on the last page of the book.

⊗ The paper in this book meets the minimum requirements of the American National Standard for Information Sciences— Permanence of Paper for Printed Library Materials, ANSI Z39.48-1984.

Contents

Preface

The title of this book calls attention to significant shifts in the debate about and the use of Critical Theory. Since about 1980, not only the parameters but also the character of the discussion have changed. Before that, by and large, the Frankfurt School and Critical Theory were perceived as part of the larger project of Western Marxism—as a revisionist version of the Marxist tradition in which Hegel's dialectic strongly resurfaced, breaking up the scientific orientation of the Second International and the neoorthodoxy of the Third International. While the evaluation of the Frankfurt School ranged from outspoken hostility to emphatic praise, there was a consensus about the locus of the Frankfurt School within the Marxist tradition.

Recently, however, the boundaries of this tradition have become more fluid. The interface and exchange with other traditions have changed our understanding of both Western Marxism and Critical Theory. The essays collected in this volume reflect as well as respond to these shifts. They attempt to reconsider the Frankfurt School from the vantage point of the contemporary debate in Europe and the United States. Although they were originally written under varied circumstances and with different purposes in mind, they share a common theme: the development of Critical Theory, in particular its history after the Second World War.

Preface

More than is usual, I have emphasized the connection with the early Lukács, a link the members of the Frankfurt School never fully acknowledged. Mediated through Lukács's prewar writings, the German romantic tradition, sometimes in its neo-romantic gestalt, left its traces on the Frankfurt School. Of crucial importance for the contemporary debate is the transition from the first to the second generation of Critical Theory, which must not be understood as a mere temporal sequence. Rather, I suggest in these essays that this transition is a complex and intertwined reconfiguration. Sometimes advances occur in the form of a return to older positions, sometimes expected directions change because of confrontations with competing theoretical traditions. For this reason, the essays cannot be organized as a linear historical evolution. Moreover, national theoretical developments rarely coincide. I try to show that the German and the American perspectives vis-à-vis Critical Theory have differed significantly during the last two decades.

With the exception of the Introduction and the final one, the chapters of this book have all appeared in journals and special collections before. An earlier version of Chapter 1 appeared in German in *Geschichtlichkeit und Aktualität*, ed. Klaus-Dieter Müller, Gerhard Pasternack, Wulf Segebrecht, and Ludwig Stockinger (Tübingen: Max Niemeyer Verlag, 1988). Chapter 2 first appeared in *New German Critique* 42 (Fall 1987). Chapter 3 came out in *The German Quarterly* 54 (1981). Chapter 4 is a revised version of an essay that appeared in *New German Critique* 35 (Spring/Summer 1985). An earlier version of Chapter 5 was published in *Telos* 69 (Fall 1986), and a version of Chapter 6 appeared in *Deutsche Literatur in der Bundesrepublik seit 1965, Untersuchungen und Berichte*, ed. Paul Michael Lützeler and Egon Schwarz (Königstein: Athenäum Publishing House, 1980). I am grateful to the editors of the journals and essay collections for the permission to reprint. Excellent draft translations of Chapters 1 and 6 were provided by Karen Kenkel and Brian Urquhart.

viii

In the final preparation of the manuscript I was assisted by Andreas Kriefall and Jeffrey Schneider, whose tireless efforts I greatly appreciate. Finally, I thank Gisela Podleski for typing parts of the manuscript.

PETER UWE HOHENDAHL

Ithaca, New York

Reappraisals

Introduction:
Marx, the Frankfurt School, and West German History

Before 1970 the term "Critical Theory," if used at all in this country, referred to the works of the Frankfurt School, that is, to the writings of Max Horkheimer and Theodor W. Adorno, Herbert Marcuse, and Leo Lowenthal. More recently, the name of Jürgen Habermas has been added to this group, although opinions are divided as to whether his work, especially his more recent theory, can be subsumed under the old term. Yet this uncertainty should be seen as a positive sign, namely as an indication that Critical Theory is alive, responding to new and different cultural and political situations. In Germany the second generation of the Frankfurt School, of which Habermas is the most prominent representative, began to develop its own and different mode of theory after the death of Adorno and the climax of the student revolution in 1969. Although there was less of an obvious turning point than in France—where the defeat of the student revolution in May 1968 also shook the foundations of the Communist party and Marxist theory—in West Germany Critical Theory entered a new phase about 1970, in which ultimately the links to the Marxist paradigm became weaker and the attachment to the Marxian text a question of critical interpretation rather than a matter of faith. Of course, a similar argument can be made for the first generation of the Frankfurt School; at no time can its members be described as orthodox Marxists. Even during the 1930s, when they still used traditional Marxist concepts, they were selective in their application of the Marxist paradigm. Still, they could always reaffirm the element of truth in Marxist theory. Not only does the culture-industry chapter of *Dialectic of Enlightenment* (1947) articulate basic Marxist concepts, but also in Adorno's latest writings, for instance in *Aesthetic Theory*, the presence of Marx is strongly felt. For the next generation this presence is less certain; the revisions are so far-reaching that Marx—as in the writings of Jürgen Habermas—becomes just one theorist among others. Even when a Marxist position is more clearly affirmed, for example in the writings of Oskar Negt and Alexander Kluge, this recuperation does not simply continue an orthodox position; rather, it opens a critical and sometimes polemical dialogue with other strands of Critical Theory.

The American situation is not altogether different.[1] During the 1970s the understanding of Critical Theory was beginning to change, both from within and from the outside. In this country it was of course more the voices of Herbert Marcuse and Leo Lowenthal that dominated the discourse of the 1960s and influenced the New Left. While it would be difficult to give a specific date for this change, both the scope and the emphasis of Critical Theory shifted during the 1970s, but not necessarily in the same direction as in West Germany. On the one hand, partly through the increasing impact of Habermas's work in the English-speaking world, there is an apparent parallel to the West German situation, that is, a reformulation of Critical Theory in terms of linguistic and pragmatic theory;[2] on the other hand, there is also an equally strong attempt to connect the thought of the old Frankfurt School with poststructuralist theory. As Catherine Gallagher observes in a recent essay, the agenda of the New Historicism can be traced back, at least in

1. See Perry Anderson, *In the Tracks of Historical Materialism* (Chicago, 1984).

2. See *Habermas and Modernity*, ed. Richard J. Bernstein (Cambridge, Mass., 1985).

part, to the New Left.[3] Thus it would be plausible to define the New Historicism as a radical revision of revisionist (Marcusian) Marxism. Obviously, in this metamorphosis, the model of the classical Critical Theory is hardly discernible anymore; it has become an atmospheric presence. For this reason the term "Critical Theory" has taken on a broader meaning in this country: it includes the Frankfurt School but also different strands of oppositional theory.

In contrast, the West German usage has been much more restricted, since poststructuralist models have been introduced in opposition to the Frankfurt School. Habermas's critical response to French theory (beginning in 1980) would only be the most obvious case in point. As long as the cohesion of the "school" dominated the German situation, the possibility of an integration of Critical Theory and poststructuralist paradigms was clearly remote. In this respect the American situation has been much more ambiguous: while the debate between Habermasians and poststructuralists has been mostly polemical, with a strong sense of defending one's own ground, the appropriation of Benjamin's and Adorno's work by American critics has been less restricted to a particular camp. Benjamin in particular has been claimed for a variety of agendas ranging from Marxism to deconstruction.[4] As a result, the boundaries of "Critical Theory" have become less clear during the last decade. Moreover, German and American theoretical discourse, in spite of a considerable amount of theoretical exchange, drifted apart during the 1970s and only recently, after the appropriation of poststructuralism in West Germany, can we speak of comparable configurations again.

The broad use of the term "Critical Theory" today reflects a trend toward blending paradigms and models with less regard for traditional boundaries and conceptional logic and more em-

3. Catherine Gallagher, "Marxism and the New Historicism," in *The New Historicism*, ed. H. Aram Veeser (New York, 1988), 37–48.
4. See Michael W. Jennings, *Dialectical Images* (Ithaca, 1987), 1–14.

phasis on the situational aspect of theories, that is, their embed-
dedness in specific cultural practices. Hence the question What
is the meaning and relevance of Critical Theory today? has to
be answered in local terms. The response in Germany will differ
from that in the United States. In West Germany, Critical Theory, after the disintegration of the Institut für Sozialforschung
(Institute for Social Research) in 1969, has positioned itself in
opposition to functionalist social theory (for instance, Niklas
Luhmann), on the one hand, and a Foucauldian approach, on
the other. Even those critics who did not follow the so-called
linguistic turn in Habermas's writings and stayed closer to the
older Frankfurt School kept a distance, by and large, from poststructuralist theory—Karl Heinz Bohrer's work might be mentioned here—while the supporters of French theory (Michel
Foucault) for the most part were no longer familiar with or
interested in the tradition of Critical Theory.[5] The exception
may be Samuel Weber, a student of Paul de Man and collab-
orator of Peter Szondi, who introduced Jacques Lacan to a German academic audience in 1978.[6] Weber prepared the transition
from Critical Theory to post-Freudian psychoanalysis, while
Szondi himself, developing a hermeneutical model in his later
work, refused to participate in this trend. More typical, however, is the break with former allegiances and the ensuing formation of a new identity, as we find it in the writings of Helga
Gallas, who started out as a Marxist and later embraced poststructuralist theory.[7]

5. Karl Heinz Bohrer (born in 1935) has been a journalist and literary
critic and a professor of German at the University of Bielefeld; in 1983 he
became editor of the important magazine *Merkur*; see his books *Plötzlich-
keit: Zum Augenblick des ästhetischen Scheins* (Frankfurt, 1981), and *Die
Entwicklung der ästhetischen Subjektivität* (Frankfurt, 1987).

6. Samuel M. Weber, *Rückkehr zu Freud. Jacques Lacans Ent-stellung
der Psychoanalyse* (Frankfurt, 1978).

7. See Helga Gallas, *Marxistische Literaturtheorie: Kontroversen im
Bund proletarisch-revolutionärer Schriftsteller* (Neuwied, 1971), and her
*Das Textbegehren des "Michael Kolhaas": Die Sprache des Unbewussten
und der Sinn der Literatur* (Reinbek, 1981).

What makes the map of contemporary West German criticism and theory difficult to read for outside observers is not so much its ambiguous pluralism, where several models compete for hegemony, but its warped temporal structure, that is, a sometimes odd reversal of the "normal" development of theory and criticism. Instead of moving in a smooth progression from traditional Marxism to revisionist models of various kinds in postwar Germany, the classics of Marxist theory had to be recuperated at various stages. This phenomenon is closely related to the impact of National Socialism in Germany, which was clearly not limited to the years 1933–1945. In more than one way it also determined the critical discourse after 1945. First of all, between 1945 and 1949 it was not for the Germans to decide what critical discourses were acceptable. Just as the Allies could not agree on the political future of Germany, they disagreed about its ideological formation. While the Soviets obviously favored orthodox Marxism in their zone, the Western Allies were less tolerant of Marxist traditions and communist organizations. Unlike Italy or France, West Germany never had a communist mass movement. In fact, the Communist party (KPD) was outlawed in 1956. By that time the political consensus of the young Republic included a strong anticommunist bias that resulted in a virtual ban of Marxist theory as it was developed in East Germany (GDR). At West German universities Marxist theory had no place, at least not during the 1950s. The notable exception was the Frankfurt School, primarily because its members returned to Germany from the United States (as American citizens) and carefully avoided traditional communist rhetoric.

Much of the contemporary German theoretical discussion on the Left, therefore, has to be understood against the background of the history of the Frankfurt School after World War II. Adorno's and Horkheimer's return to Frankfurt and the ensuing reopening of the Institute for Social Research was overshadowed by two concerns: a legitimate apprehension about anti-Semitism in postwar Germany and considerable anxiety about the position of Critical Theory vis-à-vis orthodox Marxism. The latter concern was motivated by internal as well as external circumstances. Already in the United States, Adorno and Horkheimer had learned to disguise their position by an avoidance of Marxist terminology. Yielding to the ideological pressure within the American political discourse after the war, they had purged *Dialectic of Enlightenment* of its Marxist terminology before its publication in 1947. Obviously, this pressure continued in West Germany, where the power of the United States was felt very strongly, and both Horkheimer and Adorno, who relied on their "American" identity, had to take this bias into consideration. Moreover, for the survival of the institute within the West German configuration, a clear distance toward orthodox Marxism was advisable. Adorno's critique of Lukács and Brecht—both very prominent figures in East Germany— has to be seen in this light.

The presence of orthodox Marxism in a hegemonic position in East Germany clearly influenced the trajectory of Critical Theory. One must not forget, however, that the metamorphosis of Critical Theory had occurred already during the early 1940s, long before Adorno and Horkheimer took up their positions in Frankfurt again. As Helmut Dubiel has shown, the essays published in the *Zeitschrift* between 1938 and 1944 indicate a growing rift between the Marxist paradigm and Critical Theory—not only in terms of its relationship to the Soviet Union under Stalin as well as the official communist explanation of fascism, but also in regard to more fundamental assumptions about the evolution of advanced capitalism and its political organization.[8] For the authors of *Dialectic of Enlightenment*, German fascism, Stalinism in Russia, and the American culture industry became part of a larger negative configuration of modernity, a configuration for which the explanatory power of

8. See Helmut Dubiel, *Wissenschaftsorganisation und politische Erfahrung: Studien zur frühen Kritischen Theorie* (Frankfurt, 1978).

traditional Marxism was inadequate. Hence neither Horkheimer nor Adorno was interested in reprinting the essays of the group published during the 1930s. Horkheimer, it seems, even objected to the republication of *Dialectic of Enlightenment* when the need arose in West Germany during the 1960s. In other words, the early writings of the Frankfurt School were not part of the postwar theoretical discourse. As Habermas has observed, the senior figures kept most of the history of Critical Theory out of sight, emphasizing philosophical and cultural questions instead.[9]

Clearly, this version of Critical Theory did fit much better into the Federal Republic than the radical beginnings of the 1930s. Still, the Frankfurt School of the 1950s enjoyed a rather ambivalent position, in certain ways (ideologically) Adorno and Horkheimer were on the margins, their cultural and social criticism undermined the conservative intellectual consensus of the Federal Republic. On the other hand, in terms of their personal influence, they represented the center. This is particularly true for Horkheimer, who served as the *Rektor* of Frankfurt University for a number of years. This ambiguity also very much shaped the reception of Critical Theory in Germany. Especially during the late 1960s, the radical student movement not only appropriated and politicized Critical Theory, they also confronted the members of the Frankfurt School as pillars of the establishment. Symptomatic of this incongruity was the bitter dispute between Adorno and the New Left over the political meaning of Walter Benjamin's work, which Adorno had helped to restore through his 1955 edition.[10] At the same time, Adorno and his disciple Rolf Tiedemann carefully restricted the

9. Jürgen Habermas, "The Dialectics of Rationalization," an interview with Axel Honneth, Eberhard Knödel-Bunte, and Arno Widmann, in *Telos* 49 (1981): 5–31; see esp. 5–6.

10. Walter Benjamin, *Schriften*, 2 vols., ed. Theodor W. Adorno and Gretel Adorno (Frankfurt, 1955); Theodor W. Adorno provided the introduction.

reading of Benjamin's writings to the orthodoxy of the Frankfurt School.[11] In this context, Benjamin's commitment to a communist position during the 1930s, as it surfaces in a number of essays and reviews, was eliminated wherever possible or rejected. Adorno referred back to (and even published) his old letters in which he had argued against the *Passagen* project (Benjamin's study of nineteenth-century culture in Paris) by criticizing its lack of mediations between material factors and literary texts.[12] The New Left, with some support from East German scholars, on the other hand, pointed out that the Frankfurt School, especially Horkheimer and Adorno, had more or less censored Benjamin's essays before they were allowed to appear in the *Zeitschrift*.[13]

In the heated debate between the Frankfurt School and the New Left it was of course not really the philological question that mattered but the political issue, that is, the repression of the Marxist tradition in the new institute in Frankfurt. This concern was shared by some of its younger members, among them Jürgen Habermas and Oskar Negt. They felt that the theory of the Frankfurt School had been truncated after its return to Frankfurt and therefore made a conscious attempt to retrieve the earlier phases of Critical Theory with its stronger emphasis on Marxian concepts and categories. The result was a curious reversal of the theoretical discourse in West Germany. While in France the events of May 1968 led to increasing skepticism toward the Communist party and its dogma, in

11. Rolf Tiedemann, *Studien zur Philosophie Walter Benjamins*, introduction by Theodor W. Adorno (Frankfurt, 1965).

12. Adorno included his own response to Benjamin in the German edition of Benjamin's letters: Walter Benjamin, *Briefe*, ed. Gershom Scholem and Theodor W. Adorno, 2 vols. (Frankfurt, 1966), 671–83.

13. Crucial for the debate are *alternative* 56/57 (Oct./Dec. 1967) and 59/60 (Apr./June 1968), two special Benjamin issues with contributions by Hildegard Brenner, Helga Gallas, and Rosemarie Heise. See also the East German edition of *Das Paris des Second Empire von Baudelaire*, ed. Rosemarie Heise (Berlin, 1971).

West Germany a similar situation led to a radical recuperation of Marx and Lenin based on a strong call for political praxis.

Habermas's essay collection *Theory and Practice* (1963) is symptomatic of this new tendency in two respects. First, Habermas openly discussed problems of social change; second, he left no doubt about his own revisionist position vis-à-vis the Marxist doctrine. Unlike Adorno and Horkheimer, who never fully articulated their position vis-à-vis orthodox Marxism, Habermas, through a renewed reading of the classical texts from Hobbes to Marx, attempted to redefine the project of Critical Theory. Partly by drawing on the later work of Herbert Marcuse, he tried to overcome what he was to coin the "pessimism" of the postwar Frankfurt School, its lack of interest in structural change. Especially in 1969, when Willi Brandt and the Social Democrats formed the West German government (together with the Free Democrats), radical reform seemed to be possible. The West German society appeared to be much more open and flexible than Adorno's theory was prepared to admit.

By the end of the 1960s, Critical Theory found itself in a curious and defensive position. Naturally, conservatives and moderate liberals made Critical Theory responsible for the student movement, calling openly for the state to subdue student unrest. On the other side, Critical Theory faced the increasing opposition of orthodox Marxism in its various forms. Finally, the tension within the Frankfurt School, among the older and the younger generation as well as between internal camps, clearly increased to the point where communication and exchange of ideas became strained—especially under the pressure from the student movement. Although certainly more "political" than Adorno, Habermas also came under attack for his lecture "Die Scheinrevolution und ihre Kinder" (The pseudo-revolution and its children), given June 1, 1968, at the VDS Congress in Frankfurt.[14] Habermas's critique of the students'

14. The VDS (Verband Demokratischer Studenten [Union of Democratic

protest rituals (what he called "Left fascism") was angrily rejected by the New Left. But the disagreement was not limited to political strategy, it was the foundations of Critical Theory that were at stake at this crucial turning point. As much as the members of the second generation disagreed about the failure of classical Critical Theory, that is, its grounding and its political function, they shared a sense that Adorno's late theory had reached an endpoint. Typical for this attitude was the early reception of *Aesthetic Theory* (1970): the positive reviews were written by conservative or moderate critics while the New Left kept a noticeable distance from Adorno's posthumous opus. Adorno's attempt to preserve Critical Theory through an aesthetic discourse met with disbelief and hostile criticism.

The charge of undue "pessimism" resurfaced in the debate of the 1980s. When Habermas criticized Horkheimer and Adorno for their use of dialectical reason—first in his *Theory of Communicative Action* (1981) and later in the essay "The Entwinement of Myth and Enlightenment" (1982)—he clearly focused on the question of rationality in the critique of rationalism.[15] During the late 1960s and early 1970s, the New Left was primarily concerned about Adorno's lack of commitment, that is, his conviction that the late capitalist society could not be overthrown without repeating the mechanisms of social domination and repression. Indeed, for Adorno's postwar theory—particularly in *Negative Dialectics* and *Aesthetic Theory*—the notion of a unified historical process served only as a springboard for the critique of historical progress. Neither Habermas nor the poet and critic Hans Magnus Enzensberger

---

Students]) was an important leftist political group formed by students in West Germany at this time.

15. Jürgen Habermas's essay "The Entwinement of Myth and Enlightenment" has appeared twice in English: in *New German Critique* 26 (1982): 13–30, and in his book *The Philosophical Discourse of Modernity*, trans. Frederick Lawrence (Cambridge, Mass., 1987), 106–30. His other important critique of Horkheimer and Adorno can be found in *The Theory of Communicative Action*, vol. 1: *Reason and the Rationalization of Society*, trans. Thomas McCarthy (Boston, 1984), 366–99.

or Oskar Negt was prepared to accept Adorno's radical critique of the enlightenment.[16] This political decision forced the next generation of theorists to redefine the structure and goal of Critical Theory.

From the typical point of view of Western Europe and the United States, it was first and foremost the work of Jürgen Habermas that articulated the post-Adornian form of Critical Theory. In *Strukturwandel der Oeffentlichkeit* (Structural transformation of the public sphere, 1962), and more forcefully in *Knowledge and Human Interests* (1969), he had already modified the project of the older generation in two ways: by reevaluating the Enlightenment tradition and valorizing European modernity and through his decision to focus on the question of grounding by showing that all forms of knowledge are based on an anthropological definition of needs and interests. The conventional view that these texts established the new form of Critical Theory, however, has to be modified for two reasons. First of all, Habermas's early books do not yet mark the decisive break with the older Frankfurt School. In the development of Habermas's work, especially in its post-Adornian gestalt, the crucial break has to be located in the early 1970s, prepared by Habermas's debate with Niklas Luhmann's systems theory: it is only with the approach to social theory as it is articulated in *Legitimation Crisis* (1973) that Habermas's method is no longer compatible with the model of the classical Frankfurt School.[17] Second, the typical approach, by favoring Habermas, tends to overlook the fact that there are also theorists who follow a different path.

In this respect, the work of Negt and Kluge and also the

16. Hans Magnus Enzensberger (born in 1929) began to write political poetry in the late 1950s and later was coeditor of the influential leftist journal *Das Kursbuch*; his essays on the avant-garde and modern media reflect the influence of Adorno as well as Brecht.

17. See Jürgen Habermas and Niklas Luhmann, *Theorie der Gesellschaft oder Sozialtechnologie—Was leistet die Systemforschung?* (Frankfurt, 1971).

writings of Alfred Schmidt and Albrecht Wellmer have to be mentioned; they remained closer to the older paradigm, though with a stronger interest in retrieving the Marxist and socialist tradition.[18] While Habermas faced Western theory—establishing his own model by working through the theories of Emile Durkheim, George Mead, and Talcott Parsons, and returning to Marx only at the end of the second volume of *The Theory of Communicative Action*—Negt and Kluge in *Oeffentlichkeit und Erfahrung* (The public sphere and experience, 1972) defined their project in terms of Marxist concepts of class and class antagonism. Their reconstruction of a proletarian public sphere, as separate from the classical liberal public sphere analyzed by Habermas in *Strukturwandel*, was politically committed to a socialist project in which the concept of the proletariat was vigorously reintroduced as a major challenge to the social structure of the Federal Republic. In 1972 Negt and Kluge placed in the foreground exactly those aspects of the public sphere that Habermas had barely touched in 1962.

Also, in contrast to Habermas, the authors of *Oeffentlichkeit und Erfahrung* deconstructed the notion of a unified public sphere as the site of ideological and political struggle, underscoring instead the multiplicity and heterogeneity of public spaces. These struggles and conflicts (conceived in terms of class antagonisms) cannot be subsumed, as Habermas argued

18. The social theorist Oskar Negt (born in 1934), a student of Adorno and Horkheimer, and the writer and filmmaker Alexander Kluge (born in 1932) collaborated on a number of important projects. Negt holds a position at the University of Hannover; Kluge began his literary career with *Lebensläufe* (1962) and *Schlachtbeschreibung* (1964). At the same time he became one of the significant representatives of the New German Cinema. Alfred Schmidt (born in 1931), a student of Horkheimer and Adorno, became a professor of social philosophy in 1972. Among his works are *Geschichte und Struktur* (1974) and *Zur Idee der kritischen Theorie* (1974). Albrecht Wellmer is presently professor of philosophy at the University of Constance. Together with Peter Bürger he reinforced the aesthetic dimension of Critical Theory. See especially his book *Zur Dialektik von Moderne und Postmoderne: Vernunftkritik nach Adorno* (Frankfurt, 1985).

in 1962, under the concept of a single, self-contained *Oeffent-lichkeit* (public sphere), a space where solutions can be worked out through rational arguments. Much more than Habermas, and certainly also as a reflection of the radical political climate of the early 1970s in West Germany, Negt and Kluge emphasized the *fictional* character of the public sphere, its strategic function for the rising bourgeoisie. They argued explicitly against the formal characteristic of the liberal model that Habermas not only analyzed but also tried to revitalize during the later Konrad Adenauer years. Consequently, they insisted on a materialist grounding of the public sphere by reconnecting the formal structure to its *Produktionsstruktur*, that is, by embedding the model in the actual social experiences of the participating agents.[19] Through this procedure, Negt and Kluge, with an obvious polemical turn against Habermas, wanted to explicate the dialectic between the critical value of the public sphere and its dependence on the actual social relations, a discrepancy that, according to Negt and Kluge, Habermas was unable to solve.

Clearly, Negt and Kluge defended Critical Theory in terms that Habermas had given up after 1969. In a certain way, they restated the hidden orthodoxy of the Frankfurt School, at least in the sense that social history has to be understood as the history of class conflicts (bourgeoisie and proletariat), a social history that is embedded in the actual relations of production. Of course, Adorno would have rejected out of hand the strong belief in the proletariat as a central political agent of political history. He never returned to this position after *Dialectic of Enlightenment*, but there are latent structural similarities—for instance, a general acceptance of the Marxian categories of forces of production and relations of production as well as their dialectical mediation. For this reason Negt and Kluge tended

---

19. Oskar Negt and Alexander Kluge, *Oeffentlichkeit und Erfahrung: Zur Organisationsanalyse von bürgerlicher und proletarischer Oeffent-lichkeit* (Frankfurt, 1971), 17.

to understand the public sphere as an epiphenomenon produced by the forces of production (whereas Habermas insisted more on its relative autonomy).

Although Negt and Kluge reinforced a class model, they did not seek an alliance with orthodox Marxist theory as it was produced and disseminated in East Germany. While a part of the New Left moved toward a more orthodox articulation of their opposition and therefore sought alliances with advanced theory in the GDR, Negt and Kluge clearly resisted this trend, mostly for political reasons. The orientation of the Frankfurt School and its theory excluded any rapprochement with orthodox Marxism and its political organizations. The politics of the second generation significantly differed from that of their teachers, especially after 1965, yet their positions only modified or radicalized the stance of the first generation and did not cancel their link with the project of Western Marxism. This became already very apparent in the debate between Habermas (who stood in for the institute) and the New Left.

In 1968, Negt, writing in response to Habermas's critique of the New Left, argued in favor of a revolutionary solution and against the resolution of social as well as ideological conflicts through public debate. He countered the Habermasian argument that the students misunderstood the historical situation and therefore ended up in subjectivist voluntarism by underscoring Habermas's own subjectivism, his unwillingness to recognize the contradictions and the ensuing instability of the West German society. It is interesting to note that Negt at this point invoked the theories of the young Lukács and of Karl Korsch in order to demonstrate the need for revolutionary action. But Negt's critique of Habermas also turned into a critique of the Leninist party and its worn-out political strategies. What Negt suggested as an appropriate response to the repression of state institutions (like universities) were decentralized, spontaneous actions. That is to say, the emphasis was placed on a praxis more suited to subvert the system. What Habermas, not unlike Adorno, perceived as "Putschismus," as pseudo-revolutionary and essentially self-serving posturing, the New Left understood as an attempt to overcome the defensive position of the Frankfurt School, on the one hand, and the rigid response of the Communist party, on the other.

In West Germany, as a result of these tensions, the at least partial identity of Critical Theory and the New Left had already lost its momentum during the early 1970s (at a time when this alliance was still much stronger in the United States). With the rise of repressive state measures after 1972 (*Berufsverbot*) and the radicalization of the protest movement (terrorism), the revised project of Critical Theory, as it was articulated in Adorno's later work, appeared less relevant, since it did not offer a clearly formulated political strategy. It was the political issue, namely the actions of the APO (the extra-parliamentary opposition), that divided the second generation of the Frankfurt School and propelled its factions into different theoretical directions. While Jürgen Habermas's formulation of the project is well known in the West, other strands of Critical Theory were only marginally received outside Germany. The names of Michael Theunissen, Herbert Schnädelbach, and Karl Heinz Bohrer, even those of Albrecht Wellmer and Peter Bürger, have no major resonance in this country.[20] As a result, the present debate about the status of Critical Theory in America is strangely incomplete, since it works with the premise that today Critical Theory is identical with Habermasian theory. Within the German context, however, Habermas's theory represents one possible response to the crisis of the early 1970s. The vitality of Critical Theory, the fact that it survived the closing of the institute is due precisely to this heterogeneity

20. Michael Theunissen (born in 1932), is presently professor of philosophy at the Free University of Berlin; among his works are *Hegels Lehre vom absoluten Geist als theologisch-politischer Traktat* (1970) and *Sein und Schein* (1980). Herbert Schädelbach (born in 1936) received appointments in philosophy at the Universities of Frankfurt and Hamburg; among his works are *Geschichtsphilosophie nach Hegel* (1974) and *Rationalität* (1984).

and the lack of a unified system. By the same token, the relationship of the younger theorists to Horkheimer and Adorno varied greatly, ranging from a systematic critique in the more recent writings of Habermas and his students to various attempts to regenerate Adorno's theory, especially his aesthetic theory.

The impact of the Frankfurt School on contemporary theoretical discourses in Germany comes in various forms and shapes. In a recent essay, Habermas argues that it is precisely the multifaceted character of Critical Theory that has allowed for new and innovative combinations with different models and discourses, among them the hermeneutic tradition, analytical philosophy, systems theory, and structuralism.[21] The most apparent continuity can be traced through the tradition of Western Marxism—for instance, in the writings of Negt and Kluge. In *Geschichte und Eigensinn* (History and self-will, 1981), they return to fundamental Marxist concepts even more rigorously than in *Oeffentlichkeit und Erfahrung*—in particular to the category of labor as the most basic relationship between humans and reality—without, however, ever reducing theory to economic theory. At the same time, there is no attempt to follow Adorno's paradigm of negative dialectics. If one can speak of indebtedness at all, the indebtedness of *Geschichte und Eigensinn* to Adorno articulates itself as a materialist approach for which Adorno's analysis of music is the model.[22] In this case and others, the explicit return of the analysis to Marx's *Capital*—certainly the exception rather than the rule within Critical Theory—serves as a constant reminder that the potential of Marxian theory has not yet been exhausted. This is a position that would not be shared by Claus Offe or Habermas, both of whom have emphasized their historical dis-

---

21. Jürgen Habermas, "Drei Thesen zur Wirkungsgeschichte der Frankfurter Schule," in *Die Frankfurter Schule und die Folgen*, ed. Axel Honneth and Albrecht Wellmer (Berlin, 1986), 8–12.
22. Oskar Negt and Alexander Kluge, *Geschichte und Eigensinn* (Frankfurt, 1981), 82.

tance from Marx.[23] For them, Marx's impact is mediated at least twice before he enters the discussion of the 1970s: first, through Lukács and Korsch; second, through Horkheimer, Adorno, and Marcuse.

According to Habermas, one can distinguish four areas in which Critical Theory partakes in the contemporary theoretical discourse: (1) an epistemological critique based on *Negative Dialectic*, (2) the project of aesthetic theory and literary criticism, as it was articulated by Benjamin and Adorno, (3) social theory, and (4) concrete interpretation through close reading.[24] What this rather mechanical enumeration does not address is the theoretical metamorphosis of the Frankfurt School during the 1970s and 1980s. Habermas's own remarks underline continuities more than breaks and discontinuities. One of the significant cases of a paradigm shift would be his own work, beginning with his appointment in 1970 as director of the Max Planck Institute, but radical challenges are also visible in the field of aesthetic criticism and social theory. Whether the various discourses in these areas can still be called Western Marxism becomes an open question. In fact, the writings of Negt and Kluge, with their strong and explicit affirmation of the Marxist tradition, are anything but typical for the approach of Critical Theory during the 1970s and 1980s. Their position appears to be marginal compared with Jürgen Habermas and his disciples (Axel Honneth, Hauke Brunkhorst) and a post-Adornian group (Karl Heinz Bohrer, Burghardt Lindner, Albrecht Wellmer, W. Martin Lüdke), which has tried to reopen a critical dialogue with *Negative Dialectic* and *Aesthetic Theory*—a dialogue that was to some extent also encouraged by the impact of poststructuralist theory. The focus of this dialogue is not on restoring Adorno's "doctrine" or even

23. Claus Offe, presently professor of sociology at the University of Bielefeld, is best known in the United States for his *Contradictions of the Welfare State* (1984) and *Disorganized Capitalism: Contemporary Transformations of Work and Politics* (1985).

24. Habermas, "Drei Thesen," 11–12.

his much-debated pessimism but, rather, on epistemological
and ontological questions that Adorno, sometimes only
obliquely, addressed in his late writings. His critique of Heidegger's ontology would be a case in point. Similarly, his analysis of the avant-garde served as springboard for the extended
discussion of modernism and postmodernism between Peter
Bürger on the one hand, and Burghardt Lindner and W. Martin
Lüdke on the other.[25]

As early as 1974, Bürger had argued in *Theory of the Avant-
Garde* that Adorno's philosophy of art was rooted in the historical avant-garde and could therefore no longer be appropriated dogmatically. Similarly, Albrecht Wellmer underscores an
inevitable distancing from Adorno's philosophy when he writes
(in 1986):

Die These vom Verblendungszusammenhang der modernen
Welt ist zwar in vieler Hinsicht aus den konkreten geschichtlichen Phänomenen herausgelesen, sie ist aber—und darin liegt
ihre philosophische Schwäche—bei Adorno zugleich in einer
Theorie des Begriffs begründet, durch deren Optik sie als a priori
wahr erscheint. A priori deshalb, weil aus der Sicht Adornos
das Andere dieses Verblendungszusammenhangs das Andere der
diskursiven Rationalität sein müsste, und daher das Andere der
Geschichte: Nur von einem messianischen Fluchtpunkt her
lässt die Analyse der *wirklichen* Vernunft noch als Kritik der
falschen sich verstehen.

[The thesis of the total obfuscation of the modern world can of
course in many respects be read out of concrete historical phenomena, but—and herein lies its philosophical weakness—in
Adorno it is grounded in a theory of the concept, through which
it appears as true a priori. A priori because, from Adorno's per-

25. The literary critics Burghardt Lindner (born in 1943) and W. Martin
Lüdke (born in 1943) represent the third generation of Critical Theory.
Both teach literature at the University of Frankfurt. See esp. *"Theorie der
Avantgarde": Antworten auf Peter Bürgers Bestimmung von Kunst und
bürgerlicher Gesellschaft*, ed. W. Martin Lüdke (Frankfurt, 1976).

spective, the Other of this total obfuscation would have to be the Other of discursive rationality, and therefore the Other of history: only from a messianic point of view can the analysis of *actual* reason still be understood as a critique of *false* reason.][26]

For Wellmer, a productive reappraisal of Critical Theory would include the earlier phases of the Frankfurt School and possibly a greater distance toward negative dialectics, as it appears in the theory of Jürgen Habermas. Yet, this is precisely the open question in the present German debate. Is Habermasian theory the only legitimate response to the unresolved problems of Adorno's late work? Or, to put it differently, how dialectical is Critical Theory allowed to be? Wellmer himself pleaded for the importance of Adorno's "mikrologisches Verfahren" (micrological method), that is, the immanent textual analysis that informed Adorno's philosophy.[27] It is significant for the present debate that Wellmer suggests a separation between Adorno's philosophical system (with its unmistakable links to the category of identity) and his method (of reading cultural artifacts)—clearly with an antisystematic intention: what Wellmer wants to rescue is the *implicit* theory of language and epistemology, especially those moments that Adorno did not fully articulate. In this formulation of the task, Wellmer goes beyond the project of a fragmentary philosophy that he defines as Adorno's legacy. Its radical nature lies in its break with Adorno's own intention. Clearly, however, this Adornian procedure is not compatible with the communication model of Habermasian theory. Hence one cannot refer to *the* discourse of Critical Theory today. In the context of the present West German debate, two models at least are competing with each

26. Albrecht Wellmer, "Die Bedeutung der Frankfurter Schule heute," in *Die Frankfurter Schule und die Folgen*, ed. Axel Honneth and Albrecht Wellmer (Berlin, 1986), 28. All translations, unless otherwise noted, are mine.
27. Ibid., 31.

Reappraisals

other: namely, Habermas's communication model and the fragmentary aesthetic model of Adorno's late work with its stress on difference. Wellmer's suggestion that this model as a fundamental critique of traditional metaphysics is not too far removed from Heidegger's project shows how much this debate has moved away from Adorno's intentions, since Adorno himself did not admit any common ground between Heidegger and his own theory.

The present tensions within Critical Theory reflect, at least to some extent, also the heterogeneity of the Frankfurt School's past. In spite of Horkheimer's repeated attempts to define the project of the institute, it was always difficult, if not impossible, to find a common theoretical ground for its members. In making his strong claim to critical rationalism, Habermas invokes the early phase of Critical Theory—especially the early writings of Horkheimer and Marcuse—in order to distance himself from Adorno's fragmentism. In contrast, proponents of the aesthetic model would go back to Adorno's early music criticism, especially *Philosophy of Modern Music,* and to Benjamin's literary criticism with its links to the early romantics. Furthermore, the tensions mentioned above are related to significant shifts in the theoretical discourse during the 1970s. The emergence of sociological functionalism as well as systems theory, on the one hand, and poststructuralism, on the other, changed the configuration of the discourse to such an extent that Critical Theory, by responding to these new models, lost its old center and split into a variety of overlapping and competing paradigms. Only one of them, represented in the work of Oskar Negt, remains squarely in the tradition of Western Marxism. Neither the theory of communicative action nor the post-Adornian aesthetic model, although they occasionally relate to Marxian theory, are in terms of their epistemology and methodology exclusively based on Marxist premises.

20

I   Neoromantic Anticapitalism: Georg Lukács's Search for Authentic Culture

In the more recent research on romanticism, Georg Lukács enjoys a reputation as a dogmatic and obstinate opponent of romantic literature. This view is certainly not without justification, for his essays of the 1930s and 1940s on authors such as Heinrich von Kleist and E. T. A. Hoffmann, as well as his *Skizze einer Geschichte der neueren deutschen Literatur* (Sketch of a history of modern German literature, 1953), reveal him to be an inexorable critic of German romanticism. Also, in his broadly conceived history of German ideology, *The Destruction of Reason* (1954), romantic philosophy (Schelling) stands at the beginning of a process of irrationalization of spirit that Lukács believed led the way into German fascism. Here we find one important explanation for Lukács's harsh critique of romantic thought: the affirmative reception of romantic themes and conceptualizations by the National Socialists determined the perspective of his criticism. For Lukács, romanticism moves in a cultural tradition that must be understood as an aberration of the German spirit. For the later Lukács, the history of German (and European) literature divides into two traditions struggling with each other: the Enlightenment stands on one side, leading by way of its liberal and democratic tendencies to a socialist literature; romanticism and its emerging irrationalism stand on the other side. Lukács believed that this irrationalism continued after 1848 in modernism and, in the twentieth century, in the avant-garde (expressionism). This conceptualization not only influenced the study of literature in East Germany up into the 1970s, it also affected in a lasting way the scholarly treatment of the Enlightenment in the Federal Republic: West Germany's rediscovery of the Enlightenment in the 1960s often contained a bias against romanticism.[1]

Lukács's attempt to deal with fascism was not the only important factor in his rejection of romanticism; another important motif for Lukács was orthodox Marxism's negative stance toward romantic anticapitalism. Orthodox Marxism's claim to an objective and scientific critique of bourgeois society seemed irreconcilable with an approach that derived its strength from a utopian alternative—even more so when this alternative project contrasted modern society and its division of labor with earlier idealized historical periods (whether antiquity or the Middle Ages). During the Second International, the romantic-utopian intellectual motifs of the Marxist tradition were forced increasingly into the background. The German social democracy supported by Engels separated itself more and more from this "utopianism" and appropriated the economic theory developed in *Capital* together with a conception of history that trusted in gradual evolution.[2] The German and Austrian socialists were justified in invoking Marx, for their theories emphasized genuine elements of his theory. At the same time, however, they repressed under the influence of this positivism other aspects of Marx's thought, more particularly those that stood nearer to the romantic conception of social critique. The crucial achievement of the early Lukács lies in his rediscovery of this dimension of Marxism even before Marx's Paris manuscripts (which illustrate this connection clearly) were published.

The materialism of *History and Class Consciousness* (1923)

1. See Klaus Peter's introduction to *Romantikforschung seit 1945*, ed. Klaus Peter (Königstein, 1980); see esp. 22–29.
2. On the question of "scientific" Marxism, see Alvin W. Gouldner, *For Sociology: Renewal and Critique in Sociology Today* (New York, 1973).

does not oppose itself to the romantic social critique as it is first formulated, for example, in the work of Friedrich Schlegel and Novalis. Instead, Lukács expands, criticizes, and renders these romantic beginnings more precise by bringing them into contact with the theories of Marx and Max Weber. Lukács thereby reexposed in 1923 genuine motifs of the Marxist tradition that had been extensively suppressed by the Second International. He was predestined for this task, as his intellectual development placed him on intimate terms with romanticism and his position toward romanticism developed against the backdrop of turn-of-the-century neoromantic tendencies. As Ferenc Feher has shown, especially important for the development of Lukács's thought was his friendship with Paul Ernst, a radical naturalist who later became an extreme nationalist.[3] Other significant influences included Lukács's acquaintance with life philosophy (Wilhelm Dilthey, Georg Simmel) and his engagement with contemporary literature (Thomas Mann). Lukács's sudden decision to join the Hungarian Communist party in 1918 and to devote his life to the revolution did not extinguish neoromantic tendencies in his thought, rather, it pushed him to integrate these tendencies into the Marxist theory of the 1920s. Lukács thus achieved an enormous transformation of Marxist theory, which, as "Western Marxism," has traveled a path separate from that of the Third International since the 1930s.

We ought not to see Lukács's turn toward Marxism, however profound its biographical significance, solely as a rupture; the moment of continuity is equally strong. It reveals Lukács's continuing reflection on problems that he had been considering since his *Entwicklungsgeschichte des modernen Dramas* (The history and development of modern drama, 1912)—a contin-

---

3. See Ferenc Feher, "Am Scheideweg des romantischen Antikapitalismus. Typologie und Beitrag zur deutschen Ideologiegeschichte gelegentlich des Briefwechsels zwischen Paul Ernst und Georg Lukács," in *Die Seele und das Leben: Studien zum frühen Lukács*, ed. Agnes Heller (Frankfurt, 1977), 241–327.

uing reflection that certainly involved self-critique and changes in his own position. The question posed in *Soul and Form* (1911), "How is authentic culture possible?" was answered by the revolutionary theory of Marxism (Rosa Luxemburg, Lenin). The following solution emerged, then, in the early 1920s: authentic (aesthetic) culture can be built only on the basis of a far-reaching social revolution that extends beyond the establishment of a new political order.

As soon as one turns to the early Lukács, his existential proximity to romanticism becomes clear, while the Enlightenment that he later regarded so highly remains in the background or, when it appears, is viewed critically as part of the alienated world. This thesis leads us to the following question: Why did Lukács turn away from his romantic tradition in the 1930s? What led him to believe that the social protest of the romantics was at best a failed attempt to deal with the modern world, a failure that must be overcome by means of the liberal-democratic tradition? Only a step-by-step analysis can possibly answer these questions. My first step consists of reconstructing, at least sketchily, the position of the middle and late Lukács. In the second step, I will indicate the tradition in which Lukács placed himself after 1930 in his discussion of romanticism. In the third step I will treat the early Lukács's reception of romantic literature (first condensed in *Soul and Form* in 1911 and *The Theory of the Novel* in 1916 and 1920), in order finally to move into his elaboration of a new revolutionary theory in *History and Class Consciousness.*

Lukács formulated his later critique of romanticism most powerfully in the essay "Die Romantik als Wendung in der deutschen Literatur" (Romanticism as a turning-point in German literature), which first appeared in the volume *Fortschritt und Reaktion* (Progress and reaction) and later in *Skizze einer Geschichte der neueren deutschen Literatur* (Sketch of a history of modern German literature, 1953). While this essay attracted little attention in the West—or at least exercised no lasting influence on its literary research—it galvanized literary criticism in East Germany. The essay's impact is easy to recognize in the early work of Hans Mayer, Hans Dietrich Dahnke, and Claus Träger.[4] Lukács criticizes romanticism so strongly because he believes that romantic literature marked that point in German intellectual history where the German tradition separated from Western Europe, embarking on a special path that would eventually end in the National Socialists' seizure of power.

In order to understand the essay fully, one must place it in the broader context of the *Sonderweg* debate (the controversy over Germany's "special destiny"), which was taken up again after the Second World War by German historians and social scientists. In the historical and social sciences since the end of the nineteenth century, as well as in literary criticism, the prevailing voices had attributed to Germany a special destiny that, beginning in the late eighteenth century, distinguished it politically, philosophically, and literarily from the general European lot.[5] The theory of Germany's *Sonderweg* was generally presented by conservative historians in an emphatic manner: the importance of this thesis did not lie in its description of a demonstrable difference but, rather, in its legitimation of a desired special position that rejected the democratic civilization of the West in the name of German culture. The fall of the Third Reich rendered this particular tradition of thought and research highly questionable. From this point forward, the affirmative *Sonderweg* thesis was associated (not only by Lukács) with pre-fascist and fascist ideologies.[6] The philosophical and literary traditions that historical and literary studies in-

4. See Hans Mayer, "Die Wirklichkeit E. T. A. Hoffmann," in his *Von Lessing bis Thomas Mann* (Pfullingen, 1959), 198–246; Claus Träger, "Novalis und die ideologische Restauration," in *Sinn und Form* 13 (1961): 618–30; reprinted in Träger's book *Erläuterungen zur deutschen Literatur: Romantik* (East Berlin, 1967).

5. Bernd Faulenbach, *Ideologie des deutschen Weges* (Munich, 1980).

6. See Jürgen Kocka, "Der 'deutsche Sonderweg' in der Diskussion," in *German Studies Review* 5 (1982): 362–79.

voked in order to ground Germany's particularity also appeared spurious. Romanticism—already read by Wilhelm Dilthey (in terms of life philosophy) as part of a specifically German movement, and assessed in the literary history of Adolf Bartels (1901/ 1902) as the true German literature—belonged to that suspect tradition.[7]

For this reason, Lukács believed in 1945 that romanticism constituted that part of the German tradition that must be eliminated in order to make possible Germany's return into the community of democratic peoples. It is remarkable that Lukács adopted this *Sonderweg* thesis while repudiating its inherent valuation. In 1945, Lukács saw only one solution: romanticism must be canceled. Thus, according to Lukács, the correct evolution of German literature led from the Enlightenment to Weimar classicism, and from there to Heine and the Left-Hegelian opposition. Bourgeois realism (only weakly developed in Germany), which appeared to Lukács as the predecessor of socialist realism, was connected to these traditions. Significantly, this construction leaves no place for modernism or the avant-garde. Lukács's version of the *Sonderweg* thesis presupposes a schematic division of good and bad traditions. Lukács does not contest the modernity of romanticism; he understands romanticism as a movement involving bourgeois men of letters who, for the first time in Germany, had to deal with a modern society in the beginning stages of capitalism. But he rejects romanticism's worldview, which appears reactionary; protesting against modern society, romanticism reaches for premodern models. It is no coincidence that Novalis's essay "Die Christenheit oder Europa" (Christianity or Europe, 1799), in which Novalis seems to recommend the Middle Ages as an answer to the fragmentation and alienation of his own time, appears as the central proof of the reactionary spirit

---

7. On this topic, see Peter Uwe Hohendahl, "Bürgerliche Literaturgeschichte und nationale Identität," in *Bürgertum im 19. Jahrhundert*, ed. Jürgen Kocka (Munich, 1988).

of romanticism. Corresponding to Lukács's protest against modernism and the avant-garde, which he considered phenomena of decay, was his assessment of early romanticism—in particular, his assessment of Friedrich Schlegel—as decadent. Schlegel's theory of romantic irony appeared dangerous to Lukács because of its disengaged worldview. Only those writers (like Ludwig Uhland) who could be proven to stand in the tradition of political liberalism or those authors (like E. T. A. Hoffmann) who neared realism in their prose (even if in fantastical terms) were exempted from this judgment.

It need hardly be mentioned that for the late Lukács, Marx and Engels are separated from German romanticism by a wide chasm—such that both appear above all as critics of the romantic worldview. In other words, from Lukács's viewpoint the classics of Marxist theory speak for a particular tradition. This tradition can be traced from a Marxist literary critic like Franz Mehring and the Left-Hegelians Arnold Ruge and Robert Prutz to Heinrich Heine and G. W. F. Hegel. The mature Lukács incorporated this tradition's critique of romanticism into his own. In 1945, his own polemic reproduced many of its motifs and conceptualizations. Hence a brief summary of this tradition is in order.

In his *Romantic School* (1835), Heinrich Heine established the Left's assessment of German romanticism as a reactionary political movement—against the more favorable judgment of Madame de Staël, who was unable from her French position to conceive of the equation of romanticism and conservatism. This distancing from romanticism continued with Arnold Ruge and Ernst Theodor Echtermeyer's manifesto against romanticism in the *Hallischen Jahrbüchern* (1839).[8] In the tradition of Hegel, both critics accused romanticism of substanceless subjectivity, of an internality that failed before reality. Ruge and

---

8. See Peter Uwe Hohendahl, "Literary Criticism in the Epoch of Liberalism," in *The History of German Literary Criticism*, ed. Peter Uwe Hohendahl (Lincoln, Neb., 1988), 179–276.

Echtermeyer suggested even more explicitly than Heine that the romantics repudiated the progressive tradition of rationalism. In philosophy, they attributed this turn primarily to Friedrich Schelling.

At the same time, we find in the *Hallischen Jahrbüchern* an opposition of classicism and romanticism to which Georg Lukács would return a hundred years later. This opposition interprets Weimar classicism as the continuation and realization of the Enlightenment; classicism appears, therefore, as a secure literary basis for the cultural evolution of the nineteenth century. This assessment largely corresponds to Gervinus's judgment, in which Goethe and Schiller represent the zenith of German literature, and romanticism (and Junges Deutschland [Young Germany]) already manifests its decline.[9] Even Rudolf Haym, who presented in 1870 the first extensive scholarly discussion of early romanticism, obviously distances himself from the romantic worldview.[10]

Conversely, renewed interest in romanticism, appearing in the 1860s in the work of Wilhelm Dilthey and increasing in the last decades of the nineteenth century, should be understood as a critique of liberalism—a critique of an interpretation of history as well as a theory of society. After 1866, interest in articulating a specific German tradition was not limited to Dilthey. One also finds the desire to integrate romantic literature into the national canon in the criticism of Wilhelm Scherer, especially after the founding of the empire. This nationalism, which understood Bismarck's unification of Germany as the fulfillment of the old liberal demands, pushed the reception of romanticism toward the right, as Klaus Peter correctly notes.[11] The positive assessment of romanticism served

9. Georg Gottfried Gervinus, *Geschichte der Deutschen Dichtung*, 4th revised ed., 5 vols. (Leipzig, 1953).

10. Rudolf Haym, *Die romantische Schule: Ein Beitrag zur Geschichte des deutschen Geistes* (Berlin, 1870).

11. Peter, *Romantikforschung*, 5–7; see in addition, Peter Uwe Hohen-

a specific ideological-political function, although it was not always explicitly expressed: insofar as one understood romanticism as a parallel to the struggle against Napoleon (Scherer), as the emancipation from cultural domination by foreign powers, it belonged to the movements that prepared the way for the new empire.

This opposition between liberal animosity toward and nationalistic enthusiasm about romanticism clarifies Lukács's position at the end of the Second World War. By returning to the liberal-democratic tradition, Lukács believed he would be able to fight the dangerous German nationalism. With this strategy, Lukács also sacrificed the neoromantic cultural criticism of his earlier work. Cultural criticism of the late nineteenth century sympathetic to romanticism served to strengthen a Right-radical nationalism, which in turn fueled, among other things, the ideology of National Socialism. In order to evoke this tendency, it is sufficient to mention the names of Paul de Lagard, Julius Langbehn, Friedrich Lienhard, and Möller van den Bruck.[12] Finally, the early work of Thomas Mann also belongs in this tradition. In his *Reflections of a Nonpolitical Man*, Mann protests in the name of romanticism against Western civilization. Common to these authors is a repudiation of modern capitalist society. They therefore followed with skepticism the modernization of Germany after 1870. One could invoke the older romanticism, which was the first to criticize the symptoms of modern society, precisely for this reason. The search for an authentic life led the neoromantic trends into a double opposition—against both the official empire nationalism and the technologically oriented ideology of

---

dahl, *Literarische Kultur im Zeitalter des Liberalismus 1830–1870* (Munich, 1985), 194–210 and 240–65.

12. See Fritz Stern, *The Politics of Cultural Despair: A Study in the Rise of the Germanic Ideology* (Berkeley, 1961), and George L. Mosse, *The Crises of German Ideology: Intellectual Origins of the Third Reich* (New York, 1964).

progress that was characteristic of positivism and the later stages of liberalism.

Paul Breines suggests with justification that this neoromantic opposition to capitalism is politically ambivalent.[13] Its critique of society can settle on either the right or the left side of the political spectrum. It can articulate itself in nationalistic or egalitarian terms. The work of the young Lukács arose within this constellation of tensions. His early treatment of German romanticism—more specifically, his discussion of Novalis, Friedrich Schlegel, Solger, and Schelling—stands as a fundamental protest against a modern world that denies any authenticity. This criticism contains, to be sure, no nationalism—an element not to be overlooked in the work of Thomas Mann. The test case was the outbreak of the First World War, when the German intelligentsia was suddenly forced to show its political colors. The majority, including Thomas Mann and Max Weber, placed themselves on the side of the Germans; a liberal minority, including Heinrich Mann, supported the Western powers. Lukács refused his fealty to both sides.[14] The reconstruction of Lukács's argument in the preface of the 1962 German edition of *The Theory of the Novel* is revealing in this regard. It reads: "the Central Powers would probably defeat Russia; this might lead to the downfall of Tsarism; I had no objection to that. There was also some probability that the West would defeat Germany; if this led to the downfall of the Hohenzollerns and the Hapsburgs, I was once again in favour. But then the question arose: who was to save us from Western civilization?"[15]

13. Paul Breines, "Marxism, Romanticism, and the Case of Georg Lukács," in *Studies in Romanticism* 16 (1977): 473–90.
14. See Andrew Arato and Paul Breines, *The Young Lukács and the Origins of Western Marxism* (New York, 1979), esp. 61–74; also Ernst Keller, *Der junge Lukács: Antibürger und wesentliches Leben* (Frankfurt, 1984), esp. 155–66.
15. Georg Lukács, *The Theory of the Novel: A Historico-Philosophical Essay on the Forms of Great Epic Literature* (Cambridge, Mass., 1971), 11;

The last sentence is above all worthy of note. The Western civilization that Heinrich Mann prescribed for the Germans held no charm for Lukács. The victory of the Western powers could not, therefore, represent the final word. At this time, the solution for Lukács lay much more in Russia, and *The Theory of the Novel* indicates the direction of this solution. When, in the last chapter of *The Theory of the Novel*, Lukács believes he has found in Dostoevsky the overcoming of the novel, he acknowledges the possible beginning of a new aesthetic culture. This obviously presented a religious-metaphysical solution that Lukács would no longer recognize a few years later. At the same time, however, this discussion was a preparation for the answer that Lukács would present in *History and Class Consciousness*.

In order to understand Lukács's conceptual position within the neoromantic trends, it is instructive to examine his relationship with Paul Ernst—a relationship that facilitated Lukács's interrogation and clarification of his own position in the period from 1910 until the writing of *The Theory of the Novel*. Lukács shared with Ernst a critical opinion of naturalism, which Lukács had already formulated in his history of modern drama. In that work, he described naturalism as a poetics of the purposelessness of bourgeois ideals, which hovered between socialism and an individualism strained to the point of sickness, between Stirner and Marx.[16] The naturalistic poet presents longing for a new life (Hauptmann), but his desire goes unrealized because the naturalist drama already contains the message that hope for change must remain unfulfilled. For Lukács, therefore, naturalism does not overcome the problems left behind by classical drama, but instead appears as an indecisive and consequently "powerless innovator."[17] Lukács and Ernst agreed that the positivistic notion of science, which the

---

in further references in the text, this work will be cited as *TN*, followed by page number.

16. On this topic see Feher, "Am Scheideweg," 246.

17. Translated from ibid., 247.

German social democracy largely appropriated, could not achieve a transition to a new way of life. Both shared—and therein lies their literary-critical alliance—an uncompromising anticapitalist position that does not rely on Marxist theory (from which Ernst much more decisively distanced himself). Of course, even from the very beginning, there lay in Ernst's and Lukács's alliance the seed of their later estrangement. Ernst, in search of a populist conception of life, moved in the direction of a nationalist worldview—and consequently approved of the war in 1914. Lukács, on the other hand, decisively rejected the possibility of a populist nationalism and saw the necessity of thoroughly rethinking the problem of authentic culture.

In his essay "Metaphysik der Tragödie: Paul Ernst," published in 1911, Lukács first articulated a program for a post-naturalist dramatic art. He called for a return to the classic form of tragedy, as it was presented in Paul Ernst's play *Brunhild* (1909). At this point in Lukács's development, Ernst's plays represented a possible solution to the problem of a new aesthetic culture—a solution that impressionism, according to Lukács, was precisely unable to achieve. For the theoretician Lukács, it was most important to carry the real life, which he emphatically separated from the empiricism of facts and data, over into the dramatic form. The irreality of the "real life," of that which leads beyond the banality of the everyday, should meet with the dramatic form. According to Lukács, this can happen only when empirical life is distanced from drama or, more accurately, when it is filtered such that it loses its historical-concrete temporality and spatiality. "Such existence knows no space or time; all its events are outside the scope of logical explanation, just as the souls of its men are outside the scope of psychology."[18] This position consistently opposes re-

---

18. Georg Lukács, *Soul and Form* (Cambridge, Mass., 1974), 156; henceforth cited in the text as *SaF*, followed by page number.

alism and naturalism. "Realism," argues Lukács, "is bound to destroy all the form-creating and life-maintaining values of tragic drama" (*SaF*, 159). Lukács believed in 1911 that Ernst's classical plays satisfied his demands, surpassing the banal empiricism of naturalism in order to condense "the pure soul-content of pure form" (*SaF*, 164), as Lukács formulated it in his discussion of *Brunhild*.

This championing of the classical tragedy by no means excluded treatment of romanticism. Exactly the opposite: Lukács's interest in tragedy is grounded, as his essay "On the Romantic Philosophy of Life: Novalis" illustrates, in a problem lying near to his detailed treatment of early romanticism. The early romantics, in their debate with the preceding generation (Goethe and Schiller), were the first to consider a question central to Lukács: in a world that has splintered into heterogeneous parts, how does the soul guard itself against falling prey to the mundane and philistine? How is poetics possible in the modern society? In his Novalis essay, Lukács takes up the culturally critical motifs of early romanticism and opens them up to debate, without deciding if the complete poetization of reality constitutes a sound solution. One can discern a note of sympathy, but also of distance, which is articulated through a quote from Heinrich Steffen's letter to Ludwig Tieck: "There was something unhealthy about the whole thing" (*SaF*, 42, 46, 51)—a sentence that will be repeated as a leitmotiv. There is thus in this early essay no lack of explicit reservations, many of which foreshadow Lukács's later objections to the romantics: the individualism of the romantics was always in danger of sinking into pettiness; the romantics, following Kant's critique of dogmatic reason, prided themselves on overcoming rationalism, but this attitude also undermined the program of Enlightenment; finally, Lukács's essay already invokes the comparison with Goethe, whose cult of self-formation he acclaims. The stereotypical liberal reproach, that romanticism was in essence no more than a literary clique, also appears in

Lukács's essay: "Of course the whole thing was really no more than a big literary salon, even if scattered over the whole of Germany" (*SaF*, 44).

It would nevertheless be overly hasty to evaluate Lukács's relationship to the romantic tradition solely on the basis of this confining and critical observation. It must instead be understood as a self-critical note—as an indication of the unsolved questions of his own life. The early Lukács took romanticism seriously—especially its search for a new mythology, which contained for Lukács the program of a new aesthetic culture. "Friedrich Schlegel believed that in the all-penetrating force of idealism ... there lay concealed a myth-engendering force which only needed to be awakened into life in order to provide a ground which would be as strong and as collective as that of the Greeks for poetry, art and every life-expression" (*SaF*, 45). This allusion to the unity of Greek culture, which can be compared with the transcendental shelter of medieval culture, is extremely important to Lukács.

A few years later in *The Theory of the Novel* (in the tradition of early romanticism), Lukács would fashion a philosophy of history in which the desire to overcome the fragmented, heterogeneous modern world determined his perspective. Lukács's claim in his Novalis essay that the romantics used ancient Greece and the Middle Ages as "makeshift symbols for this new longing" (*SaF*, 46) is also true of his own understanding: *The Theory of the Novel*'s outline of Homeric culture as a closed and organic totality is a preliminary symbol for aesthetic culture not yet achieved. It does not occur to the young Lukács to understand the romantic interest in the Middle Ages, for example, Novalis's famous essay "Die Christenheit oder Europa," as a literal glorification of that period. The Novalis essay is in this regard remarkably free from the interpretive clichés that slipped into the writing of liberal literary history. Lukács similarly avoids the aestheticized interpretation of early romanticism easily accessible about 1900, which saw in the poetic theory of Schlegel above all an anticipation of symbolism.

Indeed, he explicitly rejects this position: "It is not art for art's sake, it is pan-poetism" (SaF, 47). Poetry is the "the One and the All." This "pan-poetism" brings life into poetry, such that the culture of romanticism includes "the whole of life" (SaF, 48). Lukács obviously uses the term "life" here in an emphatic sense, rather than as a referent for the everyday and its depressing facticity.

Lukács refers in a central passage of his Novalis essay to the dream of a golden age. This reference must be understood as a cipher for the utopian claims of romanticism: romanticism as the program for a utopian culture, in which the soul and life are in accordance. This is the viewpoint through which the young Lukács approached the early romantics, through which he imagined himself in their position, without entirely identifying himself with them. This process of approximation holds at the same time an element of critical resistance. The ambivalence reveals itself in Lukács assessment of romantic subjectivity—of the internality so rebuked by the liberal camp. Lukács makes clear that he accepts this internality as a legitimate expression of the romantic program: "Yet this path was the only possibility open to their longing for the great synthesis of unity and universality. They looked for order, but for an order that comprised everything, an order for the sake of which no renunciation was needed; they tried to embrace the whole world in such a way that out of the unison of all dissonances might come a symphony" (SaF, 48). On the other hand, Lukács is not willing to entrust himself completely to this dream. The romantics identified the longed-for organic world with the real one. "This gave their world the quality of something angelic, suspended between heaven and earth, incorporeally luminous; but the tremendous tension that exists between poetry and life and gives both their real, value-creating powers was lost as a result" (SaF, 50). To be sure, this objection hits the romantic synthesis squarely on the head; the synthesis reveals itself to be a mere semblance that exists at the expense of the resistance with which life opposes poetry—and here we should probably understand the expression "life" as the empirical everyday. But it is not fully clear at this point if it is only the romantic synthesis that proves problematic, or if it is the assumption of a poetic synthesis per se; for when Lukács objects that the romantics failed to realize the border between poetry and action (such that it became necessary for them to awake as from a dream), the question arises whether the assumption of such a border, the insistence on the limited character of all life-praxis, must not in the end position itself against utopia altogether.

As is commonly known, the mature Lukács broke with the utopian approach of his early years and focused the question of life-praxis on the problem of proper collective action. In the course of his expressionism debate with Ernst Bloch, Lukács decisively formulated this realist position.[19] Lukács rejected the subjectivized notion of reality that guided Bloch's defense of the expressionist avant-garde and that was traceable to a (romantic) utopianism. Whether *History and Class Consciousness* already contains such a critique of the panpoetic utopia needs to be investigated. It undoubtedly does not appear in *The Theory of the Novel*, however, which, it must be remembered, was originally planned as the first chapter in a study of Dostoevsky. In the theory of the novel that Lukács wrote after the outbreak of the war, he cogently develops a utopian conception of history—which was only hinted at in the essays of *Soul and Form*—such that the depiction of Dostoevsky approached that of a conqueror of the modern world abandoned by God.

Lukács completes the step from life philosophy to philosophy of history in *The Theory of the Novel* without rejecting the life-philosophical or aesthetic-theoretical motifs of his earlier writing. His position regarding romanticism also changes with this transition. If the final objection to romanticism in the

---

19. See Georg Lukács, " 'Grösse und Verfall' des Expressionismus," in *Probleme des Realismus* (Berlin, 1955).

Novalis essay focuses on the biography of Novalis himself, who managed as an individual thoroughly to poeticize his life and death, then the historical process offers the starting point for a critique of romanticism in *The Theory of the Novel*. This critique realizes itself no longer in the form of an opposition between achievement and failure but, rather, as a critique of the history of spirit. The beginnings of this view are already evident in Lukács's essay "The Bourgeois Way of Life and Art for Art's Sake: Theodor Storm," which describes the poet Storm as an outmoded romantic in a bourgeois world. Under the conditions of a developed bourgeois society, as Lukács emphasizes, the work of art arises no longer through poetization but rather in connection with the capitalist ethic of work performance. With such an approach, the poet consciously abandons the synthesis of poetry and life. Memory replaces hope in the work of Storm; his is a "poetry of decay" (*SaF*, 63), exposed to the danger of sentimentality, which accompanies the attitude of retrospection. This viewpoint becomes central in *The Theory of the Novel*. This historical-philosophic construction stresses the loss of totality and thereby positions itself differently vis-à-vis the romantic epoch. First and foremost, it is important to note that Lukács introduces in his theory of the novel a notion of romanticism that is more extensive spatially as well as temporally. By expanding his view of European literature and at the same time including the later phases of romanticism, romantic literature appears in a different light. At this point, the contours of romanticism in Lukács's interpretation stand much nearer to Nietzsche's conception than they did in 1911.[20] In *The Theory of the Novel* the emphasis shifts from the moment of utopia to the modern character of romantic literature—that is, to the tension between abandonment by God and resistance to the prosaic.

20. For Nietzsche's conception of romanticism, see Ernst Behler, "Nietzsche und die frühromantische Schule," *Nietzsche Studien* 7 (1978): 59–87.

This transition was prepared for in Lukács's never-completed project, "Die Romantik des 19. Jahrhunderts" (Nineteenth-century romanticism), the plans for which have resurfaced in his posthumous works. This project was not only supposed to begin—in typical German fashion—with the philosophy of Fichte and Schelling, moving from there to a discussion of the Schlegels; it included also Baudelaire, Kierkegaard, Flaubert, and Storm.[21] Furthermore, Lukács evidently wanted to extend the project to deal with postromantic authors such as Ibsen, Holz, Tolstoy, and Dostoevsky. This plan clearly illustrates that Lukács wanted to articulate the connection between romanticism and his own epoch. In other words, romanticism is placed here explicitly in relationship to modern literature; it is understood as the beginning of that literature—as the first attempt to express poetically the postclassical situation. Remarkable in Lukács's organization of this project is not so much the inclusion of late romanticism, which appears simultaneously in the work of Ricarda Huch, and which even literary historians like Wilhelm Korsch and Gustav Roethe desired (out of nationalistic-populist motivations).[22] Far worthier of note is Lukács's explicit mention of Flaubert and Baudelaire. Such a conception embraces the modern, distancing itself decisively from the picture sketched by Dilthey in *Das Erlebnis und die Dichtung* (1905) and Oskar Walzel in his concise treatment of the subject (1908).[23]

Dilthey, whose efforts in this regard decisively influenced succeeding German interpretations of romanticism, was primarily concerned with integrating the romantic authors into the canon of the great German tradition. To this end, in his inaugural lecture at Basel (1867) Dilthey had already advocated a continuity between classicism and romanticism. Romanticism appeared as a part of a larger cultural movement that

21. See Keller, *Der junge Lukács*, 134–36.
22. Ibid., 136.
23. Wilhelm Dilthey, *Das Erlebnis und die Dichtung*, 14th ed. (Göttingen, 1965); Oskar Walzel, *Deutsche Romantik* (Leipzig, 1908).

extended from 1770 to 1830. From this perspective, romanticism and idealism proved to be the fulfillment of the German spirit—precisely in their difference from the West European Enlightenment. For this reason Dilthey explicitly declares his interest in "find[ing] in him [Novalis] several of the most important motifs of a world view that emerges in the generation following Goethe, Kant, and Fichte."[24]

The young Lukács had no intention of describing early German romanticism as the culmination of the German spirit. Instead, the sketches he left behind of his romanticism project anticipate *The Theory of the Novel*, in which the motif of disillusionment—of an irreconcilable discrepancy between the hopes and expectations of the subject, and the indifference of an external world which the individual can no longer infuse with meaning—moves to the forefront. Romantic theory of art, especially the romantic theory of irony, plays an important role in this context. By appropriating the romantic notion of irony—presumably on the basis of his extensive preliminary research for the book on romanticism—Lukács creates an odd situation in which he achieves his critique of historical romanticism with the help of an idea placed at his disposal by that same romanticism. But matters don't stop there: the critique of historical romanticism, which appears in *The Theory of the Novel* as a discrete stage of spirit to be overcome, salvages at the same time the utopian impulse that Lukács, in his Novalis essay, identified as the essence of the romantic program. The utopia of the good life and authentic culture were displaced by Lukács into the future: instead of the plans and programs of romanticism, it is the novels of Dostoevsky that act as ciphers for the golden age that must be rewon.

In order to illustrate this shift, we must first investigate the historical construction that lies at the basis of *The Theory of*

---

24. Translated from Dilthey, *Das Erlebnis und die Dichtung*, 188, my interpolations.

the Novel. In the preface to the second edition (written in 1962), Lukács emphasized that *The Theory of the Novel* represented the transition in his development from life philosophy to Hegel's philosophy of history (*TN*, 16). While motifs of Hegelian thought, such as the historicization of categories, should not be overlooked, it would nevertheless be a mistake to understand *Phenomenology of Spirit* as the basis of Lukács's theory. Lukács's theory emphasizes the loss of organic totality and the longing for a new age without alienation to an extent irreconcilable with such a claim. Lukács appears to stand nearer at this point to a romantic conception of history, similar to the one Novalis designed in "Die Christenheit oder Europa," than to the Hegelian logic of history. In order to legitimize the form of the novel, Lukács invokes the difference between antiquity and the modern world. The world of Homer, out of which the Greek epic emerged, represents a closed, organic totality in which "the essential difference between the self and the world, the incongruence of soul and deed" (*TN*, 29) do not yet exist. "It is a homogeneous world, and even the separation between man and world, between 'I' and 'you,' cannot disturb its homogeneity. Like every other component of this rhythm, the soul stands in the midst of the world; the frontier that makes up its contours is not different in essence from the contours of things" (*TN*, 32–33). This closed world is for Lukács the exclusive historical-philosophical locus of the epic. As soon as the organic totality of the antique world dissolves—and this begins already in Greek history—the epic loses its grounding and transforms into an abstract form that, although capable of being imitated, has nevertheless lost its authenticity. Thus the period of Greek tragedy, and even more the period of Greek philosophy (Plato), mark both the loss of "Homer's absolute immanence of life" (*TN*, 35) and the development of a transcendence that divides phenomena and ideas.

Lukács describes the novel as the suitable genre for a world in which unity has disintegrated, in which, consequently, there is no more "spontaneous totality" (*TN*, 38). This point is reached in the history of the genres with Cervantes. The jump from antiquity to the modern age appears to leave the question of how Lukács would classify the verse novel of the Middle Ages unanswered. The predominance of Christian metaphysics, with its strict division between the present world and the world to come, makes the assumption of an immanent totality of existence difficult. For the early Lukács, however, the decisive loss obviously first occurs when a metaphysical construction of reality becomes impossible. In this sense, the medieval world of a Dante or a Wolfram is indeed clearly differentiated from Homer's immanence of life. This difference, however, is smaller than that between Dante and Cervantes or Goethe. Lukács argues that the theology of the Catholic church, even though it strongly insists upon the transcendence of God, creates anew a complete world in which sensuality is preserved. "In Giotto and Dante, Wolfram von Eschenbach and Pisano, St. Thomas and St. Francis, the world became round once more, a totality capable of being taken in at a glance; the chasm lost the threat inherent in its actual depth; its whole darkness, without forfeiting any of its somberly gleaming power, became pure surface and could thus be fitted easily into a closed unity of colours" (*TN*, 37). The Middle Ages thus drew closer to antiquity under the aspect of totality and completeness; the break first enters with the dissolution of the Catholic world. This break, though, is final; every attempt to regain the Greek world (humanism) remains at the level of a "hypostasy of aesthetics into metaphysics—a violence done to the essence of everything that lies outside the sphere of art and a desire to destroy it" (*TN*, 38).

One popular notion of romanticism stresses the poets' turning back to the Middle Ages; one can refer in this regard to Wilhelm Heinrich Wackenroder and Tieck as well as to Novalis's "Die Christenheit oder Europa"—in which the modern age is compared with the closed world of the Middle Ages. According to conventional classification, classicism, in opposition to romanticism, refers to Greek culture. If we follow this classification, the early Lukács appears as a classicist—his championing of Paul Ernst's tragedies affirms this judgment. Upon closer examination, however, this association proves to be only superficially accurate. Lukács's construction of history draws upon the difference between the immanence of existence and the loss of that immanence; it stresses the opposition of a world in which the individual has his secure place to a world (the modern) in which the ego knows no pre-given coordinates.

The transcendental homelessness of the individual is the existential situation that Lukács assumes for the beginning and development of the novel. The novel is, according to Lukács's powerful formulation, "the epic of an age in which the extensive totality of life is no longer directly given, in which the immanence of meaning in life has become a problem, yet which still thinks in terms of totality" (*TN*, 56). The novel is for Lukács the form in which the internal and external worlds have separated, in which the ego can no longer recognize the external world as its own. With this formulation, the preeminence of the subject in the form of the novel is decided for Lukács. While the Homeric epic knew heroes but no individuality, the novel is distinguished by an individuality that corresponds only formally to the idea of the hero—and then often with ironic intent (Goethe).

Lukács succeeds romantic theory in more than one aspect here, probably most clearly with regard to his historical conception.[25] Still, Lukács's theory of the novel establishes a connection with ideas of early German romanticism. Liberal historians, reading the romantic interpretation of history as a conservative turn to the past, often misunderstood early romantic conceptualizations. It has become clear, most recently in the work of Hans-Joachim Mähl and Wilfried Malsch, to what extent the nineteenth-century liberal critique misperceived the romantic conception of history and its political im-

---

25. See also Michael Löwry, *Marxisme et romanticisme revolutionnaire* (Paris, 1979).

plications.[26] Malsch proves in detail that Novalis's Europa speech—still considered by Träger in 1961 to be the decisive anti-Enlightenment turning point—must be understood as a typological figure of thought.[27] Novalis perceives "in the old-new 'dialectical' perversion of history the effects of an opaque poetics, which wins its freedom through self-recognition as self-design. For this reason, he could begin the 'new' history of the self-recognizing poetics with the French Revolution, and he could take the 'old' path of history toward freedom from the revolution out of its 'conscious' transition into the 'old' realm of self-knowledge or of 'belief and insight.' "[28] In this typological interpretation of history by Novalis, the seemingly lost past is rediscovered as the future. Malsch rightly draws attention to the fact that the typological form of thinking found its continuation in the twentieth century in the philosophy of Ernst Bloch. Malsch could have just as accurately cited Lukács's early work, had it not been hidden by Lukács's later opposition to romanticism.

Continuing Richard Samuels's research, Mähl brings to the forefront even more thoroughly the crossing of past and future in the historical thought of Novalis. Mähl powerfully under-scores the difference between this vision of history and the linear-progressive Enlightenment conception (Lessing, Kant): "For Novalis, by contrast, the process of history lies between that primitive state of humanity, which is characterized by

26. Wilfried Malsch, *"Europa" Poetische Rede des Novalis: Deutung der Französischen Revolution und Reflexion auf die Poesie in der Geschichte* (Stuttgart, 1965); Hans-Joachim Mähl, *Die Idee des goldenen Zeitalters im Werk des Novalis: Studien zur Wesensbestimmung der frühromantischen Utopie und zu ihren ideengeschichtlichen Voraussetzungen* (Heidelberg, 1965).

27. Claus Träger, "Novalis und die ideologische Restauration," reprinted in *Erläuterungen zur deutschen Literatur: Romantik.*

28. Translated from Malsch, *"Europa,"* 119. With this statement, Malsch moves Novalis nearer to Hegel and consciously removes him from the sphere of romanticism. He wants to distinguish a critical-orphic classicism (Goethe, Schiller, Novalis, Schlegel, Hegel) from romanticism (Brentano, Tieck, Hoffmann). On this point, see esp. 121.

childlike innocence and a fantastical harmony of the natural and spiritual world, and that desired end condition of humanity, which re-produces this innocence and harmony on a higher plane and cancels the limitations of time and eternity."[29] Novalis's triadic understanding of history incorporates mystical elements while nevertheless denying the possibility of a mystic unification outside of history; this conception sees in the present signs of loss, but also of hope—and indeed, hope in the sense of an openness toward the future. Therefore, the golden age lies not only in the past but also in the future. "Memory" and "anticipation" are interwined. "Nothing is more poetic than memory and anticipation or representation of the future. The representations of previous times draw us toward death, toward disappearance. The representations of the future drive us toward animation, toward abbreviation, toward an assimilating efficacy." Thus wrote Novalis in Blüthenstaub-Fragment of 1798.[30] Between the poles of the past and future lies the present, whose critical negation Novalis demands. "Annihilation of the present—apotheosis of the future, this truly better world."[31] Malsch and Mähl both stress the prophetic, future-oriented character of the romantic critique of the present. "Poetics preserves in the midst of a decayed present, dulled by understanding, the memory of the 'previous time,' so that out of it, as out of the death, out of the mystic, the idea of a true future, the common golden age, may arise."[32]

The idea of conquering the world crisis through poetry—a central idea of early romanticism—is preserved in Lukács's *Theory of the Novel*, although Lukács had treated the project of the Jena school with skepticism in his Novalis essay a few

29. Translated from Mähl, *Die Idee des goldenen Zeitalters*, 305.
30. Translated from Novalis, *Schriften*, ed. Paul Kluckhohn and Richard Samuel, 2d expanded ed. (Stuttgart, 1965), 2:461.
31. Cited (and translated by Karen Kenkel) from Mähl, *Die Idee des goldenen Zeitalters*, 318. All translations of quotations in this essay by Karen Kenkel.
32. Translated from ibid., 319.

years earlier.[33] Possibly, Lukács can maintain this idea because from this point forward he places it at a distance from historical romanticism and associates it with the novels of Dostoevsky. Between the publishing of *Soul and Form* (in 1911) and *The Theory of the Novel* (in 1916), Lukács shifted his interest in romanticism. Already in his unrealized attempt at thoroughly representing European romanticism, the emphasis had shifted from German early romanticism to European late and postromanticism. The inclusion of Baudelaire and Flaubert in the arrangement of the work is characteristic. *The Theory of the Novel* continues in the same vein when it presents the disillusionment novel as the representative novel type of the nineteenth century, for the disillusionment novel, demonstrated by Lukács above all with the example of Flaubert's *Education sentimentale*, thematizes a postromantic situation, a situation in which the dream of a correspondence between the ego and the world is lost, but the desire for such a correspondence is not. If the form of the novel is first constituted through the separation of the ego and the world, which occurs in the *Neuzeit*, then the disillusionment novel is an extreme manifestation of this separation. "The elevation of interiority to the status of a completely independent world is not only a psychological fact but also a decisive value judgment on reality; this self-sufficiency of the subjective self is its most desperate self-defense; it is the abandonment of any struggle to realise the soul in the outside world, a struggle which is seen *a priori* as hopeless and merely humiliating" (*TN*, 114). The content of the disillusionment novel maintains the desire for the fusion of the ego and the world, the desire for a life filled with meaning. This is nevertheless a utopia that is "based from the start on

---

33. See also Friedrich Schlegel in his *Ideen* from 1800: "Humanity becomes an individual through the artists, for it is they who combine past worlds and coming worlds in the present. They are the higher organ of the soul, where the life-spirits of all of external humanity meet, and in which inner humanity has its first effects" (translated from *Kritische Friedrich-Schlegel-Ausgabe*, ed. Ernst Behler [Munich, 1967] 2:262).

an uneasy conscience and the certainty of defeat" (*TN*, 116). The coherence of Lukács's position with romanticism is preserved, however. For example, the poetization of life, an essential aspect of Friedrich Schlegel's and Novalis's theories of the novel, appears renewed in the disillusionment novel, of course only to be disappointed. "Life becomes a work of literature; but, as a result, man becomes the author of his own life and at the same time the observer of that life as a created work of art" (*TN*, 118). The "fulfilling itself" (*TN*, 118) of the ego is no longer possible. It therefore amasses and confines its energy in the internal, enriching internality at the cost of the external world, which has disintegrated into heterogeneous fragments. "The novel remains a beautiful yet unreal mixture of voluptuousness and bitterness, sorrow and scorn, but not a unity; a series of images and aspects, but not a life totality" (*TN*, 120).

For all that, the lost totality of life remains the unshakable focus of Lukács's theory; it is precisely with this focus that he maintains the project of early romanticism. According to the logic of *The Theory of the Novel*, however, totality can be attained only after the present, which is distant from God, is overcome. Between the years 1914 and 1916, Lukács conceived of this victory in terms of a new faith.[34] We need to remember that *The Theory of the Novel* contains not only a structural analysis of the novel but also a criticism of Lukács's own era. In 1914, this assessment of the present took a position against the civilization of the West, anticipating salvation from the East—especially from Russia's literature. At the end of his essay "Aesthetische Kultur," Lukács speaks of the "sanctified

---

34. See Ernst Keller, *Der Junge Lukács*, 172–75. Keller protests against the assumption that Lukács stood primarily under the influence of Hegel when he composed *The Theory of the Novel*, as Lukács himself later claimed; Keller emphasizes instead Lukács's agreement with the Neoplatonic understanding of history and connections with the thought of early romanticism.

names of our epic poets."[35] He is referring to Dostoevsky. Lukács joined his vision of an authentic life, in which Western individualism is overcome by community, with the work of this novelist. The focus of this program is the "greater closeness of nineteenth-century Russian literature to certain organic natural conditions, which were the given substratum of its underlying attitude and creative intention" (*TN*, 145). According to Lukács, it is this nearness that permits the Russian writers—first Tolstoy, but primarily Dostoevsky—to return to the form of the epic. Lukács remarks in this regard: "It is in the words of Dostoevsky that this new world, remote from any struggle against what actually exists, is drawn for the first time simply as a seen reality. That is why he, and the form he created, lie outside the scope of this book. Dostoevsky did not write novels, and the creative vision revealed in his works has nothing to do, either as affirmation or as rejection, with European nineteenth-century Romanticism or with the many, likewise Romantic, reactions against it" (*TN*, 152).

That Lukács settles the Russian novelist on the other shore, beyond the "perfected iniquity" of his own age, emphasizes once again how much he adheres to the utopia of the golden age while repudiating European romanticism. In the "Ethische Fragmente" (Ethical fragments, 1914–17), utopia does not concretize the idea of a just society but a conception of human solidarity. "Each one of us is guilty for everyone else and everything in the world—not only because of the common sins of the world, but also, each solitary individual is responsible for all of humanity and each member of it on this earth. Recognition of this is the climax of life."[36]

After entering the Communist party, Lukács rejected *The Theory of the Novel*. Accordingly, he describes this early work,

---

35. Cited and translated from ibid., 203.
36. Cited and translated from ibid., 214.

in the preface to the new edition of 1962, as abstract-utopian, searching for a resolution to the historical crisis of the First World War without being able to develop it theoretically or conceptually (*TN*, 12, 17). It is certainly correct that Lukács would soon radically alter his substantiation of the change, of the entrance of a new world condition. Still, this certainly does not mean that Lukács's utopian patterns of thought lost their power. Paul Breines rightly stresses that the decisive turn of Marxist theory, expressed in *History and Class Consciousness*, originates in the romantic impulse.[37] Lukács's success in breaking through the positivistic Marxism of the Second International is more easily explained by the fact that his thought did not originate in economic theory—theory that proved to be primarily antirevolutionary in the hands of the German Social Democrats. Instead, Lukács's thought derived from a romantically influenced theory of culture, in which the category of reification, though not developed out of social history, was nevertheless already contained in idealistic form. The central chapter on reification and proletariat consciousness in *History and Class Consciousness* was miles distant in its political objective from the vague hopes of *The Theory of the Novel*; conceptually, however, Lukács could follow closely his early theory of culture. The notion of totality (in its historical expression), as well as the concept of reification, which Lukács from this point on explicitly attributed to Marx's *Capital*, bear witness to the continuity of the (neo)romantic impulse.[38] Lukács became with this work the founder of Western neo-Marxism without ever belonging to it.

As soon as one has rendered visible the connection be-

---

37. On the question of this continuity, see Arato and Breines, *The Young Lukács*, 75–96; Ursula Apitzsch, *Gesellschaftstheorie und Aesthetik bei Georg Lukács bis 1933* (Stuttgart, 1977), esp. 83–85; and Michael Grauer, *Die entzauberte Welt: Tragik und Dialektik der Moderne im frühen Werk von Georg Lukács* (Königstein, 1985), esp. 67–69.

38. Breines, "Marxism, Romanticism, and the Case of Georg Lukács," 428–30.

tween a neoromantic theory of culture and a Marxist theory of revolution, a further question confronts us: How does Lukács's avowed hostility toward romanticism come about? After 1930, sympathy for romanticism is hardly detectable. Prior to Lukács's essay "Die Romantik als Wendung in der deutschen Literatur" (1945) and his studies of Kleist and E. T. A. Hoffmann, his antiromantic position is indirectly articulated in the expressionism debate of the 1930s. The attack on Ernst Bloch (and his defense of expressionism) constituted an attack on a position that Lukács himself had held between 1910 and 1920 but from this point forward repudiated as abstract utopianism.[39] In his critique of expressionism, Lukács draws attention to the political dangers of this position: that is, its potential proximity to fascism. His engagement with National Socialist literary scholarship—for instance, its Büchner and Kleist studies—strengthened these reservations toward the romantic tradition. Fascism's appropriation of romantic and neoromantic ideas and terms legitimized the fundamental decision that Lukács had already made in the 1920s. Coming to terms with the Marxist orthodoxy of the Third International, Lukács retracted the romantic motifs in his theory of society and revolution (without giving them up entirely) in order to maintain his connection with the party.[40] Accordingly, in 1933 (in his autobiographical portrayal "Mein Weg zu Marx" [My path to Marx]), Lukács had already identified and abandoned as error his own proximity to romanticism and his participation in neoromantic cultural criticism (Simmel, Bergson).[41]

Nevertheless, Lukács's essay "Heinrich Heine als nationaler

39. On this topic see Sandor Radnoti, "Bloch und Lukács: Zwei radikale Kritiker in der 'gottverlassenen Welt,' " in Heller, ed., *Die Seele und das Leben*, 177–91.
40. On the debate about Lukács, see Arato and Breines, *The Young Lukács*, 163–89; on Lukács's development, see Apitzsch, *Gesellschaftstheorie*, 112ff. and 139ff.
41. Georg Lukács, *Schriften zur Ideologie*, ed. Peter Ludz (Neuwied, 1967), 323–29.

Dichter" of 1935 illustrates that he preserved a continuity with his early work. It was not difficult for Lukács to rescue Heine politically: Heine was one of the Jewish authors banned by the National Socialists, and Heine himself had harshly criticized German romanticism in his *Romantic School* in a way that corresponded in part to Lukács's critique. Still, Lukács could not overlook the fact that within a European perspective, Heine had to be placed in the romantic canon. Therefore, Lukács argues—in a fashion similar to that of *The Theory of the Novel*—that Heine (as a member of the second generation of romanticism) had to destroy the illusion of the romantic utopia in light of a social situation in which emerging capitalism also increasingly determined literary relationships. Heine develops as an answer a poetic process of radical subjectivity that itself criticizes romantic subjectivity. According to Lukács, Heine does not simply continue to write romantic irony but instead critically overcomes it with an irony that always again rends the hope for a harmony of ego and world. The result is an ideological pessimism that Lukács nevertheless justifies as the last self-critical bourgeois position before the appearance of socialism. In other words, Lukács is able thoroughly to appreciate Heine's romantic, though self-critical, impulses. According to Lukács, Heine reaches his limit only when he comes into contact with Marxist socialism: "Heine had no idea of the socialist revolution as a concrete-historical process. In this regard he remained throughout his life at the methodological standpoint of utopianism: Socialism is for him a condition, an impending condition of the world."[42]

It is remarkable, however, that in his Heine essay Lukács assesses the postromantic—that is, modern—situation so much more cautiously than in his other studies of the same period. In other works (the contributions to the *Linkskurve*,

---

42. Translated from Georg Lukács, *Deutschen Realisten des 19. Jahrhunderts* (Berlin, 1952), 107; henceforth cited in the text as *DR*, followed by page number.

for example), he positions himself directly against modernism and the avant-garde. Although Lukács registers his negative assessment of romanticism ("reactionary character of German romanticism," *DR*, 126), he alters his evaluation of the historical context. Lukács attributes to Heine a deeper understanding of the connection between romanticism and modern literature. "But secondly, Heine sees the inner connection of romanticism with the modern movement of literature.... For example he belongs to those few who have grasped the ideological and methodological significance of the German philosophy of nature. He also understands that the return of romanticism to the popular (*Volkstümliche*), despite any reactionary tendencies it contained, was an indispensable movement for the development of modern literature and culture in Germany" (*DR*, 127). Although it is questionable whether Heine believed that romanticism could be saved by a notion of the popular, he undoubtedly viewed himself as the progeny, critic, and executor of the last testament of romantic literature. The equally important question, to what extent Heine can be understood as an architect of modernism, is touched upon by Lukács, but significantly, he does not fully explore it.[43] Instead, he stresses the parallel to Balzac in order to describe Heine's place "in the development of West European bourgeois literature of the 19th century" (*DR*, 131). According to Lukács, both authors distinguish themselves as still standing before the threshold of modernism. In short, in its overall judgment, the Heine essay corresponds to Lukács's basic antiromantic position of the 1930s and 1940s. The opportunity to deviate from predetermined tracks, however, lay above all in the person and the work of Heine. Heine's critique of romanticism allowed Lukács to return his consideration, at least indirectly and partially, to the romantic sources of his early work.

43. See Peter Uwe Hohendahl, "The Emblematic Reader: Heine and French Painting," in *Paintings on the Move*, ed. Susanne Zantop (Lincoln, Neb., 1989), 9–29.

In the case of Georg Lukács it is appropriate, if not almost necessary, to distinguish between his opposition to romanticism and his (objective) relation to it. While his position vis-à-vis romantic philosophy and literature changed many times during his life, his objective relation to the romantic tradition remained to a large extent constant. It exists even when Lukács expresses his antiromanticism, for instance, in his enmeshment in and duty to the philosophical tradition that enabled him radically to reformulate Marxist theory in the early 1920s. From the viewpoint of structural Marxism, which places renewed emphasis upon the scientific character of Marxist theory, Lukács's entire oeuvre appears to be romantic. From this perspective it makes no difference whether one speaks of the early or late Lukács. That Lukács begins in the 1930s to stress the line from the Enlightenment via Hegel to Marx does not alter the basic assessment of his thought, in that Marx, read through the philosophy of Hegel, appears idealistic and "romantic."

There are three ways in which Lukács, even in his antiromantic phase, remained bound to the romantic tradition (in the broadest sense): his adherence to the notion of totality as an indispensable tool for the materialistic interpretation of history; his insistence upon the Marxist notion of alienation (objectification) as a central concept in the Marxist critique of society; and finally his emphasis on a theory of consciousness in which both literature and art could play an important role in the historical process—not only as reflections of objective relationships, but also as factors that intervene and effect change. The distance toward Hegelian neo-Marxism brought about by the structuralist Marxism of the 1970s allows the romantic components of Lukács's work to appear more clearly than they did in the 1950s, when the debate between Western Marxism (Sartre, the Frankfurt School) and Lukács almost entirely obscured Lukács's affiliation with the romantic Marxist tradition.

2 Art Work and Modernity: The Legacy of Georg Lukács

The debate between Georg Lukács and the Frankfurt School after the Second World War did not occur in a climate of mutual understanding. Even before they left Germany in 1933—Lukács emigrating to the Soviet Union and most of the members of the Frankfurt School to the United States—there were theoretical differences and disagreements on major political issues; after 1945, especially after the political division of Germany, there was even less of a basis for fruitful discussion. While Lukács became the most influential spokesman of orthodox Marxism in Hungary and East Germany (whether this role was an appropriate one is another matter), the members of the Frankfurt School, particularly Horkheimer and Adorno, moved far away from the Marxist premises of their early work, no longer sharing many assumptions with the Hungarian critic. At least this is what each side felt about the other when they looked at the work of their respective opponents. We remember Lukács's remark about the "Hotel Abyss" into which the members of the Frankfurt School had settled all too comfortably;[1] we also remember, of course, Adorno's essay "Reconciliation under Duress," written in 1958 as a response to Lukács's book *Realism in Our Time.*

1. Georg Lukács, *The Theory of the Novel* (Cambridge, Mass., 1971), 22; henceforth cited in the text as *TN*, followed by page number.

This highly polemical essay certainly helped to discredit Lukács as a philosopher and critic among young West German intellectuals of the 1950s and early 1960s. Offering a rigorous and vicious critique of Lukács's theory of realism, this text is in one way clearly a product of the cold war. Adorno, for instance, refers to the socialist countries behind the Iron Curtain only as the *Ostbereich* (Eastern sphere). Yet the essay goes beyond a mere rhetorical dismissal of the orthodox Marxist theory of art, containing at least elements of a more positive appreciation of Lukács, a reading which tries to situate the difference between Adorno's approach and Lukács's method within a broader philosophical context. Adorno, for instance, excludes Lukács's early work, especially *The Theory of the Novel*, from this negative verdict and acknowledges its major impact on the leftist intelligentsia of the 1920s and 1930s. As we shall see, the link between the early Lukács and the Frankfurt School was never entirely severed. Just as the project of Western Marxism can hardly be defined without reference to *History and Class Consciousness*, Adorno's theoretical endeavors can be understood only against the background of Lukács's early work—those texts their author transcended when he became a Marxist. While Lukács viewed his early literary essays as part of a phase that would ultimately lead him to the fundamental insights of orthodox Marxism, Adorno came to the opposite conclusion in "Reconciliation under Duress."[2] The real Lukács is not the mature Lukács, the proponent of the theory of realism and the advocate of the *Volksfront* (popular front) during the 1930s and 1940s, but the early Lukács, whose collection of essays, *Soul and Form*, established him as a major literary critic in Germany and whose *History and Class Consciousness* fundamentally changed the European understanding of Marx.

2. Theodor W. Adorno, "Reconciliation under Duress," in *Aesthetics and Politics*, ed. Ronald Taylor and Fredric Jameson (London, 1980); henceforth cited in the text as "RD," followed by page number.

If we were to focus exclusively on Lukács's literary theory or his philosophy of art, we might possibly disregard Adorno's polemic. Since it is our task to explore the relationship between Lukács and the Frankfurt School, however, we cannot overlook Adorno's critique. His essay provides a forceful, although certainly not neutral, statement about the two opposing positions. While Adorno occasionally, particularly at the end of the essay, attempts an intrinsic understanding of Lukács's theory, his attack for the most part measures Lukács's work against his own concepts and presuppositions. Hence he vehemently disagrees with Lukács's central thesis that modernism and the avant-garde must be seen as a phase of artistic decline when compared with nineteenth-century realism and twentieth-century socialist realism in the Soviet Union. Where Lukács sees a basic tendency toward literary and cultural deterioration after the failure of the 1848 revolutions, a loss of vigor he does not hesitate to call "decadence," Adorno emphatically insists that nineteenth-century modernism and the avant-garde movements of this century—Adorno does not systematically distinguish between these concepts—provide (precisely through their nonrealistic method) the moment of aesthetic truth that Lukács wrongly finds in realism. Modernist works of art unveil, without imitating, empirical reality. It is not progressive works of art—for example, the compositions of Arnold Schönberg—that fail to grasp and explore the social reality of their time, but rather, as Adorno emphasizes, the belated attempts to capture this reality through the method of bourgeois realism.

Adorno's opposition to Lukács centers on the latter's concept of the work of art, especially his insistence on defining the interconnection between art and social reality in terms of representation. Adorno argues against this. We have to understand the relationship between art and reality first and foremost as an opposition. Only by conceiving art as an antithesis to social reality can one unfold the inner connection between them. Adorno notes: "Art exists in the real world and has a function in it, and the two are connected by a large number of mediating links. Nevertheless, as art it remains the antithesis of that which is the case" ("RD," 159). Consequently, one cannot treat the content (*Gehalt*) of art works as a simile of historical reality, as if aesthetic presentation were no more than a vehicle that critical analysis quickly transcends in order to reach the essential core of the art work.

This criticism—we shall have to come back to it later—leads to two important points. First, Adorno argues that in his later work Lukács underestimates the significance of *artistic technique*. In reducing its importance, Lukács necessarily misunderstands the nonmimetic tendencies of modern art. In order to fend off this reduction, Adorno underscores the logic of aesthetic form. Progress in the realm of art does not result from proper imitation; rather, it stems from the intrinsic unfolding of technique. As Adorno remarks: "But can he really close his eyes to the fact that the techniques of art also develop in accordance with their own logic? Can he rest content with the abstract assertion that when society changes, completely different aesthetic criteria automatically come into force?" ("RD," 162).

Adorno's theory of the aesthetic forces of production developing their own historical logic through artistic techniques then necessarily turns—and this is the second point—against Lukács's normative concept of realism. Undercutting the opposition of formalism and realism, Adorno argues that the formal construction of the work of art, the relationship of its elements to each other, precedes the representation of empirical reality. The concept of realism, which is indeed crucial for the later Lukács, appears in Adorno's writings only as a dominant literary convention of the nineteenth century. Thus, for Adorno, the realism of Balzac, as it was praised by Lukács, turns out to be much less realistic than generally assumed—an argument that Adorno, however, does not use to belittle the literary importance of Balzac. For Adorno, Balzac's significance lies in his radical use of themes and formal elements, rather than in the reflection of contemporary French society.[3]

Obviously, the fundamental disagreement between Lukács and Adorno concerns the mediation of art and society in their respective theories. This confrontation can be traced on two levels. First, they disagree about the correlation between art and social reality. Whereas Lukács conceptualizes this correlation on the level of content, Adorno insists on the priority of form; and while Lukács introduces the concept of *reflection* at this juncture, Adorno refers in his aesthetic theory to the notion of a *monad*. As he reminds us, the Leibniz monad is without windows, yet the inside contains the outside.[4]

On a second level, Lukács and Adorno also cannot agree on the evaluation of social reality. As far as the perils of late capitalism are concerned, they come to more or less the same conclusions (reification and alienation). They part ways, however, in their understanding and evaluation of the future. Adorno no longer accepts Lukács's conviction that the reification of advanced capitalism can be overcome through the proletarian revolution. Adorno's critique of Lukács's aesthetic theory has its exact parallel in his critique of Lukács's social theory, especially of the socialism of the Soviet Union and its Eastern allies. Therefore, in Adorno's eyes, Lukács's concept of socialist realism is no more than the expression of Stalinist terror. It effaces, among other things, the essential category of aesthetic autonomy.

Still, as a reader of *Realism in Our Time*, Adorno is also careful to accentuate those elements of Lukács's theory that do not support the official literary theory of Hungary or the GDR. At the end of his essay, he tries to rescue some of Lukács's concepts, but this does not get very far, since Adorno basically judges the work of the mature Lukács by the standards of the

3. Theodor W. Adorno, "Balzac-Lektüre," *Noten zur Literatur II* (Frankfurt, 1961), 10–41.

4. Theodor W. Adorno, *Aesthetic Theory* (London, 1984), 257–60; henceforth cited in the text as *AT*, followed by page number.

early Lukács. The last sentence of his essay makes this very clear: "The magic spell which holds Lukács in thrall and which prevents his return to the utopia of his youth that he longs for, is a re-enactment of that reconciliation under duress he had himself discerned at the heart of the absolute idealism" ("RD," 176). At least Adorno is willing to admit that Lukács's aesthetic theory cannot be dismissed as a simplistic concept of thematic reflexion. Structural and formal questions are important for Lukács as well. As Adorno concedes, Lukács's critique of certain forms of socialist realism contain elements of critical resistance that, if elaborated rigorously, could be used to defend the avant-garde. When Adorno makes this point, incidentally, he does not fail to refer again to Lukács's early work, with its emphasis on the crucial difference between intensive and extensive totality.

This, then, is precisely the common ground between Lukács and Adorno. When Adorno develops the difference between theoretical and aesthetic knowledge, he introduces the concept of totality. "A work of art only becomes knowledge when taken as a totality, i.e. through all its mediations, not through its individual intentions" ("RD," 168). As much as Adorno distances himself from Lukács's preference for the cognitive aspect of the art work, they share the category of totality, although not its construction and application in the realm of aesthetic theory. Obviously this category refers to their common heritage in Hegel's philosophy as it was reformulated by Marx and the Marxist tradition. We might, as Peter Bürger does, conclude from this intertextual relationship that both Lukács's and Adorno's theories are variations of the same basic Hegelian model.[5] This approach, however, obscures the historical difference between Lukács and Adorno; it represses the historical causes that discouraged Adorno from simply explicating Lu-

5. Peter Bürger, *Theory of the Avant-Garde* (Minneapolis, 1984), 83–94.

kács's theory. Both Lukács and Adorno are indebted to the Hegelian tradition, but their debt must be understood in terms of transformation and modification. Adorno's transformation of Lukács results in a position to which the latter is fundamentally antagonistic. To put it differently: Adorno's critique of Lukács makes use of concepts and categories that were partly taken from Lukács's early work and in which Lukács had to recognize himself. In the prefaces to the second edition of *The Theory of the Novel* (1962) and the reprinted edition of *History and Class Consciousness* (1967), Lukács makes it very clear that he fully understands this intertextual connection.

The Theory of the Novel is key to the debate between Lukács and the Frankfurt School; both sides refer to it explicitly or implicitly. Only with this text in mind can we fully understand both the Frankfurt School's compatibility and its conflict with Lukács. This claim, however, must be specified. The members of the Frankfurt School did not simply read *The Theory of the Novel* as a continuation of Lukács's earlier work; rather, they read it backward, so to speak. Their interpretation included the social theory of *History and Class Consciousness*, especially the concept of reification. In the late 1920s, Benjamin and Adorno gave *The Theory of the Novel* a revisionist Marxist reading, but in doing so they repressed certain parts of Lukács's theory. This is particularly true of Adorno's aesthetic theory, which fails to pick up Lukács's attempt to return to the totality of the epic in the closing discussion of Tolstoy and Dostoevsky. Instead, Adorno uses Lukács's concept of the novel—the form that articulates the condition of the modern world—as the basis for his own theory. When Lukács developed the idea that the novel is historically grounded in an age marked by alienation, he provided Adorno's theory with two significant elements. First, he insisted on the historicity of aesthetic forms—an important step toward a sociology of forms; second, he underscored the legitimacy of the structure of the novel, that is, the legitimacy of its fragmentary, nonorganic character. Adorno's thesis that technique is more important than content was already anticipated in Lukács's emphasis on the nonorganic structure of the novel.

It is important to unpack this aspect of *The Theory of the Novel*. Lukács delineates the concept of the novel by differentiating the homogeneous world of the Greek epic from the modern world. While the early Greek age is characterized by a life-world filled with immediate meaning, this extensive totality has become problematic in the postmedieval modern world. The individual faces an alienated reality; the meaning of life is no longer guaranteed by traditional social practices. Still, the demand for totality does not vanish. It is precisely this historical configuration that generates and determines the novel form. "In a novel, totality can be systematized only in abstract terms, which is why any system that could be established in the novel—a system being, after the final disappearance of the organic, the only possible form of a rounded totality—had to be one of abstract concepts and therefore not directly suitable for aesthetic form-giving" (*TN*, 70). The early Lukács, precisely because he emphasizes the concrete, rounded totality of the world of the Greek epic, insists on the modern world's lack of rounded totality. Organic form therefore has been replaced by abstract structure, an abstract form that can only allude to the rounded totality of the epic, since the "immanence of being" (*TN*, 71) no longer coincides with empirical reality. To put it differently, there is an unbridgeable hiatus between the immanent meaning of life and outer reality, between the subject and the objective world. The novel responds to this configuration by articulating this hiatus through its formal structure. As Lukács remarks: "The composition of the novel is the paradoxical fusion of heterogeneous and discrete components into an organic whole which then is abolished over and over again" (*TN*, 84).

Two aspects of this formulation must be underlined. On the one hand, Lukács points out that the form of the novel differs significantly from the epic form yet is not illegitimate. In fact,

Lukács insists on the historico-philosophical necessity of its abstract, nonorganic composition. On the other hand, Lukács suggests that there is a longing for an organic whole that can only be suggested and must be repeatedly canceled in the context of the modern world. In *The Theory of the Novel*, Lukács is primarily concerned with the legitimation of the novel, yet we also find an attempt to stipulate organic composition as the ultimate goal of history. Lukács articulates this idea in a more pronounced fashion especially when confronting the question of whether and how the novel form can be overcome in the final chapters.

Let us look at this problem more closely. If the structure of the novel cannot reach the authentic organic form of the epic, then the question becomes how abstract elements can form a whole at all—and here we do not speak of a conceptual but of an aesthetic unity. The early Lukács clearly separates these two aspects. While he grants the feasibility of systematically constructing an extensive totality through concepts, he assumes that the attempt to grasp this extensive totality through aesthetic means would be problematic. It can be realized, however, at least approximately. Lukács solves this dilemma by introducing the concept of *irony*, although his concept must not be confused with the rhetorical figure where the true meaning is simply the opposite of what is said. In *The Theory of the Novel*, irony describes the attitude of the creative subject (the writer) toward reality after he has realized his own problematic status in this world. This self-consciousness—the insight into the discrepancy between his own desire for a meaningful life and the alienated reality—articulates itself in the novel as the reflexivity of the narrator. The form of the novel, the patterns of its composition, grows out of the tension between the reflexivity of the narrator and the world as it appears in the narrative (the given material). The never-completed but always-anticipated synthesis of abstract elements is brought about through the narrator's self-awareness, which thematizes the gap between the interior and the outer world, between the longing for meaning and a trivialized empirical reality. As Lukács notes, irony "extends not only to the profound hopelessness of the struggle, but also to the still more profound hopelessness of its abandonment—the pitiful failure of the intention to adapt to a world which is a stranger to ideals, to abandon the unreal ideality of the soul for the sake of achieving mastery over reality" (*TN*, 85–86). Hence the plot, narrating the development of the hero, is not the final word. Through the reflexivity of the narrator, the narrative transcends itself. The form of the novel, therefore, is not only abstract but also self-critical. The aesthetic appearance, as it materializes in the characters and the plot, is not the ultimate level of meaning. "Irony, the self-surmounting of a subjectivity that has gone as far as it was possible to go, is the highest freedom that can be achieved in a world without God. That is why it is not only the sole possible *a priori* condition for a true, totality-creating objectivity but also why it makes that totality—the novel— the representative art-form of our age: because the structural categories of the novel constitutively coincide with the world as it is today" (*TN*, 93).

Again, I want to underscore that the form of the novel does not cancel the longing for rounded totality. Lukács, as we remember, insists on the longing for totality; yet this totality is not a given essence. Rather, it is an attempt that is regularly undermined through irony. The appearance of organic wholeness is no more than a suggestion to be problematized by the narrator. At the same time, we have to keep in mind that for Lukács the novel is only a transitional genre. It is the form that corresponds to the age of alienation. As soon as this age has been overcome and the rupture between the subject and reality has been healed, the novel form loses its raison d'être. Thus, at the end of *The Theory of the Novel* Lukács is faced with the question: What will be the adequate genre after the demise of the novel? In certain ways, Lukács argues, the novels of Tolstoy already transcend the structure of the novel and return to the epic mode, although in Tolstoy it is more a matter of intent and *gestus* than a question of historical necessity. Lukács further suggests that Dostoevsky's narratives are no longer novels, without, however, explaining what the basis of this transformation might be. Still, the underlying argument becomes quite apparent: under certain historical conditions, the problematic totality of the novel will be replaced by a renewed organic totality of the epic.

It is evident that Lukács's later Marxist position deviates significantly from this theory. As he points out in the preface to the 1962 edition of *The Theory of the Novel*, his early theory looks like a utopian construct without historical and social foundations. The hope for a restoration of epic totality and organic form is not firmly grounded in social history. Nonetheless, I would argue, this motif does not entirely disappear from Lukács's work. He brings it into his later criticism by redefining the task of the novel. Adorno and Benjamin, on the other hand, who in many ways stay much closer to the impetus of *The Theory of the Novel*, do not follow Lukács when he later emphasizes the need for organic form in the novel. Adorno asserts the abstract character of modern art; and in his criticism, the nonorganic composition of the novel becomes the model for the advanced work of art in general.

This strategy can be studied by looking at Adorno's music criticism of the 1930s and 1940s. The prime example is the essay "Schönberg und der Fortschritt" later incorporated into *The Philosophy of Modern Music*. In a different way, the same argument prevails in the famous chapter on the culture industry in *Dialectic of Enlightenment*, where Adorno works out the difference between administered art and authentic autonomous works of art. First, Adorno continues the move toward historical understanding of forms and genres, as it was introduced by the early Lukács (who, of course, already inherited this idea from Hegel's aesthetics); second, Adorno sharpens the focus and transforms the philosophical interpretation of form into a sociological one. This revision is closely connected to Lukács's own development. The changes in Lukács's position

when he wrote *History and Class Consciousness* clearly left
their traces in the work of the Frankfurt School. In particular,
Lukács's theory of reification, as synthesized from the writings
of Marx and Weber, had a major impact on the work of Benjamin and Adorno. Whereas the concept of commodity fetishism in Marx's *Capital* refers primarily to the material practices
of human beings, Lukács extends the concept by fusing it with
Weber's notion of rationalization in modern societies and applies it to cultural configurations as well. The philosophy of
German idealism, for instance, the epistemological theory of
Kant, comes as much under the spell of reification, Lukács
argues, as the social relations between human beings.

This is the early Adorno's point of departure in the 1930s.
His essays on music—for example, his famous essay on the
regression of listening in advanced capitalist societies—concentrate their effort on the social context of musical production
and reception under late capitalism.[6] Adorno means to demonstrate that neither the production nor the reception of music
can be treated as natural and transhistorical phenomena. Listening is determined by the fact that modern society is almost
totally reified. The process of reification extends to culture as
well. Works of art are transformed into cultural goods that have
only exchange value and no use value. I do not wish to pursue
the later development of this argument in *Dialectic of Enlightenment;* instead, I want to have a closer look at its other side,
the fate of the autonomous work of art under advanced capitalism.

Adorno's analysis of Schönberg's music combines the historical definition of modernity set forth in *The Theory of the
Novel* with the theory of reification unfolded in *History and
Class Consciousness.* While the early Lukács was concerned
with the legitimation of the aesthetic form of the novel,

6. Theodor W. Adorno, "On the Fetish Character in Music and the
Regression of Listening," in *The Essential Frankfurt School Reader,* ed.
Andrew Arato and Eike Gebhardt (New York, 1978), 270–99.

Adorno, using Schönberg's music as an example, wanted to legitimize the experiments of the avant-garde vis-à-vis traditional romantic music. Adorno argues that the decline of romantic music, that is, the transition from tonal to atonal methods of composition, is a logical process justified by the material itself. This material, which confronts the artist in previous works of art, calls for the destruction of tonal conventions as soon as the artist defines his or her task vis-à-vis a postliberal capitalist society. For Adorno, exterior and interior motives (social context and intrinsic structure) are of equal importance.

In *The Philosophy of Modern Music*, Adorno insists on the impossibility of an organic work of art in the modern age, much as Lukács did in *The Theory of the Novel*. Schönberg only followed the internal logic of evolution in music when he diverged from the late romantics and refused to compose rounded and closed works of art. Adorno notes: "Under the coercion of its own objective consequences, music has critically invalidated the idea of the polished work and disrupted the collective continuity of its effect."[7] Hence, the only legitimate works of art are those compositions that are no longer works of art in the traditional sense. Adorno uses this insight when he criticizes Alban Berg's opera *Wozzeck*: its final form returns to a more traditional notion of an opera, especially in comparison with the first draft.

Lukács's idea of the fragmentary and artificial character of the modern novel becomes even more radical in the writings of Adorno. Adorno favors the idea of a thoroughly fragmented, open work of art, a text emphatically distanced from a cultural tradition that has been integrated into the culture industry. Where Lukács emphasized the heterogeneous nature of the aesthetic elements that have to be fused by the novelist's creative subjectivity, Adorno uses the concept of the material following

7. Theodor W. Adorno, *Philosophy of Modern Music* (New York, 1973), 29; henceforth cited in the text as *PhMM*, followed by page number.

its own logic. The composer's sensibility has to differentiate between those forms that have become obsolete and those that are adequate responses to the social context. Thus Adorno remarks on the historical logic of musical harmony: "The isolated appearance of chords does not in itself decide their correctness or incorrectness. These are to be judged only from the perspective of the level of technique adhered to at a given time" (*PhMM*, 84). Consequently, the technique applied in a work of art—and this is the other side of the coin—would also elucidate its social meaning and function. In other words, for Adorno the social meaning of the work of art is expressed through technique rather than through specific themes and motifs.

In music, the concept of representation or imitation as a way of correlating art and reality is not particularly fruitful. Yet Adorno's preference for formal, technical analysis is by no means limited to the field of music. In his literary essays, Adorno later uses the same concept of technique in reading novels and poems. The idea of mimesis plays only a very minor role in Adorno's literary criticism. Instead, Adorno's theory is centered on the concept of aesthetic autonomy. Modernism and the avant-garde are particularly determined by their radical separation of the aesthetic realm from social and political reality. The more modern society is defined by reification—a situation that has become reality under monopoly capitalism—the more the work of art has to distance itself from its social as well as its political context. Its critical power derives from its refusal to participate in a largely commercialized tradition. Therefore, Adorno already radicalizes the concept of aesthetic autonomy in his 1940 Schönberg essay to such an extent that it ultimately undercuts the traditional notion of aesthetic appearance. Art, as Adorno later notes in *Aesthetic Theory*, "challenges its own essence, thereby heightening the sense of uncertainty that dwells in the artist" (*AT*, 2). This element of heightened uncertainty does not, however, encourage Adorno to retract the claim that truth is expressed in art. In *Aesthetic*

Theory, Adorno emphatically opposes the Kantian approach to art, which views the act of aesthetic judgment purely as a matter of taste. Adorno, following the early Lukács, insists on the objective truth content of art works, although this truth value cannot be reduced to the level of cognitive knowledge.

Although Adorno's authentic work of art, particularly that of the avant-garde, may be isolated and far removed from the cultural tradition, it is nevertheless closely connected with reality through its *Gehalt* (Adorno's concept of the synthesis of form and content). Hence the concept of totality, which is central to Lukács's criticism, is crucial to Adorno's as well. In *Aesthetic Theory*, this emphasis must not be understood as a plea for affirmation. Rather, Adorno needs this category to situate the fate of the modern work of art. Especially when Adorno moves from an intrinsic analysis to a contextual interpretation that brings the historical configuration to bear on the reading of the art work, the category of totality becomes essential. Without it, the relationship between the aesthetic sphere and empirical social reality (including its organizations and institutions) would be reduced to monocausal correlations. The relationship between art and reality, Adorno argues, cannot be reduced to a field of causal connections. Rather, art works are to be conceived as monads that contain and therefore mirror the totality of social reality. For this reason, Adorno is not interested in the communicative aspect of art. The notion of communication would result, as Adorno maintains against empirical sociology, in affirmation. For Adorno, the relationship of the art work to the whole of the social system can be understood only as concrete negation (*bestimmte Negation*).[8]

In emphasizing the importance of the concept of totality in Adorno's work, we have to underscore at the same time the particular nature of this category in his writings. In his study *Marxism and Totality*, Martin Jay correctly points out that the

8. For an explication of this concept, see Theodor W. Adorno, *Negative Dialectics* (New York, 1973).

Frankfurt School moved away from the concept of totality developed in *History and Class Consciousness*.[9] This category loses its dogmatic character, especially in Adorno's work. Hegel's dialectical struggle for synthesis is replaced by a negative dialectic that refuses the completion of synthesis and thereby continually calls the notion of stable truth into question. Truth and totality are mutually exclusive. The whole, according to Adorno, is the false. Still, the concept of totality has a place and a function in *Aesthetic Theory*. It serves as a reference point for the mediation between art and reality, the aesthetic and the social realm. But the totality of the social system absolutely cannot serve as a goal. For the modern artist, reconciliation is strictly prohibited. The concept of totality must be restricted to the sphere of art. As Adorno remarks in *Aesthetic Theory*: "The road to the integration and autonomy of the art work leads to the death of its moments in the totality. As art works transcend their own particularity, they flirt with death, the epitome of which is the totality of the work" (*AT*, 78). Even this use of the category distances itself from Hegel's affirmative dialectic. For Adorno, Lukács's Hegelian concept of totality in *History and Class Consciousness* is only the negative foil against which he defines his own approach.

With this point we return to where we began. Adorno's "Reconciliation under Duress" made it very clear that the Frankfurt School was unable to identify with the critical writings of the later Lukács. Yet this rigid opposition calls for scrutiny, because the hostility between Lukács and Adorno is grounded in a shared tradition of concepts and categories. There are three ways to understand and evaluate this common ground. If one maintains the unity of Lukács's oeuvre, if one stresses the continuity of his writings from the early essays to his late aesthetic theory, the position of the Frankfurt School appears to be an unfortunate deviation from the path of Western Marx-

9. Martin Jay, *Marxism and Totality* (Berkeley and Los Angeles, 1984), 241–75.

ism. Fredric Jameson at least comes close to this point of view. For him, Lukács's writings can be understood as the continuous unfolding of a basically identical theory.[10] The contrary position is more prominent among Adorno's disciples in Frankfurt. They accept Adorno's critique of Lukács as a premise of their own work and therefore eliminate Lukács's writings after 1930 from any further consideration. Consequently, Lukács's heritage is limited to his early work, especially to *The Theory of the Novel* and *History and Class Consciousness*. In *Marxism and Totality*, Martin Jay takes a similar position when he stresses the fact that the Frankfurt School criticized and transformed Lukács's concept of totality.[11]

In his *Theory of the Avant-Garde*, Peter Bürger challenges this point of view, maintaining that it stays too close to the subject matter and therefore takes the differences between Lukács and Adorno as absolutes. According to Bürger, it is not difficult to show that both critics share basic presuppositions— exactly those elements that remain outside the controversy. Hence Bürger insists that the theories of both Lukács and Adorno, though they seem contradictory, are actually cut from the same cloth. They share certain limitations that must be articulated and overcome. In order to transcend these limitations, we have to historicize not only Lukács's writings, but Adorno's as well. Thus Bürger argues: "the intention of the theory sketched here is to demonstrate that the debate itself is historical. To do so, it must be shown that the premises of the two authors are already historical today and that it is therefore impossible to simply adopt them."[12]

According to Bürger, both Lukács and Adorno basically developed theories of the art work without attending to the institutional context. "The dispute between Lukács and Adorno concerning the legitimacy of avant-gardiste art as outlined

10. Fredric Jameson, *Marxism and Form* (Princeton, 1971), 160–63.
11. See Jay, *Marxism*, 196–219 and 241–75.
12. Bürger, *Theory of the Avant-Garde*, 86.

above is confined to the sphere of artistic means and the change in the kind of work this involves (organic versus avant-gardiste).''[13] Since both theories are grounded in the concept of aesthetic autonomy, their authors underestimate the avant-garde's challenge to the principle of autonomy. Arguing about the specific character of the modern art work, both overlook the fact that the avant-garde movements fundamentally problematized the status of art. These movements aimed, as Bürger holds, at the cancellation of the institution of art in general. They meant to destroy the very institution that served as the foundation for the ongoing debate about modern art.

This is not the place for an extensive discussion of Peter Bürger's theory. His thesis that both Lukács and Adorno have become historical has lost much of its shock effect. It would be difficult today to find many orthodox students of Lukács's literary theory, nor are there dogmatic practitioners of Adorno's philosophy of art. Our problem is not so much to achieve distance but to come to terms with this heritage, the tradition of Western Marxism. Is it superfluous baggage to be thrown overboard in order to get the boat floating again? Or would it be better to rescue parts of Lukács's and Adorno's theories? Bürger's solution to this problem, the move toward historical distance, is not sufficient, since it is basically negative, a warning against the dogmatic use of Lukács's and Adorno's theories. Bürger does not discuss the usefulness of revisions, and his solution is schematic. Lukács's and Adorno's theories do not occupy the same historical space (as it may have appeared in West Germany during the 1960s). Rather, we must note the historical filiation: the aesthetic theory of the early Lukács, together with the social theory of *History and Class Consciousness*, is the basis for the Frankfurt School and Adorno. As we have seen, Adorno appropriates and develops a position that Lukács sketched in *The Theory of the Novel* (the nonorganic work of art), while Lukács himself later favored different

13. Ibid.

aspects of his early theory, for instance, the notion that the crisis of bourgeois society has to be overcome—in both the social and the aesthetic sphere. Since the proletarian revolution in Russia has transformed the structure of a bourgeois society, Lukács suggests, we may also expect a new organic art form. Socialist realism is this new organic art that differs so significantly from the formal experiments of bourgeois modernism. We must not overlook the correlation between the political and the aesthetic development in Lukács's theory. Similarly, Adorno's resistance to Lukács's normative theory of realism is grounded in a different assessment of the class conflict and its outcome in the twentieth century. Adorno is convinced that the emancipatory potential of the proletarian revolution failed. In Germany, the fascists seduced the proletariat; in Russia, the revolution resulted in Stalinism. Thus Adorno's aesthetic theory is confronted either with late capitalism or with pseudo-socialism. According to Adorno, neither system allows change.

This assessment of the condition of modern society has a major impact on Adorno's aesthetic theory. Adorno wants to constitute a realm of critical resistance against the overwhelming power of the reified social system. Therefore he emphatically embraces the concepts of aesthetic autonomy and aesthetic appearance. For the same reason he is less interested in those tendencies of the avant-garde movements that would undermine and ultimately destroy the institution of art, for this thrust could only weaken the resistance against the pressure of the system.

As I have tried to demonstrate for both Adorno and Lukács, the problem of cultural tradition cannot be separated from political theory and the evaluation of the concrete political situation. Yet recent history has not exactly supported either theorist. In this respect, Peter Bürger has rightly emphasized that their theories are no longer immediately applicable to the present situation. The political and literary practices of the socialist countries could legitimize socialist realism only for a limited time. The most advanced authors of these countries have moved closer to the formal structures of modernism and the avant-garde, particularly since the 1970s. These tendencies must be understood as signals that the social reality of these countries cannot be grasped through the concept of epic totality. On the other hand, the literary practices of Western countries after the Second World War do not easily conform to the concept of the avant-garde. Adorno was aware of these changes when he discussed the evolution of modern music. He defined these changes as a process of aging without, however, adjusting his aesthetic theory in major ways. In this case, the correlation between aesthetic and social theory functions as a block. Since Adorno stresses the reified character of the social system—that is, the lack of dynamic change—he is unable to anticipate new forces that would break with the status quo. Hence the work of art is locked into place, and aesthetic autonomy must be the final answer to the pressure of the system of late capitalism.

Our historical distance from Lukács and Adorno is hard to deny. It restricts dogmatic readings of their theories and unmediated application of their theses. Since the institutional structure of art has changed, and with it the function of art, we can no longer share some of Lukács's and Adorno's implicit presuppositions. For instance, our view of the relationship between authentic art and mass culture has changed. Both Lukács and Adorno—in this they are heirs of romantic theory—have a defensive attitude toward mass culture. They exclude that which cannot be subsumed under the category of autonomy from the concept of art. This aggressive stance, especially in Adorno's case, always risks becoming a defense of an affirmative elite culture. This danger should not, however, blind us to Lukács's and Adorno's theories. Adorno's critical procedure, negative dialectic, is still a powerful and decisive instrument for critical analysis of our present social and cultural reality. And, although Adorno would find this difficult to admit, it has incorporated a good deal of Lukács's theory.

Adorno's model of negative dialectic reflects Lukács's concept of totality—totality not as reconciled reality (as in the age of the Greek *epos*) but as a hypothetical concept that refers to a notion of wholeness. This hypothesis then allows the critic to understand and criticize the individual and concrete moment. In other words, the element of deconstruction in Adorno's theory, his insistence that the individual moment is not identical with its concept, cannot forgo the category of totality, because without it the critical approach would be reduced to the collection and ordering of facts or the phenomenological description of individual elements. This emerges, for instance, in Adorno's strong criticism of empirical sociology of art. In his essay "Theses on the Sociology of Art," he states: "Sociology of art, in the strict sense of the word, contains all aspects of the relationship between art and society. It is impossible to reduce this discipline to one aspect, for example the social impact of art works. This impact is only one moment in the totality of this relationship."[14] Lukács would have agreed with this, as much as he differs from Adorno when it comes to working out the mediation between an art work and society.

Adorno's concept of totality does not, however, imply the notion of an organic construct. Organic totality is only a hypothetical model, and in his historical analyses of modern art, Adorno clearly does not use such a concept. It could be argued that Adorno's category of immanence makes the presupposition of totality superfluous. This would lead to a defense of Adorno's intrinsic method of reading against Lukács's historical reading, which apparently transcends the text. This dichotomy cannot do justice to the problem at hand, however, since Adorno's emphasis on an intrinsic procedure is a matter of methodological priority rather than an attempt to restrict the interpretation to the text and exclude historical reality. Adorno does not mean to dissolve history. His concept of the monad makes this very clear. When we understand the art work as a monad, we assume that the totality of the social system

14. Theodor W. Adorno, "Thesen zur Kunstsoziologie," in *Ohne Leitbild* (Frankfurt, 1967), 94.

(against which we read the text) is not simply outside but inside as well. At the same time, this model retains a notion of objective meaning—it retains the concept of the truth content (*Wahrheitsgehalt*) of the work of art, which, since it is "begriffslos" (conceptless), challenges decoding.

3 Autonomy of Art: Looking Back at Adorno's *Aesthetische Theorie*

Theodor W. Adorno's major contribution to the philosophy of art, his *Aesthetische Theorie*, appeared in 1970.[1] The work was almost completed when the author died in 1969. Adorno meant to rewrite the introduction, but otherwise the text needed only stylistic revisions, which were carried out by Rolf Tiedemann, Adorno's faithful disciple and editor. Tiedemann rightly felt that *Aesthetische Theorie* deserved immediate publication, since it was the legacy of Critical Theory. Yet it was precisely this aspect that marred the reception of the book. Except for a few voices in the liberal and conservative camp, the response was surprisingly negative. One might have expected that the East German critics would denounce Adorno's theory as a typical example of Western ideology—which they did; more alarming was the unfriendly or at least cool reception among the West German Left. If the members of the Frankfurt School considered *Aesthetische Theorie* Adorno's legacy, it turned out to be a legacy that was clearly unwelcome. The charges varied,

1. For a full account of the genesis of *Aesthetische Theorie*, see Rolf Tiedemann's "Editorisches Nachwort" (editorial afterword), in Theodor W. Adorno, *Gesammelte Schriften: Aesthetische Theorie* (Frankfurt, 1970), 7:537–44. The quotations and page numbers cited in the text will be translations from this edition, which will be abbreviated as *AT*, followed by page number. An English translation has been published as *Aesthetic Theory* (London, 1984).

but there was almost a consensus among the critics of the Left that Adorno's last book did not offer the materialist theory of art that everybody was looking for. It was particularly Adorno's insistence on the autonomy of the art work and his well-known indictment of *Tendenz* (tendentiousness) and political art that angered the Left. Adorno evidently had not changed his position. In his last work he reiterated his critique of unmediated engagement and once more presented modernism and the avant-garde as the only viable responses to the increasing brutality of advanced capitalism. His renewed claim that, in the final analysis, only the authentic work of art overcomes the stultifying atmosphere of the culture industry met with disbelief and outspoken disapproval. The hostility was so strong that the German Left dismissed the book out of hand and left the appropriation to the conservatives, who at this point were inclined to use some of Adorno's arguments for the defense of their aesthetic and moral beliefs.

What were the reasons for this bizarre development? After all, the leftist movement in Germany owed most of its theoretical insights to the Frankfurt School and especially to Theodor W. Adorno, who taught the younger generation the critical approach to literature and music. When *Aesthetische Theorie* came out, the West German student movement had reached the climax of its public influence. At the same time, it faced its first major crisis. The remarkable public recognition did not translate into a lasting, serious impact on the social system they critiqued and attacked. Unlike the American students, the West German students tried to solve this problem by forming more structured political organizations or moving closer to established political parties. In 1970 the student movement, entering its second phase, turned against its initial belief in spontaneous political expression and rallied around more orthodox leader figures like Lenin, Trotsky, or Mao Tse-tung. As much as these various groups fought among themselves and disagreed about strategy, they had one thing in common: their dislike of the Frankfurt School and its interpretation of Marxism.[2] They redefined their goals in terms of immediate political action and tried to establish a closer connection with the working class. Critical Theory became the victim of this reorientation. Since the New Left had been under the influence of the Frankfurt School at least until 1969, this critique was more than anything else a self-critique and therefore carried out with uncommon harshness. The members of the Frankfurt School were openly condemned as bourgeois, and their theory was denounced as liberal middle-class ideology. The liberal element in Adorno's writing—not only his concept of genuine culture, which clearly owed much to the eighteenth and nineteenth centuries and showed the *Bildungsbürger* in Adorno, but also his defense of individual freedom against the demands of the state and political parties—made him definitely unpopular with a movement that struggled to transform the social structure of West Germany.

Using the yardstick of orthodox Marxism, Adorno's leftist critics found it easy to dismiss his late work, especially *Aesthetische Theorie*, as irrelevant for the Marxist project. It was either Lukács or Brecht and Benjamin who became the new cultural heroes, and their theoretical work was appropriated to develop an alternative position. Ever since the famous Benjamin issue of *alternative* in 1967 (no. 56/57), the extremely complicated personal relationship between Walter Benjamin and the younger Adorno, who became Benjamin's disciple, critic, and editor, was presented as a clear-cut opposition: on the one hand, the smug Adorno who tried to suppress certain parts of Benjamin's oeuvre because they did not agree with his understanding of Benjamin's essential philosophy (an accusation that cannot be denied); on the other hand, Walter Benjamin, who moved closer to Brecht, transcended idealism and developed a truly materialist theory of art. We have to under-

2. For the development of the West German student movement and its impact on literature, see *Literatur und Studentenbewegung*, ed. W. Martin Lüdke (Opladen, 1977); also see *Nach dem Protest: Literatur in Umbruch*, ed. W. Martin Lüdke (Frankfurt, 1979).

stand this emotionally charged debate as a political rather than philological discourse. The heart of the matter for the New Left was a defense of Benjamin's oeuvre against the authority of Adorno and its integration into the dogma of the Frankfurt School.[3]

The interest in Benjamin, particularly in his essays of the thirties, which support the Communist party, reflects the yearning of the New Left to grasp and revive the element of political praxis in aesthetic theory. Since the Left placed the emphasis primarily on those elements in Benjamin's work that agreed with Brecht and overlooked other traditions, Adorno's critique of these essays, which he advanced already in letters during the 1930s, could only fuel the aversion toward the devious influence of Adorno's aesthetic elitism.

Although this debate has not yet come to an end—the question of Benjamin's Marxism seems to be as undecided as ever—there is a growing consensus among the Left and its various factions that the initial approach and the way it shaped the discourse has lost its usefulness and its critical edge. While Benjamin scholars have realized that we have to get out of the old mold if we want to appropriate Benjamin's writings for the present time, the discussion about Adorno's theory seems to linger without any direction.[4] It is time to take another look at *Aesthetische Theorie* and Adorno's essays on literature. This is not to make Adorno less controversial and thereby more acceptable to the established forces of the academy. The per-

---

3. See Jürgen Habermas, "Bewusstmachende oder rettende Kritik: Die Aktualität Walter Benjamins," in *Zur Aktualität Walter Benjamins* (Frankfurt, 1972), 175–223; also see Philip Brewster and Carl Howard Buchner, "Language and Critique: Jürgen Habermas on Walter Benjamin," *New German Critique* 17 (1979): 3–14.

4. Among the contributions to Adorno research, see especially Richard Wolin, "The De-Aestheticization of Art: On Adorno's *Aesthetische Theorie*," *Telos* 41 (Fall 1979): 105–27; and Anson Rabinbach, "Critique and Commentary/Alchemy and Chemistry: Some Remarks on Walter Benjamin and This Special Issue," *New German Critique* 17 (1979): 3–14.

spective that guided the interpretation and critique of Adorno in the early 1970s was rooted, as I have tried to show, in a singular historical situation—the struggle between the student movement and the West German establishment. The historical distance from these events, which only the nostalgic observer can overlook, calls for a reappreciation. In this rereading we cannot simply dismiss the arguments of the early 1970s and pretend to face the text for the first time, but we must be conscious of the limitations imposed on the interpretation at that time.

According to the Left, Adorno refused to apply his own theory to the political realm. He indulged in pessimism. Indeed the social theory of the Frankfurt School, which started out in the thirties as a Marxist project, became increasingly pessimistic with respect to Marx's prognosis that capitalism would ultimately self-destruct and give way to a socialist society. Faced with fascism in Germany and Italy and monopoly capitalism in the United States, Horkheimer and Adorno concluded in the 1940s that the Enlightenment, which was supposed to bring freedom and emancipation, had resulted in barbarism and slavery, not as an accidental relapse—as the liberal mind preferred to see this development—but rather as the logical outcome of the historical process. In their *Dialectic of Enlightenment* Horkheimer and Adorno argued that the political unfolding of *ratio* would lead to the increasing domination of nature by man, who then would become the victim of his own structure of domination. Since Horkheimer and Adorno, unlike Lukács, had given up the belief that the proletariat would revolutionize the given social structure, their analysis of advanced capitalism did not include the revolutionary perspective of traditional Marxism.

The Frankfurt School reached the position that man can analyze the logic of history but not organize political opposition. As late as 1969, shortly before his death, Adorno defended this stance against the demands of the students. The unity of theory and praxis, he argued, tends to privilege action.[5] And this emphasis becomes irrational when imposed on philosophy. Adorno denounced the call for praxis as dogmatic and insisted that the uncompromising rigor of theory that defends its realm against the onslaught of positivism offers the truly critical opposition. This last effort to preserve the priority of theory came close to the very position that the Frankfurt School castigated as traditional in the 1930s. Adorno's use of the category of negation became abstract and thereby lost its critical edge.

Although Adorno refused to view his attitude as pessimistic, we cannot overlook the widening of the gap between theory and praxis in his later writings. His late work tends to dwell on the importance of art. It is not accidental that Adorno's last book deals with aesthetic rather than social problems. His concern with social questions leads to aesthetic rather than political theory. Adorno's philosophy of art is his final answer to the dilemma of social praxis. Adorno offers the authentic work of art as that emphatic opposition that can no longer materialize in political organizations. This perspective might look more attractive today than twenty years ago when there appeared to be hope that the age of capitalism might come to an end. But is this kind of relevance a good reason for us to return to Adorno's criticism? Is Adorno perhaps becoming fashionable again because his aestheticism and pessimism appeal to the readers of the troubled 1990s? By asking these questions I do not want to discredit the legitimacy of our present interests and simply restore the authority of Adorno and the Frankfurt School. Still, the question of what *Aesthetische Theorie* offers us today should be coupled with the complementary question of what we offer to Adorno's theory and from where we look at it.

Let me begin with a broad description of Adorno's philosophy. His oeuvre is clearly grounded in the tradition of German

5. Theodor W. Adorno, "Resignation," in his *Kritik: Kleine Schriften zur Gesellschaft* (Frankfurt, 1971), 145–50.

idealism, particularly in Hegel. The same can be said about Georg Lukács, but the results are strikingly different. When Lukács moved from an idealist to a Marxist position and attempted to work out a materialist basis for his criticism, he adopted Lenin's reflection theory, which is supposed to support Lukács's concept of the organic work of art as the only authentic form of art. Adorno rejects this more traditional part of Hegel's aesthetics and insists that the rigorous historical approach should be extended to basic aesthetic norms and rules. Lukács also historicizes art and literature. Coming from reflection theory and a general concept of realism, however, he favors those forms of literature that express the interest and concerns of the proletariat—in other words, social realism. Adorno, who admired the early Lukács, refused to accept this argument. In his essay "Erpresste Versöhnung," he distances himself from Lukács's theory of realism and at the same time harshly critiques Lukács's concept of the organic work of art.[6] Adorno denounces Lukács's struggle against modernism—writers like Kafka and Joyce—as the regressive part of Hegel's influence—a reduction of the work of art to considerations of content. Adorno on the other hand defends modernism precisely because he shares the historical approach with the Hegelian tradition. To put it more concretely: he rejects the attack on modernism because it is rooted in an ontological, ahistorical understanding of the organic work of art. Modern writers are not decadent and therefore unable to synthesize content and form; rather, they try to work out the dialectic of social change and aesthetic innovation. What we call the history of literature, changes of style and genres, is not just a sequence of facts and events; it consists of a dialectical process in which the individual work is seen against the background of conventions and norms. Authenticity is reached only through the negation of

6. In Theodor W. Adorno, *Gesammelte Schriften* (Frankfurt, 1974), 11:251–80; an English translation has appeared as "Reconciliation under Duress," in *Aesthetics and Politics*, ed. Ronald Taylor and Fredric Jameson (London, 1980).

the affirmative tradition. This stress on novelty should not be mistaken for an apology of the fashionable, it rather indicates that the aesthetic material itself is drawn into the historical process.

Adorno follows the idealist tradition of Kant, Schiller, and Hegel and emphasizes the autonomy of the art work. Unlike the aesthetic theory of the later nineteenth century in Germany, which tends to view aesthetic principles as metahistorical, Adorno is much closer to Hegel's intention when he applies the historical critique also to the basic aesthetic categories—including the concept of autonomy. The legitimacy of this category is limited to the period between the eighteenth and twentieth centuries, although Adorno is never quite clear whether this period has come to an end. In his famous lecture in 1957 on poetry and society, Adorno refers to the collective *Grundstrom* (deep undercurrent) in the poems of Brecht and Lorca, without indicating whether this grounding in a collective spirit marks the beginning of a new progressive era or the decline of poetry as a medium of philosophical truth.[7] I shall come back to this ambiguity later. First I would like to develop another important aspect of Adorno's theory: the correlation between the aesthetic and the social sphere.

When literary theory in the late eighteenth century developed the notion that art is autonomous, the intention was to free the art work from the demand of social praxis. The result is an abstract opposition between the social and aesthetic sphere. By historicizing the major categories of aesthetic theory Adorno brings these realms closer together again. Ultimately art and society belong to the same stream of history. This insight is certainly not new. The Left-Hegelians, beginning with Heine, used Hegel's model of history to understand the evolution of literature as representative for the development

7. Theodor W. Adorno, "Rede über Lyrik und Gesellschaft," in *Gesammelte Schriften* (Frankfurt, 1974), 11:48–68; translated as "Lyric Poetry and Society," in *Telos* 20 (Summer 1974): 56–71.

of social and political history. Adorno's approach stands in this tradition, but he is very much aware of its dangers. While he insists on the dialectic of art and society (the art work is also a social fact), he does not, like Lukács, conceive of it in terms of reflection. Adorno's *Aesthetische Theorie* is his final effort to grasp and theoretically refine the dialectic of the social and the aesthetic spheres.

Adorno's theory not only defends and legitimizes modernism and the avant-garde, it may well be called a theory of the avant-garde. Its author is clearly on the side of those historical forces that undermine the rule of European classicism. Adorno is a distant and skeptical observer of the ideas of Johann Winckelmann. Looking back at Greek classicism Adorno points out the material conditions of Greek history, which were anything but ideal: brutal warfare, slavery, and oppression are the reality that have to be suppressed before we can enjoy the notion of perennial beauty and harmony in Greek art.

> Neoclassicism presented a unity of the general and the particular which already in the Attic period could not be attained, much less later. It is why the classic statues gaze at us with those empty eyes which, instead of radiating noble simplicity and silent greatness attributed to them by the neoromantic period, give us an archaic scare. What is forced upon us as classicism has nothing to do with corresponding European classicism in the era of the French Revolution and of the Napoleons, not to speak of the time of Baudelaire. (*AT*, 241)

The object of this critique is the neohumanism of Weimar and its glorification of Greek art. This seemingly historical polemic has a methodological aspect that I want to bring to the foreground: Adorno, at least implicitly, speaks here against the model that was used by the early Lukács to situate the novel form. Adorno undercuts the fundamental assumption of Lukács's *Theory of the Novel* that early Greek literature was grounded in social conditions that were free of alienation.

This critique of classicism becomes important because it is

83

at the same time a critique of a model that was further developed by Lucien Goldmann. For Goldmann the task of the critic and sociologist of literature is to establish a homology between the social and the literary structure.[8] Adorno's theory looks similar, yet this similarity is deceptive. While Adorno shares with Goldmann the interest in formal structure and rejects any kind of *Inhaltssoziologie* (sociology of content) as vulgar materialism, he is careful not to press the correlation into the homology model. The difference becomes apparent when Adorno defines his approach as *immanent*. The critic is starting out from the text rather than beginning with an analysis of the social structure. It is the explication of the work of art that offers insight into the social conditions that defined the production of the work of art. In his essay "Rede über Lyrik und Gesellschaft" (Lyric poetry and society) he unfolds the notion that the social meaning of the poem is expressed through its language. The poem relates to social history only indirectly. Adorno calls the poem a philosophical and historical sundial; by deciphering the structure of the poem the critic decodes the meaning of social history. Again, this sounds like Goldmann's theory, but we have to note the distinction: the interpretation of the poem refers to the meaning of history, not to the facts or objective structures. The two realms are mediated by philosophy—more specifically the philosophy of the early Marx. Unlike Goldmann, Adorno would never identify the work of art with an individual social group or class. This procedure, which is typical of Goldmann's criticism, is unacceptable to Adorno on principle. The correspondence between art and society, the aesthetic and the social meaning, transcends the particular group or class. Authentic are only those works representative of the whole. The choice of the sundial as the key metaphor signals that for Adorno the important element in the text is its expressive force and not so much the author and his

8. Lucien Goldmann, *Pour une sociologie du roman* (Paris, 1964); see also his *Recherches dialectiques* (Paris, 1959).

or her intentions to build up a coherent vision of the world. The individual author enters the sphere of criticism only as the human voice, the historical subjectivity that objectifies the expression through the work. Thus the emphasis is placed on the objective side: the authentic work of art is given the status of a permanent testament of human history—it embodies the hopes and sufferings, the expectations and contradictions, of the human race.

In *Aesthetische Theorie* Adorno tries to unfold this argument: "If [the authentic work of art] stands in opposition to empirical reality by means of its formal moment—and mediation between form and content cannot be comprehended without this differentiation—then a certain degree of mediation is to be found in the fact that aesthetic form is but a sediment of content" (*AT*, 15). Or another definition: "Only by separating itself from empirical reality—a separation possible, based on the need of art to manipulate the relationship between the whole and its parts—can a work of art become a being of second power" (*AT*, 14). Here Adorno, following Walter Benjamin, introduces the concept of the monad. By comparing art works with monads, Adorno tries to explore the dialectic of art and reality. Monads are closed—they have, so to speak, no windows and therefore offer no immediate access to reality. This, as it turns out, is quite necessary, since the outside world is already contained in a monad. Adorno then applies this idea to the understanding of aesthetic forms: "The unresolved antagonisms of reality recur in the works of art as immanent problems of its form. This and not the introduction of concrete moments define the relationship of art and society" (*AT*, 16). These unanswered questions provide literary and art history with their dynamic force. The increasing contradictions of reality show up as dissonances of form, they propel the evolution of art to the point where the avant-garde artist negates the very principle of the art work itself. Thus only those works deserve to be called authentic that question their own formal structure.

By stressing the formal aspect of literary history Adorno arrives at a position close to that of Russian formalism. He also argues that aesthetic criticism should be primarily concerned with questions of technique. The detailed analysis of seemingly technical points, in other words close readings, throws light on the social meaning. The comparison with Russian formalism is fruitful with respect to considerations of form. There are also important differences. Adorno would have rejected the formalist notion that literary history can be fully understood in terms of its intrinsic evolution. As we shall see, Adorno insists on the totality of history no less than Hegel or Lukács. Therefore the approach of Tynjanov—that the critic has to look first at the literary sequence, then at the political or economic evolution, and finally try to relate these sequences—would be shunned as undialectical and positivistic.[9] While Adorno shares the concern of the Russian formalists with technique, his interpretation of history follows a model that is quite different.

In spite of his outspoken critique of the traditional dialectic, which moves from thesis to antithesis and finally ends with a synthesis, Adorno's philosophy is still grounded in Hegel's philosophy of history. The concept of history proposed by the formalists, although analytically sound, is unacceptable to Adorno because it deprives the work of art of its emphatic truth value (*Wahrheitsgehalt*). Adorno's interest in literary evolution is not that of the historians who are satisfied when they have demonstrated how a genre changes or a motif is expressed in different ways. Adorno's theory puts a high premium on aesthetic innovation. Patterns, forms, genres, are not fixed entities but historical categories. The notion of change and innovation, however, must not be fetishized. Its meaning can be understood only as a part of a larger historical context. Close reading is for Adorno, strange as this may sound, a contextual reading. When Adorno postulates that the sociologist of art must begin with

9. Jurij Tynjanov, "Ueber die literarische Evolution," in *Texte der russischen Formalisten*, ed. Jurij Streidter (Munich, 1969), 1:393–431.

the text, he presupposes a model of history in which the various spheres—social, political, philosophical, aesthetic—are part of a unified process. Thus Adorno's claim to *Immanenz* should not be interpreted as a German version of New Criticism, the equivalent of Emil Staiger, for instance. Stressing the intrinsic approach means the opposite: it is the attempt to overcome the reification of traditional interpretation. Formalized professional scholarship insists on the rigorous definition of its object, the separation of the researcher and his or her material, without paying attention to their dialectical relationship in which the subject is very much part of the object and the seemingly objective material is the result of the subject's activities. When we talk about Adorno's approach we have to realize that he refuses to offer an objectified scientific method that can be abstracted from the individual act of understanding and then applied to various works.

Among the three approaches to the work of art, the interest in the origin and production of art, the interest in its structure, and the interest in its impact and reception, Adorno favors, as we have seen, the structural procedure. He is less sympathetic to studies that try to understand art in terms of communication. Adorno argues:

> The objectification of art [from a social standpoint, its fetishism] is in itself a social product of the division of labor. Thus, an examination of the relationship between art and society should not zero in on the sphere of reception as it precedes reception: it is to be found in the sphere of production. The interest in the social de-coding of art should turn to production and not be satisfied with analysis and classification; for societal reasons, they often are completely divergent from the works of art and their objective social content. (*AT*, 338)

This hostile remark against reception studies is primarily directed against positivism in musicology, which tried to develop a quantitative method to demonstrate the success and significance of music.[10] Adorno himself was clearly interested in reception and wrote a number of important essays on the sociology of listening.[11]

Adorno's emphasis on production as the key to the understanding of the art work deserves closer scrutiny. What does he mean? Certainly not the kind of studies popular in the late nineteenth century, when the critic explained the work of art by documenting its sources and demonstrated the roots in the biography of the author. In Adorno's criticism the individual author and his or her intentions rarely receive more than fleeting attention. Biography is in most cases treated on the anecdotal level. Adorno would agree with Lukács's argument that Balzac's intentions and the meaning of his novels were not identical. He carefully refrains from praising the genius, knowing well that this category is part of the liberal ideology: the self-promotion of the artist who has to deal with the marketplace. Adorno defines production of art in terms of the general economic and social conditions under which the artist has to work—feudal patronage, the competition of the capitalist market, or the situation of the culture industry in advanced capitalist societies. Second, Adorno wants to emphasize artistic labor: the concrete struggle of artists with the techniques available at a certain time. By focusing attention on the process of production the critic at the same time reveals its meaning and truth value.

An example from *Aesthetische Theorie* will serve to demonstrate what Adorno has in mind. There is no doubt that Adalbert Stifter was a conservative author. Both his critical prose and his works of fiction express a moderate and cautious stance. It is not accidental therefore that Stifter's reading public consisted to a large extent of educated conservative German

10. Theodor W. Adorno, "Thesen zur Kunstsoziologie," in *Ohne Leitbild* (Frankfurt, 1970), 94–103.

11. See Theodor W. Adorno, *Einleitung in die Musiksoziologie* (Frankfurt, 1962); translated as *Introduction to the Sociology of Music* (New York, 1976).

Bürger (bourgeois citizens), while the leftist camp remained indifferent or hostile. Typically enough, Lukács denied Stifter the status of a major German writer. Adorno agrees with neither side. His interpretation wants to rescue Stifter's work from his conservative admirers, who find their own ideology confirmed in the message of the novels. Adorno is fully aware that this effort is problematical when he notes: "The strata which granted him his somewhat esoteric popularity has since disappeared. This is not the last word about him, however. Especially in his late period, there is too much of reconciliation and reconcilability. Objectivity becomes a mere mask and the conjured life a ritual of resignation. But throughout his middle period, we perceive the suppressed and renounced suffering of the alienated subject and an unreconciled situation" (*AT*, 346). This statement, however, is followed by another one that demonstrates Adorno's understanding of the authentic value within the conservative ideology: "The ideological overtension present lends [Stifter's] work its mediated nonideological truth content and guarantees its superiority over literature that can offer only solace and the overrated privacy of the countryside. It gives him the authentic quality Nietzsche so admired" (*AT*, 346). Adorno clearly differentiates between the meaning Stifter wanted to express in his writings and the *Gehalt* (Adorno's adaptation of the Hegelian idea of a synthesis of form and content) hidden in the structure of the work. In the case of Stifter, Adorno sets the utopian element apart from the conservative ideology of the author. This is a significant move. The sociologist who concentrates on the plot and the characters of, say, *Nachsommer*, can read this novel as a typical example of the conservative mood of the 1850s. The overriding themes offer plenty of evidence for this thesis. Adorno, to be sure, does not deny the validity of this aspect, yet ultimately the thematic conservatism of Stifter's novels is seen as part of a larger context. Adorno's reading links the conservative component to the industrial revolution of the 1850s. The legitimacy of *Nachsommer* is its negation of the new industrial society.

The category of negativity is crucial for Adorno's philosophy. Through its negativity the work of art secures its authenticity and sets itself apart from the conventions of its time and genre. Indeed, Adorno de-emphasizes conventions because, as socially accepted models of artistic expression, they indirectly also affirm the social status quo. This is the reason why Adorno never feels quite comfortable with older literature or music. The works of the sixteenth and seventeenth centuries rely heavily on conventional devices and moreover fulfill immediate social functions. They are still embedded in social and cultural traditions of individual social groups and classes. For Adorno they are less valuable because they belong to a specific social setting and are not fully autonomous. Their truth value appears to be more limited.

This bias shows that Adorno's criticism is not just another form of criticism of ideology. In this respect Goldmann's theory is certainly closer to Marxist orthodoxy. Goldmann focuses on a specific social and historical situation—for instance, the situation of the *noblesse de robe* in France—and then relates his findings to the structure of individual works of literature, Racine's tragedies, for example. In the final analysis he maintains a base-superstructure model. Adorno, on the other hand, makes use of the critique of ideology to undermine ossified structures and reified thought patterns. He firmly holds that those works of art that deserve to be called *gelungen* (that is, genuine and excellent) cannot be reduced to the status of documents that reflect the ideas of a particular class. Although the authentic work of art is grounded in its historical moment, its truth value (*Wahrheitsgehalt*) transcends the historical moment. This truth value, on which their rank ultimately rests, Adorno argues in a key passage of *Aesthetische Theorie*, is historical through and through: "Truth value is not related to history in a way that it, together with the status of works of art, changes with the passing of the period. To be sure, some variations are possible; works of art of high quality, for example, may unfold throughout history. This does not mean, however, that truth value and quality devolve on historicism" (*AT*, 285). Against any relativistic notion, Adorno maintains that there is an objectively correct historical consciousness: "Ever since the potential for freedom disappeared, correct consciousness...will be advanced consciousness about contradictions, with their possible reconciliation on the far horizon" (*AT*, 285). The aesthetic analogies of this advanced consciousness are the forces of production within the art world, the craftsmanship of the artist, mastering the material, struggling against the general trend toward conformity. Artistic innovation, in other words, is the equivalence of the advanced historical consciousness.

It should be obvious by now that Adorno's theory summarizes the development of the last century. Its examples are the composition of Schönberg and his disciples and the evolution of modern poetry since Baudelaire. Whether this philosophy can be applied to medieval art seems doubtful, since the category of autonomy is central to the basic argument. This brings us back to my initial question. After outlining what Adorno "has to offer," we must ask ourselves where we stand and how we relate to this theory today. If we mean to take Adorno's philosophy of art seriously, we cannot evade this question, because theory itself is no less historical than literature and music. And Adorno was quite aware of this problem. In the introduction to *Aesthetische Theorie* he states, "Just as the concept of system or moral, the notion of a philosophical aesthetics today seems antiquated" (*AT*, 493). Then the question arises: How can we develop a systematic aesthetic theory when most of the traditional categories on which this theory was built have become obsolete? The fact that recent history has liquidated basic concepts like the beautiful makes any attempt to systematize aesthetics highly problematical.

Thomas Baumeister and Jens Kulenkampff have argued that Adorno could no longer follow Hegel's philosophy of art, which places the emphasis on content rather than form, because it privileges rational discourse and therefore imposes its concepts on art in such a way that art loses its status as an independent mode of expression.[12] Those elements of the work of art that cannot be grasped by theoretical concepts are indeed most meaningful ones for Adorno, who is distrustful of rational discourse. By the same token Adorno cannot hark back to a more traditional genre theory that rests on metahistorical norms. Nor can he turn to Kant's aesthetic theory, which is concerned with aesthetic experience. Still, Adorno is convinced that modern art and literature are in need of aesthetic theory. Appreciation as a mode of criticism is not enough. Since philosophical criticism aims at the truth value of art, the critics must not confine themselves to subjective experience. The task is to decipher objective meaning and this can be accomplished only with the help of a theoretical framework. Especially the complexity of modern art calls for a theoretical approach. Adorno notes: "Precisely those moments of art which cannot be reduced to subjective experience and cannot be comprehended in their plain immediacy need consciousness, that is, philosophy. It is part of every aesthetic experience as long as it is not barbaric, alien to art. Art expects its own explication" (*AT*, 524). So Adorno, in spite of his skepticism against rational discourse, clearly relates back to the tradition of philosophical aesthetics and turns explicitly against the concept of experience offered by positivism and pragmatism. He defines the goal of aesthetic theory as follows: "Aesthetics today should be above the controversy between Kant and Hegel without trying to form it into a synthesis" (*AT*, 528).

This reference to Kant and Hegel—Adorno's shorthand for two types of aesthetic theory—locates the realm in which Adorno tries to work out the tension between theory and history. He suggests that the categories of idealism still help us capture the emphatic meaning of modern art and literature, although modernism and the avant-garde are no longer

12. Thomas Baumeister and Jens Kulenkampff, "Geschichtsphilosophie und philosophische Aesthetik: Zu Adornos Aesthetischer Theorie," *Neue Hefte für Philosophie* 5 (1973): 74–104.

grounded in idealism. Adorno is fully aware of the dilemma. The philosophical concepts of criticism are at the same time indispensable and inadequate. Because of this ambiguity the late work of Adorno tends to identify philosophy and art, since the process of deciphering and preserving—in other words, criticism—is the only way in which truth in an emphatic sense can be revealed. Genuine art, for Adorno the last bastion that has not yet capitulated, is the sphere where the deception of instrumental reason is without consequence. This vision owes its force to Hegel, although it does not share Hegel's negative attitude toward postclassical art. For Adorno, art and philosophy are inseparable but not identical. This position allows him to cling to the concepts of the work of art and truth value as his categories. When philosophy in the phase of late capitalism has lost most of its emancipatory functions, as Adorno claims, it becomes the task of the authentic art work to stand in and defend the tower of truth.

I started this essay with some remarks about the hostile reception of *Aesthetische Theorie* in the early 1970s. This animosity was partly caused by the frustration of the student movement. The students were looking for a leader in their political struggle and had to realize that Adorno was unwilling and also unprepared to step into this role. This explanation, however, is insufficient. The lack of appreciation the younger generation showed in 1970 must be related to a broader phenomenon. Between 1967 and 1970 West Germany witnessed an almost unparalleled breakdown of the literary system. The radicals called for the end of literature and criticism, since the capitalist system had turned them into meaningless toys of the establishment. This crisis undermined the belief in the autonomy of art, which Adorno defended against *Tendenz*. This debate is only the foreground for a deeper problem that had been lingering since the Second World War. I mean the fate of the avant-garde. Adorno's philosophy of art is closely related to the avant-garde of the early twentieth century. He takes most of his examples from works written or composed between

1890 and 1930. Seldom does he refer to later works. His literary criticism favors authors of the nineteenth and early twentieth centuries, such as Heine, Balzac, Joseph Eichendorff, Stefan George, Frank Wedekind, Karl Kraus, and Benjamin. The notable exception is his interpretation of Beckett's *Endgame* (1957)—a play that speaks very much to the mood of Adorno's late years.[13] Occasionally Adorno would play with the idea that the concept of autonomy of art might not be fully appropriate for the period that followed the Second World War. Here and there he cautiously alludes to the end of the avant-garde, yet he fails to pursue this perspective with any rigor.

Today it would be futile to suppress this question: Did the neo-avant-garde still have the same critical edge Adorno saw in the works of the previous generation? The New Left answered in the negative. They appropriated the arguments of Horkheimer and Adorno's *Dialectic of Enlightenment* that there is no room for genuine culture in advanced industrial societies and therefore rejected the notion of aesthetic opposition. As I mentioned earlier, they discovered Benjamin's writings and followed his thesis that the autonomy of art, which was grounded in its ritual function, faded away with the advent of mechanical mass reproduction. Benjamin had argued: "But the instant the criterion of authenticity ceases to be applicable to artistic production, the total function of art is reversed. Instead of being based on ritual, it begins to be based on another practice—politics."[14] This thesis guided the theoretical efforts of the student movement. They wanted to tear down the walls of the aesthetic ghetto and apply the arts to the political realm. By 1975 it was clear that this movement had failed to reach its goal. The literary system slowly but surely returned to its earlier status quo. I cannot go into the political and philosoph-

13. Theodor W. Adorno, "Versuch das Endspiel zu verstehen," in *Gesammelte Schriften*, 11:281–331; translated as "Trying to Understand Endgame," *New German Critique* 26 (1982): 119–50.

14. Walter Benjamin, *Illuminations*, ed. Hannah Arendt, trans. Harry Zohn (New York, 1969), 224.

ical reasons for this failure.[15] My argument is exclusively concerned with the critique of Adorno's *Aesthetische Theorie* as it emerged from the crisis of the literary system.

As soon as we focus on this question we begin to realize what separates our situation from that of Adorno in the 1960s. We notice that Adorno's philosophy of art has become historical. Adorno stresses the precarious state of modern art and emphasizes the negative impact of capitalism on culture, yet he maintains that the function of art has not changed since the advent of modernism. To put it differently: Adorno's theory takes the institution of art for granted. Peter Bürger advanced the argument in his *Theory of the Avant-Garde* (1974) that Adorno failed to provide a critique of the concept of autonomy.[16] It was the aim of the avant-garde movement, according to Bürger, to overcome the gap between the aesthetic and practical spheres and regain political impact by eliminating the traditional aesthetic autonomy. Bürger convincingly demonstrates that Adorno, in spite of his hostility toward Lukács, shares basic philosophical assumptions with him. Their disagreement about realism and modernism is based on a common notion of the autonomous work of art. While Lukács tilted toward a model of organic works of art, Adorno placed the emphasis on the raison d'être of tensions and contradictions. In Bürger's analysis the sharp edge of the historical dialectic finally turns against Adorno himself. Following Benjamin, Bürger describes the avant-garde movement in terms of a self-critique that denounces the complacency of modern aestheticism. Compared with this radical stance, where art moves toward its own destruction, Adorno's aesthetic theory reads

15. See Peter Uwe Hohendahl, "Politisierung der Kunsttheorie: Zur ästhetischen Diskussion nach 1967," in *Deutsche Literatur in der Bundesrepublik seit 1965: Untersuchungen und Berichte*, ed. Paul Michael Lützeler and Egon Schwarz (Königstein, 1980); Chapter 6 in this volume is a translation and reworking of this essay.

16. Peter Bürger, *Theorie der Avantgarde* (Frankfurt, 1974), 117–27; translated by Michael Shaw as *Theory of the Avant-Garde* (Minneapolis, 1984).

like a somewhat belated summary of modernism—a recapitulation that is not quite ready to accept the extreme conclusions of the twentieth-century avant-garde.

Not all critics and theorists have agreed with Bürger's thesis. W. Martin Lüdke for instance, in a response to Bürger, questioned whether *Theory of the Avant-Garde* does justice to Adorno's category of modernism (*Moderne*).[17] He takes issue with Bürger's presentation of Adorno's theory of aesthetic innovation, and finally tries to show that Bürger's critique is not really intrinsic but, rather, inspired by the social theory of Jürgen Habermas. Lüdke's rejoinder is persuasive as an interpretation of *Aesthetische Theorie*, but it is ultimately beside the point. Adopting a Habermasian position, that is, looking at the Frankfurt School from a stance that has modified some of the basic tenets, enables Bürger to situate Adorno's aesthetic theory historically. Precisely because he stands outside of Adorno's theory he can point out that the logic of this theory is limited to a specific period of European art. Although it may not be obvious at first sight, this argument has far-reaching consequences. It undercuts Adorno's key metaphor: the art work is no longer the sundial of history. The period after 1945, according to Bürger, is marked by a legitimate coexistence of different styles and tendencies. There is no stringent correlation between social and art history.

Bürger's critique and its strategy are sound and convincing. Yet I would like to go one step further. To some extent Bürger himself still operates within the confines of Adorno's model. His major thesis—that the production and reception of literature between 1780 and 1910 were determined by the concept of autonomous art—is obviously derived from Adorno. Looking back at this period today and viewing it within the broader context of preceding and following literary history, we realize

17. W. Martin Lüdke, "Die Aporien der materialistischen Aesthetik— kein Ausweg? Zur kategorialen Begründung von P. Bürgers *Theorie der Avantgarde*," in *Antworten auf Peter Bürgers Bestimmung von Kunst und bürgerliche Gesellschaft*, ed. W. Martin Lüdke (Frankfurt, 1976), 27–71.

that Adorno's idea of autonomy, which was then historicized by Bürger, never covered more than a part of the actual literary production of the nineteenth century. Much of the Restoration period (1815–48), with Heinrich Heine as the prime example, would not fit. Aesthetic autonomy as an episode of history: this perspective looks more familiar to us than to Adorno. He was not prepared to accept this interpretation, because it would have deprived him of any meaningful approach to history. In his essay "Das Altern der Neuen Musik," Adorno is ready to concede that modern music was more radical in its beginnings than in its later phases.[18] Still, he refuses to unfold the implications of this argument. He laments this development as a loss. His remark about Béla Bartók's later work is typical of this attitude: "Partial responsibility for this is borne by the naiveté of the professional musician who goes about his business without partaking in the movement of the objective spirit."[19] This reference to the objective spirit indicates that Adorno, in the final analysis, relies on a Hegelian model of history in which all strands relate to one single center. The application of this model, however cautiously Adorno proceeded, seems to blind him with respect to the divergence of artistic trends and movements. While Adorno certainly rejected a reductive reading of history and was also skeptical of historical laws, his thinking is deeply rooted in the concept of a unified historical process. This idea, then, since the project of the Enlightenment has failed, leads him to the notion that the evolution of modern music is regressive because there is less personal freedom and an increasing amount of alienating bureaucracy in our society.[20] In a way, this argument puts the blame on history for not following the course that the philosopher has mapped out for it.

What is problematical in Adorno's philosophy of art, in other

18. This essay has been translated as "The Aging of the New Music," and has appeared in *Telos* 77 (Fall 1988): 95–116.

19. Theodor W. Adorno, *Dissonanzen* (Göttingen, 1972), 140.

20. Ibid., 157.

words, comes from the historical determinism he inherited from the Hegelian and Marxian tradition. The link between this tradition and the Frankfurt School is the work of Georg Lukács, especially *History and Class Consciousness*. Those orthodox Marxists who denounced Adorno's theory as liberal ideology failed to notice that they did not share his concept of the work of art and his approach to criticism but based their aesthetic theories on the same understanding of history: history as a dialectical process in which the concrete is by definition part of the whole. For Adorno there is no philosophy without *Universalgeschichte* (universal history). As Russell Berman puts it, "This historical scheme, an attempt to retain the universal history of Hegel and Marx, evidently precludes the possibility of perceiving the qualitatively new, for the new is only more of the old."[21] Although Berman underestimates the difference between Adorno and orthodox Marxism, he has a valid point.

What are we to learn from this critique? Does it mean that any project of defining aesthetic theory in historical-philosophical terms has become impossible, as Rüdiger Bubner claims?[22] Or are we to take the advice of Hans R. Jauss and turn to a system of aesthetic experience? Both Bubner and Jauss are prepared to eliminate history.[23] This way they hope to regain a less problematical theory of art. I would not be willing to pay this price, for the loss of history would imply a fragmentation of experience, decreasing its meaning.

21. Russell Berman, "Adorno, Marxism, and Art," *Telos* 34 (Winter 1977–78): 165.

22. Rüdiger Bubner, "Ueber einige Bedingungen gegenwärtiger Aesthetik," *Neue Hefte für Philosophie* 5 (1973): 38–73.

23. Hans R. Jauss, *Kleine Apologie der ästhetischen Erfahrung*, (Constance, 1972).

4   *Dialectic of Enlightenment* Revisited: Habermas's Critique of the Frankfurt School

A well-known newspaper caricature, printed some twenty years ago, pictures the Frankfurt School as a closely knit group with Max Horkheimer as a large father figure watching over the other members of the school, among them Theodor W. Adorno and Jürgen Habermas. This view of the relationship between the members of the Frankfurt School was quite common in Germany at that time: Habermas was seen not only as a member of the school but more specifically as a disciple of the older generation, someone who had started out from the position of Critical Theory, as it was developed in the 1940s and 1950s by Horkheimer, Marcuse, and Adorno. Although this interpretation cannot account for all of Habermas's early work, notably not for his *Strukturwandel der Oeffentlichkeit* (Structural transformation of the public sphere, 1962), it was plausible enough to find wide acceptance. Yet it was no accident that Habermas's first major study, which traces the evolution of the public sphere from the eighteenth to the twentieth century and stresses the need for an enlightened and rational reconsideration of the public sphere under advanced capitalism, never found Adorno's and Horkheimer's complete acceptance. Their own critique of the process of Enlightenment differed so markedly from the position Habermas outlined that there could be no full consensus. In a certain way, I would argue, the later differences, especially those between Adorno and Habermas, were already foreshadowed in *Strukturwandel,* although Habermas, when describing the decline of the liberal public sphere under organized capitalism, made use of the critique of mass culture formulated by the older generation and certainly did not indicate that he was in disagreement with the analysis offered in *Dialectic of Enlightenment.* On the whole, however, conventional wisdom, treating Habermas as a junior member of the Frankfurt School, was justified for the 1960s, when Habermas, for instance, defended the position of the Frankfurt School in the Positivism Dispute against Karl Popper and his allies of the Cologne school. While Adorno and Popper in their addresses to the German *Soziologentag* (sociology conference) of 1961 decided to suppress rather than highlight their theoretical and methodological differences, the younger generation, represented by Habermas and Hans Albert, did not hesitate to use a highly polemical rhetoric, in order to undermine the position of the enemy camp.[1] Habermas's insistence on the limitations of rational positivism and his emphasis on the need for a grounding of the humanities and the social sciences that is different from the methods of the natural sciences, clearly defended the position of Adorno. At least it was much closer to Adorno's understanding of the social sciences than that of Popper and the Cologne school.

The change of paradigm: Seen against the background of the rivalry between the Frankfurt and the Cologne schools during the 1950s and 1960s in Germany, there can be no doubt that Habermas's early work from *Theory and Practice* (1963) to *Knowledge and Human Interests* (1969) is part of the Frankfurt School, since it makes use of and relies on the analyses of the older generation, especially those of Horkheimer and Herbert Marcuse. Not only does Habermas share with classical Critical Theory a goal—the search for an

---

1. Jürgen Habermas, *Zur Logik der Sozialwissenschaften* (Frankfurt, 1970), 9–38 and 39–70.

emancipated and free society—he also continues, although not without modifications, the discourse of his teachers. More openly than Adorno and Horkheimer, Habermas returns to the Marxist problematic of Critical Theory, attempting to clarify the validity and function of Marxian theory vis-à-vis advanced capitalism. It is precisely this critical reexamination of Marxian theory, I would argue, that propels Habermas during the 1970s on a trajectory that distances him more and more from the position of Horkheimer and Adorno. By the end of the decade, friendly gestures notwithstanding, this process reaches a point from which, given the systematic development of Habermas's own theory, a return to the discourse of the old Frankfurt School is no longer possible. It seems that at this juncture Habermas wants to stress the break rather than the continuity. While the chapter devoted to Horkheimer and Adorno in *The Theory of Communicative Action* is still characterized by critical sympathy, his reassessment of *Dialectic of Enlightenment*, published under the title "The Entwinement of Myth and Enlightenment" in 1982, not only sharpens the critique of Horkheimer and Adorno but also displays a certain amount of acrimony absent from Habermas's earlier essays.[2] Habermas states in no uncertain terms that something went wrong in the evolution of Critical Theory during the 1940s. This harsh verdict is directed against Horkheimer's and Adorno's work from *Dialectic of Enlightenment* on. In particular, it is directed against Adorno's *Negative Dialectics* and *Aesthetic Theory*.

This turn in Habermas's appreciation of the older generation definitely calls for an explanation. I believe that there is more involved than just an increasing theoretical estrangement be-

2. Jürgen Habermas, "The Entwinement of Myth and Enlightenment: Re-reading *Dialectic of Enlightenment*," *New German Critique* 26 (Spring/Summer 1982): 13–30; reprinted in *The Philosophical Discourse of Modernity*, trans. Frederick Lawrence (Cambridge, Mass., 1987), 106–30.

tween the older and the younger generation. Habermas's earlier attempt to reformulate Marxian theory, by discarding a number of orthodox dogmas on the one hand and differentiating between labor and interaction on the other, did not result in a break because the open revision of Marxian theory in many ways simply spelled out what Horkheimer, Marcuse, and Adorno had already tacitly changed in their own theories since the early 1940s. Equally, the turn toward a theory of communicative action, the so-called linguistic turn in Habermas's work after *Legitimation Crisis* (1973), did not in itself necessitate the noticeable distress. There is an additional element that, taken together with Habermas's attempt to work out a communicative grounding of his theory, intensified the disagreement. What is ultimately at stake for Habermas is no less than the idea of rationality and the notion of a legitimate rational society. Rereading *Dialectic of Enlightenment*, Habermas discovers that Horkheimer's and Adorno's critique of reason owes as much if not more to Nietzsche than to Marx and the Marxist tradition. It is the Nietzsche connection that is, I think, responsible for the somewhat hostile tone, especially in the second essay. Again, I will argue, it is not Nietzsche's work in itself that creates the distress—Habermas had offered a critique of Nietzsche as early as *Knowledge and Human Interests*—but the intellectual atmosphere of the late 1970s and early 1980s in West Germany, where the revival of interest in Nietzsche was largely caused by the emergence of poststructuralism. As we shall see, it is Foucault's interpretation of Nietzsche that fuels Habermas's critical rereading of *Dialectic of Enlightenment* and of the later work of Horkheimer and Adorno.

Using explicit statements and implicit arguments from Habermas's systematic writings, I first want to document the growing rift between Habermas and the orthodoxy of the Frankfurt School. In a second step I want to look more specifically at the above-mentioned chapter in *The Theory of Communicative Action* and the essay on *Dialectic of Enlightenment*.

This should finally lead us to a reexamination of the fundamental problems involved in the grounding of Habermas's own
theory. My interest in Habermas's reassessment and critique
of Horkheimer and Adorno, to state it explicitly, is not primarily historical. The question whether Habermas's interpretation is historically correct or not is, in the context of my
argument, secondary at best. The evidence, for instance, that
Habermas misunderstands the intention of Horkheimer and
Adorno in *Dialectic of Enlightenment*—a case that could possibly be made—will not be used as an argument against the
critique of a specific position attributed to Horkheimer and
Adorno.

Habermas's critique of the Frankfurt School: Axel Honneth has
given a persuasive account of the changes of paradigm within
Critical Theory.[3] "Habermas implicitly takes the first step toward a reorientation of social criticism to re-establish critical
theory's tenuous claims within the present historical context."[4] Honneth rightly states that Habermas's own essays
dealing with Marcuse, Adorno, and Benjamin do not systematically address the reasons why Habermas turned away from
the position of the Frankfurt School in a late phase and challenged its historical and theoretical presuppositions. There are,
however, clear indications that I want to bring into the foreground. While Habermas admires the aphoristic and stylistic
qualities of Adorno's writings in his short essay "Theodor W.
Adorno: Ein philosophierender Intellektueller" (A philoso-
phizing intellectual, 1963)—which was, incidentally, not included in the later English edition of *Philosophical-Political
Profiles*—the second essay on Adorno, published in 1969, already focuses on the problem that was to become crucial for
Habermas's later reading of Adorno (and Horkheimer): Haber-

3. Axel Honneth, "Communication and Reconciliation in Habermas'
Critique of Adorno," *Telos* 39 (Spring 1979): 45–61.
4. Ibid., 46.

mas concentrates on the dialectic of reason and Adorno's pessimistic conclusions.

As Habermas points out, for Adorno, "mastery of nature is chained to the introjected violence of humans over humans, to the violence of the subject exercised upon its own nature."[5] Thus the Enlightenment, since it remains unreflected, cannot attain the level of rationality that it claims for itself; rather, this process stays on the level of self-affirmation gone wild (*verwilderte Selbstbehauptung*). Habermas then suggests that he has some doubts about this view and hints that he would not necessarily concur with the analysis of reason lying behind it, but in 1969 he does not fully develop these thoughts because he seeks to understand Adorno's position as the result of his biography and the historical experience of his generation. He traces Adorno's concept of negative dialectic, concentrating on its challenge to both formal logic and orthodox Hegelian dialectic, which favors synthesis, but he does not emphasize the difference between his own project and Adorno's philosophy. In the final paragraphs Habermas merely touches on these differences when he problematizes his own psychological interpretation of Adorno and calls for a more systematic treatment of the fundamental epistemological questions raised by Adorno's concept of negative dialectic. He points out that Adorno cannot overcome the basic contradiction between his insistence on negativity (*bestimmte Negation*) and his use of the idea of reconciliation (*Versöhnung*), a state that would transcend the gesture of negation.

At this juncture the alternative project, as it was announced and partially developed in *Knowledge and Human Interests*, comes into the foreground. Habermas argues: "The idea of truth, already implicit in the first sentence spoken, can be shaped only on the model of the idealized agreement aimed for in communication free of domination. To this extent the truth

---

5. Jürgen Habermas, *Philosophical-Political Profiles* (London, 1983), 101.

of a proposition is bound up with the intention of leading a genuine life."[6] This statement, in which free communication becomes the basis for an authentic life, implicitly cancels the logic of reification on which Adorno's negative dialectic is modeled. Habermas is keenly aware that Adorno would not have accepted his premises and tries to explain why the older generation of the Frankfurt School would have resisted the idea of communication without domination as a real possibility for social organization. *Versöhnung*, the key term for Adorno's gesture toward an authentic social totality, must be grounded in a prerational understanding of nature, an understanding in which the dichotomy between subject and object does not exist. In Habermas's words, "Adorno (and also Benjamin, Horkheimer, Marcuse and Bloch) entertained doubts that the emancipation of humanity is possible without the resurrection of nature."[7] Habermas concluded in 1969 that the "dialectic of Enlightenment," that is, the historical logic of rationality, is profoundly ambivalent with respect to the chances of humanity's escaping the logic of domination.

So the question arises: Is universal reconciliation ultimately no more than an extravagant idea? Habermas's cautious statements seem to indicate that he differs from the older generation in two respects. First, he is unwilling to accept the logic of total reification that dominates *Dialectic of Enlightenment*, and second, he distances himself from a concept of reconciliation based on the notion of primal nature. In philosophical terms, Habermas at this point has moved away from the philosophical discourse of Hegel and the various schools that depend on the model of dialectical mediation.

By the late 1970s this critical stance becomes much more explicit in Habermas's work. This change, however, does not occur as a leap from one model to another, but rather as a critical reexamination that results in the development of a

6. Ibid., 107.
7. Ibid.

radically transformed discourse, using linguistic theories, theories of social action, and systems theory. The new model, which I cannot even sketch here, both replaces the Marxist Hegelian foundations of the Frankfurt School and calls for a systematic critique of these foundations. In *The Theory of Communicative Action* Habermas undertakes this reevaluation by tracing the concept of reification from Weber through Lukács to Horkheimer and Adorno. The charge is that Horkheimer and Adorno, by taking over and even broadening Lukács's concept of reification, maneuvered themselves into a position that did not allow them to conceptualize forces of resistance against the totally administered society.

In his reconstruction Habermas comes to the conclusion that Horkheimer's and Adorno's radical critique of reason (in its subjective and objective version) ultimately undermines the possibility of critical reflection itself. If critical thought, as Horkheimer and Adorno maintain in their later work, cannot formulate truth because it is already contaminated by the logic of instrumental reason, then the force of critical arguments is endangered. Critical reflection in its Adornian version can only hint at truth in the form of mimesis, but it cannot be developed as a theory with formal and methodological consequences. Habermas states this aporia in the following way: "The paradox in which the critique of instrumental reason is entangled, and which stubbornly resists even the most supple dialectic, consists then in this: Horkheimer and Adorno would have to put forward a theory of mimesis, which according to their own ideas, is impossible."[8] To put it differently, according to Habermas the critique of instrumental reason through the concept of reification makes it impossible to ground theory in communicative interaction. The business of philosophy would come to an end because discursive methods would lose their

---

8. Jürgen Habermas, *The Theory of Communicative Action*, vol. 1: *Reason and the Rationalization of Society*, trans. Thomas McCarthy (Boston, 1984), 382.

validity under the spell of identifying thought. By the same token—and this should be kept in mind—without discourse there is no space left for social praxis. It is precisely for this reason that Habermas does not follow Horkheimer's and Adorno's critiques. Instead, he wants to show how the Hegelian-Marxist tradition, relying heavily on the concept of reification, must end up in an aporetic situation.

Before I retrace the line of Habermas's argument, I want to call attention to its context. The critique of the Frankfurt School at the end of the first volume of *The Theory of Communicative Action* is part of a larger argument explaining the change of paradigm from a theory of teleological action to a theory of communicative action. The point of reference is the potential of rationality embedded in speech and linguistic communication, a rationality that remains, as Habermas claims, undeveloped in Max Weber's theory of action. Specifically, Habermas refers to the difference between rationality in the life-world and the rationality of systems and subsystems (economy, political system). By reconstructing the tradition of Western Marxism, Habermas wants to demonstrate that the heritage of Max Weber's theory of rationalization, as it can be found in Lukács well as in Horkheimer and Adorno, ultimately explodes the bounds of the philosophy of consciousness. The point of his argument is that the Frankfurt School, because of its dependence on the Weberian model of rationalization, fails to do justice to the problematic of the life-world—despite its own intentions.

Focusing on Horkheimer's *Eclipse of Reason*, Habermas underlines the similarity between Weber's and Horkheimer's interpretation of modern capitalist societies: their theories share an essentially identical model of rationalization. The history of modernity is seen as a process of disenchantment, with reason undermining the unquestioned validity of religion and ontology. Thus modern consciousness is characterized by a growing rift between knowledge and belief systems. This implies that morality and art are decoupled from the scientific pursuit of truth. Modern reason functions primarily as a tool for the promotion of self-interest and survival. Similarly, both Weber and Horkheimer stress the loss of individual freedom in modern society, Weber by calling attention to the impact of increasingly complex bureaucracies, Horkheimer, favoring psychological arguments, by pointing to the growing pressure of the social system on the individual. Habermas rightly acknowledges, however, that Horkheimer's conclusions differ significantly from Weber's reading of modern social organizations. He argues that these differences have to do with the impact of Lukács's theory of reification on the Frankfurt School.

Lukács, relying equally on Marx's theory of commodification and on Weber's theory of rationalization, fuses the concepts of reification and rationalization. As Habermas reminds us, this move in *History and Class Consciousness* allows Lukács to go beyond Weber and at the same time, I would add, to supplement Marxian theory. Habermas, however, is primarily interested in the theoretical limitations of this approach that are caused by Lukács's Hegelian reading of Marx. He sees two major deficiencies. First, Lukács's concept of reification relies exclusively on the concept of exchange value in *Capital* and therefore reduces all forms of rationalization in modern Western societies to a variation of reification caused by capitalism. As long as capitalism dominates social organization, reification is inevitable, not only in the sphere of social organization, but also in the realm of philosophy. Lukács argues, however, that this logic can be overcome because there are epistemological as well as social limits to the reification of reason. Also, this argument, in Habermas's opinion, depends on the use of Hegel's logic, a form of metaphysical thought that cannot be resurrected after its critique by post-Kantian philosophy.

Against Lukács's thesis of total reification under capitalism Habermas suggests that instrumental reason "establishes itself at the cost of practical rationality."[9] Then he concludes:

9. Ibid., 363.

"Thus it makes sense to ask whether the critique of the incomplete character of the rationalization that appears as reification does not suggest taking a complementary relation between cognitive-instrumental rationality, on the one hand, and moral-practical and aesthetic-practical rationality, on the other, as a standard that is inherent in the unabridged concept of practice, that is to say, in communicative action itself."[10] To put it differently, Hegel's logic of reconciliation, applied by Lukács to the problem of rationalization, remains a fiction, as long as it is carried out in the realm of theory only. This brings us to the second criticism: Habermas is equally opposed to the political solution of Lukács. He calls Lukács's notion of a proletarian revolution guided by Marxian philosophy a mistake, because the revolutionary avant-garde as the standard-bearer of theory would need a knowledge of the total structure of society that is empirically not available.

Habermas's critique of Lukács emphasizes two points: he challenges the reduction of rationalization to the level of reification caused by the capitalist economy, and he refuses to depend, as Lukács does, on a Hegelian reading of Marx that tries to solve the problem of practice in the sphere of philosophy. As we shall see, this critique reiterates many of the explicit or implicit arguments of the older Frankfurt School against Lukács—though I would like to add that a crucial part of Habermas's argument is not based on his reading of Horkheimer and Adorno but on his own theory of social practice. As much as he attempts to carry through an immanent critique, using the nexus of intellectual history, he reverts occasionally to the systematic framework of his own theory. This is equally true of his reading of *Dialectic of Enlightenment*.

The following steps of the argument unfold in a rather straightforward manner. Since the Frankfurt School, especially Horkheimer and Adorno, find it difficult to follow Lukács's Hegelian solution of the reification problematic, they have to

10. Ibid., 363–64.

reconsider the question of rationalization. They do this by de-
coupling the concept of reification from the historical development of capitalism. It seems that Habermas, who accuses
Lukács of a reductive interpretation of rationalization and reification, approves of this criticism, yet at the same time he
insists that this very move leads to the aporia I mentioned
before. Habermas is distressed not so much by the way in which
Horkheimer and Adorno de-historicize the concept of reification when they uncover the emergence of instrumental reason
already in early Greek history, as by their tendency to blur the
contours of the concept of reason itself. His criticism is carried
out on two levels. He presents historical arguments in order
to explain the strategy of the Frankfurt School, and he offers
theoretical arguments to show why this strategy could not be
successful.

The historical thesis, based on the work of Helmut Dubiel,
can be summarized in the following way: (1) the Frankfurt
School was faced with the peculiar development of Marxism
in Russia, that is, Stalinism; (2) in Germany and Italy they
encountered fascism, a political system that proved that capitalism could overcome its crisis by reorganizing the political
order; and finally (3) they experienced in the United States the
success of a capitalist system that integrated the underprivileged masses through organized mass culture (the culture industry).[11] As a result, so the argument goes, Horkheimer and
Adorno could no longer rely on Lukács's theory of reification.
While they still shared with Lukács the notion of a modern
society largely determined by alienation, they could not share
Lukács's view that this situation could be changed by the consciousness and the revolutionary action of the proletariat. To
put it succinctly, their theory of fascism demonstrated why
the consciousness of the masses would support advanced capitalism under the disguise of a new social order, and their theory

---

11. Helmut Dubiel, *Wissenschaftsorganisation und politische Erfahrung* (Frankfurt, 1978).

of the culture industry shows how the commodification of culture supplied the means for the integration of the masses into the existing social system.

The theoretical line of the argument is built on these historical considerations. In particular, Habermas wants to clarify why Horkheimer and Adorno, by radicalizing the theory of reification and/or rationalization, undermine the basis of their own critique. Habermas suggests that the rejection of Hegel's logic of mediation, to which Lukács could still resort in order to solve the problem of reification, leaves a vacuum that weakens the structure of the theory. Critical reflection in its attempt to grasp and break through the barriers of reified social relations is left only with the procedure of negative dialectic—a procedure that forgoes the attempt at reconciliation. The suspicion that even Lukács's critique of the reified mind is based on a philosophy grounded in the concept of identity (Hegel) leads to the eclipse of reason altogether. There are no weapons left to fight against the phenomena of reification, at least not within the sphere of rational discourse.

This is the center of Habermas's criticism, an argument I have to unfold. The question is, How can critical theory, fighting against positivism on the one hand and attacking ontology on the other, grasp and demonstrate its own validity? Habermas suggests two possibilities: either this critical reflection must be grounded in a general theory "that elucidates the foundations of the modern natural, social, and cultural sciences within the horizon of more encompassing concepts of truth and knowledge," or it has to be linked to a form of self-reflection "that reaches down into the lifeworld foundations, the structures of action and the contexts of discovery, underlying scientific theory-construction or objectivating thought in general."[12] The second alternative is clearly the one favored by Habermas. Yet this observation is of secondary importance in my context. More important, by

12. Habermas, *Theory of Communicative Action*, 375.

setting up this opposition, Habermas prejudges the following reading of Horkheimer and Adorno. He argues that Horkheimer's response to the theoretical dilemma does not fit into his classification of the possible solutions, for Horkheimer calls for a self-reflection that demystifies the social processes that determine the boundaries of systematic thought. Habermas takes this statement as a first step toward a self-reflection of scientific theory, as it was carried out by the next generation of social scientists and philosophers. Yet he rightly stresses that the Frankfurt School did not pursue this project. Rather, Horkheimer and Adorno insisted on a radical critique of reified subjective reason, of instrumental reason.

Habermas suggests that this critique was doomed because it destroyed the basis of critical reflection altogether. The first step of his argument reconstructs the strategy of Horkheimer and Adorno in *Dialectic of Enlightenment*. Habermas arrives at the following conclusion:

> Horkheimer and Adorno detach the concept [of reification] not only from the special historical context of the rise of the capitalist economic system but from the dimension of interhuman relations altogether; and they generalize it temporally (over the entire history of the human species) and substantively (the same logic of domination is imputed to both cognition in the service of self-preservation and the repression of instinctual nature). This double generalization of the concept of reification leads to a concept of instrumental reason that shifts the primordial history of subjectivity and the self-formative process of ego-identity into an encompassing historico-philosophical perspective.[13]

In his second step Habermas extrapolates the historico-philosophical horizon of Horkheimer's and Adorno's strategy. Through instrumental reason the human race attained

13. Ibid., 379–80.

the domination of nature, but the price it had to pay for this achievement was the repression of subjectivity. This dialectic works against the traditional notion of Enlightenment as a process of human emancipation. Instead, history turns into a self-imposed catastrophe from which there is no escape. Confronted with the failure of reason, Horkheimer and Adorno attempt to anchor their own critique of this process in an approach that is not trapped in the dialectic of instrumental reason. They mean to overcome the constraints of rational discourse by moving to a procedure that retraces a state without the separation between subject and object. In the words of Horkheimer and Adorno: "But the constellation under which likeness is established—the unmediated likeness of mimesis as well as the mediated likeness of synthesis, assimilation to the thing in the blind discharge of life as well as the finding of likenesses in what has been reified in the process of scientific concept formation—is still the sign of terror."[14]

Habermas rejects this move to philosophical hyperspace, since it does not provide the basis for rational discourse, for communicative interaction. In other words, Habermas claims that this radical critique of instrumental reason cannot be validated in theoretical terms. It has accepted the distinction of classical philosophical systems on the one hand and has disclosed the horrifying consequences of instrumental reason on the other. As a result, it finds itself in limbo. In order to criticize modern positivism, it must revert to the fundamental concepts of classical philosophy such as truth; in order to show the ideological nature of the older philosophical tradition, it uses the instruments of modern rationality. Habermas concludes that the Frankfurt School paid a very high price for its skeptical turn during the 1940s. In this context his own project can be understood as a return to the problematic of the early Frankfurt

---

14. Max Horkheimer and Theodor W. Adorno, *Dialectic of Enlightenment* (New York, 1972), 181.

School, though he definitely does not mean to rely on their position in any dogmatic sense.

The dangerous influence of Nietzsche: Before I turn to Habermas's answer to the dilemmas of Horkheimer's and Adorno's later work, I want to address his essay "The Entwinement of Myth and Enlightenment" of 1982, which not only radicalizes his critique but also develops more clearly the contemporary background of the debate. In *The Theory of Communicative Action* Habermas suggested in passing that the later writings of Adorno were not too far removed from the philosophy of Heidegger—in spite of their own intentions. This suspicion is intensified in Habermas's rereading of *Dialectic of Enlightenment* in 1982. Although the essay is just as much concerned with the problematic of the foundations of a critical theory, both the strategy and the rhetoric differ significantly. The emphasis is placed on the critique of ideology and its increasing radicalization in modern European history. Again Habermas means to demonstrate that the approach of Horkheimer and Adorno in *Dialectic of Enlightenment* leads to a paradoxical situation: it results in a critique denouncing reason, though it is based on reason itself. Thus Habermas insists that Horkheimer and Adorno cannot fend off the consequences of Nietzsche's critique of rationality, whatever their own intentions may have been. "Nietzsche's critique," as Habermas puts it, "consumes the critical impulse itself."[15]

To position Nietzsche and his significance for Horkheimer and Adorno, Habermas describes the history of modern consciousness as a three-phased process. Whereas the initial intention of the Enlightenment aimed at the explosion of traditional worldviews, the second and third phases used a different model, namely the critique of ideology. The older model of ideology critique (Marx) works with the assump-

---

15. Habermas, "Entwinement of Myth and Enlightenment," 23.

tion that the truth claims of theories can and must be questioned because these claims possibly rest on premises not derived from principles of reason but from presuppositions that reflect the self-interest of the theorist and his or her social group. This model maintains the ideas of the Enlightenment and uses them as the critical standard for the evaluation of existing social practices.

The following, more radical model of ideology critique extends the suspicion to the procedures of reason itself. "With this type of critique Enlightenment becomes reflexive for the first time; it now carries out the project on it own products, i.e. its theories. But the drama of Enlightenment reaches its peripeteia or turning point when the critique of ideology itself is suspected of no longer producing truth—it is only then that Enlightenment becomes reflexive for a second time."[16] This final phase is that of Nietzsche and of *Dialectic of Enlightenment*. In *Dialectic of Enlightenment* "this critique of ideology describes the self-destruction of the critical faculty."[17] More specifically, Habermas argues that *Dialectic of Enlightenment* owes its dangerous force to Nietzsche's philosophy; from Nietzsche, Horkheimer and Adorno take over the interpretation of reason as a mere instrument of self-preservation and power.

In this context I can develop neither Nietzsche's theory of truth nor Habermas's reading of it. It must suffice to summarize Habermas's arguments. Habermas emphasizes the aesthetic turn in Nietzsche's philosophical writings, a move that cancels established values of knowledge and morality. Nietzsche, Habermas suggests, "enthrones taste, 'the Yes and No of the palate' as the sole organ of knowledge beyond Truth and Falsity, beyond Good and Evil."[18] This move consistently undercuts the rationality of Yes/No positions. Thus both descriptive and

16. Ibid., 20.
17. Ibid., 22.
18. Ibid., 25.

normative statements are reduced to expressions of evaluation. (The sentence "x is true" should be read "I prefer x.") In Nietzsche these value judgments are no longer grounded in cognitive principles that can be demonstrated; rather, they express a claim to power. The core of this approach is an aesthetic sensibility and productivity, the excitement of the will by the beautiful. The theory of the will to power, however, is untenable, Habermas argues, because it is contradictory. It is unable to valorize its own claims. In Habermas's words: "If, however, all proper claims to validity are devalued and if the underlying value judgments are mere expressions of claims to power rather than to validity, according to what standards should critique then differentiate? It must at least be able to discriminate between a power which deserves to be esteemed and a power which deserves to be disparaged."[19]

The section on Nietzsche in Habermas's Adorno essay is of crucial importance in two respects: it serves to demonstrate the deficiencies of a totalizing critique of ideology, and it calls attention to the present poststructuralist debate. Habermas holds that Horkheimer and Adorno, under the impact of Nietzsche's theory of power, end up in an aporia similar to that of Nietzsche. Thus their own version of Critical Theory loses its critical edge because it follows a self-contradictory strategy. This conclusion concurs with the analysis presented in *The Theory of Communicative Action*. In the Adorno essay of 1982, however, Habermas stresses the impact of Nietzsche rather than the Marxist heritage because he wants to bring into the foreground an unresolved problematic embedded in *Dialectic of Enlightenment*. The procedure of unmasking the Enlightenment, showing that reason ultimately reverts to myth, leads to a theory of power deprived of possible strategies to overcome the impasse. Negative dialectic, always turning back to the abyss of yet another turn of suspicion, cannot address this problematic. It remains unresolved.

19. Ibid., 27.

Habermas and Foucault: Habermas comes to almost identical conclusions in *The Theory of Communicative Action* and his Adorno essay of 1982, although in the first case he puts the blame on the heritage of Western Marxism (reification), whereas in the second he makes the influence of Nietzsche responsible for the wrong turn of the Frankfurt School. This convergence is slightly puzzling: from the point of view of intellectual history, the two traditions that Habermas uncovers in *Dialectic of Enlightenment* are not easily reconcilable. In theoretical terms the two arguments do not necessarily belong together. The thesis that Horkheimer and Adorno, under the influence of Nietzsche, developed a totalizing critique of ideology is not identical with the thesis that Horkheimer and Adorno, by generalizing the concept of reification, arrived at a radical critique of instrumental reason. One could argue, however, that the two claims at least support each other. When we describe the history of modern consciousness as stages of an increasingly radical critique of its own presuppositions, we can also use this framework to position the transformation from Lukács's theory of reification to the critique of instrumental reason in the writings of Horkheimer and Adorno. We observe the same move toward a totalizing critique of reason undercutting the rationality that was used to carry out the project in the first place. Still, the logic of reification, as it was first fully developed in *History and Class Consciousness*, is significantly different from the theory of power in the writings of Nietzsche and Foucault. For Habermas, however, who is primarily looking at the strategical aspect, the two positions converge because they both aim at the destruction of rationalism.

Historically, I feel, Habermas is on safer ground when he develops the problematic of the late Frankfurt School out of the tradition of Western Marxism. For the strategy of his own project, on the other hand, the confrontation with the poststructuralist interpretation of Nietzsche, particularly that of Foucault, has become more crucial. The reason for this turn is as follows: since Habermas has consistently maintained that

Lukács's solution to the problem of reification is no longer viable, the defense of rationalism has become at the same time more difficult and more urgent. If Foucault's critique of reason is correct, Habermas's own theory of communicative action built on rational consensus through speech acts is in jeopardy. The skepticism of Foucault's geneaological history is a position that Habermas has to challenge in order to secure the viability of rational discourse. By the same token, incidentally, Habermas has to confront Luhmann's systems theory, which argues in favor of social systems without subjects and meaning (*Sinn*). The common denominator is "positivism," or the elimination of claims for meaning and validity.[20] Foucault's radical rereading of history results in relativism, since the genealogical historian cannot sustain his or her position when confronted with the question why a specific view of history should be preferable to another one (the same problem that Habermas found unresolved in Nietzsche).

Hence Habermas uses a similar strategy against Foucault: the inner logic of genealogical historiography becomes the target of his critique. Specifically, he wants to demonstrate that the seemingly objective approach of discourse analysis simply represses the fundamental hermeneutic configuration involved in the encounter between the historian and the material. The historian, whether it is explicitly stated or not, always takes a position. If we follow Foucault's position and assume that all knowledge is power and therefore critical only vis-á-vis other forms of knowledge/power, we undermine the basis of genealogical history. In this case the knowledge provided by critical historiography is as much part of the will to power as the practices under investigation. Habermas concludes: "Every counter-power moves within the horizons of the power which

---

20. See Jürgen Habermas, "Genealogische Geschichtsschreibung: Ueber einige Aporien im machttheoretischen Denken Foucaults," *Merkur* 38 (Oct. 1984): 745–53.

it opposes, and as soon as it is victorious transforms itself into a power complex which then provokes a new counter-power. The genealogy of knowledge cannot break out of this vicious circle."[21] As soon as critical knowledge has successfully challenged established knowledge/power, it becomes power, a vicious circle from which the genealogy of knowledge cannot escape. Hence, Habermas concludes that a critique that does not reflect on its own methods and theoretical premises is chained to this aporia.

While I think that Habermas's formal argument is persuasive, I am less certain whether it is strong enough to challenge Nietzsche's and Foucault's assumption that there is no ultimate meaning in history. To put it differently: the proof that Foucault's project is contradictory in terms of its own logic is not the same as proving that his pessimistic view of history is wrong. The rational critique can demonstrate the contradictions, but this strategy does not automatically secure the meaning of history. In particular, it does not prove that social practices are embedded in reason. The rationality of social practices, especially the validity of certain social practices in comparison with others, and the assumption that human history can be deciphered as a meaningful process toward a goal, have to be grounded in a different way. Foucault, who does not share Habermas's conviction that human practices are determined by rationality (in its emphatic sense), makes a different use of rational methods. His genealogical analysis seeks to undercut the presumed foundations of knowledge and the teleological constructs of history relying on unquestioned notions of continuity and logical sequence. "The search for descent," Foucault writes in his discussion of Nietzsche, "is not the erecting of foundations: on the contrary, it disturbs what was previously considered immobile, it fragments what was thought unified; it shows the heterogeneity of what was imagined consistent

21. Ibid., 749.

with itself."[22] In this context the concept of emergence takes on a meaning different from Habermas's usage. While Habermas seeks to understand genealogy in Nietzsche as the search for validity (the validity of the older forms), Foucault wants to stress the dangers of historical reconstructions along the lines of development or evolution. "As it is wrong to search for descent in an uninterrupted continuity, we should avoid thinking of emergence as the final term of an historical development. ... These developments may appear as a culmination, but they are merely the current episodes in a series of subjugations."[23] Yet Foucault overstates his claim when he goes on to say that history is the "endlessly repeated play of dominations" and concludes: "The domination of certain men over others leads to the differentiation of values; class domination generates the idea of liberty; and forceful appropriation of things necessary to survival and the imposition of a duration not intrinsic to them account for the origin of logic."[24] This view of history totalizes the process of history as much as the liberal view stressing progress. While we can possibly agree that in all historical situations known to us human interaction has been determined by domination, it does not *eo ipso* follow that this insight can be generalized and extrapolated into the future. This, then, is the case that one can make for Habermas's position: granted that human practices have been shot through with violence, granted further that history has been propelled by the drama of power, we cannot logically exclude the possibility of change, unless we believe in eternal laws of history for which we would need more than empirical examples. The question then arises whether and how human beings can escape the fate of power, how they can become masters of their own history. This is obviously the central Marxian question.

Let me briefly state Habermas's answer. He infers from his

22. Michel Foucault, *Language, Counter-Memory, Practice* (Ithaca, 1977), 147.

23. Ibid., 148.

24. Ibid., 150.

analysis of Horkheimer's and Adorno's writings that the approach of the philosophy of consciousness to a subjectivity not contaminated by instrumental reason has failed and cannot be restored. Attempts by Dieter Henrich and others to rescue subjectivity by differentiating between subjective and instrumental reason result in the same aporia already diagnosed by Adorno. Hence, this approach has to be replaced with an intersubjective orientation undercutting from the very beginning the logic of reification inherent in instrumental reason. This project, Habermas believes, can be developed out of existing social theories, especially those of George Mead and Emile Durkheim. So Habermas proposes a shift of focus rather than a new philosophy. "The focus of investigation thereby shifts from cognitive-instrumental rationality to communicative rationality. And what is paradigmatic for the latter is not the relation of a solitary subject to something in the objective world that can be presented and manipulated, but the intersubjective relations that speaking and acting subjects take up when they come to an understanding with one another about something."[25] Habermas understands this approach as the alternative to systems theory as well as the genealogy of knowledge, approaches where concepts like subject and object can be replaced by system and *Umwelt* (environment) and the problematic of subjectivity hence can be reformulated in terms of complexity aimed at self-preservation. Instead, Habermas offers a different reading of modernity. The process of disenchantment, the "decentration of our understanding of the world and the differentiation of various universal validity claims," seen by Luhmann as the historical background of systems theory, prepares the way for a reconsideration of intersubjective relations.[26] The very lack of fixed, overarching worldviews calls for an intersubjective interpretation of reality. Only a theory of communicative action, Habermas is con-

25. Habermas, *Theory of Communicative Action*, 392.
26. Ibid., 397.

vinced, can combat the reduction of subjectivity to the level of mere self-preservation (and power games). Obviously, this theory, unlike systems theory, cannot limit itself to the explanation of facts and structures; it is involved in claims for validity. Habermas emphasizes this element when he states: "The utopian perspective of reconciliation and freedom is ingrained in the conditions for the communicative sociation (Vergesellschaftung) of individuals; it is built into the linguistic mechanism of the reproduction of the species."[27]

Systems theory and the life-world: It is not my task in this book to analyze the foundations of this theory. Still, I want to discuss some of its aspects. In contrast to Parsons's systems theory, Habermas suggests a dual focus: he differentiates between system and life-world. The concept of the life-world, taken from phenomenological sociology (Schütz), refers to ordinary social situations where human beings interact. The life-world can be described in terms of narrative presentations of historical events and social situations. Among them are cultural events, for instance, aesthetic projects the function of which is to express the worldview of a social group and thereby help to integrate its members. The phenomenological analysis of the life-world primarily uses a hermeneutic approach; it reconstructs the life-world from the point of view of the participating actors. (The meaning of the events is seen through the eyes of the involved actors.) The actors, operating inside of their life-world, are involved in reaching a common understanding about the facts, the experiences, and the norms of their reality. Hence, it is also the transcendental horizon of their agreements and disagreements, their disputes and their claims. This pertains especially to language and culture. The actors cannot distance themselves from culture and language in the same way they can detach themselves from the objective

27. Ibid., 398.

reality of facts. Since communication is based on speech acts, the actors are always involved in the use of language.

Now, Habermas's thesis is this: a theory of communicative action must be grounded in the hermeneutic understanding of the life-world, but it cannot stay on this level because social relations cannot be reduced to social interaction. Therefore, the view from the inside has to be supplemented by the external perspective offered in systems theory. "I would like to suggest conceiving societies as simultaneously system and life-world."[28] Societies are conceived in terms both of systems and of life-worlds. This dual approach would also apply to the cultural sphere. While hermeneutic theories (Gadamer) interpret the relationship between the subject and the work of art as a dialogue between two subjects (both raise questions and give answers), Habermas insists on the systematic and functional character of culture as well. By this I mean that culture has to be treated as a part of the social system in which it operates. When the analysis moves to this level, we step out of the commonly acknowledged cultural tradition of our life-world and shift to a functional reading of the events, norms, and objects in which we normally participate as actors. Yet, Habermas does not simply want to replace the first perspective by the second—which would be a structuralist notion. Rather, he wants to combine them. He calls attention to the shortcomings of the phenomenological interpretation of the life-world (the bias for cultural aspects) and postulates a reorientation that would include the legitimate aspects of systems theory.

On the other hand, Habermas reminds us that the life-world cannot automatically be subsumed under the system. More specifically, he argues that the historical differentiation of the social system resulting in increased complexity leads at the same time to a situation where system and life-world are clearly

28. Jürgen Habermas, *Theorie des kommunikativen Handelns,* vol. 2 *Zur Kritik der funktionalistischen Vernunft* (Frankfurt, 1981), 180.

detached from each other. The process of differentiation implies a rift between system and life-world. "The social system definitively explodes the horizon of the life-world, removes itself from the pre-understanding of communicative everyday praxis, and remains accessible only to the counter-intuitive knowledge of the social sciences that have developed since the eighteenth century."[29] The result is the *Versachlichung* (reification) of the life-world; this would apply not only to the spheres of morality and law, but also to the cultural sphere. System differentiation, then, leads to the formation of new institutions dealing with specific problems in terms of their own logic.

Let us consider the implications for the realm of art more closely. As soon as the differentiation occurred in the sphere of art and literature in the eighteenth century, we observe the emergence of a new institution. This institution, the institution of art, performs specialized functions that cannot be duplicated by other social institutions. Thus validity claims in the sphere of art do not have the same meaning as claims made by moral or scientific theories. Specifically, Habermas, following Parsons, defines the claims of art to meaning as expressive values. Accordingly, the autonomous institution of art prescribes the reception of the individual work of art. That work is primarily received under the auspices of *Wahrhaftigkeit* (authenticity), as distinguished from *Wahrheit* (truth). The process of differentiation within the social system, in other words, assigns art a specialized function. This reorientation both sharpens and limits art's specific validity claims. To put it bluntly: as part of the cultural subsystem, art loses the central place it occupied in traditional societies, where it was bound to religion and morality.

Literary criticism and the life-world: We have to contemplate the consequences of this strategy. The grip of systems theory

29. Ibid., 258.

marginalizes art by insisting on its expressive function as the primary one. The aesthetic experience is detached from cognitive and moral truth. In Habermas's work, however, this analysis should not be understood as a plea for aestheticism. On the contrary, Habermas is well aware of the critical force of modern artistic movements. In his critique of Daniel Bell he argues—and this brings him close to Adorno again—that the avant-garde of the twentieth century fulfilled an important critical task. He writes: "These discontents [of modern societies] have not been called into life by modernist intellectuals. They are rooted in deep seated reactions against the process of *societal* modernization. Under the pressure of the dynamics of economic growth and the organizational accomplishments of the state, this social modernization penetrates deeper and deeper into previous forms of human existence."[30] In this context, Habermas stresses the critical function of modern art and vigorously defends it against the neoconservative praise of unquestioned tradition. He calls on communicative rationality in order to undercut the power of the economic and administrative logic that determined the historical process of modernization. Yet, on the level of systems analysis, he accepts the separation of art from science and morality. Hence, the standards for the appreciation and evaluation of art are different from those developed by ethical and scientific theories. In the realm of theoretical analysis (dealing with the system) we are left therefore with an unbridgeable gap between the specialized institution of art (as part of the cultural subsystem) and the life-world. (Like Peter Bürger, Habermas is convinced that the attempts of surrealism to destroy the institution of art and reconnect art and life-world have failed.)[31] Still, as we have seen, the task for Habermas is to relink system and life-world. In our example this would mean the specialized institution of

30. Jürgen Habermas, "Modernity versus Postmodernity," *New German Critique* 22 (Winter 1981): 7.
31. See Peter Bürger, *The Theory of the Avant-Garde*, trans. Michael Shaw (Minneapolis, 1984).

art and the use of art in everyday life have to be brought together again; the alienated analysis of the expert and the impoverished experience of the layperson have to be reintegrated. But how good are the chances for this project? Habermas is cautious enough to voice his doubts because the logic of the social system has been more powerful than the resisting forces within the life-world.

It seems that Habermas has maneuvered himself into a difficult position: on the one hand, using systems theory, he traces the process of social differentiation that leads to the institutional detachment of art from the life-world; on the other hand, he postulates the revival of the life-world and with it the revival of a common aesthetic experience that can be connected to other modes of experience, such as the moral sphere. Yet, this task of relinking is not an easy one because the differentiation of values, as it has been accepted by the institution of literary criticism, denies an immediate integration of the various modes of experience. This was one of the reasons why Adorno in his aesthetic theory heroically refused to support a strictly Kantian interpretation of art (through the category of taste) and insisted on the *Wahrheitsgehalt* of the work of art, on a moment of truth that is at least equivalent to, if not more valid than the truth claims of philosophical discourse. Thus Adorno does not acknowledge the dichotomy between the life-world and the institution of art. His analysis, which is clearly that of an expert critic, relies on hermeneutic procedures that must satisfy the institutional level as well as the experience of the life-world. The truth claims of the work of art cannot be restricted to one level. In fact, Adorno maintains that the redemption of the reified life-world can be conceived only through the understanding of the authentic work of art. This claim, of course, leaves him with the problem of explaining how the extreme complexity of the modern work of art can be related to our daily experience. The more Adorno emphasizes the validity of modern art by contrasting its aesthetic structure with the depraved language of everyday communication, the more he widens the gap between the work of art and the general public. Obviously Habermas does not want to pursue this approach, primarily, as we have seen, because he does not share Adorno's notion of a completely reified reality under advanced capitalism. He clearly means to redeem the life-world in its various modes. But how can this be done in the realm of art?

Two strategies are conceivable for the solution of this problem: either one has to find a mediating element between the system and the life-world, between the institution of art and everyday aesthetic experience, or one has to undercut the dichotomy by showing that it is a false one, by showing, in other words, that the use of language in ordinary communication and its use in fictional literature are not fundamentally different. In the second case the autonomy of art would be erased. Brecht's aesthetic would be a step in this direction. Habermas has not favored this approach, however. In his most recent essay on the distinction between philosophy and literary criticism, he has argued instead that the leveling of language in the project of deconstruction leaves us with no means to confront and solve the problems we encounter in our life-worlds. Most notably, he argues that Richard Rorty's notion of language as a permanently floating process would destroy the possibility of a meaningful practice because this concept of language cancels the yes and no of communication. "The yes and no of communicatively acting players are so prejudiced and rhetorically overwhelmed by linguistic contexts, that the anomolies that appear in phases of exhaustion are depicted only as symptoms of a diminishing vitality, as part of the aging process, as processes analogous to nature—and not as the result of failed solutions to problems and inadequate answers."[32] Against the"holistic" approach of Jacques Derrida and Richard Rorty, Habermas emphasizes the process of linguistic differentiation:

---

32. Jürgen Habermas, "Exkurs zur Einebnung der Gattungsunterschiede zwischen Philosophie und Literatur: Ueber Idealisierungen im Alltag" (1985, manuscript), 34–35.

the discourses of science, law, and morality have become separate and therefore each has developed according to its own logic. Consequently, Habermas in his attempt to relink system and life-world must favor a model of mediation. Literary criticism, to give an example, has the task of mediating between the literary system, as it is articulated in the institution of art, and the ordinary language of communication. Since modern art beginning with romanticism is increasingly inaccessible to the general public, it becomes the mission of the critic to translate the *Erfahrungsgehalt* (experience content) of the art work into the language of ordinary communication. A similar function, incidentally, is assigned by Habermas to philosophy. It is supposed to mediate between the expert discourses of science, law, and the like, and ordinary communication.

My reservations about this model are twofold: first, I have some doubts about the chances for the success of this translation. Given the complexity of expert discourse, it is problematic to assume that ordinary language is adequate for the articulation of subtle aesthetic problems. This is, of course, one of the reasons why literary criticism has lost its mediating function between the advanced work of art and the general reading public. The rhetoric of modern criticism is no more accessible than the structure of advanced works of art. Second, Habermas's approach, much like that of the Young Hegelians, is a one-way street: it traces only the flow from the level of the system to the level of the life-world. Yet it would be crucial also to explore the possible impact of ordinary language on expert discourse. What can ordinary language contribute to the discourse of the experts?[33] In what way is the analysis of the critic also grounded in his or her daily experience? In certain ways Adorno's aesthetic theory can do justice to this dialectic by holding on to a notion of aesthetic truth that integrates the expert discourse and ordinary experience through the idea of

33. See Peter Uwe Hohendahl, *The Institution of Criticism* (Ithaca, 1982).

mimesis—an idea that Habermas wants to limit to the prerational phase of human development. In a different way Derrida's project of deconstruction undercuts the logocentric tradition of European philosophy. Habermas seems to underestimate its critical potential when he charges that Derrida reduces philosophical and literary writing and reading to the problem of rhetoric. Instead of assuming with Habermas that deconstruction aestheticizes all language (everything becomes literary criticism), one can also argue that deconstruction is an attempt to relink the formal discourse of the experts and ordinary language by problematizing both. In the realm of literary criticism this means, as Habermas notes critically, that the special status of poetic language is denied. But it is not quite evident why Habermas is not willing to use the critical force of deconstruction against the logic of differentiated systems. It seems that Habermas overstates his case when he describes deconstruction as a purely literary approach without concern for problem solving in the realm of the life-world. Thus my suggestion would be: if we want to free the life-world from the contraints of the overarching system and its institutions, there is room for the project of deconstructive criticism, precisely because it questions the logic of systems.[34]

One reason why premodern literary criticism—say that of the seventeenth century—could more easily connect literature and life in its discourse is that ordinary language and poetic language were not yet conceived of as fundamentally different. Both followed the same rules of rhetoric. Only with the emergence of the concept of aesthetic autonomy in the eighteenth century does the transition from poetic to ordinary language become problematic. Although it is not likely that we can return to the literary system of premodern classicism, its historical existence should remind us that the autonomy of art is

---

34. See, for instance, Michael Ryan, *Marxism and Deconstruction: A Critical Articulation* (Baltimore, 1982), and the critical remarks of John O'Kane, "Marxism, Deconstruction, and Ideology: Notes toward an Articulation," *New German Critique* 35 (Fall 1984): 219–47.

not a transhistorical category but rather a concept grounded in specific historical conditions. Looking back at the evolution of the institution of art from the eighteenth to the twentieth century we can understand the claim for the autonomy of poetic language as a critical response to the process of differentiation at the level of the social system. Yet this process had its own dialectic: as soon as the concept of autonomy was firmly installed in the institution of art, it became conventional. Today it hardly has the subversive force it had about 1800. Similarly, Habermas's attempt to rescue the autonomy of art as the sphere where language playfully creates new worlds and thereby offers counterfactual possibilities—as Habermas emphasizes against Mary L. Pratt—no longer has the same critical edge.[35] The whole issue of the life-world, I suggest, is still an open question in Habermas's recent work—a question that definitely deserves further attention and possibly has to be reformulated to reach the goal that Habermas has in mind.

35. Mary L. Pratt, *The Speech Act Theory of Literary Discourse* (Bloomington, Ind., 1977).

Habermas's *Philosophical Discourse of Modernity*

In September 1980, when he accepted the Adorno Prize from the city of Frankfurt, Jürgen Habermas provoked his audience by insisting that the discourse of modernity, which supposedly had collapsed, was by no means obsolete; moreover, he stressed that it was still waiting for its ultimate fulfillment. Habermas openly attacked the notion that we have reached the age of postmodernism, because this assumption would necessarily result in a flawed assessment of our future. Instead, Habermas insisted on the continuation of the Enlightenment project, even if this project, as he readily conceded, should not be pursued through the use of instrumental reason or in the mode of traditional subject philosophy. The reason for Habermas's polemic was his fear that the contemporary critique of rationalism would play into the hands of conservative forces—not only in West Germany but also in the United States. Habermas's provocation was answered in similar fashion: both in France and in the United States poststructuralist theorists angrily rejected the positing of a logical link between postmodernist theory and political neoconservatism. Jean-François Lyotard, for instance, responded by arguing that it was Habermas's logocentric theory that should be called conservative and hopelessly outdated.[1]

1. Jean-François Lyotard, *The Postmodern Condition: A Report on Knowledge* (Minneapolis, 1984).

It seems as if Habermas had entered a debate for which he was ill-prepared. Before 1980 he had not had many serious encounters with French theory. He had acknowledged neither Foucault nor Derrida and his deconstructionist disciples in this country. His own interest in the Anglo-American and French tradition had clearly favored theories that came out of the European Enlightenment, among them analytic philosophy and the pragmatism of John Dewey, Charles Peirce, and George Herbert Mead. In *The Theory of Communicative Action* (1980), French structuralism and poststructuralism are simply absent. There are biographical and historical reasons for this gap. For a German intellectual who grew up during the Third Reich, the most influential forerunners of contemporary French theory—Nietzsche and Heidegger—are politically dubious because of their impact on or their involvement with German fascism. This distrust of the Nietzsche-Heidegger connection continues in Habermas's latest book. His doubts concerning the validity and the political implications of poststructuralist theory are grounded in his hostility toward the German mastertexts on which French theory is based. Between 1980 and 1985, however, Habermas clearly moved away from the relatively simple opposition of Enlightenment versus postmodernism, or of progressive versus conservative traditions. The distance between Frankfurt and Paris decreased, although it would be misleading to call Habermas's position poststructuralist. It can be said, however, that Habermas's intensive readings of George Bataille, Foucault, and Derrida have resulted in a more precise and also more fruitful statement of the theoretical differences between Paris and Frankfurt. Whether his French colleagues would agree with his interpretations of their texts is another matter. The recent attempt to bring "German" and "French" theory together in Paris was, as Rainer Rochlitz has suggested in his instructive account of the meeting, unsuccessful.[2] Both

2. Rainer Rochlitz, "The Missed Meeting—A Conference Report of French and German Philosophy," *Telos* 66 (Winter 1985/86): 124–28.

sides were ultimately unwilling to make a leap and familiarize themselves with the opposing arguments. It seems doubtful that Habermas, who participated in the meeting only as an observer, could have prevented the disaster. Even his *Philosophical Discourse of Modernity* would in all likelihood have been rejected by Derrida and his disciples as a defense of a position that still relies on the unquestioned premises of European rationalism.[3] After all, Habermas did not change his position in the process of reading French theory. Still, there is one major agreement. It concerns the critique of the philosophy of consciousness, which Habermas fully shares with Foucault and Derrida. Thus, Habermas welcomes their attempts to move beyond the problematic concept of modern subjectivity, although his own critique of the subject differs significantly from the poststructuralist approach. Habermas shares with contemporary French theory the preference for a linguistic paradigm, yet he clearly does not support an understanding of language in which words function as a chain of signifiers for which a signified can never be established with certainty. This rhetorical interpretation of the function of language is unacceptable to Habermas because it makes intersubjective understanding and consensus impossible.

Some critics have argued that one cannot equate poststructuralism and postmodernism because poststructuralist discourse remains closer to modernism than to postmodernism. Poststructuralist theory is concerned with the texts of classical modernism. When Habermas refers to modernism (*Moderne*) he has a broader historical period in mind. He means the phase from roughly 1500 to the present, for which German historians have coined the term *Neuzeit* (as opposed to *Mittelalter*). More specifically, he refers to the philosophical discourse that began with the Enlightenment of the eighteenth century and reached

3. Jürgen Habermas, *The Philosophical Discourse of Modernity: Twelve Lectures*, trans. Frederick Lawrence (Cambridge, Mass., 1987); cited henceforth in the text as *PD*, followed by page number.

its maturity in the philosophy of Hegel. This is the moment when the theoretical awareness of historical modernity is fully developed. Hence, for Habermas the question of whether the present age is still part of modernity or whether it is already a phase of postmodernity can be answered only by addressing the accumulated philosophical problems of the last 150 years. This approach differs rather drastically from that of either Heidegger or Derrida, who argue that the problem of modern thought, that is, its logocentricity, goes back to ancient philosophy (Plato). Here, Habermas seems to be closer to Foucault, who assumes a fundamental epistemological break in the late eighteenth century. Even in this case, however, the differences are undeniable: while Foucault insists on the rupture between the classical episteme and modernism, Habermas views the German idealism of the early nineteenth century as a continuation of the Enlightenment, which began with Descartes.

Habermas defines modernity in the narrow sense (*Moderne* as opposed to *Neuzeit*) as the second stage of a philosophical discourse stretching from German idealism to the present. Modernity is understood as that historical moment when philosophy, by fully appropriating its own history, calls for its own cancellation (Marx) or at least radically questions the unproblematic continuation of its project (Left-Hegelians). Therefore, Habermas claims that the philosophical discourse following Hegel's system—both its more conservative and its more radical branches—is still relevant today. Although they hardly offered lasting solutions, the positions developed in Germany during the 1840s still have a (mostly unacknowledged) impact on present philosophical discussion.

For this reason, Habermas's debate with French theory begins with its German forerunners in the nineteenth century. At the center of this discussion we find Nietzsche, who clearly influenced Heidegger and also directly and indirectly had a major impact on contemporary French thought. It is not accidental that Habermas calls Nietzsche's work a *Drehscheibe* (turntable) of European philosophy. In the fourth chapter, which deals with Nietzsche's critique of the Enlightenment, Habermas underscores the radical nature of this polemic, which not only questions the content of previous philosophical discourse but attacks the episteme of rationalism itself—its method and its function. While Hegel saw reason as "reconciling self-knowledge" and the Left-Hegelians defined reason as "emancipatory appropriation" by and for human beings, Nietzsche decides to cancel the project of rational critique. "Nietzsche ...renounces a renewed revision of the concept of reason and *bids farewell* to the dialectic of enlightenment" (*PD*, 86). When Nietzsche undertakes a critique of the Enlightenment he does this with the "goal of exploding modernity's husk of reason as such" (*PD*, 86).

This formulation may remind us of Lukács, for whom Nietzsche was one of the most important precursors of German fascism. Still—and this makes a major difference—Habermas does recognize the importance and validity of the historically accumulated epistemological problems, and he also differentiates much more clearly between Nietzsche's utopian project and its reactionary appropriation by the German fascists. In order to demonstrate the problematic nature of Nietzsche's program, Habermas links Nietzsche's thought with German romanticism (with Richard Wagner as the connecting link). He tries to explain the difference between Nietzsche's position and the romantic approach to the problem of truth. As specifically romantic, Habermas defines the concept of a new mythology, a program to which Nietzsche remains indebted. "The idea of a new mythology is of Romantic provenance, and so also is the recourse to Dionysius as the god who is coming. Nietzsche likewise distances himself from the romantic use of these ideas and proclaims a manifestly more radical version pointing far beyond Wagner" (*PD*, 88). It is not the interest in Dionysius that is original in Nietzsche's writings but, as Habermas underscores, the displacement and revision of the Dionysius figure. In Nietzsche the god Dionysius is clearly separated from the Christ figure—a separation that does not occur in roman-

tic thought. By cutting the link with Christian mythology—
the presence of which he criticizes in Wagner's writings—
Nietzsche redefines the utopian program in purely aesthetic
terms. Thereby he undermines the liberal claim for an understanding of history that should culminate in the emancipation
of humanity. "And as a counterauthority to reason, Nietzsche
appeals to experiences that are displaced back into the archaic
realm—experiences of the self-disclosure of a decentered subjectivity, liberated from all the constraints of cognition and
purposeful activity, all imperatives of utility and morality"
(*PD*, 94). To put it differently, Habermas views Nietzsche—
and, of course, he is not the first critic to see Nietzsche in this
light—as the proponent of a radical aestheticism that rejects
all cognitive and moral norms.

Expectedly, Habermas is highly critical of this position. He
is especially critical of Nietzsche's theory of power, which later
resurfaces in Bataille and Foucault. This theory, Habermas
maintains, is ultimately unable to legitimate itself because its
major thesis (everything is grounded in power relations) makes
it impossible to ground theory rationally. As Habermas points
out, this type of radical critique of rationality necessarily ends
in an aporetic situation: the critique undercuts the ground on
which the proof of its validity must be based. This fundamental
contradiction reappears in various forms in Nietzsche's disciples. It can be traced in Bataille, Lacan, and Foucault, who
continue the critique of subject-centered reason through anthropological, psychological, and historical arguments. It can
also be found in Heidegger and Derrida, who follow Nietzsche's
attack on metaphysics and therefore want to return to pre-
Socratic philosophy. The most radical questioning of philosophy, however, may well turn into a defense of the status quo.
He uses the case of Heidegger to demonstrate the link between
a radical critique of rationality and German fascism, and later
he uses the case of Foucault to show the contradictions involved in a theory of power that borrows from Nietzsche.
Within the context of this theory no critique of existing power

structures can escape the argument that it is itself involved in claims for power. At the end of his chapter on Nietzsche, Habermas suggests that Heidegger at the same time continues and surpasses Nietzsche's critique of rationality. Heidegger takes over Nietzsche's aestheticism, the attempt to rescue philosophy by transforming it into art, but at the same time he wants to limit this program and moves toward a restitution of philosophy proper. Unlike Nietzsche, Heidegger does not appreciate the provocation of modernist art, its subversive function vis-à-vis a professionalized discourse of philosophy.

Here it is useful to provide a more detailed analysis of Habermas's criticism of Heidegger, because this polemic serves as the background for his reading of Derrida and the American deconstructionists. Heidegger and Bataille, as far as they follow Nietzsche's lead, face the same problem: they want to carry out a radical critique of reason which "attacks the roots of the critique itself" (*PD*, 101). In his presentation of Heidegger's philosophy, Habermas follows the traditional division between Heidegger's early thought, which was still under the impact of Edmund Husserl's philosophy of consciousness, and the late philosophy of the 1940s and 1950s. But he does not follow Heidegger's own interpretation of this development, which reads the later writings as a *Kehre* (turn) that reinterprets the problems and questions presented in *Being and Time* (1928). Habermas's resistance to the late Heidegger's humanism is clearly motivated by political considerations. More than once Habermas points to the dangerous political implication of Heidegger's position, that is, its closeness to fascism. This connection is not simply a matter of Heidegger's dubious personal decision; rather, it is Heidegger's very discourse that is involved in thought patterns and arguments that affirm the power of the National Socialists.

Still, Habermas's critique cannot be reduced to a narrow political polemic. His aim is to demonstrate the inherent connection between Heidegger's specific philosophical criticism of traditional metaphysics and the historical circumstances in which this discourse was developed. In other words, Habermas offers a radical historical reading of Heidegger, while Heidegger himself thought of his philosophy as being above historical events. This interpretation throws a different light on Heidegger's position. His critique of *Seinsverlassenheit* (abandonment of being) appears as a mystification—an empty shell that can be filled in different ways according to changing historical circumstances. Thus, while Heidegger's position in *Being and Time* does not yet actively support the doctrine of National Socialism, neither does it preclude it. This political problem is grounded in a philosophical argument. Habermas stresses again and again that Heidegger remained much closer to a philosophy of consciousness (*Subjektphilosophie*) than he was willing to admit. While the genesis of *Being and Time* has to be seen in the context of the neo-ontological movement of the 1920s, it is apparent that Heidegger could not return to pre-Kantian ontology. His own project grew out of neo-Kantian philosophy and the problems of *Lebensphilosophie* (philosophy of life). Thus, Habermas notes: "He [Heidegger] makes use of the vocabulary of the neo-ontological turn in order to further the dissolution of the concept of the transcendental subject; but even in this radicalization he holds on to the transcendental attitude of a reflective illumination of the conditions of the possibility of the being of the person as a being-in-the-world" (*PD*, 142). Not only are Heidegger's pro-fascist statements between 1933 and 1935 (when he still believed in the revolutionary power of the movement) compatible with the language of *Being and Time*, but so is his later critique of fascism, where he stresses the critique of technology.

Habermas presents Heidegger as a German intellectual whose biography and philosophy participated in the fascist movement. Such an involvement cannot be found in Heidegger's French disciples. Derrida's interest in Heidegger's critique of metaphysical thought, for instance, is clearly unrelated to Heidegger's 1933 political decision. What Derrida appreciates in Heidegger's position is the emphasis on the end of European history and the decline of traditional European philosophy. Thus, Derrida continues Heidegger's later writings, but at the same time he returns to Husserl's phenomenology, which he interprets as the final expression of European logocentricity. Habermas describes Derrida's project as an anarchist and subversive struggle that aims at undermining the foundations of Western metaphysics (*PD*, 161–62)—a strategy Habermas acknowledges as an important contribution, although he does not believe in its efficacy. According to Habermas, Derrida's critique of European metaphysics remains dependent on the very structures he wants to criticize. The attempt to explode the foundations of logocentric thinking only leads to the search for ever deeper foundations (*écriture*). This fundamentalism in reverse cannot, therefore, escape the structure of a philosophy of origin (*Ursprungsphilosophie*). Hence, Derrida is closer to Heidegger than he himself would admit.

What are Habermas's arguments, and what are their implications? In his chapter on Derrida, Habermas focuses his analysis on Derrida's critique of Husserl. From a critique of Husserl's theory of language and his thesis that an ultimate grounding of pure philosophy should be possible through intuitive *Anschauung* (perception), Derrida reaches a position that favors *écriture* rather than phonemes. As Derrida notes: "The rationality which governs a writing thus enlarged and radicalized, no longer issues from a logos. Further, it inaugurates the destruction, not the demolition but the desedimentation, the de-construction, of all significations that have their source in that [signification] of the logos. Particularly for the signification of truth" (*PD*, 164). Habermas traces the argument Derrida presents in *Speech and Phenomena* in detail; his strategy, in other words, aims at an immanent critique. The point of his reconstruction is to show that in Derrida *écriture* rather than Logos becomes the starting point. Habermas appears to be willing to follow Derrida's critique of presence and his insistence on difference. At the end of his argument he notes: "Thus, Derrida achieves an inversion of Husserlian foundationalism inasmuch as the originative transcendental power of creative subjectivity passes over into the anonymous history-making productivity of writing" (*PD,* 178).

This is where Habermas finally inserts his criticism. He understands Derrida's movement as a reversal rather than an overcoming of *Ursprungsphilosophie.* The history of Being is replaced by a complicated mirror image: the mirroring of a text in another one, which again is mirrored in a third one. Each text can only directly or indirectly point to the original text without ever reaching the *Urschrift* (original text). This search for the original text, however, which for Derrida takes the place of the search for the transcendental subject, is for Habermas both a continuation and a radicalization of Heidegger's program. "Against his will, he [Derrida] lays bare the inverted foundationalism of this thought by once again going beyond the ontological difference and Being to the differance proper to writing, which puts an origin already set in motion yet one level deeper" (*PD,* 181).

The weakness of Derrida's approach, Habermas argues, lies in its dependence on the very kind of *Ursprungsphilosophie* that Derrida means to criticize. Thus, Derrida ends up with a "formulalike avowal of some indeterminate authority" (*PD,* 181). It is obvious that Habermas does not expect Derrida's project to result in a viable political praxis. Strangely enough, however, he does not make this criticism explicit. Rather, when dealing with the sociopolitical consequences of Derrida's philosophy, Habermas emphasizes the positive value of deconstruction in comparison with Heidegger's endorsement of archaic Greek culture. Following Susan Handelman, Habermas argues that Derrida's approach has to be seen against the background of Jewish mysticism and its heretical hermeneutic theory.[4] Hence, Derrida's deconstruction belongs to a tradition

---

4. Susan Handelman, "Jacques Derrida and the Heretic Hermeneutic,"

that opposes the hegemony of Christian logos and its hermeneutics in Paul's teaching. The attempt to rescue writing from
the hegemony of the spirit suggests Derrida's proximity to Benjamin's anarchist philosophy of history. For Habermas this
comparison clearly implies both respect and distance. Habermas has never concealed his admiration for Benjamin; at the
same time he has made it clear that he does not believe in the
feasibility of Benjamin's project.[5]

In an extended footnote to a passage concerning the relation
between philosophy and literature (*PD*, 408–409) Habermas
makes a very important general point: he argues—not only
against Derrrida but also against Adorno and Benjamin—that
they read and write philosophy as if they were only one generation removed from Hegel. These critics, insofar as they see
themselves as disciples of Nietzsche, remain caught in those
universal problems they received from the philosophical tradition extending from Plato to Hegel. Habermas, on the other
hand, wants to remove philosophy from this need for an ultimate grounding (*Letztbegründungen*) and to limit its project.
According to him, the business of philosophy does not differ fundamentally from other disciplines—all results are fallible
in principle, they are grounded in praxis and history, and
therefore they have to be reconsidered under different circumstances. In this claim for a pragmatic position, Habermas is not
far from someone like Rorty, whom he explicitly mentions in
this context. This position, however, does not imply a repudiation of normative claims, as one might read the move against
Letztbegründungen. This is precisely the point where Habermas disagrees with Foucault, with whom he shares more common ground than with Derrida.

---

in *Displacement: Derrida and After*, ed. M. Krapnick (Bloomington, Ind.,
1983), 98–129.

5. See Jürgen Habermas, "Walter Benjamin: Consciousness-Raising or
Rescuing Critique," in his *Philosophical-Political Profiles* (London, 1983),
129–63.

Apparently Habermas was seeking a dialogue with Foucault before the latter unexpectedly died in 1984.[6] In his obituary, Habermas openly expressed a feeling of appreciation, without, however, suggesting at any point that he was in agreement with Foucault's theory. Habermas's proximity to Foucault's work, which also clearly comes through in the two chapters devoted to him in *The Philosophical Discourse of Modernity*, is grounded in the nature of the questions that Foucault would ask, especially in Habermas's interest in Foucault's critique of the philosophy of consciousness. Reading *The Order of Things* and *The Archeology of Knowledge*, Habermas could not fail to notice the similarity with (but, of course, also the difference from) his own attempts to overcome the transcendental approach (which was still dominant in *Knowledge and Human Interest*) by moving closer to the epistemology of systems theory. This comparison would also, however, reveal the similarities of Foucault's and Luhmann's positions with respect to fundamental methodological assumptions—for instance, their basic common antagonism to hermeneutics. Thus, Habermas's analysis of Foucault's work concentrates on two related aspects: the antihermeneutic attitude of archaeological and genealogical history and the move toward a general theory of power in Foucault's late writings. For Habermas this theory of power is the bold but ultimately unsuccessful attempt to establish a new kind of subject-decentered historiography without metaphysical foundations.

While the ninth chapter primarily introduces Foucault's theory, the tenth chapter, entitled "Aporias of a Theory of Power," presents Habermas's critique of Foucault's theory. Here, the focus will be on three questions: (1) what does Habermas mean by his claim that Foucault is undercutting the hermeneutic approach, (2) how does Foucault's general theory of power grow out of this antihermeneutic strategy, which replaces the con-

---

6. See Jürgen Habermas, "Mit dem Pfeil ins Herz getroffen," in his *Die neue Unübersichtlichkeit* (Frankfurt, 1985), 126–31.

cept of interpretation (*Verstehen*) with the concept of discourse, and (3) why does Habermas so emphatically object to the theory of power?

Foucault, so Habermas argues, wants to move away from the historical paradigm that favors the present (as the point of departure) and understands the writing of history as a form of self-understanding. This strategy also necessarily undercuts the hermeneutic approach. "Hermeneutical effort is aimed at the appropriation of meaning; in each document, it hunts out a voice reduced to silence that should be roused into life again. This idea of a *document* pregnant with meaning has to be called into question just as radically as the business of interpretation itself" (*PD*, 250). This implies that the perspective of the observer replaces the perspective of the participant. Closely connected with this stance are the attack on any totalizing form of history, which attempts to understand the process from a central concept, and the renunciation of expressive causality, which argues that the divergent phenomena of a given period can be related to a center containing the essential meaning of the period. Foucault replaces historical interpretation with the analysis of discourse—a method that deliberately keeps its distance from the material under consideration.

Readers familiar with Foucault will find little new in the ninth chapter. Yet, the reconstruction of the argument (as usual in Habermas) is no more than a preparation for the systematic discussion that follows in chapter 10. Again, Habermas begins his critique of Foucault's theory of power with a close reading of the text. Then Habermas suggests that discourse analysis is faced with a fundamental problem. "What then counts as fundamental are the rules (accessible to archeology) that make possible the ongoing discursive practice. However, these rules can make a discourse comprehensible only as regards its conditions of possibility; they do not suffice to explain the discursive practice in its actual functioning—for there are no rules that would govern their own application" (*PD*, 268).

Foucault is faced with the problem that a discursive practice controlled by its rules cannot determine the context in which it functions. Foucault responds to this problem with a general theory of power. The archaeology of knowledge is therefore subsumed by a genealogy of knowledge "that explains the emergence of knowledge from practices of power" (*PD*, 268). Still following Foucault's strategy Habermas acknowledges two advantages of this move in Foucault's theory. First, this strategy allows Foucault to distance himself from the philosophy of consciousness, and second, it provides the various discourses of knowledge with a common ground. The general theory of power is supposed to explain the operation of theoretical discourses. Habermas, however, argues that this strategy is doomed to failure; he holds that Foucault's theory of power does not escape the quandaries of subject-centered philosophy. According to Habermas, the theory of power itself is ambiguous because it is supposed to operate on two different levels. On the one hand, it is expected to analyze empirical power constellations; on the other hand, it has to function as a transcendental theory explaining the very possibility of theoretical discourses. As Habermas notes: "In his basic concept of power, Foucault has forced together the idealist notion of transcendental synthesis with the presuppositions of an empiricist ontology" (*PD*, 274). Consequently, Foucault faces the following aporia: If we assume with Foucault that the concept of truth is based on the concept of power (rather than the other way around, as idealism presupposes), then we cannot explain successful action, since successful action can be measured only in cognitive terms, that is, according to its adequacy vis-à-vis specific circumstances. Of course, in using this argument against Foucault, Habermas presupposes the priority of the acting subject—a subject that relates to the world either in terms of cognition or in terms of practice. Foucault, on the other hand, reverses this relationship: Subjectivity is the result of discourses grounded in power relations.

Although Foucault and Habermas strive toward a similar goal, a critique of the philosophy of consciousness, their solutions to this problem differ significantly. While Foucault (following Nietzsche) treats normative considerations (*Geltungsansprüche*) as purely functional aspects and reduces them to power relations, Habermas insists that this strategy does serious harm to the definition of social praxis. Moreover, he claims that Foucault's theory rests on basic contradictions. The most fundamental one is this: genealogical historians must make a truth claim for their research and presentation. As soon as they apply the genealogical method to their own project, it leads to an unresolvable contradiction. Habermas distinguishes three aspects of this aporia (*PD*, 276): genealogical historians are part of a temporal context; an analysis of history grounded in a specific moment of history itself can make only relative truth claims; and genealogical historians, no matter how much they try to distance themselves from the material (documents, facts, and so on), remain partisans. Foucault's method suppresses the hermeneutic aspect of historical analysis. In his early work Foucault simply does not reflect on the position of the cognitive subject, the perspective of the historian. In his later work, under the influence of Nietzsche, this objective stance results in general skepticism—an attitude Habermas somewhat viciously calls "professing irrationalism" (*PD*, 278). He observes: "The unmasking of the objectivist illusions of *any* will to knowledge leads to an agreement with a historiography that is narcissistically oriented toward the standpoint of the historian" (*PD*, 278). If we limit the concept of truth to the specific discourse in which it is used, if, in other words, we limit the category of truth to the impact it has within a specific discourse, then Foucault's theory cannot be universalized and would have no more than local relevance. This conclusion, however, frustrates Habermas because it takes Foucault's project seriously and supports his attempt to undermine any form of power (also those forms that dress up as scientific truth). Hence, Habermas insists (against Foucault) on a universal concept of truth that cannot be derived from power relations. (This claim, of course, does not exclude the possibility that concrete scientific projects may be motivated by considerations other than the search for truth). Clearly, for Habermas power and truth operate on different levels. Specifically, truth cannot be grounded in power. In the end, Habermas disagrees with Foucault's claim that all norms and standards are ultimately relative; he disagrees with the thesis that the historian must therefore refrain from value statements in order not to be affected by the influence and power of existing discourses. With good reasons, Habermas argues that this position cannot be carried out consistently. Foucault's discourse—as a radical critique of the humanities and social sciences (*Geisteswissenschaften*)—contains implicit value judgments. Habermas wants to show that Foucault, as much as he steers clear of an explicit statement, occasionally admits that normative criteria are unavoidable (*PD*, 284).

At this point Foucault and his disciples might ask Habermas, How do you explain these norms and values (in the social as well as in the scientific sphere)? Do you not fall back on a position that emphasizes the need for these values and covers up their origin in power relations? These questions would force Habermas to account for his own position and to examine the basis from which he launches his critique of poststructuralist theory. In the concluding chapters he tries to answer these questions by restating his own theory. Most of all, he wants to demonstrate that there is a third way—besides philosophy of consciousness and poststructuralism (chapter 11). Furthermore, he wants to illuminate why the project of modernity cannot simply be canceled (chapter 12).

As one would expect, in these final chapters Habermas basically refers back to his theory of communicative action. He considers this theory a realistic and pragmatic approach— equally distant from the dangers of logocentric philosophy of consciousness with its problems of *Letztbegründungen* and from the pure rejection of metaphysics in the work of Foucault, Derrida, and their disciples—a rejection that easily results in irrationalism. This claim also throws more light on Habermas's understanding of the project of modernity (*Aufklärung*). What he has in mind is not, contrary to what some of his critics have claimed, simply the continuation of the idealist tradition. Habermas thinks in terms of a third alternative that would avoid the dangers of logocentrism and deconstruction. In this search, he feels close to a philosopher like Rorty who tries to rewrite the history of philosophy in terms of a radical critique of modern philosophy and its development from Descartes to Heidegger. Habermas could hardly share this program fully because he would have to cut himself off from the tradition in which he was trained, but it is apparent that today he has more affinities with thinkers like Dewey or Mead than with German idealism or even with the philosophy of the early Marx. Like Foucault and Derrida, Habermas insists on a paradigm change because he concurs with them that the metaphysical tradition of European philosophy is exhausted. In his opinion, the old paradigm is to be replaced with the model of communicative action in which neither the subject nor factual relations are the basis. Instead, the point of departure is communicative interactions. In particular, Habermas wants to undercut the opposition of an empirical and a transcendental subject, an opposition that even the critics of logocentrism have retained in their attacks.

How can this program be grounded? How can it be defended against the criticism that it remains part of the old paradigm of subject philosophy (Lyotard's criticism)? Habermas decided to ground his theory in language theory, especially speech-act theory. In the eleventh chapter he restates his arguments for this approach. Habermas believes that language itself contains the premises for a theory of communicative action. In other words, the explication of speech acts is not only supposed to explain how actual human communication works, but it is also supposed to demonstrate why consensus and thereby human solidarity is possible at all. It is impossible here to discuss this theory in detail. The following will, rather, focus primarily on its implications for the understanding of modernity. Habermas argues that the linguistic approach allows a rereading of the project of the Enlightenment in a different light and thereby reappropriates its semantic content. This revisionist tendency in Habermas's interpretation of modernity has to be emphasized more strongly than usual. As Habermas notes, "By contrast, as soon as we conceive of knowledge as communicatively mediated, rationality is assessed in terms of the capacity of responsible participants in interaction to orient themselves in relation to validity claims [*Geltungsansprüche*] geared to intersubjective recognition. Communicative reason finds its criteria in the argumentative procedures for directly or indirectly redeeming claims to propositional truth, normative rightness, subjective truthfulness, and aesthetic harmony [*Stimmigkeit*]" (*PD*, 314). To put it differently: the use of reason is not conceived anymore in terms of an absolute origin; rather, it unfolds within the context of an intersubjective exchange of arguments, an exchange that will necessarily raise normative claims. But these claims are not absolute: they can be questioned at any given time.

Habermas's use of speech-act theory contains a descriptive and a normative aspect. On the one hand, the analysis of speech acts explains how human communication actually works. On the other hand, it is also used by Habermas to ground his social theory, which emphasizes human emancipation. Habermas has been accused by his critics of idealizing the actual use of language in human communication. This reproach, however, misses the real problem. The weak spot in Habermas's argument is the dual function of language. By pointing to the actual operation of linguistic and social communication, Habermas conceals that these empirical conditions are ultimately turned into a normative understanding of language. This dualism results in an aporetic situation, which, incidentally, is not very different from the contradictions in Foucault's theory of power—although with a different turn. By insisting that linguistic communication, as it functions in the real life-world, provides the basis for the new paradigm, Habermas distances himself from a transcendental argument. But this move has a price: the rigid equation of facts and norms. As Habermas notes: "Inasmuch as communicative agents reciprocally raise validity claims with their speech acts, they are relying on the potential of assailable grounds. Hence, a moment of *unconditionality* is built into *factual* processes of mutual understanding" (*PD*, 322). Those norms to which we have recourse in our everyday interaction are, as Habermas suggests, context-bound, but there is another important aspect, which "serves as the foundation of an existing consensus" (*PD*, 323). This thesis seems to be close to a transcendental argument. To put it differently: if we want to avoid the quasi-transcendental structure of the argument, it might be safer to drop the use of universal norms and favor a purely local, context-bound use of rationality. Obviously, Habermas is not inclined to draw this conclusion, since universal normative claims (*Geltungsansprüche*) are of great importance for the structure of his emancipatory social theory.

The last chapter, then, tries to make two points: it shows why Habermas in the final analysis refuses to subscribe to the presuppositions of poststructuralist theory, and it sketches the outline of an alternative theory. It becomes quite clear, incidentally, that Habermas does not speak out in favor of a continuation of classical Critical Theory. In fact, he sees the later work of Adorno, for instance *Negative Dialectics* and *Aesthetic Theory*, as part of a tendency from which he wants to distance himself. Why, then, does Habermas, after a full-scale analysis of its major texts, decide to draw a line between himself and French theory? He argues that the poststructuralist critique of reason reduces the concept of rationality to such an extent that significant distinctions become irrelevant. In particular, Habermas turns against the undialectical critique of subjectivity—the general attack on logocentricity. This polemic has reduced the ambiguity of modernity by stressing the negative elements without considering the positive side of the account. The frontal attack has thereby repressed the progressive potential of modernity. As Habermas observes:

> Not only the devastating consequences of an objectifying relation-to-self are condemned with this principle of modernity, but also the other connotations once associated with subjectivity as an unredeemed promise: the prospect of a self-conscious practice, in which the solidary self-determination of all was to be joined with the self-realization of each individual. What is thrown out is precisely what a modernity reassuring itself once meant by concepts of self-consciousness, self-determination, and self-realization. (*PD*, 337–38)

This statement clearly defines the direction of Habermas's program. It differs significantly from the project of his teachers (Horkheimer and Adorno) and also from those traditions within Marxist theory that want to reemphasize the category of human praxis. Unlike Horkheimer and Adorno, Habermas can positively relate to Max Weber's work. While *Dialectic of Enlightenment* reads modernity—through the eyes of the early Lukács—primarily as a process of increasing reification, Habermas sees Weber's description of modern history (a process of disenchantment) also as a positive and encouraging tendency. Since *Legitimation Crisis*, Habermas has maintained that modern society has developed through a process of *Ausdifferenzierungen* (differentiations), which results in a system consisting of relatively autonomous subsystems and spheres. Thus he writes about the cultural system: "These knowledge systems of art and criticism, science and philosophy, law and morality, have become the more split off from ordinary communication the more strictly and one-sidedly they each have to do with one linguistic function and one aspect of validity. But they should not be considered on account of this abstraction per se as the phenomena of decline symptomatic of subject-centered reason" (*PD*, 339). It is fairly obvious that this sentence also contains a critical indictment of Adorno's philosophy. For Habermas, the fundamental development on which his reflections on modern society are based is the difference between the life-world and system, as it begins to surface during the eighteenth century. In this context he encourages the rehabilitation of reason (*Vernunft*)—a project beset with problems, as Habermas knows so well. Hence, his defense of reason must chart its course most carefully in order not to succumb to the dangers of instrumental, or to the lure of "inclusive," reason—both of which have a totalitarian character.

It is precisely poststructuralist objections to the specter of a totalizing rationalist norm that, as one might have expected, have made *The Philosophical Discourse of Modernity* a highly controversial book in America, once it was available in English (1987).[7] The battle lines were predictable: they pretty much followed the division between the Critical Theory camp and the poststructuralist camp. Also predictably, the reception revealed a considerable amount of misunderstanding about Habermas's position, especially his conception of rationalism and his defense of modernity. To some extent, Habermas's earlier essay ("Modernity—an Incomplete Project")—with its strong indictment of implicit conservative tendencies within postmodernism/poststructuralism—blocked an adequate appropriation of Habermas's *Philosophical Discourse*, in which the epistemological problems figure much more prominently than the political ones. Among poststructuralists—John Rajchman for instance—it was simply assumed that Habermas extended his argument in order to reinforce his earlier position.[8]

There is no need to trace the details of this rather acrimonious debate, in which received opinions and stereotypes have overshadowed the discussion of the substantive issues. Instead, I hope to bring these issues more to the foreground by turning the tables on the prominent poststructuralist discourse in this

7. See esp. John Rajchman's review article "Habermas's Complaint," *New German Critique* 45 (Fall 1988): 163–91.
    8. Ibid.

country; rather than challenging Habermas on the basis of poststructuralist models of analysis, I would like to raise the question What can Habermas's theory contribute to the discourse on power and truth? Can the Habermasian version of Critical Theory throw light on poststructuralist positions? Further, considering the debate between Habermas and Foucault, another crucial issue is the distinction commonly made between normative and descriptive levels. If we accept this distinction as useful, how do we justify it and ground it theoretically? While Habermasian theory has tended to privilege the normative use of reason, Foucault's writings have strongly emphasized the descriptive level of particular historical analysis. This tension leads us to the core of the debate over Habermas's rationalism and his defense of modernity.

Once one has stripped away the polemical rhetoric, the question about norms is, I believe, at the bottom of the debate between John Rajchman and Richard Wolin.[9] Although I will not trace this discussion in detail, in general, the argument in favor of Foucault's (and against Habermas's) position can be presented in the following way: philosophical discourses, like all cultural discourses, are culture-bound and historical. Consequently, one can no longer theorize about modernity in the same manner as in the eighteenth century, when people were seeking for universal structures of knowledge. Habermas, since he continues to use the theoretical apparatus of the Enlightenment, fails to understand the historical end of the project of modernity, with its stress on teleological history (evolution). Once we grant that history is a construct rather than an actual (linear) process, we no longer have an Archimedian point from which to judge progress and reaction, good and bad. This situation necessitates a new approach (and a new definition of "critical"): instead of confronting "bad" reality with "good"

9. See Wolin's response to Rajchman's review essay (cited above), entitled "On Misunderstanding Habermas: A Response to Rajchman," as well as Rajchman's "Rejoinder to Richard Wolin," *New German Critique* 49 (Winter 1990).

norms in order to improve society, one "tries to explore what we take for granted as necessary and fixed in our existence as something that has been happening to us, and which we may refuse to accept."[10] Foucault's theory wants to eliminate the normative aspect of rationality because it tends to interfere with our access to historical events (in their specific function). Norms and standards are there to be questioned. Concepts like justice must not be trusted; rather, a critical approach analyzes actual discourses of justice to demonstrate how the use of this concept depends on particular social practices. According to Rajchman's account, Habermas fails to recognize Foucault's project and therefore superimposes his own categories on Foucault's writings.

In the final analysis, for Foucault, reason and rational behavior are always defined in local terms: "there is no such thing as Objectivity or Rationality in general."[11] Consequently, the distinction between true and false statements relates only to rules grounded in a specific discourse. Still—and this is where I would locate the weakness in the Foucauldian argument— the description and analysis of particular discursive practices, which lead to a recognition of the plurality of discourses, always require a comparative rationality that in itself can never be merely local. How do we make rational decisions when we have to address competing and conflicting discourses, let us say, of social justice? Habermas offers a solution by arguing that there are formal universal norms available that can serve as a guide for a rational discussion. The formal character of these norms has to be underscored: they are not supposed to deal with specific contents; rather, they are expected to map the parameters and define the character of public communication. Hence it is possible to argue that the concerns and problems of marginalized groups can be dealt with most successfully when rationality is restricted to principles of formal

10. Rajchman, "Habermas's Complaint," 174.
11. Rajchman, "Rejoinder to Richard Wolin," 158.

procedure. In other words, the distinction between universal and local aspects of reason, between generalizable norms and culture-bound questions of the good life, is necessary. For this reason, Habermas criticizes Foucault's attempt to reduce rationality to the level of a cultural context.

In his desire to overcome a relativistic position and to secure the possibility of rational discussion (but not through deductions from a priori knowledge, as some of his critics have maintained), Habermas tends, I feel, to underestimate the epistemological strength of local reason and, conversely, to overrate the need for overarching norms of rationality. Although Habermas agrees that most of the practical questions with which we are confronted in our life-worlds cannot be solved through demonstrative arguments, he tries to transcend an unstable pluralism, where individual needs and interests cancel each other, and wants to hold out the possibility of a normative and rational consensus that is stronger than a rationally negotiated, pluralist compromise. According to Habermas, this outcome can be achieved by separating formal procedure from substantive content. When we are faced with fundamental divergences in value orientation, however, this distinction tends to break down. The boundaries between procedural rationality and cultural rationality (concerning the "good life") are less stable than Habermasian theory assumes. To put it differently, demonstrative norms—even norms of formal procedure—that transcend specific cultural contexts are not available in the public sphere where political and social issues are debated. Yet this does not mean that there is no room for rational debate. Particular and local rationality does not claim to provide a conclusive mechanism for creating a consensus, but it offers a comparative analysis of needs and values so that a compromise can be reached. This means that rational debate does not have to be based on demonstrative universal norms. At the same time, we have to note that this argument does not eliminate the difference between the normative and the descriptive aspects of rationality, as Rajchman appears to assume; the move from a problematization of Habermas's claim for demonstrative norms to a rejection of norms and procedures is not persuasive. It is flawed because it makes the problematic assumption that these norms cannot be questioned, overlooking the fact that Habermas's formal notion of communicative norms stresses precisely the process of questioning and debate.

6 The Politicization of Aesthetic Theory: The Debate in Aesthetics since 1965

In West Germany the politicization of aesthetic theory and literary criticism began during the second half of the 1960s. If one were to describe everything that took place in the fifteen years between 1965 and 1979, the resulting recitation of names and projects would contribute little to our understanding of the matter.[1] I have therefore chosen to focus on themes and categories that can aid us in laying out the internal logic of the theoretical discussion. This approach assumes that one can organize the processes of theory formation into a historical pattern. As a consequence, the years between 1965 and 1979 are presented as comprising a unified epoch or phase that differs from the preceding and following years. The legitimacy of this assumption can be assessed only by critically examining the theoretical material itself. My approach thus relies on a schema whose validity can be demonstrated only by investigating its contents.

In 1969 Hans Robert Jauss alluded to Thomas Kuhn by speaking of a paradigm shift in literary criticism.[2] Jauss foresaw a new theoretical model emerging from reception aesthetics. As Jauss himself later admitted, this claim proved rash; yet, in the

---

1. Please consult the Postscript to this chapter for some remarks on the decade of the 1980s in Germany.

2. Hans Robert Jauss, "Paradigmawechsel in der Literaturwissenschaft," *Linguistische Berichte* 3 (1969): 44–56.

mid-1960s, significant changes do indeed begin to occur in West Germany.[3] Nevertheless, these changes do not so much take place because new theorems are developed; rather, they result more from a rediscovery of older, obscured approaches and positions. In retrospect, this turn can be characterized as a break with the modernist and avant-gardist aesthetics variously represented by Theodor W. Adorno and Gottfried Benn. This is not to claim that Adorno's theory played no role in influencing later developments. On the contrary, it is precisely his theory that became extraordinarily important to the debates and self-understanding of the 1970s. This initial break is instead a matter of rejecting particular elements of Adorno's thought: his attachment to the great names of modernism like Franz Kafka, James Joyce, and Samuel Beckett, and his conception of the social function of art as it is expressed in his essays on Jean-Paul Sartre, Georg Lukács, and Bertolt Brecht. Those who opposed the modernists' aesthetics concentrated on the defensive stance of postwar modernism vis-à-vis the contemporary social contradictions that became evident in West Germany with the formation of the Great Coalition in 1966. This division was a thoroughly painful and, for the most part, deeply traumatic event for both sides, for the student movement's theory of art was profoundly indebted to the crucial stimulus of Adorno's work.

I will not even attempt to sketch out Adorno's aesthetic theory here; it is enough to name those features of his theory that were received by the New Left and then wielded against him:

1. In contradistinction to traditional academic aesthetics, Adorno's theory is historically oriented, both in relation to its object and in respect to its own position. In each case, it ad-

---

3. Hans Robert Jauss, "Racine und Goethes *Iphigenie*—Mit einem Nachwort über die Partialität der rezeptionsästhetischen Methode," *Neue Hefte für Philosophie* 3 (1973): 1–46.

dresses the work of art only in the context of its historical emergence and reception.

2. We are not dealing with a historicist but an ideologically critical historical approach. This means that the encounter with the work of art that deserves the name of criticism interrogates the structure of the work of art by attending to the element of historical truth it contains.

3. Adorno is indebted to the Marxist analysis of commodities for crucial insights into the conditions of aesthetic reception and production under capitalism. The rubric of "culture industry" summarizes this approach, which ultimately relates the aesthetic to the economic sphere.

4. Lastly, Adorno formulates a theory of aesthetic autonomy that radically departs from the concept of the organic work of art and the notion of aesthetic reflection.

This extremely broad characterization nevertheless allows for a more precise delineation of the paradigm shift. Adorno's theory denies itself a political application of its own insights and negates the step from a contemplative to a practical attitude. This can in no way simply be attributed to personal idiosyncrasies. Adorno rejects the politicization of aesthetics, which would of course include his concept of art, because his social theory ruled out any essential transformation in the global system of organized capitalism. In the face of the proletariat's integration into existing society, the resistance of late Critical Theory was confined to the level of reflection. This political resignation dramatically affects the aesthetic sphere, which for Adorno becomes the sole realm in which freedom from and opposition to the omnipresent system can be articulated.

The theoretical kernel of this position is already formulated at an early stage in Adorno's thinking. In the essay "On the Fetish Character in Music" from the year 1938, which should be understood as a confrontation with Walter Benjamin's essay "The Work of Art in the Age of Mechanical Reproduction," Adorno resists his friend's attempt to draw political conclusions from the destruction of the aura—that is, of aesthetic autonomy.[4] Adorno expressly repudiates Benjamin's hope that the technical grounding of art as it was emerging in film might have progressive political implications. The theory of the culture industry anticipated here by Adorno is not interested in technology as a new force of production but in the exchange value of art, an exchange value that unswervingly guarantees art's degradation. This difference of opinion between Adorno and his older friend is not mentioned out of caprice, for precisely this conflict becomes a crucial catalyst in the confrontation between Adorno and the New Left. The rediscovery of Benjamin's later writings, which were only partially represented in the 1955 edition of his works overseen by Adorno, changed the emphasis of the debate with help from theories that had already been developed in the 1930s—most significantly by Benjamin and Brecht. The increasingly embittered 1967 debate between the Frankfurt School and the journal *alternative* over the authentic form of Benjamin's writings is symptomatic of the intensification of what I would like to designate as the political aesthetics of the 1960s.[5] It would certainly be precipitous at this point to trace back this materialist aesthetics, which clearly relies on Marx, exclusively to the rediscovery of Benjamin. The search for a materialist theory of art leads in the late 1960s to a series of different, to some extent conflicting, efforts that take issue with Critical Theory.

In a schematic way, one can distinguish between four different schools of thought. During the first phase of the movement, that is, between 1967 and 1969, Herbert Marcuse and his writings were particularly important for the self-understanding of the Left, for they directly met the demand for

---

4. Theodor W. Adorno, "On the Fetish Character in Music and the Regression in Listening," in *The Essential Frankfurt School Reader*, ed. Andrew Arato and Eike Gebhardt (New York, 1982), 270–99; Walter Benjamin, "The Work of Art in the Age of Mechanical Reproduction," in *Illuminations*, ed. Hannah Arendt (New York, 1969), 217–52.

5. See *alternative* 56/57 (Oct./Dec. 1967) and 59/60 (Apr./June 1969).

a political aesthetics. Marcuse answered the question In what way can art and literature play a role in transforming society? Although Marcuse's theories certainly receded into the background after 1969, they continued to exercise a considerable degree of influence in the 1970s, particularly among those who continued the tradition of Critical Theory. Nevertheless, after 1972—above all with his *Counterrevolution and Revolt* (1972)—Marcuse revised his thesis of the total transposition of art into praxis and spoke out against a desublimated praxis, thus preparing the way for the turn against political aesthetics. Christian Enzensberger's literary theory, for instance, which strictly separates political praxis and utopia, is deeply indebted to Marcuse's approach despite its polemic against Critical Theory.

Commodity aesthetics, which likewise arose from Critical Theory, took a different path. The commodity aesthetics developed by such authors as Wolfgang Fritz Haug, Hans Heinz Holz, and Friedrich Tomberg grappled with Horkheimer and Adorno's *Dialectic of Enlightenment*. At first, these efforts followed Adorno's use in his aesthetic theory of Marx's analysis of commodities; yet, over time, commodity aestheticians clearly distanced themselves more and more from the premises of the Frankfurt School in their stringent development of a materialist commodity aesthetics. By 1970 this process resulted in these theorists' seeing themselves in pronounced opposition to the Frankfurt School. The debate over commodity aesthetics dwindled away over the course of the 1970s after Hannelore Schlaffer contributed what she viewed as the critical conclusion to this debate, until W. Martin Lüdke renewed the discussion in 1977.[6] A similar process of rediscovery, in this

6. See Hannelore Schlaffer, "Kritik eines Klischees: 'Das Kunstwerk als Ware,' " in *Erweiterung der materialistischen Literaturtheorie durch Bestimmung ihrer Grenzen*, ed. Heinz Schlaffer, Literaturwissenschaft und Sozialwissenschaften 4 (Stuttgart, 1977), 264–87; and W. Martin Lüdke, "Der Kreis, das Bewusstsein und das Ding: Aktuell motivierte Anmerkungen zu der vergangenen Diskussion um den Warencharakter der

instance of Georg Lukács and Bertolt Brecht, encouraged the group around the journal *Argument* to draw closer to an orthodox Marxist position. This retrospective reflection on buried traditions, whose onset can be dated at about 1967, intensified theoretical discussion even as it simultaneously problematized anyone's claim already to possess a consistent materialist theory. The intensive appropriation of these materialist traditions necessarily led to the insight that an avant-gardist position, as it was represented by Benjamin and Brecht in the 1930s, could not be reconciled with the theory of Georg Lukács. The treatment of the expressionism debate and the later concern with the polemics of the *Linkskurve* made it evident that absolutely no consensus obtained in the Marxist camp about essential theoretical questions such as the problem of realism, the function of art, the assessment of specific artistic means, and so on. Helga Gallas's work *Marxistische Literaturtheorie* (1971) created a historical explanation, even as it deepened the conflict by taking up a pronounced Brechtian position while critically distancing itself from Georg Lukács and East German literary criticism.[7]

Thus, it is difficult to find a common denominator in the literary theory produced within the leftist camp during the 1970s. One does encounter fragments of and approaches to a materialist theory that clearly share a certain hostility to academic literary criticism and its aesthetics. This opposition was not least aimed at the Constance school, which fielded a phenomenologically grounded reception aesthetics as an innovative alternative to orthodox Marxism.[8] Otherwise, one can only

---

Kunst," in *Lesen, Literatur und Studentenbewegung*, ed. W. Martin Lüdke (Opladen, 1977), 124–57.

7. Helga Gallas, *Marxistische Literaturtheorie: Kontroversen im Bund proletarisch-revolutionärer Schriftsteller* (Neuwied, 1971).

8. For a summary of reception theory, see *Rezeptionsästhetik*, ed. Rainer Warning (Munich, 1975). For the Marxist position, see Bernd Jürgen Warneken, "Zu Hans Robert Jauss' Programm einer Rezeptionsäthetik," in *Sozialgeschichte und Wirkungsästhetik*, ed. Peter Uwe Hohendahl (Frankfurt, 1974), 290–96. For a discussion of reception theory in East

note the variety of opinions and viewpoints that were promulgated in such journals as *Kursbuch, alternative, Das Argument,* or *Aesthetik und Kommunikation.* One could make similar statements about the situation in France or the United States at the beginning of the 1970s. Yet when one carefully examines the period between 1965 and 1979 and compares the developments in the German debate with those taking place in French or American discussions, profound differences appear in the objects granted critical attention, the premises granted validity, and the methods that form the basis of discourse. If one wishes to grasp the aesthetic theory of the 1970s as a historical process, one must concentrate on the points where contradictions and oppositions become immediately apparent.

I begin with the political aesthetic that, primarily under the influence of Herbert Marcuse, radicalized the Frankfurt School's theory of art. Marcuse's earlier works, such as his famous 1937 essay on the affirmative character of culture, characteristically centered on a critique of ideology that opposed the concept of an autonomous culture transcending social pressures.[9] After his intensive study of Freud, however, Marcuse's interests began to focus on the utopian element of art. In *Eros and Civilization* (1955) Marcuse construes the opposition between art and reality found in classicism's aesthetic concept of autonomy in such a way that art comes to have an essential role in the emancipation of humanity. Art undermines the reality principle of analytical reason by advocating the principle of sensuousness. Marcuse develops the theory of a sensual liberation through aesthetic experience that prepares the way for political emancipation. What was chiefly a theoretical problem

---

Germany, see Peter Uwe Hohendahl, "Aesthetik und Sozialismus: Zur neueren Literaturtheorie der DDR," in *Literatur und Literaturtheorie in der DDR*, ed. Peter Uwe Hohendahl and Patricia Herminghouse (Frankfurt, 1976), 100–162.

9. Herbert Marcuse's famous essay, first published in the *Zeitschrift für Sozialforschung* in 1937, has been translated as "The Affirmative Character of Culture," in Herbert Marcuse, *Negations* (Boston, 1968), 88–133.

at the time *Eros and Civilization* first appeared became an immediate political problem in the late 1960s. In the preface to his *Essay on Liberation* (1969), Marcuse not only ascertains that his position accords with that of the radicals in France and the United States, he also emphasizes the utopian character of their demands: "The radical utopian character of their demands far surpasses the hypotheses of my essay; and yet, these demands were developed and formulated in the course of action itself; they are expressions of concrete political practice."[10] Marcuse achieves the transition from art to politics by attributing the character of social praxis to the new sensibility and aesthetic experience. The way in which Marcuse develops this thesis explains the initially surprising claim that the new sensibility itself already possesses the quality of praxis. Marcuse's gaze is no longer primarily directed at the artistic product, but at the moment of experience, which, as sensual reason, opposes instrumental reason. City planning, conservation, and ecological reforms are subsumed under the aesthetic sphere, which itself thereby becomes a political sphere. With Marcuse, aesthetics becomes political by freeing us from conventional politics. At the same time, this liberation embodies the sublimation of art. Art and reality coincide as soon as art gives up its autonomous status and becomes the daily practice of human beings. In 1969 Marcuse approaches Benjamin's conception of a postauratic art that belongs to the masses.

Among the German journals of the Left, the *Kursbuch* represented—at least temporarily—Marcuse's political aesthetics. Peter Schneider's 1969 essay "Die Phantasie im Spätkapitalismus und die Kulturrevolution" (Fantasy in late capitalism and the cultural revolution) exemplifies this tendency within the *Kursbuch*.[11] Writing under the influence of the failed May revolt in Paris, Schneider draws a distinction between the

10. Herbert Marcuse, *Essay on Liberation*, (Boston, 1969), ix.
11. Peter Schneider, "Die Phantasie im Spätkapitalismus und die Kulturrevolution," *Kursbuch* 16 (1969): 1–37; reprinted in Peter Schneider, *Atempause* (Reinbek, 1977), 127–61.

economic-political and the cultural revolution. He then follows Marcuse by concluding:

Simultaneously, De Gaulle's tanks have shown what the economic-political revolution cannot do. It cannot beget the revolutionary consciousness which corresponds to the state of development of industrial productive forces; it cannot transform the emancipation of the oppressed class into the emancipation of the individual; it cannot develop the liberation of society from capital further into the liberation of fantasy from the performance principle; and it cannot win if it does not begin as a cultural revolution and become a cultural revolution once more.[12]

In this instance, the cultural and aesthetic sphere is designated the realm in which revolutionary praxis must develop if it is to shatter the organization of late capitalism, for this system is comprised not only of classes and organizations but also of elements of consciousness that serve oppression. Schneider thus views the cultural revolution as a culminating step: "After the demolition of the state apparatus and the socialization of the means of production, it [the cultural revolution] transforms the emancipation of society from private property into the practical supercession [*Aufhebung*] of all relations of servitude which are modifications and consequences of alienated labour."[13] Again, Marcuse's theory serves as a bridge between the repressive culture of capitalism and ultimate liberation.

The union of Marx and Freud proposed by Schneider in 1969 obviously relies on Marcuse. It is certainly remarkable how Schneider, who was probably not yet aware of the *Essay on Liberation*, politically hones the position of *Eros and Civilization*. Whereas in 1955 Marcuse had addressed the utopian moment of art as art's political dimension, Schneider sharply

12. Translated from Schneider, *Atempause*, 127. All translations from articles and books in German, here and throughout the chapter, are provided by Brian Urquhart unless otherwise noted.

13. Ibid., 128; first interpolation, mine.

separates these aspects and notes a contradiction between the practice-free utopia of bourgeois art and the revolutionary action upon which a political aesthetics should be founded. With this distinction, Schneider breaks with Marcuse, whom he accuses of formalism. It is evident that the step with which Schneider would like to surpass his predecessor is precisely the one Marcuse himself takes in 1969—the desublimation of art into social praxis. In the words of Schneider: "Under late capitalism, the progressive, usable phantasy is absolutely no longer at home in art; instead, it is at home where it seeks its satisfaction in the revolutionary, rather than imaginary, transformation of society." According to Schneider, both traditionalist and avant-gardist works of art have lost their revolutionary force in late capitalism. "Form in art no longer expresses the promise of a future realization of desires; on the contrary: form makes a kind of promise out of real suffering and the real destruction of desires by still allowing the promise to become an object of imagination."[14]

From this criticism of Adorno's and Marcuse's aesthetics, Schneider draws the conclusion that in the context of late capitalism, one can identify only two meaningful functions for art: the agitative and the propagandistic. This conclusion remains noteworthy for its theoretical grounding. Although Schneider's approach remains beholden to Marcuse and Critical Theory, his social theory relies more on an orthodox position, such as Lenin's or Paul Sweezy's theory of imperialism. This attempt to modify the aesthetic theory of the Frankfurt School and simultaneously provide it with a new theoretical foundation seems characteristic of the situation of the New Left after 1969.

The same holds true of commodity aesthetics, which does not proceed so much from political as from economic analysis. The first attempts to develop a materialist commmodity aesthetics link up with Critical Theory, namely, with Horkheimer and Adorno's *Dialectic of Enlightenment*. This is true of Wolf-

14. Ibid., 146, 152.

Reappraisals

gang Fritz Haug's 1963 essay "Zur Aesthetik von Manipulation" (Toward an aesthetics of manipulation). Intent on providing an ideological critique, the essay tracks down the
purpose and form of advertising in late capitalism: "The ad-
vertisement appears with the deceptive appearance of mediating universality," whereas in reality it only represents the
interests of capital.[15] The use of aesthetic signs boils down to
channeling the existing needs of the population in such a manner that they benefit consumption and, as a result, profit. Commodity aesthetics clearly became significant only in its second
phase, when it departed from Critical Theory. In the 1970 preface to *Kritik der Warenästhetik* (Critique of commodity aesthetics), Haug settles accounts with the approach of the
Frankfurt School by rebuking it for proceeding from surface
phenomena and ignoring essential structures. According to
Haug, this produces a speculative theory in which the particular and the whole are related to one another in an unmediated
fashion. Nevertheless, the target of his critique is not the concept of totality, which Haug in no way relinquishes, but the
ontologization of a particular phase of late capitalism by the
Frankfurt School. The materialist grounding called for by Haug
from that point on relies on the Marx of *Capital* and not on
the Paris manuscripts of 1844, whose emphatic concept of alienation provided the basis for the project of Critical Theory.
"The task which I set myself," commented Haug in 1970, "was
therefore to derive the phenomena of commodity aesthetics
economically and to develop and present their systematic
connection."[16]

Haug's theory, which proceeds from Marx's analysis of commodities, can scarcely be considered a theory of art; the scope
of the aesthetic realm is defined in much broader terms than
is the case with Adorno. Haug uses the concept of the aesthetic

15. Wolfgang Fritz Haug, *Warenästhetik, Sexualität und Herrschaft*
(Frankfurt, 1972), 32.
16. Wolfgan Fritz Haug, *Kritik der Warenästhetik* (Frankfurt, 1973), 11.

on the one hand to designate sensuous knowledge (as does Kant) and on the other hand to designate the realm of the beautiful. The subject matter is clearly not primarily works of art but commodities that use the semblance of the beautiful in order to sell themselves. Since works of art certainly have offered themselves on the market as commodities ever since the eighteenth century, however, the next obvious step would be to apply the aesthetics of the commodity to the work of art.

Hans Heinz Holz took this step by formulating an argument that closely resembles Benjamin's analysis of the aesthetic aura and its disappearance. He follows Benjamin in discerning a precapitalist phase in which the work of art appears above all as a cultic object. When the cultic value of the object vanishes and the work of art's new function centers on display, then the work of art approaches the commodity:

> The work of art become commodity now shares all features of the essence of the commodity: it participates in an art market which is subject to the play of supply and demand, and in which the sales practices are in principle no different than those found in the market dealing in commodities of utility [*Gebrauchsgüter*]. The sales strategy employed in the two markets differ only in that the art market does not claim that the commodities it offers possess an immediate use value, but a spiritual value for the purchaser.[17]

Yet, at the same time the reception of the work of art changes, so too does its form of production: that is, the artist must offer his or her works to an anonymous market in order to make his or her way. The artist becomes "constrained by a product form which is compatible with the market." For Holz, the essential significance of commodity aesthetics lies in its refusal to examine the work of art without reflecting on the context in which it is rooted. In his view, commodity aesthetics is concerned with "analyzing the structural determinants which lie

17. Hans Heinz Holz, *Vom Kunstwerk zur Ware* (Neuwied, 1972), 16.

in the relations of production and distribution." This analysis of art as a commodity does not lead to political aesthetics, since, like Critical Theory, Holz places great emphasis on the commercialization of art. Yet the concept of aesthetic autonomy familiar to Critical Theory no longer plays a decisive role for Holz. Under developed capitalism, loss of autonomy is the fate of works of art: "The degradation of the work of art to a commodity implies the loss of the particularity of the aesthetic: from now on, the aesthetic object can only be exalted above other, random objects of utility by a decisionistic act of arbitrariness."[18]

Evidently, Holz goes one step beyond Haug's position. Whereas Haug still attributes some significance to the aesthetic sphere—that is, the realm of art—Holz stresses that criticism may not stop at the level of the work of art. In other words, the theory of art will dissolve into art history and the sociology of art. "The relative autonomy of the aesthetic," he argues against Adorno, "is annulled [*aufgehoben*]; instead of serving as a medium of reflection, the aesthetic becomes a mere function of society, an ideological simulacrum."[19] According to Holz's definition of art's present crisis, art has lost its authentic function. Moreover, in contrast to Marcuse, Holz promises art no new function. Holz extends the scope of commodity aesthetics by denying any difference between works of art and objects of utility.

This all-inclusive identification, which could not draw on Adorno for support, becomes the main target of Hannelore Schlaffer's critique, mentioned above.[20] Her goal is to do away with commodity aesthetics by proving that the autonomy of art was left essentially untouched by the development of a capitalist market. According to Schlaffer, it was only in the area of distribution that the work of art was pulled into the

18. Ibid., 25, 27, 37.
19. Ibid., 10.
20. Schlaffer, "Kritik eines Klischees," 264–87.

market and transformed into a commodity. Indeed, neither production nor reception were substantially affected by these conditions: "A commodity is the union of exchange value and use value provided that it is transferred in the exchange between buyers. The artist and the purchaser only apparently enter into an exchange relation, for artistic value cannot be determined and clearly cannot be paid for."[21] Against commodity aesthetics, Schlaffer argues that artistic labor or aesthetic production is not socialized and therefore not subject to the laws of the market. Since aesthetic production is not alienated, the autonomy of the work of art is in principle secured. The commodity aspect is secondary. This argument, as Lüdke rightly objected, underestimates the social character of artistic production. Lüdke refers to the historically changing context influencing the work of the artist and his or her artifacts.[22]

Generally speaking, one must ask whether the opposition between aesthetic autonomy and social determination can be specified on an abstract level. Indeed, it would appear that this relationship must be understood as a historical one that changes qualitatively between the eighteenth century and the present. It matters less, then, that the work of art cannot become an object of utility because it is spiritual, than does the circumstance that the work of art's function—like its reception—changes over time. Hence the category of autonomy, which Schlaffer derives from the very nature of works of art, itself proves to be historical. In this respect, Holz appropriately grasps the present situation as a historical crisis that cannot simply be resolved on the level of theoretical reflection. Holz's argument nevertheless clearly lacks a careful distinction between material and aesthetic production. Schlaffer's much-needed objection to this form of commodity aesthetics critically questioned precipitous, globalizing judgments and theoretical clichés. Lüdke's contribution demonstrated that the

---

21. Ibid., 277.
22. Lüdke, "Der Kreis, das Bewusstsein und das Ding," 133.

discussion did not come to an end with Schlaffer; he not only summed up the debate, he also articulated the possibility of its theoretical solution.

With good reason, Lüdke stresses that, as a rule, earlier approaches apply categories from political economy too directly to the aesthetic realm and do not sufficiently take into account the process of reification. At this juncture, however, the discussion is referred back to its starting point, namely, the reification theory of the early Lukács, which supplies the basis for the Frankfurt School. Thanks to Lüdke's attentive reconstruction, Adorno's theory of art again becomes visible as the starting point of the debate. It appears that the polemical turn against the Frankfurt School did not necessarily overcome it; rather, it led to an elaboration of certain possibilities already present in Adorno's thought. Both the thesis that in late capitalism all art is degraded to the status of a commodity and the thesis that the autonomy of art is inalienable can be found in Adorno. Thus, the discussion returns to Adorno, where the original formulation of the problem could be found. Lüdke argues that the critique of commodity aesthetics cannot restrict itself to specific conclusions, such as those put forward in the thesis of the commercialization of art or its autonomy vis-à-vis the market. On the contrary, this critique must deal with the Marxian concept of the commodity and the reification theory derived from it: "The thesis of the commodity character of art only obtains its real explanatory value by relying upon the Marxian conception of the fetish-character of commodities. In the meantime, it has become problematic for the thesis of the commodification of art to draw upon a reification theory developed from the fetish-character of commodities."[23] Lüdke's critique here is directed against the hidden orthodoxy of Critical Theory. Considered systematically, commodity aesthetics rests upon the theory of reification, which in turn is

23. Ibid., 150.

derived from Marx's analysis of the commodity in *Capital*. As a result, any doubt about Marx's economic theory must correspondingly affect commodity aesthetics and the theory of reification.

Lüdke brings this critique to bear in his discussions of Habermas, Claus Offe, Wolfgang Pohrt, and Luhmann. Lüdke would like to fill the gap in the argument with a theory of pure aesthetic experience that "could break through the reified structures of contemporary experience"; but because Lüdke quite clearly perceives that aesthetic experience always is mediated socially, he cannot relinquish the category of reification he just repudiated.[24] This contradiction becomes clearer as soon as Lüdke outlines his program. He would like to avoid the rigid conclusions of a theory that can offer only the concepts of degradation or autonomy to aesthetic experience. In other words, he wants to develop a theory that does justice to immediate experience and the subjective aspect of social reality. "If need be, the agenda can be expressed in a formula: to attain a maximum of immediate experience with a minimum of instrumental mediation."[25] This formula nevertheless simply displaces the problem, since it refers to the opposition between subjective experience and positivistically formed objective concepts. The primary focus of commodity aesthetics, however, is on the "historical" dialectic in the relationship between material relations of production and aesthetic creations. This problem cannot be solved by recourse to the concept of immediate experience, the current feasibility of which would first have to be demonstrated. Lüdke's proposed solution ignores the social mediation of experience and thereby becomes not so much untheoretical as unhistorical.

Let me briefly summarize the outcome of the first phase of the theory discussion. About 1970 a consensus existed in the leftist camp on the inadequacy of the aesthetic theory of the

24. Ibid., 152.
25. Ibid., 153.

Reappraisals

Frankfurt School. Furthermore, both political and commodity-aesthetic theories were in agreement that the work of art as an artifact no longer could remain the central object of aesthetic theory. For both approaches, although for differing reasons, it was no longer immediately evident that the work of art possesses a self-sufficient value. The discussion of the 1970s can be grasped as a response to this zero-point situation. The assertion that the theory of art had to abandon the category of the work of art turned out to be hasty; and the elimination of Critical Theory proved to be easier to demand than to accomplish theoretically. The ensuing development certainly cannot be understood as a mere restoration of an earlier state of affairs. Instead, the unsolved problems of materialist aesthetics forced a revision. This is above all true of the thesis that art can continue to claim legitimacy only as propaganda or agitation. I will use three examples to introduce the possibilities and limits of the West German theoretical debates of the 1970s: in the case of Thomas Metscher's theory I will discuss the reclamation of the concept of art under the aegis of Marxist orthodoxy; in connection with Christian Enzensberger's study I will look at the critique of political aesthetics; and lastly, I will examine the work of Peter Bürger, his historicization of Critical Theory, and the problems it leaves unresolved.

Since Bürger's historicization of Critical Theory also encompassed Lukács's theory of art, a conflict between Metscher's and Bürger's positions was unavoidable. I would like to begin with this debate, which was carried out in 1975 in the journal *Das Argument*. At the core of this debate stands the question What approach should the aesthetic theory of the 1970s acknowledge as its legitimate theoretical predecessor? Metscher, after turning away from Adorno, decides to fall back on Lenin's reflection theory and from there develop a theory of the work of art that is in close proximity to Lukács. Bürger, by contrast, responds to the same set of circumstances by drawing the conclusion that only historical reflection—that is, the continuation and radicalization of Critical Theory—can resolve the aporias of the situation. In his reply to Bürger's polemic, Metscher sums up the orthodox position and stands by the theory of reflection and an aesthetics of realism.[26] Relying on the reception theory of East Germany, Metscher argues that the Leninist theory of reflection embraces both productive and reproductive aspects of society and, as a result, takes into account more than Peter Bürger admits. Art production based on reflection has an effect on reality through its product—the work of art. This concession to reception theory's arguments does not prevent Metscher from subsequently expounding his position without responding in any greater depth to the core of Bürger's objections. The argument that aesthetic theory is tied to certain historical preconditions and that, as Bürger asserts, it is finished as a normative theory is not accessible to Metscher because his conceptual apparatus is produced deductively and lays claim to logical correctness. This does not mean that Metscher is not aware of his historical situation—on the contrary, he understands the return to reflection theory as part of a strategy that is important for West Germany in particular; even so, this political task cannot simply be assigned to a theory that derives from general epistemological principles rather than reflection upon a specific historical situation.

Metscher's designedly abstract approach is indicative of his theory's systematic character: "The epistemological approach necessitates a procedure which in the first instance proceeds not historically but systematically. Since it remains largely abstract, it may be capable of breaking through to the concrete only sporadically.... The epistemological principles of Marxism-Leninism possess a degree of generality which continually stands in need of concretization." Metscher integrates the theory of art into the general theory of reflection by conceptualizing aesthetic production as a "cognitive act," that is,

26. Thomas Metscher, "Aesthetische Erkenntnis und realistische Kunst," in *Das Argument* 90 (May 1975): 239–58; reprinted in his *Kunst als sozialer Prozess* (Cologne, 1977), 221–57.

as a particular form of knowledge—the aesthetic.[27] The tradition of Hegelian aesthetics is perceptible here: like Hegel,
Metscher places his emphasis on the truth content of works
of art. In Metscher's own formulation: "According to Hegel, in
beauty the idea is actualized in the form of appearance [*Schein*]
as the 'concrete intuition' [*Anschauung*]—that is, a sensuously
objective appearance in which, as Lenin said, the 'entire wealth
of the world' is enclosed." Lenin's materialist reinterpretation
of the Hegelian idea allows Metscher a definition of art that
finds the essential preserved in the representation reflecting
reality. "Art is therefore not—in the Platonic sense—a copy
reproducing empirical phenomena but an articulation of the
concrete 'concept' constituting the world of the empirical; art
is the sensuous manifestation of the lawfulness of social processes."[28] In short, the truth content of works of art does not
refer to empirical objects but to the totality of reality. Metscher's aesthetic theory of reflection is unmistakably close to Lukács's theory of realism, even though it does not follow Lukács
rigorously.

Metscher expressly supports Lukács against Ernst Bloch and
the objections of radical leftists while he also, as might be
expected, strictly defends Lukács's use of the category of totality. Metscher's critique of Lukács commences at the point
where Lukács conceptualizes totality as something closed. For
Metscher, Lukács's inability to do justice to the work of Brecht
marks the one-sidedness of his theory, which does not sufficiently take into account the active role of consciousness. Certainly, one should not overlook Metscher's tendency to
integrate Brecht's theory in a harmonizing rather than critical
manner into his own theory, which is more influenced by Lukács. As a result, Metscher ends up taking the bite out of

---

27. Thomas Metscher, "Aesthetik als Abbildungstheorie," in his *Kunst als sozialer Prozess*, 150–52, 156.
28. Ibid., 160, 161.

Brecht's polemic against Lukács. Since Metscher commits himself to Leninist reflection theory and passes it off as the logical continuation of Marxian theory, the dialectic of being and consciousness is brought to a standstill. Theory ossifies into a doctrinal edifice from which one then makes deductions. In the following formulation, Metscher collapses art and historical praxis, imitation, and activity: "Art is a concretion of social experience, of historical praxis in the form of a sensual copy, whereby the particular structure of this copy is primarily determined by the structure of the duplicated reality."[29] It is noteworthy that Metscher places more value on the structural homology than on the act of producing. As a result, for Metscher the objective dialectic of a specific social situation becomes decisive for the representation (*Darstellung*). Without wanting to, Metscher here inherits Lukács's objectivism.

Bürger's critique of this position is above all directed against its deductive approach, which in his view must repress problems essential to present-day aesthetic theory. "Preliminary decisions [*Vorentscheidungen*] are arrived at which are not secured by historical investigation, but legitimated solely through the appeal to Leninism."[30] The neoorthodox theory of art suffers from simply appropriating the classics rather than taking up a historical-hermeneutic—and therefore critical—stance. For Bürger, in contrast, the evolution of art is itself the historical precondition upon which every theory must reflect: "An aesthetic theory which does not reflect this radical change [brought about by the modernists and the avant-garde] in its categories, cuts off its access to its object from the very start." Furthermore, concludes Bürger, such a theory is not in a position to orient itself in the present. Bürger then criticizes Metscher as follows: "What is missing from Metscher's dis-

29. Ibid., 202.
30. Peter Bürger, "Was leistet der Wiederspiegelungsbegriff in der Literaturwissenschaft?" *Das Argument* 90 (May 1975): 227.

cussion is a precisely articulated standpoint in the present."[31] What is at stake in this debate is the Marxist legacy. While Metscher takes the classical texts as his models and renovates them for the present day, Bürger deprives them of their unquestioned normative status by consistently following his historical-hermeneutical approach. For Bürger, who thereby radicalizes the method of Critical Theory, historical reflexivity also applies to theory itself. Theory is therefore precluded from having recourse to older positions in its search for a materialist aesthetics. Bürger finds historical reflection lacking already in Lukács's invocation of the authority of reflection theory to denounce modernism and the avant-garde as decadent. The struggle between historical critique and normative aesthetics, which in Lukács is ultimately resolved in favor of the latter, is nonetheless—as Bürger rightly points out—the central problem of every aesthetic theory that directly or indirectly rests on Hegel. Historical criticism must object to Lukács's theory on the grounds that the historical logic of art had to lead, not to realism, but to the emergence of new forms and the transformation of the function of art altogether.

Like many aesthetic theories in the 1970s, Bürger's own attempt to resolve the problems of the materialist theory of art starts out from a critique of Adorno's aesthetics. This critique develops the approach of Critical Theory up to the point where Adorno's philosophy of art proves to be just as historical as that of Lukács. Since Adorno's theory is considered the appropriate theory for the avant-garde, it simultaneously takes on the role of a theory whose validity is historically determined and qualified. Adorno puts forward a theory of the nonorganic, avant-gardist work of art that does not yet take into account the obsolescent character of the avant-garde: "The debate between Lukács and Adorno concerning the legitimacy of avant-gardiste art is confined to the sphere of artistic means and the change in the kind of work this involves (organic versus avant-

---

31. Ibid., 220 (my interpolation), 221.

gardiste). Yet the two authors do not thematize the attack that the historical avant-garde movements launched against art as an institution."[32] In other words, Adorno upholds a normative aesthetics no less insistently than Lukács and does not carry out the historicization of the theory of art that begins with Hegel to its logical conclusion. This is precisely what Bürger attempts to do when he reduces theoretical conflicts to outdated, dogmatic struggles and incorporates them into the history of the institution "art."

The decisive step in this historical argument is the following: the avant-gardist movements of the early twentieth century did not simply radicalize the demand for aesthetic autonomy; rather, they furnished a self-critique of art and urged the sublimation of the traditional division between art and life-practice. Bürger concludes, "But once the historical avant-garde movements revealed art as an institution as a solution to the mystery of the effectiveness or ineffectiveness of art, no form could any longer claim that it alone had either eternal or temporally limited validity." The legacy of Hegel's and Marx's philosophies of history liquidates the possibility of a normative aesthetic theory: "the normative examination is replaced by a functional analysis, the object of whose investigation would be the social effect (function) of a work, which is the result of the coming together of stimuli inside the work and a sociologically definable public within an already existing institutional frame."[33]

Bürger's historicization of aesthetic theory changes the character of the discussion vis-à-vis the 1960s. In the first and second phases of the student movement, the search for a materialist aesthetics was carried out in the form of a polemical confrontation between certain given positions (Adorno, Lukács, Brecht, Benjamin), while in the third phase—which has

32. Peter Bürger, *Theory of the Avant-Garde*, trans. Michael Shaw (Minneapolis, 1984), 86.
33. Ibid., 86, 87.

been exemplified in this essay by Bürger's *Theory of the Avant-Garde*—one encounters an increasingly pronounced conscious-ness of the contemporary historical situation and, as a result, a growing distance from the earlier models. Bürger warns, for example, against the unmediated appropriation of Brecht's the-ory.[34] It is clear that neoorthodox theory did not take this warn-ing to heart. It ended up paying a dear price for this disregard. Neoorthodox theory disengaged from the specific literary and political situation in West Germany and displayed features of a certain alexandrine hermeticism absent even from East Ger-man theory once it had parted company with Lukács.

Ultimately, as the example of Christian Enzensberger's *Lit-eratur und Interesse* (Literature and interest, 1977) makes clear, this revision also takes hold of the political aesthetics of the student movement. The central thesis of political aesthetics held that belles lettres had lost the socially critical function that Adorno imputed to it and that it therefore had to be re-placed by an agitational literature that could exercise direct political influence. Enzensberger's theory can be understood only against the background of this thesis. In contrast to Marx-ist orthodoxy, Enzensberger's theory reflects West German cir-cumstances much more concretely. The unnamed starting point of this theory is the failed leftist cultural revolution. Enzensberger did not embark on the privatization of literature under way at that point, but instead—and in this respect he became the consummate successor to Critical Theory—ex-amined the aporias of political aesthetics: the failure of liter-ature to induce social change and the rigid instrumentalization of literature for the class struggle. Marcuse had already repu-diated the radical desublimation of art into social praxis and returned to the concept of the work of art in his 1972 book *Counterrevolution and Revolt*. Enzensberger expands this skepticism into a general theory by making the category of lack of meaning (*Sinndefizit*) into the starting point of aesthetic

34. Ibid., 88.

production. According to Enzensberger, all known societies manifesting division of labor and social differentiation suffer from lack of meaning. The unequal distribution of resources and opportunities leads to inadequacies that then, in order to appear meaningful, demand legitimation. "The lack of meaning consequently remains; it derives from social shortcomings, cannot be eliminated by ideology, and fundamentally asks for redress."[35] At least deficiencies can be overcome in fantasy. As the product of fantasy's activity, literature has the function for Enzensberger—as for Freud—of compensating for inadequacies. This compensation theory is obviously at odds with the tradition of Critical Theory, particularly with Adorno's philosophy of art, since it essentially disputes the claim of purposelessness. For Enzensberger, aesthetic production is always already and primarily responding to an unsatisfactory state of affairs. It is therefore part of the ideological consciousness that serves to legitimize this condition. Furthermore, where the Frankfurt School continued to maintain the oppositional power of the authentic work of art, Enzensberger views the aesthetic coherence of the work of art as more of an argument for its affirmative character. The opposition between art and reality typically found in Critical Theory is reinterpreted in such a way that art furnishes what reality withholds. In Enzensberger the beautiful appearance becomes deception: the emergence of literature begins with a need for deception about reality. Ineluctably harnessed to this set of relations, literature serves privileged interests. The core of this theory is the function of art; for this reason, Enzensberger's theory is fundamentally concerned with the question of reception, even if he completely repudiates the reception aesthetics of the Constance school. The act of reading or seeing (in the theater) is for Enzensberger always an act of identification: the reader sympathizes with the heroes, takes on their points of view, and in this way

35. Christian Enzensberger, *Literatur und Interesse* (Munich, 1977), 1:52.

achieves gratification. The intention of this description of reception is to prove that literature can have no real effect. Contrary to the assumptions made by political aesthetics or reception aesthetics, since literature appeals to needs that demand immediate satisfaction, the recipient's consciousness remains unchanged.

This pessimistic conclusion may correspond with what came to be known in the West German discussion as the *Tendenzwende* (change in tendency or commitment). Yet Enzensberger does not limit himself to recanting political aesthetics. He simultaneously attempts to redefine the social contribution of aesthetics and thereby continues to follow the model of Critical Theory in spite of himself. Nevertheless, this is done with the help of new methodological instruments. Enzensberger relies on phenomenology in order to illuminate and clarify the concept of meaning (*Sinn*). By drawing a distinction between the category of meaning and the concept of interest, Enzensberger creates a utopian realm where art reposes: "Art shares the structure of utopia and the redeemed relation of meaning, but not their content."[36] As would be expected, this constellation has crucial consequences for the definition of the work of art and the beautiful in art. In conspicuous proximity to classical aesthetics, Enzensberger defines the work of art as a self-referential, self-contained organism. Part and whole stand in a necessary relation to one another. The language of literature does not refer to reality in a traditional way and does not fulfill any pragmatic function, while the work of art is removed from any historical referent.

What Enzensberger refers to as the utopian structure of art is, as aesthetic autonomy, thoroughly familiar to aesthetic theory. Because it is elevated above social history and the realm of interest, the work of art manifests its negation of lack (*Mangel*) as a fictitious fulfillment of meaning. The question then arises, what separates Enzensberger's theory from Schiller or

36. Ibid., 131.

The Politicization of Aesthetic Theory

Herbert Marcuse? Enzensberger reproaches utopian idealism for being largely determined by class interests. While this argument can be used against Schiller because in his case his social agenda and his aesthetic theory do not coincide, the same can hardly be said for Marcuse. What separates Enzensberger from Schiller and Marcuse is, upon closer inspection, not so much the different definition of utopia as the oppositional function of the utopian moment in literature. Enzensberger conceptualizes the contents of literature as basically ideological; they are replicas of the bad status quo. "Art is there to superscribe the bad status quo with utopias." Only aesthetic structure allows one to understand the experience of living a life which has a consistent meaning. "Aesthetic mimesis is not in the first instance concerned with the objects, but with the structural imitation of social utopia."[37] Enzensberger thus concludes that art is free from ideology only when it is pure structure, form, or figure. By way of contrast, the transfiguration of contents necessarily proves ideological because there the received elements of reality are idealized until the contradictions disappear.

It is evident that Enzensberger cannot be interested in the real effects of literature. They have no place in his theory. It is precisely the utopian structure that is the reason for literature's "profound indifference toward current politics."[38] Literary theory in this instance manifestly reflects on its own task: it criticizes the demand it had articulated during the 1960s. Enzensberger renounces political aesthetics as well as ideology critique and withdraws to a metahistorical theory that is first developed in purely phenomenological terms and only subsequently applied to history. The result of this move is an irresolvable contradiction: from a systematic philosophical perspective, the abolition (*Aufhebung*) of aesthetic autonomy cannot take place simply because works of art in principle cannot

37. Ibid., 145, 147.
38. Ibid., 150.

be assimilated to life-practice. Yet, in the conclusion of the theoretical section of his work this is precisely the move that Enzensberger heralds as the political solution to the aesthetic problem. In his view, the revolt of the Parisian students in May of 1968 completed what had only been anticipated in trivial literature: "Art and life have become one and the same." These historical reflections, which bear on the manifestations of crisis in art during the 1960s, burst the systematic framework of Enzensberger's theory. As a result, one encounters the following comment: "Art has become boring, and ideology hackneyed."[39] Art's traditional social function—to demand that the social lack of meaning be remedied—has lost its power of conviction. Yet for Enzensberger, in contrast to Adorno, this disappearance of art (*Entkunstung*) is not a regression but the sign of a positive societal turn. For, through its decline, art at the same time loses something of its complicity with hegemonic consciousness.

Was there a common denominator in West German theories of art at the conclusion of the 1970s? As one can see from the examples discussed above, this was certainly not the case at the doctrinal level. There is no new aesthetic theory that occupies the same central position as the theories of Lukács and Adorno did during the 1950s and early 1960s. It is more relevant to speculate on why the kind of philosophy of art represented by Lukács, Bloch, Adorno, and Marcuse—who all inherit the legacy of Hegelian aesthetics—became exhausted. With reference to Adorno's *Aesthetische Theorie*, Otto K. Werckmeister speaks of subjective conceptual studies that are no longer capable of asserting a general claim to validity.[40] In other words, theory decays to the level of private confessions. With the use of a concept from Adorno, Dieter Wellershoff described the situation more generally as the de-aestheticization of art (*Ent-*

39. Ibid., 178, 179.
40. Otto K. Werckmeister, "Das Kunstwerk als Negation: Zur geschichtlichen Bestimmung der Kunsttheorie," in his *Ende der Aesthetik* (Frankfurt, 1971).

kunstung der Kunst): "The posture of the consumer is the subjective correlate of the untrammeled character of art arising from the disappearance of any normative expectation which would limit the expansion of production. The last phase of this production is to dismiss the prerogative of art itself."[41] Wellershoff allows the various positions to pass review once more (Bloch's utopianism, Marcuse's philosophy of praxis, and Adorno's theory of autonomy), without expecting a breakthrough from any of them. For Wellershoff, this means the end of the aesthetics informed by the philosophy of history, the aesthetics that always assumed, regardless of the approach it took, that the work of art—to borrow Adorno's metaphor—is the sundial of history. Although neither Lukács nor Adorno wants to admit it, art has shifted to the periphery; its emphatic significance has diminished along with the cultural traditions (religion, morality) that customarily nourished it. It was only in the course of the 1970s that these problems of aesthetic theory turned out to be the significant ones. At the end of the 1970s it was no longer a matter—as it was for Lukács and Adorno—of the structure of the work of art under the conditions of progressing capitalism, but a matter of taking stock of the crumbling or already lost cultural traditions that gave rise to art in the first place.

This point of view first gained primacy in Habermas's 1972 essay on Walter Benjamin.[42] Upon its appearance this essay was wrongly read as a defense of Adorno's position against a materialist interpretation of Benjamin. If one scrutinizes Habermas's comments on Adorno more closely, however, it is impossible to overlook the fact that Habermas no longer sees any future for Adorno's theory of art. For Habermas, Adorno's theory belongs to an earlier epoch by reason of its pessimistic

---

41. Dieter Wellershoff, *Die Auflösung des Kunstbegriffs* (Frankfurt, 1976), 81.

42. Jürgen Habermas, "Walter Benjamin: Consciousness-Raising or Rescuing Critique," in his *Philosophical-Political Profiles*, trans. Frederick G. Lawrence (Cambridge, Mass., 1983), 129–64.

esotericism. It offers nothing that could help confront the problems arising from the radical loss of tradition in late capitalist societies. Philip Brewster and Carl Howard Buchner have rightly pointed out that the Benjamin essay must be regarded as preparing the way for Habermas's theory of legitimation crisis.[43] To the extent that Habermas distances himself from the Marxian concept of praxis and distinguishes more clearly between labor and communication, the problem of language advances into the foreground. And in this connection, Benjamin's contribution becomes important for Habermas by virtue of precisely that element of Benjamin's thought that does not fit into the orthodoxy of the Frankfurt School.

Both Lukács and Adorno, to a certain degree, still assumed the bourgeois legacy in the concept of culture as a matter of course. Culture must be critically examined insofar as it drags along false consciousness; however, the authentic core of culture can in each case be reconstructed in the autonomous work of art. The ties to the aesthetic theory of idealism have not yet been severed. Within the framework of his crisis theory, Habermas throws open an issue whose radical nature was not anticipated in the classical form of Critical Theory: the achievement of conditions under which cultural traditions in late capitalist social systems can no longer renew themselves. In light of this situation, not only traditional hermeneutics but also the classical critique of ideology turn out to be ways of appropriating cultural tradition. "To this extent, critique is no less a form of appropriating tradition than hermeneutics. In both cases appropriated cultural contents retain their imperative force, that is, they secure the continuity of a history through which individuals and groups can identify with themselves and with one another." Habermas compares this situation to others in which culture is either strategically-

43. Philip Brewster and Carl Howard Buchner, "Language and Critique: Jürgen Habermas on Walter Benjamin," *New German Critique* 17 (Spring 1979): 15–29.

functionally organized or historically-objectively refashioned. The conclusion thus presents itself: "Apparently traditions can retain their legitimizing force as long as they are not torn out of interpretive systems that guarantee continuity and identity."[44]

Yet this process of extraction occurs when the state systematically intervenes in the cultural realm by subjecting longstanding traditional relations to rational planning. A lack of meaning arises which cannot be compensated for. Habermas maintains the thesis that capitalist societies were "always dependent on marginal cultural circumstances" and that bourgeois culture "was never able to reproduce itself from itself."[45] Bourgeois culture is not completely compatible with the capitalist system—it is, on the contrary, largely tied to traditionalistic worldviews. This interpretation puts Habermas markedly closer to Benjamin than to Adorno, whose theory of modernity highlights its correspondence to the capitalist market. According to Habermas, who in this instance follows Arnold Hauser as well as Benjamin, the radicalization of aesthetic autonomy in the theory and praxis of modernity leads to the division between the bourgeoisie and the avant-garde. "Under the sign 'art for art's sake,' the autonomy of art is carried to the extreme. The truth thereby comes to light that in bourgeois society art expresses not the promises but the irretrievable sacrifice of bourgeois rationalization, the plainly incompatible experiences and not the esoteric fulfillment of withheld, but merely deferred, gratifications."[46]

With this sentence Habermas definitively parts company with Adorno's and Marcuse's theories of art, which adhered to art's esoteric promise despite the prevailing deprivation. Like Benjamin, Habermas assumes that the art of the avant-garde has lost the aura and forfeited its autonomous status. "Modern

44. Jürgen Habermas, *Legitimation Crisis*, trans. Thomas McCarthy (Boston, 1973), 70, 71.
45. Ibid., 77, 76 (translation modified).
46. Ibid., 85 (translation modified).

art had already shed the aura of classical bourgeois art by making the process of production evident and presenting itself as something that was produced. But art infiltrates the ensemble of use values only when it surrenders its autonomous status."[47] Without slavishly committing himself to it, Habermas absorbs essential elements of Benjamin's theory, particularly the connection between avant-garde movements and the decay of the aura, which Habermas interprets as an important aspect of the motivation crisis of the late capitalists. This occurs not least of all because Habermas in some degree appropriates the critique of the cultural heritage Benjamin had advanced in the "Theses on the Philosophy of History." Habermas not only makes use of the critique of historicism—one could also find this in the works of Horkheimer and Adorno—he also brings to bear Benjamin's critique of tradition as the conception of historical continuity.

Habermas conceives of the liquidation of autonomy as a consequence of the societal process of rationalization Max Weber had described. Naturally, Habermas is aware of the fact that Adorno never accepted this step when Benjamin took it. Habermas sums up Adorno's position once again so that he can append the following comment: "In contrast, for arts received collectively—architecture, theatre, painting—just as for popular literature and music, which have become dependent on electronic media, there are indications of a development that points beyond mere culture industry and does not *a fortiori* invalidate Benjamin's hope for a generalized secular illumination."[48] Habermas concludes from Benjamin's theory that postautonomous art harbors within it the possibility that the experience of happiness residing in mimetic behavior can become exoteric and universal. In the context of this essay, the question of whether Habermas's solution is sound is not under discussion; it is much more significant that here, in confront-

47. Ibid., 86.
48. Habermas, "Walter Benjamin," 142.

ing Walter Benjamin, the theory of postautonomous art is recognized as the central theme of the 1960s, and indeed, not simply as a continuation of the discussion about the de-aestheticization of art (*Entkunstung der Kunst*)—as Wellershoff would have it—but as an articulation of contemporary possibilities.

Postscript

When I assessed the development of German aesthetic theory in 1979, the question of politics was being raised mainly within the Marxist tradition. Hence the discussion took place among various Marxist positions while traditional criticism (historicism or formalism) maintained its distance from political questions. Even reception aesthetics (Jauss, Iser, and the Constance school), after initially competing with Marxist theory, soon relegated these issues to the background and focused on the "implied reader," that is, the relationship between textual structures and reading processes. In doing so, reception theory formalized the critical moment of the art work at the level of individual reader consciousness. Already during the early 1970s, Jauss's theory took an anthropological turn that de-emphasized his partial sympathy with Adornian theory, and consequently turned away too from attention to a historical grounding of aesthetics.[49] On the whole, reception aesthetics, after claiming a radical position during the late 1960s (as both a response to the student movement and an antidote to Marxism), returned to a more moderate position, a stance that acknowledges its indebtedness to the hermeneutical tradition.

Looking back at the theoretical debates of the late 1970s and 1980s, it seems to me that, by and large, they did not follow and develop the discussions of the previous decade. Much of radical Marxist theory (orthodox as well as neo-Marxist) dis-

49. See Hans Robert Jauss, *Aesthetic Experience and Literary Hermeneutics* (Minneapolis, 1982).

Reappraisals

appeared without leaving many traces in the current discourse. The exception is Critical Theory, especially the work of Jürgen Habermas, which tends to overshadow the other disciples of Horkheimer and Adorno. Yet Habermas, particularly during the 1980s, has been more interested in problems of moral and political philosophy than aesthetic theory. As a result, the discussion about the political meaning of aesthetic theory has not advanced significantly among his students. The recent resurgent interest in Adorno's theory, on the other hand, has shifted its emphasis more toward the problems of grounding and epistemology at the clear expense of social questions, which stood at the center of the debate between 1965 and 1975. The return to Adorno, in other words, has to be seen in the context of the influx of a poststructuralist discourse from France, beginning in the late 1970s and gaining some momentum during the mid-1980s. In the context of this new discourse, the political question has resurfaced in a different form: whereas the previous debate centered on the political implications of the art work and then searched for the appropriate theoretical articulation of the problem, the discussions of the 1980s focused on the political character of theory itself, bringing into the foreground not only the politics of theory (the political position of a specific theory) but also the political meaning of the internal structure of theories.

This became particularly apparent in the Habermas/Foucault debate in which Habermas took initially the position that poststructuralist theory implicitly supported the conservative forces by embracing a postmodernist stance.[50] While the exchange between Habermas and Lyotard or Derrida received a great deal of attention also in this country, both its political and its philosophical contexts have not been fully understood, since the theoretical and political configuration in West Ger-

50. Jürgen Habermas, "Modernity—An Incomplete Project," in *The Anti-Aesthetic: Essays on Postmodern Culture*, ed. Hal Foster (Port Townsend, Wash., 1983), 3–15.

many only partly overlaps with the American situation. What has to be taken into consideration here is the growing tension among the disciples of Adorno and Horkheimer, on the one hand, and the emergence of a poststructuralist camp, on the other. The political debate of the 1980s has occurred primarily between Habermasian theory and a Foucauldian position, as it was developed by critics like Friedrich A. Kittler, Heinrich Fink-Ertel, and Harro Müller. This discussion was certainly not limited to the status of art and literature; in fact, these traditional questions played a relatively minor role. Even for the hermeneutic camp, which had been almost invisible during the early 1970s, the theory of interpretation did not focus primarily on the work of art. The involvement of post-Gadamerian hermeneutics in Germany with poststructuralist theory—in the work of Manfred Frank, for instance—clearly radicalized the hermeneutic project in various ways, though not always in clear alignment with the main debate as it was carried out between Habermasians and Foucauldians.[51]

As these few remarks indicate, the discursive map of West Germany has changed so radically during the 1980s that the positions of the 1960s and early 1970s can hardly be recognized anymore, even within Critical Theory. Most obvious is the lack of an orthodox Marxist position. To some extent, this is the result of external forces—namely the purge of German universities of radicals after 1972. *Berufsverbot* certainly helped to marginalize orthodox Marxism (Leninist or Maoist). On the whole (and this assessment includes the New Left), the Marxist paradigm, which so clearly shaped the debates of the 1960s, lost its momentum after 1980. A good indication of this phenomenon is the fate of social history in German literary criticism. The idea of politicizing literary history through the paradigm of social history, leading to a number of major mul-

51. See Manfred Frank, *Das individuelle Allgemeine: Textstrukturierung und -interpretation nach Schleiermacher* (Frankfurt, 1977); and his *Das Sagbare und das Unsagbare: Studien zur neuesten französischen Hermeneutik und Texttheorie* (Frankfurt, 1980).

tivolume projects, came under increasing criticism from various sides when the first volumes appeared.[52] By 1985, there was almost a consensus that the project had failed because of its problematic theoretical core. Progressive literary history collapsed under a critique coming from two theoretical positions, namely Foucauldian discourse analysis and post-Gadamerian hermeneutics. In both cases, the central categories of the project—historical evolution, social totality, classes, mediation, and so on,—came under attack. In the field of literary criticism, these scattered debates were, I think, more important than the exchange between Habermas and French post-structuralists.

The most crucial development in the political dimensions of literary theory, however, and therefore a good starting point for an overview of the 1980s in West Germany, is the appropriation of Foucault's work, which began in the late 1970s: the reception of Foucault rather quickly changed the parameters of the debate and with it the nature of the political. Helga Gallas's work can serve as a good example of this transition. While her early work, especially her discussion of German Marxist criticism of the 1920s and 1930s, drew on the authority of Karl Korsch and Brecht (in opposition to Lukács), her later readings of Heinrich von Kleist retreat from traditional political issues, focusing instead on the nature of writing and the subject in the text.[53] In this transition, the former commitment to Marxist theory seems to disappear, or is even replaced by hos-

52. A number of prominent publishing houses, among them Hanser, C. H. Beck, and Metzler, planned multivolume literary histories. None of these was completed. The best example of this type would be the volume edited by Rolf Grimminger, *Deutsche Aufklärung bis zur Französischen Revolution 1680–1789*, vol. 3 of *Hansers Sozialgeschichte der deutschen Literatur*, 11 vols. (Munich, 1980). For a detailed analysis, see Peter Uwe Hohendahl, "Bürgerlichkeit und Bürgertum als Problem der Literatursoziologie," *German Quarterly* 61 (Spring 1988): 264–83.

53. See Helga Gallas, *Marxistische Literaturtheorie: Kontroversen im Bund proletarisch-revolutionärer Schriftsteller* (Neuwied, 1971); and her *Das Textbegehren des "Michael Kolhaas": Die Sprache des Unbewussten und der Sinn der Literatur* (Reinbek, 1981).

tility toward historical criticism. This gesture of rejection is equally strong in the early writings of critics like Horst Turk and Friedrich A. Kittler in their attempt to establish a counterdiscourse in German criticism.[54] To a large extent, their energy went into deconstructing the critical models of the previous decade. This critique would also include the concept of the political, as it was used by the New Left or orthodox Marxists. Much of the leftist polemic against the West German state was now discarded as merely "utopian."

This anti-utopian element has shaped the understanding of political issues, both on the level of academic politics (political position of camps or groups) and the level of theoretical models. It is primarily the concept of discourse analysis, taken over from Foucault, that informs the critical debate of the 1980s. Exemplary is the introduction of Jürgen Fohrmann and Harro Müller to the volume *Diskurstheorien und Literaturwissenschaft* (1988), which defines the agenda of the collection of essays by a critique of Hans Robert Jauss's reception model, one version of the post-Gadamerian hermeneutic approach. In defining the Jaussian model (they could have used Iser's model as well) as "Sinn-Bildungsprozess," that is, as a model in which reading is supposed to create *meaning*, they link it to the hermeneutic tradition that dominated the nineteenth and early twentieth centuries.[55] Its goal, Fohrmann and Müller argue, is to make the text speak, to answer the questions of the inquiring critic. Hence critical reading results in a commentary that claims to be a reconfirmation of the text. Fohrmann and Müller intend to deconstruct this model, first, by linking it with a dialogical model grounded in a traditional concept of the subject and, second, by questioning the viability of this concept of the subject (invoking Luhmann's systems theory).

54. See *Austreibung des Geistes aus den Geisteswissenschaften: Programme des Poststrukturalismus*, ed. Friedrich A. Kittler (Paderborn, 1980).

55. Jürgen Fohrmann and Harro Müller, eds., *Diskurstheorien und Literaturwissenschaft* (Frankfurt, 1988), 9.

The reduction of the subject to the level of an element in the social process has significant implications. It tends to deflate, for instance, the political rhetoric of the New Left that emphasized subjectivity as the core of political praxis. Yet, this new political stance is also directed against the Habermasian version of Critical Theory, in particular its assumption that society can be defined in terms of communicative interaction. The attack on the "autonomous subject," legitimized by the authority of Lacan, Derrida, Foucault, and Luhmann, undermines the terms of the theoretical discourse of the 1960s and 1970s.

The American reader will find most of this familiar. Fohrmann's and Müller's introduction sums up and repeats many of the theoretical developments that took place in the United States in the 1970s. More interesting and important than this parallel, however, is the question How does this paradigmatic leap affect the conception of the political? One would look in vain for an explicit answer. For Fohrmann and Müller, there is no reason to believe in the oppositional force of the art work itself, nor is it plausible to have faith in the impact of the work (Jauss, Iser), not to mention the critical force of the author (Sartre, Lukács) or the critical community (Habermas). What remains is *Diskursanalyse* (discourse analysis): "This entry ticket into discourse analysis conceives of constellations and hence also of texts as *constructed* and *artificially* closed-off, dispersed unities, which arise out of differences. In this sense, one can speak of the plurality of a text, which is always constituted out of the judgment-statements [*Aussagen*] of various discourses, and even in its solitary existence always already attests to *intertextuality* or *interdiscursivity*."[56]

In other words, textual analysis can be identified as part of the social process but not used as a lever to engage in political action. In fact, Fohrmann and Müller do not offer a political agenda; their questions are concerned primarily with the in-

56. Ibid., 16.

192

ternal structure of the discourse model (definition of rules and relations). It is not accidental that among the contributors both Manfred Frank, as the proponent of hermeneutics, and Peter Bürger, as a critic close to the Frankfurt School, directed their polemic against the category of *discourse*. Frank, after examining Foucault's concept of the discourse, tries to show that the elimination of the subject is the result of a restrictive methodology, a repressive act that confronts Foucault with a considerable contradiction: on the one hand, Foucault declares discourses to be *unhintergehbar* (something one cannot "get behind"); on the other, he asks for an enlightened critique of these discourses in spite of the fact that this critique cannot be grounded (without a subject).[57] Bürger is even more explicit in his critique: Foucault's decentered theory is constructed in such a way that it creates its own center. In the attempt to break away from transcendental philosophy Foucault is bound to return to his premises.[58]

Obviously, in this exchange the focus of the political debate has shifted: since the beginning of the 1980s, that is, after the impact of poststructuralism, political issues have been articulated as *epistemological* issues or, conversely, epistemological problems have been treated as political questions. This modification occurred not only in the poststructuralist discourse; it is equally noticeable in the post-Gadamerian hermeneutic debate, where the conservative celebration of tradition (as a pre- and postsubjective position) has been replaced by a radical examination of the subject and/or individual.

It was especially Manfred Frank, a student of Gadamer, who defined the new task of literary criticism already in 1977 as a dialogue between the hermeneutic tradition (coming from Schleiermacher) and the semiotic tradition (following Saussure). What makes this dialogue important and meaningful for

57. Manfred Frank, "Zum Diskursbegriff bei Foucault," in ibid., 25–44.
58. Peter Bürger, "Die Wiederkehr der Analogie: Aesthetik als Fluchtpunkt in Foucaults *Die Ordnung der Dinge*," in Fohrmann and Müller, *Diskurstheorien*, 45–52.

Frank is the challenge of the structuralists and poststructuralists, their polemical stance toward the hermeneutic tradition.
Yet, Frank—and this is noteworthy—refuses to perceive this
exchange as a conflict between conservative and radical (progressive) forces; rather, in *Das individuelle Allgemeine* (1977)
these political terms are cautiously avoided, since Frank wants
to underscore the dialectic link between hermeneutics and semiotics. For this reason, Frank carefully outlines the contemporary debate before he returns to Schleiermacher's theory,
emphasizing the intrinsic connections between positions that
have been described as incompatible. In any case, the epistemological discussions remain completely abstract. It was only
almost a decade later that Manfred Frank, in his lectures *Was
ist Neostrukturalismus?* (1984), more explicitly put the political implications of the debate between "French" and "German" theory into the foreground. In 1984, Frank claimed for
the hermeneutic tradition "critical and utopian potentials,"
which had left their traces on the radical students of 1968.[59]
Also, Frank at least alludes to the Frankfurt School and its
oppositional character. He suggests that only a combination of
existential-ontological hermeneutics (Heidegger) and Critical
Theory could articulate a progressive political critique of the
contemporary situation. The dialectical treatment that Frank
offered in his lectures is supposed to overcome the humanism/
antihumanism opposition that defined the theoretical and political agenda of the 1980s. In this respect, but only in this,
Frank's introduction is comparable to the agenda of the New
Historicism—an attempt to bring together and integrate structuralist and hermeneutic approaches, clearly not by adding
their elements but, rather, through a historical critique of the
conflicting positions.

What remains unsaid and unexamined in this articulation of
the task is its exclusion of theoretical positions that were central during the 1960s and 1970s. While the orthodox Marxist

59. Manfred Frank, *Was ist Neostrukturalismus?* (Frankfurt, 1984), 9.

tradition has disappeared almost entirely in Manfred Frank's program, Critical Theory is allowed to survive as a marginal position through its connection with hermeneutics (Karl Otto Apel, Habermas). Even those West German critics (like Kittler) who would strongly disagree with Frank's agenda (the structure/subject relationship) would share Frank's chart of the contemporary debate, marked by the surprising absence of Marx. In other words, the critical discourse has returned to its philosophical beginnings, articulating a strong preference for epistemological issues over social problems.

The notable exception would be the feminist movement(s) in West Germany, although even here the nature of the political involvement, as inside observers have noted, has undergone considerable changes. Still, compared with the general discourse of literary criticism, feminist approaches have retained a more explicit political agenda, ranging from the struggle against section 218 (the law against abortion) to poststructuralist criticism, in which the work of leading French feminists (Hélène Cixous, Luce Irigaray, Julia Kristeva) has been appropriated. The political impetus of the West German women's movement expressed itself both in the peace movement and the ecological movement (the Greens), where it reached larger segments of the population. At the same time, the project of emancipation, as it was formulated during the late 1960s and early 1970s by leftist women's groups, has lost its impact. In a recent essay, Cornelia Klinger concludes that a theory of emancipation and human progress has been relegated to the past.[60] Klinger, who is ready to defend such a project—at least up to a point—considers herself as somewhat "old-fashioned," since this defense entails also a defense of the subject and subjectivity—precisely the categories that have come under attack.

60. Cornelia Klinger, "Abschied von der Emanzipationslogik: Die Gründe, ihn zu fordern, zu feiern oder zu fürchten," in *Autonome Frauen: Schlüsseltexte der Neuen Frauenbewegung seit 1968*, ed. Ann Anders (Frankfurt, 1988), 293–329.

The continuing politicization of German feminism thus owes its force to a new agenda in which Critical Theory plays only a marginal role. Aesthetic theory in particular, the legacy of Adorno and Benjamin, is no longer central to the political debate.[61] To some extent—and here we see a clear parallel to the general discourse in literary criticism—poststructuralist theory has taken its place and simultaneously redefined the meaning of the political. Among other things, this approach has resulted in a far-reaching critique of the concept of emancipation as it was used by the New Left. Under the influence of Gilles Deleuze and Félix Guattari, Lyotard, and Lacan, the notion of the subject has come under attack; also, with the growing impact of Lacan and Foucault, the question of power has been revised in a different way and with it the definition of women's political struggle.[62] In this new constellation, the question of power refers to knowledge, its acquisition and dissemination, rather than traditional political conflicts, which were carried out under the banner of equality. Since poststructuralist theory, especially through its critique of the subject, is not compatible with more traditional women's demands based on the idea of emancipation and since these demands have not been fulfilled in West Germany, the German women's movement has witnessed considerable tensions about the nature of the political struggle during the 1980s.

In this context, aesthetic theory in its post-Adornian form has contributed to the subversion of conventional politics, but

61. This distance is due, to some extent, to the initial rejection of the male-dominated New Left in 1968, which was very much under the influence of the Frankfurt School. The gap has never quite closed again. As a result, the fruitful elements in Critical Theory, for instance, the Odysseus excursus in *Dialectic of Enlightenment*, were never appropriated. For an account of the feminists' rejection of the Sozialistischer Deutscher Studentenbund, see Helke Sander, "Rede des Aktionsrechts zur Begründung der Frauen," in Anders, *Autonome Frauen*, 35–47.

62. See, for instance, Marianne Schuller, "Vorgabe des Wissens. Notizen zum Verhältnis von 'weiblicher Intellektualität' und Macht," in Anders, *Autonome Frauen*, 174–99.

the general relation of aesthetics and politics as it was conceived in Critical Theory stands in an uncertain position. It remains to be seen whether the new political criticism—whether in its feminist, its Habermasian, its Foucauldian, or its poststructuralist form—will continue its heavily epistemological course, or if different questions about art and late capitalist society will reopen the central issues in Critical Theory.

7 Reappraisals of Critical Theory: The Legacy of the Frankfurt School in America

The participants in any discussion about Critical Theory in the United States have to keep in mind that Critical Theory is not identical with the Frankfurt School, at least not with the work of Horkheimer and Adorno or their disciples in postwar Germany. In this country, Critical Theory, particularly during the 1950s and early 1960s, was primarily associated with Herbert Marcuse, Erich Fromm, and Leo Lowenthal, originally members of the Institute for Social Research, who decided to stay in America after World War II. Clearly, the American New Left was informed and shaped by the work of Herbert Marcuse, rather than that of Adorno or Walter Benjamin. Of course, it is also true that Marcuse's *Eros and Civilization* and *One-Dimensional Man* prepared the way for the reception of Adorno's and Benjamin's more complex and demanding oeuvres during the 1970s. As Martin Jay has shown, the reception and integration of Adorno's work was a slow and uneven process, which, with good reasons, can be called incomplete even today.[1] Much of Adorno's and Benjamin's writings are not yet available in English and are still waiting to be discovered by American critics. Still, it would be misleading to argue that

---

1. Martin Jay, "Adorno and America," in his *Permanent Exiles: Essays on the Intellectual Migration from Germany to America* (New York, 1986), 120–37.

the theory of the Frankfurt School is not known in the English-speaking world. English editions, especially of Jürgen Habermas's writings, and numerous critical studies attest to its visibility. In fact, during the last decade, the presence of the "German" brand of the Frankfurt School has to some extent eclipsed the "American"contribution of Marcuse and Lowenthal, because the work of Adorno, Benjamin, and Habermas participates more openly in present theoretical discourse. This presence today clearly transcends the level of primarily historical interest, which had guided Martin Jay's first attempt to map the ideas and concepts of the Frankfurt School in *Dialectical Imagination* (1973) and Susan Buck-Morss's intricate analysis of the early Adorno in her book *The Origin of Negative Dialectics* (1977).[2]

Today, we have to assess the presence of Critical Theory in different ways. We have to appraise its function within the contemporary configuration, which has radically changed since the initial reception of the Frankfurt School during the late 1960s. At that time, the work of Adorno, Benjamin, and the early Habermas was integrated into the American discussion as a way of reinforcing the project of Western Marxism. The oppositional and critical force of these writers was directed against the formalist preferences of the New Critics and liberal social theory, for instance, the theories of Talcott Parsons and his students. The emphasis was clearly placed on the aspect of radical intervention to be carried out by marginal social groups. In *Marxism and Form* (1971), Fredric Jameson articulated this concern by bringing together the voices of Adorno and Benjamin with those of Lukács and Sartre. Jameson's attempt at a synthesis underscored the refunctioning of Critical Theory in the American context. While the Frankfurt School in Germany was quite unwilling to join with Lukács, in the United States,

2. See Martin Jay, *The Dialectical Imagination: A History of the Frankfurt School and the Institute of Social Research, 1923–1950* (Boston, 1973); and Susan Buck-Morss, *The Origin of Negative Dialectics: Theodor W. Adorno, Walter Benjamin, and the Frankfurt Institute* (New York, 1979).

Critical Theory was brought in as a supplement to more traditional Marxist theory. This supplemental role—in the case
of Jameson ultimately predicated on a Lukácsian model—had
two strategic functions: first, Critical Theory was expected to
provide Marxist literary criticism with a more refined model
in which the mediation between social and aesthetic forces
would be worked out in a more satisfactory manner; second,
the influx of Critical Theory was expected to counter the growing influence of structuralist Althusserian Marxism, whose
most visible proponent became Terry Eagleton.

It would suffice to glance at the reviewer section of *Telos*,
on the one hand, and that of *New Left Review*, on the other,
to get an impression of the ongoing struggle within the leftist
camp. The relentless polemic of *Telos's* contributors against
the new "orthodoxy" under the disguise of French structuralism relied implicitly and occasionally explicitly on the rhetoric
of the Frankfurt School against orthodox Marxism. For the *Telos* circle, Marx could be rescued from the dead weight of the
Third International only through the rigorous emphasis on the
critical and subversive moment in his works. In this context,
Critical Theory served as a weapon to undermine the structure
of reified dogma. Yet even the Frankfurt School was not critical
enough; the writings of its members too had to be purged of
hidden orthodox elements. In his introduction to the *Essential
Frankfurt School Reader* (1978), Paul Piccone outlined what he
considered the essential aspects of the Frankfurt School. More
important, Piccone underscored the need for a critique of Critical Theory in its own spirit. He argued: "Contrary to Left
conventional wisdom, according to which the quandaries of
critical theory are the result of its having jettisoned fundamental Marxist assumptions, the real problem was the exact
opposite: the unwarranted retention of too much traditional
Marxist baggage."[3] This indictment, apart from the question

---

3. Paul Piccone, "General Introduction," in *The Essential Frankfurt*

of its historical truth, reflects a very specific moment in the history of the New Left, namely the realization that its project had failed. The struggle for political and social emancipation was now perceived as a myth that had to be exploded—with the help of Critical Theory, especially Adorno's micrological criticism. At this juncture, Piccone resolutely rejected Marcuse's attempts at theorizing on a macrological level, which he saw as confirming, at least implicitly, the Lukácsian project of *History and Class Consciousness*. From this vantage point, the failure of Critical Theory has to do with the central flaw of *Dialectic of Enlightenment*, its inability to articulate the dialectic of advanced capitalist societies in specific historical terms. As a result of this inability, "the dialectic becomes dehistoricized to cover the whole of Western civilization as the genesis of the domination of the concept. Consequently, critical theory does not even attempt to prefigure the future by elaborating the mediations necessary to bring it about, and becomes purely defensive: it ultimately retreats to defend particularity, autonomy and nonidentity against an allegedly totally administered society where thinking itself appears as a dispensable luxury."[4]

Piccone's critique focuses precisely on those moments that would resurface in the debate of the 1980s: subjectivity, autonomy, and nonidentity. What Piccone holds against Adorno is the unchallenged presence of a concept of totality that would necessarily marginalize nonidentity. In the totally planned society, resistance is antiquated from the beginning. Piccone's attempt to recuperate Critical Theory emphasizes oppositional impetus at the expense of content. For Piccone, the future of Critical Theory lies in its radically undogmatic rethinking of advanced capitalist societies, especially their political and cul-

---

School Reader, ed. Andrew Arato and Eike Gebhardt (New York, 1978), v, xv.

4. Ibid., xvi.

tural systems. This radical critique includes the Adornian category of negativity, since the characteristic of postwar state
capitalism is its ability to create and tolerate its own opposition. In this context, *Telos* for many years gave its support to
the Habermasian version of Critical Theory, since *Legitimation
Crisis* (1973) seemed to offer the kind of analysis that Piccone
had sketched out in his introduction. The journal's more recent
return to Adorno, and its simultaneous growing hostility toward Habermas, reflects yet another turn in the definition of
"Critical Theory," a turn that articulates the interface of Critical Theory and poststructuralism.[5] Within the theoretical discourse of the 1980s, a new configuration has begun to emerge.
Perhaps the crucial aspect of this new constellation is the
breakup of Critical Theory, particularly the separation made
between Habermas, on the one hand, and Adorno and Benjamin, on the other. Hence, the work of these theorists, despite
the common background they share, has functioned in rather
different ways.

The most obvious case is the theory of Jürgen Habermas,
which in some quarters has been identified with Critical Theory. It is interesting to note, however, that its reception during
the 1980s, highly controversial as it was, took a separate path
from the Frankfurt School. Not only did Habermas's work address problems of social and political theory that the older
generation had not articulated, but it also redefined the parameters in such a way that it opened a dialogue with theorists
who would not have responded to Horkheimer's and Adorno's
writings. The American discourse of the 1980s locates Habermas, and quite justly so, as a consistent defender of modernity.
It is not accidental, therefore, that Thomas McCarthy's introduction to *The Theory of Communicative Action* (1984) invokes the modernity/antimodernity opposition in order to
outline the Habermasian project. The defense of reason must

5. See Robert Hullot-Kentor, "Back to Adorno," *Telos* 81 (Fall 1989):
5–29.

Reappraisals of Critical Theory

articulate itself as a critique of reason. More specifically, McCarthy situates this project and its relevance in the context of a post-Heideggerian and post-Wittgensteinian age that has thoroughly deconstructed the categories of the Western tradition.[6] While the details of McCarthy's introduction are of no particular importance in this context, the crucial question for someone who wants to introduce a theory based on linguistic consensus is its locus in the American discussion. For McCarthy, Habermasian theory indeed corrected and superseded the older Frankfurt School by exposing the decisionism of Max Weber's sociological model, which Horkheimer and Adorno took over too uncritically. Therefore, McCarthy suggests that Habermas was right to criticize Western Marxism, including the Frankfurt School, and replace it with a system/subsystem model. "He seeks to demonstrate that this model can make good the failure of orthodox Marxism to comprehend central features of advanced capitalism—in particular, government interventionism, mass democracy, and the social-welfare state." McCarthy concurs with Habermas's premise that the problems of modernity are not "rooted in rationalization as such" but are connected with failures of institutionalization, in particular with the colonization of the life-world by instrumental rationality.[7]

It is interesting to note that McCarthy's introduction to Habermas's *Theory of Communicative Action* refers only in passing to Habermas's earlier work. By contrast, Richard J. Bernstein's introduction to *Habermas and Modernity* (1985) offers a much broader historical perspective, beginning with the philosopher's early experience. Yet his account also places the emphasis on the "mature" work and the question of rationality/modernity (the Weberian connection). Not unlike McCarthy, Bernstein argues that the unresolved problem of

6. Thomas McCarthy, "Translator's Introduction," in Jürgen Habermas, *The Theory of Communicative Action*, vol. 1: *Reason and the Rationalization of Society* (Boston, 1984), viii.
7. Ibid., xxxiii, xxxvii.

rationality (the Weberian cage of modern society), as it resurfaces in Lukács and later in Horkheimer and Adorno, propelled Habermas beyond the frame of the old Frankfurt School toward a better solution. This solution would overcome the aporias of *Dialectic of Enlightenment*. Clearly, the Habermas debate of the 1980s gravitates toward *his Theory of Communicative Action*, his *Philosophical Discourse of Modernity* (English edition, 1987), and his writings on moral theory; this tendency pushes his early work toward the background. In keeping with this trend, Bernstein criticizes *Knowledge and Human Interest* (1969) as a flawed transitional work whose unresolved problems forced Habermas radically to reconceptualize his theory. The quasi-transcendental grounding of his theory clearly invoked criticism from the analytical and the poststructuralist camp. In 1969 Habermas's theory was still rooted in the tradition of a philosophy of consciousness (Descartes). What Bernstein observes and supports in Habermas's more recent work is a reworking of the older concerns with a system of human interests on the basis of a theory of universal pragmatics. Most important, however, as Bernstein points out, Habermas has left the realm of a philosophy of consciousness and turned to a dialogical model. For Bernstein and the Habermasians in North America—among them Thomas McCarthy and Seyla Benhabib—the rational defense of reason and modernity is possible and clearly desirable. By the same token, Critical Theory is wedded to a conception of rationality that clearly transcends instrumental reason.

Hence, in the Habermas debate of the 1980s it is generally taken for granted that the theory of communicative action supersedes negative dialectics. Even those who invoke the work of Adorno and Horkheimer, like Albrecht Wellmer and Martin Jay, by and large do not call for a return to the Frankfurt School. As a result, in the American discussion Critical Theory has become polarized. Its Habermasian version, certainly more prominent among social scientists and philosophers, speaks to a community with rather different concerns than the first gen-

eration of the Frankfurt School. Thus, the critics of Habermasian theory are not necessarily the critics of Benjamin or
Adorno, as we will see later. Their objections have little in
common with the orthodox Marxist critique of the Frankfurt
School (even that of the praxis group) or the polemic of empirical sociology, as it was articulated by Karl Popper in the
Positivismusstreit of the early 1960s. The criticisms of Thomas
Lukes or Richard Rorty bring categories to bear on Habermas's
work that would hardly be applicable to either Adorno or Benjamin.[8] Both of them draw on the Anglo-American philosophical tradition in their critical discussion of Habermasian social
theory. What is characteristic for their ongoing debate is that
its participants (we can add the names of Nancy Fraser, Seyla
Benhabib, and Thomas McCarthy) are basically sympathetic to
the Habermasian project, although they are in many instances
not satisfied with its arguments and therefore highly critical
of its results. By and large they share with Habermas a skeptical
attitude toward poststructuralist models and approaches.

In this respect, Richard Rorty's contribution stands out, since
it makes an explicit attempt to bring Habermas into the orbit
of French theory and the postmodernism debate. Rorty summarizes the controversy between Habermas and Lyotard in the
following way: "So we find French critics of Habermas ready
to abandon liberal politics in order to avoid universalistic philosophy, and Habermas trying to hang on to universalistic philosophy, with all its problems, in order to support liberal
politics."[9] Habermas's reluctance to give up metanarrative as
a form of legitimation, Rorty feels, is related to his aversion to
a form of social and political criticism that is "context-
dependent" (instead of generalizable). Vis-à-vis these two pos-
itives, he argues—and more recently McCarthy has presented

8. Richard Rorty, "Habermas and Lyotard on Postmodernity," and An-
thony Giddens, "Reason without Revolution? Habermas's *Theorie des
kommunikativen Handelns*," in *Habermas and Modernity*, ed. Richard
J. Bernstein (Cambridge, Mass., 1985), 161–76, 95–124.
9. Rorty, "Habermas and Lyotard," 162.

similar arguments—that there is no need for a metanarrative, that the legitimation crisis of the modern age resulted from Kant's interpretation, especially his move to split "high culture up into science, morality, and art."[10] Rorty strongly opposes this interpretation, since it valorizes a metanarrative of modernity that is too narrow (German) and too pessimistic. What is more important, however, than Rorty's cultural evaluation of Habermas's tradition is his insight that French poststructuralism—for instance, Foucault's theory—shares some of Habermas's problems insofar as it buys into the Kantian definition of modernity and therefore also into the Habermasian agenda (although of course not into his solutions). Hence his critique addresses both Lyotard (and Foucault) and Habermas, insisting on a new canon without subject philosophy and metanarrative but with a strong commitment to liberal (Habermasian) politics.

In terms of its historical significance, Rorty's essay helped to clarify not only Habermas's position vis-à-vis the continental philosophical tradition but also to map the fundamental conflict of the postmodernism debate that was initiated by Habermas's 1980 essay "Modernity versus Postmodernity" and later fueled by his *Philosophical Discourse of Modernity* (1987). Since Habermas includes Horkheimer and Adorno in his fundamental critique, this debate has had an impact on the recent reception of Adorno as well. It was not entirely accidental that Rorty suggested a return to Adorno and Horkheimer as one way of getting away from metanarratives. On the other hand, it would be difficult to see Adorno outside the continental philosophical tradition that Rorty wants to cancel. For that reason, a philosophical alliance between Adorno and Rorty's pragmatism is unlikely—except for isolated points, such as the avoidance of dogmatic metanarratives and the need for mi-

---

10. Rorty, "Habermas and Lyotard," 166; Thomas McCarthy, "Practical Discourse and the Relations between Morality and Politics" (Paper read at a Habermas conference at the University of North Carolina, Chapel Hill, Oct. 1989).

crological criticism. Much of recent Adorno criticism has used similar issues in order to recover aspects of Critical Theory that were lost or repressed in Habermasian consensus theory.

Of significant import in this context is Joel Whitebook's attempt to reconstruct the contribution of Freud and psychoanalysis to Critical Theory.[11] While the primary interest of his essay is the reworking of psychological aspects of Critical Theory in Habermas's work, Whitebook resists the tendency of much recent Habermas criticism simply to discard the older Frankfurt School as "superseded" by Habermasian theory. To be sure, Whitebook's reconstruction of the Freudian components of Critical Theory is anything but uncritical. It points, among other things, to the limitations of id theory, as it was favored by Adorno and Marcuse, and to the somewhat pessimistic tone of id psychology. Whitebook specifically relates the "pessimism" of *Dialectic of Enlightenment* to the authors' inability to come to terms with and integrate ego psychology. Yet, at the same time, he underscores the importance of the original agenda of the Frankfurt School by pointing out that Habermas, in his attempt to overcome the theoretical impasse of the early Critical Theory, also tends to shortchange the initial project.

Whitebook criticizes the Habermasian project for its neglect of the central concern of Adorno and Benjamin with happiness, a concern not grounded in abstract norms but linked to the concept of mimesis. As a consequence of its "linguistic turn," Habermasian theory of communicative action loses the sense of an "inner foreign territory," which defines Freudian theory and also its appropriation by Marcuse and Adorno. Hence for Habermas the category of alienation becomes less central and the problem of happiness a secondary one. His systematic distinction between happiness and social justice allows him to

11. Joel Whitebook, "Reason and Happiness: Some Psychoanalytic Themes in Critical Theory," in Bernstein, *Habermas and Modernity*, 140–60.

place in the foreground a notion of progress in the realm of morality, possibly at the expense of happiness. We should note that Whitebook acknowledges the theoretical advances of Habermasian theory over the older Frankfurt School, but he also wants to discuss the price for this gain. His critique boils down to the question of external reality and, more specifically, the question of the body. Thus he concludes: "we cannot defend the project of modernity—which must be defended—at the price of sacrificing the naturalistic tradition that runs from Feuerbach throughout the young Marx and Freud to the early Frankfurt School."[12]

Much of the recent discussion of Critical Theory has focused on the question Whitebook brings up in his assessment of Habermas's theory: Can one assume (with Bernstein, McCarthy, and others) that the theory of communicative action canceled older Critical Theory, or is there a need for a return to Adorno and Benjamin? To some extent, this question itself reflects the limited reception of post-Adornian Critical Theory in this country, for within the context of the German discussion it would not be plausible to perceive Habermas as the only heir to the Frankfurt School. Under these circumstances, resistance toward Habermasian theory can easily take the form of a "return" to older models, just as the dissatisfaction of the second generation of the Frankfurt School in West Germany articulated itself as a "return" to the Marxist origins of the Frankfurt School in the 1930s. This strategy of going back to the roots is sometimes linked to another move: the suggestion that the essence of Critical Theory is closely related to theoretical positions such as deconstruction or New Historicism. In this case, Adorno and Benjamin can be played out as potential allies against the Habermasian version of Critical Theory, or, on the other hand, Adorno can be framed—as in Bernstein's account—as a crypto-Heideggerian.

It may be appropriate at this point to examine the stakes of

12. Ibid., 160.

the debate. It goes without saying that the request for a return to Adorno and Benjamin has little to do with the historical moment of their writings. The contributors to *Telos*—where the call for a return has been most consistent in recent years—are not ultimately interested in a historical reconstruction of the Frankfurt School, for instance, its program of the 1930s and its evolution during the 1940s and 1950s. The core of the agenda involves a rejection of Habermasian theory, of its definition of progress, modernity, and social justice. In other words, the politics of Habermasian theory, its function within the American academy, has aroused the suspicion of the Left. By the same token, the decidedly more positive evaluation of Habermas in the writings of Perry Anderson (at Adorno's expense) reflects a significant change in the configuration of British Marxism.[13] Here it is deconstruction that serves as the negative force for the reevaluation. In both cases, the reappraisal of Critical Theory also involves reconfigurations in the understanding of oppositions and alliances. The political agenda, however, is rarely spelled out; typically, it is couched in epistemological and methodological terms. Unlike the 1960s and early 1970s, when theoretical issues were frequently reduced to political ones, during the 1980s we find a tendency to discuss political conflicts under the disguise of theoretical models. For this reason the contemporary contribution of Critical Theory is best assessed in the context of specific themes and issues.

My own discussion will focus on three areas, namely, conceptions of culture, the postmodernism debate, and the theoretical articulation of feminism. Obviously, these thematic concerns are interrelated, though they operate on different levels: among them, it is primarily the theory of culture that serves as a metalevel for the discussion of the other two, feminism and postmodernism. In its more differentiated conception of culture, Critical Theory is said to have made major gains in

13. Perry Anderson, *In the Tracks of Historical Materialism* (Chicago, 1984).

comparison with traditional Marxism. In different ways, Benjamin, Adorno, and Marcuse criticized reductive base/superstructure models. For Habermas, a return to a traditional model was never in question; at the same time, however, from his early work on, his conceptualization of culture differs significantly from Adorno's attempts. These differences have left their traces in the American debate of the 1980s—not only in the encounter between Critical Theory and poststructuralist approaches but also in the less pronounced dialogue with Cultural Marxism and the New Historicism.

In certain ways both Marcuse's and Adorno's definitions of culture stayed very close to a rather narrow traditional conception of high culture (*Kultur*). Their work can positively invoke "culture" as the canonical tradition in literature or music. When Adorno practiced his method of close reading, the typical focus remained masterpieces of the high-culture tradition, for instance, Beethoven's late sonatas or Goethe's *Iphigenie*. Needless to say, this exclusive definition of culture, with its close proximity to a conservative understanding of culture as an autonomous aesthetic realm, has not attracted much attention lately. More important are two aspects of Adorno's theory that have informed the discourse of the New Left and more recently seem to resurface in the work of the New Historians. First, the autonomy of culture is not absolute but mediated through social conventions and institutions. Such a conviction rejects as ideology the abstract concept of culture and considers the cultural criticism based on such an abstract notion dogmatic and uncritical. Second, the relationship between high culture and mass culture must not be understood as an opposition but rather as a dialectical relationship that has to be examined as part of the social formation. It was precisely this aspect of Adorno's theory of mass culture that was not fully understood in the American mass-culture debate of the 1940s and 1950s, since this debate treated the opposition as an abstract dichotomy. The Frankfurt School's critique of mass culture not only undermined this dichotomy but, in doing so, also broadened the concept of culture, bringing into prominence aspects that traditional criticism had constantly excluded from critical scrutiny. The recent canon debate is clearly indebted to Critical Theory, although the connection is rarely explicit, since the immediate impetus for the discussion frequently comes from studies of ethnic subcultures and women's studies.

Obviously, it would be misleading to describe the critical discourse of the 1980s as a straight continuation or even modified extension of the Frankfurt School—or of Western Marxism, for that matter. What current critical approaches have retained, however, is a sense of the intrinsic relation between cultural interpretation and social theory. In fact, in the present debate, the classical distinction between them, which still informed the work of the older Frankfurt School, has vanished. Cultural theory has subsumed social theory, primarily under the rubric of cultural practices. Conversely, forms of domination and coercive practices are no longer exclusively or primarily located at the level of the social system. The concept of affirmative culture, introduced by Herbert Marcuse in 1937, captures part of this shift but not all of it. His own work, as well as that of Adorno, remained linked to the category of the autonomous art work as the bearer of oppositional and utopian forces and thus could not embrace a broad anthropological concept of culture. For Marcuse and Adorno the "core" of culture, the advanced art work, escapes cultural hegemony through its own formal structure, which articulates the opposition against the social relations in which it is embedded.

For the ongoing critical debate in the United States, the differentiated concept of culture of the Frankfurt School has been fruitful, yet by no means binding. Classical Critical Theory becomes one of a number of voices; frequently it is used—for instance, in John Brenkman's *Culture and Domination* (1987)—as a critical force for the discussion of thematic problems. For Brenkman, a critical definition of culture has to hark back to the writings of Marx and Engels. In this historical unfolding of the cultural problematic, the contribution of the

Frankfurt School becomes a significant moment (but no more than that) in the history of Western Marxism. Moreover, on a critical note, Brenkman suggests that Western Marxism (and the Frankfurt School) remains bound to the tradition of scientific Marxism, that is, to "the reduction of culture to consciousness and of social relations to relations of production."[14] As a result, culture becomes eclipsed and depoliticized.

While this assessment is useful in the case of Adorno, it certainly misses the core of Benjamin's later writings, which are precisely concerned with the political moment in culture. Brenkman, however, is certainly justified in underscoring the need for a political definition of culture. Of course, in this statement not only is the concept of culture at stake, but so also is the concept of the political. The typical dismissal of Adorno's philosophy of art during the 1970s as quietistic was predicated on a notion of politics as radical opposition rather than self-reflexive subversion. In more recent definitions of the political, the micrological aspect of culture and the literary text—favored in Adorno's approach—plays a more important role. It is not accidental, therefore, that Brenkman in his reading of Blake's poetry comes back to the notion of internal contradictions and language practice. Where he turns away from Adorno is the latter's understanding of the art work as an autonomous construct. Instead, he wants to focus on the double movement of a reading that responds to overdetermined and multivalent poetic language. By invoking Freudian interpretation, he wants to stress the suspended or floating attention of Blake's reader. But this strategy of reading and situating the literary text is much closer to Adorno than Brenkman seems to realize. Where he does indeed transcend the Adornian scope of criticism is in his notion that interpretation, even in its ideal form, always contains a moment of resistance, that the ideal reader is always engaged in social practices that codetermine the act of reading.

14. John Brenkman, *Culture and Domination* (Ithaca, 1985), 100.

What emerges in Brenkman's discussion is a fundamental dissatisfaction with the social theory of the older Frankfurt School. Indeed, for Brenkman the most apparent weakness of Adorno's later theory stems from the fact that he and Horkheimer failed to develop a more flexible model of capitalist societies after 1944. While Adorno considerably refined his aesthetic theory and criticism during the 1950s and 1960s, his concept of the advanced capitalist society as a totally administered society froze and did not take in later developments. The moment of reification becomes the final word for all social practices. Therefore, the subjective moment, unable to express itself socially, moves into the art work. This, however, means that the true locus of Adorno's late social theory is his aesthetic theory. The definition of the art work as a monad contains more than Adorno's explicit formulations of the relationship between society and art; it is the core of Adorno's theory, namely, the complete entwinement of the social and the aesthetic. To this we have to add the political aspect. The work of art is the site of political resistance. Still, Brenkman's critique addresses an important point. In Adorno's later theory the social agent is underprivileged; or, to put it differently, the social structure dominates the individual and his or her social practice. By harking back to Raymond Williams and British Cultural Marxism, Brenkman means to insert a different understanding of cultural practice, which undercuts the society/art dichotomy. The political significance of this strategy deserves attention. Its intent is to mobilize the interaction between poetry and society as an interaction between two discursive practices in such a way that the outcome is not already predetermined. In order to reestablish the political thrust of the Marxist tradition, Brenkman abandons Adorno's social theory as well as the premises of his micrological analysis, turning to a psychoanalytical approach instead.

If the political aspect of culture is at the center of the recent debate (and the case for this emphasis can be made), the legacy of Critical Theory comes into play in various and contradictory forms. Different strands and phases can and have been played out against each other. Clearly, the concept of the political in Benjamin's criticism figures differently from that in Habermas's theory, for instance. But in spite of considerable differences of emphasis and outspoken disagreement about the legacy of Critical Theory, one is struck by a common element in more recent essays and books. Whereas the tenor of the discussion in the 1970s stressed the distance toward the older Frankfurt School for political reasons, the critical discussion of the 1980s has recuperated the political force of Critical Theory, especially in the writings of Benjamin, but also, more surprisingly, in the work of Adorno. For example, in *Modern Culture and Critical Theory* (1989), Russell A. Berman argues that Horkheimer and Adorno's *Dialectic of Enlightenment* contains a political message that speaks to the contemporary situation, though mediated through a historical analysis of the mid-1940s. The radical move, Berman suggests, consists of educating the individual for autonomy. "For critical theory, autonomy is the project of the subject who has not yet escaped heteronomous determination but who might do so, a potential indicative of the openness of history not closed off by the idealism of an epistemic logic of genealogy."[15] We should note that the target of this polemical formulation is no longer a conservative defense of freedom or an orthodox Marxist conception of class struggle but Foucault's concept of genealogy with its stress on power. What Berman wants to bring into the foreground are the different political implications of two positions that seemingly concur in their critique of the Enlightenment. The point of this comparison is that Critical Theory, unlike Foucauldian genealogy, is not satisfied with a pessimistic account of structures of domination. Instead, it marks the moment of freedom in the resistance of the victim. This

---

15. Russell A. Berman, *Modern Culture and Critical Theory: Art, Politics, and the Legacy of the Frankfurt School* (Madison, Wis., 1989), 15.

reading of Adorno stands in clear although unacknowledged opposition to that of Habermas in the *Philosophical Discourse of Modernity*, notwithstanding that it shares the turn against genealogy. Clearly, the attempt to revitalize Adorno, particularly in the area of cultural criticism, has created a division in the appropriation of Critical Theory. This strain becomes more visible in the postmodernism debate—a debate that has been labeled as an exchange between "German" and "French" theory, represented by Habermas and Foucault.

This is not the place to review the entire debate.[16] My observations will focus on the role of Critical Theory as a force in the definition of postmodernism. In this context, it is important to remind ourselves that Critical Theory is not identical with Habermasian theory. This is especially true in regard to the analysis and evaluation of modernity. The voices of the Frankfurt School have to be carefully distinguished. The intervention of Jürgen Habermas in 1980, which has made for a great deal of agitation in various camps, must also be understood as part of an ongoing debate within the Frankfurt School about the Enlightenment and its implications. It was prefigured already in the controversy between Benjamin and Adorno about the loss of aura and the function of mass culture and the new media (film).

For a number of reasons it is not entirely surprising that the response to Habermas's project has been ambiguous and strained among American critics, who are fundamentally sympathetic to Critical Theory. Moreover, from the vantage point of the American discourse on postmodernism, the contribution of Habermas came at a rather late stage of the debate. As Andreas Huyssen points out in his essay "Mapping the Postmodern," the debate about the end of modernism emerged in the

16. Two recent contributions questioning postmodernism in a Marxist frame are David Harvey, *The Condition of Postmodernity* (Oxford, 1989), and Douglas Vellner, ed., *Postmodernism/Jameson/Critique* (Washington, D.C., 1989).

United States during the 1960s.[17] Critics like Leslie Fiedler and Ihab Hassan introduced the term to examine contemporary literature. It was only during the late 1970s that the concept of postmodernism surfaced in France and Germany, where it took on a much broader meaning. The initial discussion dealt with the fate of the avant-garde after World War II and focused on the expansion of the literary and artistic opposition during the 1950s. The postmodernism debate of the 1980s, on the other hand, fueled by the contributions of Lyotard and Habermas, addressed a much larger issue, for the opposition modernism/postmodernism was now linked to another opposition, namely, modernity/postmodernity.

In his by now notorious essay "Modernity—an Incomplete Project," Habermas boldly subsumed the aesthetic debate under the historical debate about the post-Enlightenment age.[18] In doing so, he implicitly invoked the entire trajectory of Western Marxism from the early Lukács to the late Adorno, since in all its stages Western Marxism had to respond to the central problem: how do we understand and evaluate the transition that occurred during the eighteenth century? Clearly, through the amalgamation of modernism and modernity on the one hand, and of postmodernism and postmodernity on the other, the stakes became much higher—as did also the ensuing confusion. While Peter Bürger's *Theory of the Avant-Garde* (1974) conceptualized the problem of the end of the (classical) avant-garde in terms of a linear development from modernism to the avant-garde and its historical demise during the 1930s, thereby historicizing both Adorno and Lukács, the expansion of the debate during the 1980s has undermined the very teleology on which Bürger's argument was predicated.[19] As a result, the his-

---

17. Andreas Huyssen, *After the Great Divide* (Bloomington, Ind., 1986), 179–221.

18. This famous essay originally appeared in *New German Critique* 22 (Winter 1981) and was reprinted in *The Anti-Aesthetic: Essays on Postmodern Culture*, ed. Hal Foster (Port Townsend, Wash., 1983), 3–15.

19. Bürger's important work came out in Germany in 1974. See Peter

toricization of Adorno, which Bürger had emphasized, became again an open question. Similarly, Leslie Fiedler's strident attack on the ideology of High Modernism, which certainly included the position of Adorno, in a curious way supported the very distinction it wanted to undermine by reversing the traditional evaluation.[20] This reception of the Frankfurt School's cultural politics had to be exploded before a new appropriation could occur.

In the American configuration of the 1980s, some of the most interesting contributions to the problem of postmodernism and postmodernity have come from those critics who follow neither Habermas's line of argument nor the chorus of Foucauldian and Derridian counterattacks. Hal Foster's volume *The Anti-Aesthetic* (1983) and the fifth issue of *Cultural Critique* (1986/87) can be understood as attempts of the American Left to respond to the ambiguous shift in the discussion brought about by Habermas and Lyotard. In this context, Fredric Jameson's essay "Postmodernism and Consumer Society" is a key to the interface between the American Left and Critical Theory. On one level, Jameson's analysis of postmodernism stays close to the thesis of *Dialectic of Enlightenment*, which links modern mass culture to advanced capitalism. Jameson views postmodernist culture as an extension of that logic: postmodernism corresponds to a change in postwar capitalism. "The 1960s are in many ways the key transitional period, a period in which the new international order (neocolonialism, the Green Revolution, computerization and electronic information) is at one and the same time set in place and is swept and shaken by its own internal contradictions and by external resistance."[21] In

---

Bürger, *Theorie der Avantgarde* (Frankfurt, 1974). It was not translated into English until ten years later. See Peter Bürger, *Theory of the Avant-Garde*, trans. Michael Shaw (Minneapolis, 1984).

20. Leslie Fiedler, "Cross the Border—Close the Gap," in *A Fiedler Reader* (New York, 1977), 170–94.

21. Fredric Jameson, "Postmodernism and Consumer Society," in Foster, *The Anti-Aesthetic*, 113.

the immediate context, the question whether Jameson's assessment is plausible is not important; what matters is the clear connection of his position with the Frankfurt School. On another level, however, Jameson breaks away from a notion of autonomous art that Adorno never gave up. By defining the postmodernist style as pastiche, as a repetition without authenticity, he undercuts the avant-garde/mass-culture opposition on which Adorno's theory was predicated. From Adorno's point of view, this would mean that the moment of resistance in culture, which for him was inevitably coupled with the advanced art work, had vanished. The consequence would be complete despair, since hope, as Adorno tells us at the end of *Negative Dialectics* (1966), is linked to the nonconceptual particular, especially to the work of art.

Interestingly enough, Adorno's "pessimism," which overshadowed the German debate of the 1970s, has not had a major impact on the American postmodernism discussion of the 1980s. As Andreas Huyssen observed in 1981, the absence of a perceived downturn after the Second World War, as well as the absence of an indigenous American avant-garde (in the radical sense of the term), provided a dynamic to the postwar years that was missing in Europe. Thus he labels American art of the 1960s as the "colorful death mask of a classical avant-garde."[22] Yet the American endgame of the avant-garde, defining itself as postmodernism, is played out as rejection of high modernism and nostalgia for the historical avant-garde. While Huyssen, very much in the tradition of Critical Theory, points to the potentially affirmative character of postmodernism (for instance, its delight in pop culture), he carefully refrains from the Adornian tendency to view the end of the avant-garde as a complete closure of history. Rather, he concludes by underscoring the need for regaining a sense of history (beyond a notion of triviality) and a conception of cultural identity. At the same time, he does not advocate a return to the classical

22. Huyssen, *After the Great Divide*, 168.

avant-garde, whose claims to cultural and social regeneration have lost their validity.

This evaluation of postmodernism takes issue with the Adornian "pessimism" but also with Habermas's defense of modernity and (by implication) modernism. Huyssen's critique of Habermas, more suggested than strictly argued, stresses two points: the need for a more differentiated and dialectical account of the modern age than Habermas offers, and a strong suspicion against a theoretical project that relies on a totalizing view of history. These suggestions, clearly formulated against the background of poststructuralist theory, can be taken as an indication that the issue of postmodernism has encouraged a reorientation within the appropriation of Critical Theory. This reorientation often involves a more or less critical turn back to Adorno, as well as a (sometimes only implicit) distancing from the Habermasian "project of modernity." A good example of this complex move is the reading of Adorno in Russell Berman's recent work, *Modern Culture and Critical Theory*. Writing in a somewhat different context from Huyssen, Berman nevertheless provides (like Huyssen) a version of the Frankfurt School legacy that does not follow the Habermasian line in responding to postmodernism.

Berman develops his position by defending aesthetic autonomy (as Adorno's theory defined it) against Peter Bürger's critique. What Berman objects to in Bürger's theory of the avant-garde is Bürger's strong claim about the necessary linear development leading toward postautonomous art. Berman considers that Bürger's model overemphasizes "the predominance of a single aesthetic model within an institutional phase."[23] He argues that Bürger's central thesis about the failure of the avant-garde (and the consequent lapse into postautonomy) is based on the problematic assumption that the avant-garde constituted the hegemonic art form of the early twentieth century. Against this, Berman contends that the avant-garde was only

23. Berman, *Modern Culture and Critical Theory*, 49.

one strand in the configuration of modernism, and that it has maintained its critical position apart from the historical logic of monopoly capitalism. Consequently, Berman can valorize the avant-garde and its critical function, thereby opposing both postautonomous decline and postmodernist indifference. This argument rescues Adornian aesthetic theory without burying itself in the mood of despair that tinges much of Adorno's later writing.

In no way do I want to imply that Huyssen's and Berman's approaches to the problematic of postmodernism are identical. In fact, they clearly disagree. While Huyssen underlines the moment of subversion in postmodernist pluralism, Berman, more in the spirit of Adorno, tends to dismiss postmodernism as affirmative eclecticism. "The cultural theory of postmodernism provides the affirmative description of that which is merely given. Although it may carefully sketch power structures and practical strategies, its rejection of emancipatory autonomy precludes any systematic critical project."[24] What they do share, however—and this is the crucial point—is a sense of resistance to theoretical constructs of the kind that Habermas's later theory offers.

Obviously, the issue of postmodernism has not only divided the American Left, it has also brought about different and conflicting receptions of Critical Theory, ranging from an acknowledgment of postmodernist pluralism to a critique of its affirmative character based either on Adorno's idea of aesthetic truth or Habermas's notion of a loss of rational criticism. Similarly, there are also different emphases in the explicit or implicit political agenda connected with these positions—though these differences seem to be less pronounced than the theoretical ones. During the 1980s, the appropriation of Critical Theory in the United States, through its contact with other theoretical traditions, has (successfully, I believe) resituated the Left within the American discourse. While the theoretical

24. Ibid., 51.

interface has not necessarily changed the epistemological models, it has clearly redefined the political position of the Left, in particular its understanding of the theory/practice relation. What the question of postmodernism has helped to clarify for Critical Theory in this country is the inadequacy of the revolutionary models of the 1960s and the need for a broader definition of cultural practice, a conception in which the cultural and political are seen as complements rather than oppositions.

In even more dramatic ways than postmodernism, feminism has challenged received conceptions of culture and politics. In the case of West Germany (East Germany followed a different path altogether), it has led to a split between Critical Theory and feminist theory, since the cultural criticism of the Frankfurt School did not address the concerns of women. As far as the United States is concerned, the major strands of feminist theory that have dominated the discourse of the 1970s and 1980s—American feminism, represented by such critics as Susan Gubar, Sandra Gilbert, and Elaine Showalter, and French poststructuralist feminism (Hélène Cixous and Julia Kristeva)—followed different epistemological and methodological trajectories.[25] Only more recently has Critical Theory become a distinct voice. In the feminist debate, however, the locus of Critical Theory appears to be rather different from that of the postmodernist debate. Its critical edge has turned, to a large extent, against the "French" poststructuralist version of feminism. Hence its position is by and large closer to, but clearly not identical with, more traditional versions of Marxist theory emphasizing the *historical* nature of women's issues.[26] In this somewhat ambivalent alliance, the work of Jürgen Habermas, frequently attacked in the cultural debate, has become a focal point for a number of important questions.

25. See Toril Moi, *Sexual/Textual Politics: Feminist Literary Theory* (London, 1985).

26. See Sara Lennox's article, "Feminist Scholarship and *Germanistik*," in *German Quarterly* 62 (Spring 1989): 158–70.

In her essay "What's Critical about Critical Theory? The Case of Habermas and Gender" (1985), Nancy Fraser squarely addresses the problem of conceptualizing gender differences in the theory of communicative action.[27] The question of gender rarely surfaced in Adorno's work and was linked with the question of revolutionary movements in Marcuse's late writings only in a very general way, but Fraser rightly insists that Habermasian theory, because of its universal claims, has to respond to feminist issues on a number of levels, namely thematic, methodological, and epistemological. One obvious difficulty for a feminist appropriation is Habermas's silence on the specific social and cultural problems of women. One possible strategy to overcome this drawback would be to mobilize the distinction between labor and communication in Habermas for a critique of the bias in traditional Marxist theory toward male-dominated production, but one has to grant that, in terms of the structure of Habermasian theory, the male/female opposition does not fit easily into the difference between labor and symbolic action. Thus, Fraser suggests a more "structural" approach to the question of women's work, grafted onto the distinction between system-integrated and socially integrated (symbolic) actions. Furthermore, Fraser refers to the Habermasian division between life-world and system (typical for modern societies) in order to mark the difference between the private and the public sphere. In short, Fraser takes over major parts of Habermas's social theory for her own project, yet with the proviso that they have to be reworked for the articulation of feminist concerns.

From the feminist point of view, the private/public distinction mirrors the distribution between "productive" work and family. By putting the category to an empirical test, Fraser tries to show that the Habermasian distinction misses the mark,

27. Nancy Fraser, "What's Critical about Critical Theory? The Case of Habermas and Gender," *New German Critique* 35 (Spring/Summer 1985): 130.

that it especially does not adequately reflect the function of the family and the role of women in it. From a normative point of view, according to Fraser, the public/private distinction equally fails to address the imbalance of the traditional family structure. Specifically, Fraser notes a contradiction between the idea of social progress in Habermas's theory (which is expressed in terms of differentiation) and the norm of social justice. While social progress is linked to a process of differentiation in which the modern family and, with it, women are limited to the private realm, the idea of social justice cannot, as Habermas would agree, tolerate gender difference. To some extent, this critique misses the tension within the Habermasian concept of the public sphere, the tension between its factual and its normative aspect, by conflating these levels in Habermas's theory. What is more important, however, is the more general charge of gender blindness of the theoretical model that has defined Habermas's work since the mid-1970s. Fraser contends that his blindspot can be traced to the "categorical opposition between system and lifeworld institutions," which contains a bias toward a male-oriented society.[28] This critique simultaneously rescues other parts of Habermasian theory, however, among them the cultural interpretation of needs and the dialogical process of satisfying them.[29] For Fraser, the reception of Critical Theory is conceived as a selective and critical appropriation in which feminist concerns define the boundaries of acceptance.

Fraser's pragmatic strategy, with its somewhat understated understanding of the common ground, addresses primarily social problems but does not take up the larger issue of cultural difference that has defined the direction of feminist literary criticism. In this context, the question of the public sphere would take on a somewhat different meaning. Using Haber-

28. Ibid., 131 (also see esp. n. 47).
29. Rita Felski, *Beyond Feminist Aesthetics: Feminist Literature and Social Change* (Cambridge, Mass., 1989), 171.

mas's *Strukturwandel der Oeffentlichkeit* (Structural transformation of the public sphere), Rita Felski has argued that the
women's movement has created an important counter–public
sphere within a male-defined society.[30] In her emphasis on the
division within the public space and the possibility of undermining the hegemonic public discourse, Felski clearly extends
Habermas's conception in a direction that moves her close to
the position of Negt and Kluge.[31] The point Felski wants to
make is that a feminist public sphere opens up new spaces of
resistance that could and should be occupied by a variety of
approaches and theories. "Given the complex interpretations
of state and society in late capitalism, one can no longer pos-
tulate the ideal of a public sphere which can function outside
existing commercial and state institutions and at the same time
claim an influential and representative function as a forum for
oppositional activity and debate."[32] By stressing the need for a
discussion arena, she moves the reception of Habermas to the
level of metatheory, a move that allows her to integrate Critical
Theory in a more general way. Felski does not limit her discussion of feminist theory to specific doctrines of the Frankfurt
School; rather, she underscores a critical perspective on the
recent American conceptualization of women's studies. In particular, her approach raises the question of how feminist studies in the field of literature affect social and political structures.
Felski rightly calls attention to the situation of late capitalist
countries where the differentiation of the cultural and the po-

---

30. Ibid., 27.
31. See the introduction to this book for a discussion of Negt and Kluge.
The position to which I refer here is developed in their book, *Oeffentlichkeit und Erfahrung: Zur Organizationsanalyse von bürgerlicher und pro-
letarianischer Oeffentlichkeit* (Frankfurt, 1971). Negt and Kluge stress the
class-based notion of a counter–public sphere, but this argument is clearly
analogous to Felski's gender-based version of resistance. Both positions
arise directly out of the critique of Habermas's more univocal account of
the public sphere.
32. Felski, *Beyond Feminist Aesthetics*, 171.

litical spheres does not encourage the immediate impact of one sphere on the other.

Unlike Fraser, who is looking for a positive social model for the application of women's concerns, Felski stresses the "Adornian" aspect of Critical Theory, that is, its mode of critical reflection, as it engages theoretical positions. Again, it is the level of metatheory that becomes relevant for feminism, for instance, in a critique of feminist aesthetics both in American and French theory. Felski's metatheoretical method is especially telling in view of attempts to construct transhistorical modes of feminist writings. Within the American discourse, this project has frequently assumed a distinctive female sensibility grounded in a gendered experience. Yet, as Felski argues, this project is open to serious criticism because it overlooks significant social and cultural differences. "There are, moreover, obvious problems with a theoretical position which enshrines existing ideologies of sexual difference through reference to the supposedly intuitive and emotional quality of female consciousness, thereby merely reaffirming rather than questioning the authority of existing gender stereotypes."[33] Coming from Critical Theory, Felski argues that the lack of a sophisticated theory of ideology has typically trapped American feminism in an undifferentiated male/female dichotomy.

Whereas Felski's criticism of American feminism targets especially its reliance on ahistorical conceptions, her objections to French theory make a very different use of Critical Theory. Here she places in the foreground the similarities with Adorno's aesthetic theory, pointing to the problems involved in a modernist aesthetics. This critique builds on the post-Adornian concept of the avant-garde (Hans Magnus Enzensberger, Bürger), which has radically deconstructed the logical connection between the political and the aesthetic avant-garde. Like

33. Ibid., 27.

this critique, an advanced feminist position also has to question assumptions about a necessary connection between "avant-garde" fragmentary writing and political subversion. Making use of Mary Jacobus's critique of Hélène Cixous, Felski argues against any attempt to ground feminist criticism in the gendered nature of language.[34] For her this construct must fail because it dogmatically separates the feminine question from the social question and thereby "reiterates and is easily assimilated into a long-standing cultural symbolization of woman in Western society."[35] If Elaine Marks's statement, "Reading becomes the subversive act par excellence," is programmatic, the proximity to Adorno's aesthetic theory is indeed of crucial importance for a critical reading of *écriture féminine* (female writing or discourse).[36] Clearly, in this respect Felski tends to side with a Habermasian position that deflates the political claims of immanent criticism and, by extension, fragmentary, subversive writing. This critique emphasizes the need for contextualization: only the specific historico-social context allows the feminist critic to make political use of negativity. This leads to a method of reading that consistently deontologizes the feminist project, deconstructing the notion of an absolute distinction between the writing of males and females. The politics of writing and reading is not predetermined by fixed gender differences, rather, they have to be negotiated in the public sphere. Furthermore, the social and political function of a literary text has to be established within the context of the actual appropriation, that is to say, its subversive moment does not mechanically translate into political opposition.

Given the centrality of the concept of the public sphere for Felski's argument, it is not surprising that she turns to Habermas's *Strukturwandel*. We have to note, however, that her

34. Mary Jacobus, "The Question of Language: Men of Maxims and *The Mill on the Floss*," in *Writing and Sexual Difference*, ed. Elizabeth Abil (Brighton, 1982).
35. Felski, *Beyond Feminist Aesthetics*, 37.
36. Quoted in ibid., 39.

appropriation of Habermas's work, like that of Nancy Fraser, is selective. She clearly does not subscribe to the entire project of the early Habermas, which was not particularly sensitive to women's issues. Instead, she integrates those aspects of the Habermasian theory of the public sphere that help her to articulate the resistance of patriarchal societies to the needs of women. It is in this context that she examines the claims of feminist aesthetics and argues that there "remains, then, both an interaction and an inevitable tension between the spheres of 'feminism' and 'aesthetics.' "[37] It is a tension that cannot be resolved in either direction. The critical edge of literary analysis has to question the autonomy of the literary text as much as the social and political ideologies that determine the institution of literature. Again, this claim is rather close to Critical Theory in its general approach, even where Felski disagrees with specific theorists.

When Eugene Lunn examined the interface between Marxism and modernism in *Marxism and Modernism* (1982), he could still safely assume that the project of Western Marxism was more or less intact. Hence his own analysis traced the trajectory of German Marxism from Lukács to Adorno and Benjamin as part of the larger project of Western Marxism. In his conclusion, he (cautiously) affirmed Adorno's position on the avant-garde and mass culture while, at the same time, leaving some space for a Brechtian or Benjaminian position. Such an affirmation is, I feel, no longer possible. During the last decade, the meaning of the four theorists whom Lunn examined (Lukács, Brecht, Benjamin, Adorno) has changed in a major way. This does not mean that their work can be discarded. The question is its appropriation. It seems that the construct "Western Marxism" has lost some of its usefulness for the present debate. For one thing, Critical Theory, even in its traditional definition, does not easily fit this term anymore. Jürgen Habermas cannot be called a Western Marxist. Furthermore, Crit-

37. Ibid., 179.

ical Theory has opened up and moved in various directions by interfacing with different theoretical traditions. As a result, the conception of critical theory itself has altered. Boundaries that used to be stable have collapsed and new borderlines have emerged. This revisionism has been most visibly carried out by the New Historicists—theoretically speaking, a blend of the neo-Marxists (Frankfurt School), poststructuralists (Foucault), and cultural anthropologists (Clifford Geertz)—but it also appears, as I have tried to show, in the postmodernism debate. There is an obvious danger in this eclectic blending—the loss of the oppositional force, the "mainstreaming" of Critical Theory. The New Historicists have not always avoided this danger. But, on the other hand, there are considerable gains. To refuse the opening, to insist on the traditional boundaries, means to get caught in the past and to close off the future. The survival of Critical Theory depends on a self-critical reappraisal of its own tradition and of its locus within different cultural and political configurations. This ongoing process implies a different attitude toward its past, namely a nonlinear view of its own development and an acknowledgment of complex theoretical constellations. Of course, the early Frankfurt School, especially Horkheimer, was striving toward an interdisciplinary project in which the Marxist model was expected to be hegemonic. Forty years later and under very different circumstances, Jürgen Habermas made another attempt using a linguistic model. Both projects failed in their desire to favor a particular model. It seems that during the 1980s Critical Theory has been most effective as a local theory in a dialogical situation with different approaches and methods, receiving its strength from concrete social conflicts and struggles.

Index

Index

Adorno, Theodor W. (cont.)
  and Lukács, 6, 53–59, 63, 68–71, 81, 157
  and Lunn, 227
  and Marcuse, 198
  and Marxism, 2, 6, 9, 13, 17, 53, 79, 84, 98, 210
  on modernism, 55, 66, 81, 83, 92–93, 95–96, 157
  on modernity, 185
  on music, 16, 63, 64–66, 72
  and Negt and Kluge, 16
  and 1970s developments, 157
  "pessimism" of, 17–18, 79, 80, 183–84, 218, 219
  and Piccone, 201
  political force of, 214
  renewed interest in, 188, 208–9
  return to Frankfurt, 5–6
  Rorty on, 206–7
  and social theory, 213
  and student movement, 79, 93, 157
  on theory and praxis, 79–80
  and Weber, 203
  Wellmer on, 18–20
  and Whitebook on Freud, 207
  and younger theorists, 16
Adorno Prize, Habermas' acceptance of, 131
Advertising, Haug on, 166
Aesthetic autonomy. See Autonomy of art
Aesthetic culture, and Lukács, 24
Aesthetic forms, historicity of, 59
Aesthetic model, and Marxism, 20
Aesthetic theory
  Adorno on, 91, 92
  and feminism, 196
  and Habermas on Critical Theory, 17
  of 1970s, 162, 171–72, 182–83, 196–97; commodity aesthet-

ics, 160, 165–72; Enzensberger, 178–82; and Habermas, 183–87, 188; Metscher-Bürger debate, 172–78; political (materialist) aesthetics, 159–60, 162–65, 172, 181; and reception theory, 187
Aesthetic Theory (Aesthetische Theorie) (Adorno), 10, 66–67, 68, 80, 83
  and Benjamin, 78
  and Habermas, 17, 101, 149
  and Marx, 2
  and production, 88
  reception of, 10, 75–76, 77, 93
  and social meaning, 85
  and truth value of art, 90
  and Werckmeister, 182
Albert, Hans, 100
Alienation
  Adorno and Lukács on, 57, 110
  and Critical Theory, 166
  and Lukács, 52, 59, 62
Althusserian Marxism, 200
Analytic philosophy
  and Habermas on Critical Theory, 16
  and *Knowledge and Human Interest*, 204
Anderson, Perry, 209
Apel, Karl Otto, 195
Art
  Adorno on, 55–57, 66–67, 68, 72, 73, 82–93, 95, 97–98, 126–27 (*see also under* Adorno, Theodor W.)
  Habermas on, 124–30
  and Lukács, 31–32, 55–57, 65, 95, 183 (*see also Theory of the Novel*)
  and mass culture, 72
  Schneider on, 165
  See also Aesthetic theory; Literary theory

230

Index

Brandt, Willi, 9
Brecht, Bertolt, 77, 174–75
　and Adorno, 6, 78, 82, 157
　and autonomy of art, 127
　and avant-garde, 161
　and Bürger, 178
　and Gallas, 190
　and Lunn, 227
Breines, Paul, 30, 48
Brenkman, John, 211–13
Brewster, Philip, 184
Bruck, Möller van den, 29
Brunhild (Ernst), 32–33
Brunkhorst, Hauke, 17
Bubner, Rüdiger, 98
Buchner, Carl Howard, 184
Buck-Morss, Susan, 199
Bürger, Peter, 12n, 15, 172–73,
　175–78
　and Adorno, 18, 58, 69–70, 71,
　95–97, 176, 216–17
　Berman on, 219
　and discourse analysis, 193
　and Lukács, 58, 69–70, 71, 172,
　176, 216–17
　and Metscher, 173–76
　and modernism/postmodernism,
　18
　and surrealism, 125

Capitalism
　Adorno on, 57, 66, 79, 213; and
　art or music, 64, 72, 158; and
　culture, 95
　advertising in, 166
　and Frankfurt School, 110
　and Holz on art, 168
　Horkheimer on, 79, 213
　Lukács on, 57, 108
　and postmodernism, 217
　and romanticism, 26, 29, 30
Cixous, Hélène, 195, 221, 226
Classicism
　Adorno on, 83–84

Weimar, 26, 28
　See also Greek culture
Commodity, art as. *See* Culture
　industry
Commodity aesthetics, 160, 165–
　72
Commodity fetishism, and Lukács
　on culture, 64
Communication
　and Adorno on art, 87
　Habermas on, 104–5, 127
Communicative action
　and gender, 222
　and Habermas, 102, 107, 121–
　22, 123, 146, 147–49; debate
　on, 204; and Foucault, 118;
　and Lukács, 109
　and Marxism, 20
Communicative interaction, and
　Habermas, 192
Communicative norms, 153–55
Communicative rationality or rea-
　son, Habermas on, 121, 125,
　148
Communist party
　and Benjamin, 78
　in France, 8
　and New Left, 15
　and West Germany, 5
Constance school, 161, 179, 187
Counterrevolution and Revolt
　(Marcuse), 160, 178
Critical reflection. *See* Reflection,
　critical
Critical Theory, vii
　and Adorno, 10, 158
　alteration in, 227–28
　ambiguous position of, 7, 9
　on art, 179
　and capitalist culture, 184
　and commodity aesthetics, 165
　current meaning and relevance
　of, 3–4

Index

Index

Index

Library of Congress Cataloging-in-Publication Data

Hohendahl, Peter Uwe.
    Reappraisals : shifting alignments in postwar critical theory / by
Peter Uwe Hohendahl.
        p.   cm.
    Includes index.
    ISBN 0-8014-2455-0 (alk. paper). — ISBN 0-8014-9708-x (pbk. :
alk. paper)
    1. Criticism.   2. Critical theory.   I. Title.
PN98.S6H6   1991
801'.95'09045—dc20   91-10127

CHIVALRIC FICTION
AND THE HISTORY OF THE NOVEL

Florida A&M University, Tallahassee
Florida Atlantic University, Boca Raton
Florida Gulf Coast University, Ft. Myers
Florida International University, Miami
Florida State University, Tallahassee
University of Central Florida, Orlando
University of Florida, Gainesville
University of North Florida, Jacksonville
University of South Florida, Tampa
University of West Florida, Pensacola

Chivalric Fiction
and the History of the Novel

CAROLINE A. JEWERS

University Press of Florida

Gainesville · Tallahassee · Tampa · Boca Raton
Pensacola · Orlando · Miami · Jacksonville · Ft. Myers

05 04 03 02 01 00   6 5 4 3 2 1

Library of Congress Cataloging-in-Publication Data
Jewers, Carolina A., 1961–
Chivalric fiction and the history of the novel / Caroline A. Jewers
p. cm.
Includes bibliographical references and index.
ISBN 0-8130-1823-4 (alk. paper)
1. Romances—History and criticism. 2. Literature, Medieval—History
and criticism. 3. Chivalry in literature. I. Title.
PN671.J49 2000
809.3'02—dc21   00-061602

The University Press of Florida is the scholarly publishing agency for the
State University System of Florida, comprising Florida A&M University,
Florida Atlantic University, Florida Gulf Coast University, Florida
International University, Florida State University, University of Central
Florida, University of Florida, University of North Florida, University of
South Florida, and University of West Florida.

University Press of Florida
15 Northwest 15th Street
Gainesville, FL 32611–2079
http://www.upf.com

For my parents, John and Joan

"And you thought you'd give me some material? Alas, I've got too much already. I've read hundreds of romances. Classical romances and medieval romances, Renaissance romances and modern romances. Heliodorus and Apuleius, Chrétien de Troyes and Malory, Ariosto and Spenser, Keats and Barbara Cartland. I don't need any more data. What I need is a theory to explain it all."

"Theory?" Philip Swallow's ears quivered under their silvery thatch, a few places further up the table. "That word brings out the Goering in me. When I hear it I reach for my revolver."

"Then you're not going to like my lecture, Philip," said Morris Zapp.

David Lodge, Small World

CONTENTS

PREFACE

There are many possible histories of the novel, and this book represents but a part of one of them. Aimed at medievalists, comparatists, and general readers contemplating the origins of the novel, it seeks to reconcile aspects of the pre-Cervantine continental romance with the august lineage of what critics define—albeit tentatively—as the modern novel. Rather than viewing the novel as reacting *against* the romance, this study argues that the romance reacted to its own conventions in important ways that contribute directly and in an integrated way to the development of the genre—and therefore to the history of the novel. Accounts of the rise of the novel tend toward the seismic and iconoclastic: individual works and authors produce singular events that profoundly alter the warp and weft of the genre, leaving it changed forever. And yet there are other possible histories of the novel that, while they may celebrate works and authors as this one does, tend toward highlighting the slower erosion and evolution of narrative and the changes that came more subtly from within. In a somewhat paradoxical critical twist, the medieval romance is often overlooked on account of its apparent sameness and conventions, and at the same time it is estranged on account of its alterity and seeming distance from the boundaries of what is deemed proper modern novelistic experience. Too familiar and yet too foreign, the result appears to be that the medieval romance is snubbed all too often, left to languish on the threshold of the literary feast, when it ought to be welcomed in and given due place.

The infinite variety of the romance attests to its popularity and plasticity as a form, and to the inventiveness of countless authors who saw in it not the iteration of clichés, but the boundless potential of resituating the horizon of narrative. It bequeathed to the modern novel its most important element: the fundamental need, beyond storytelling, to quest for itself, to be engaged on a fundamental and ontological level in search of its own metafiction. Here again, even given the limits of this study within the boundaries of a few works of chivalric fiction, the potential directions are many: the present aim is simply to analyze the parodic intertextuality that manifests itself in the literary allusions and parodic lists that characterize some key works, not only in order to show important aspects of their fiction and friction but also to demonstrate that these parodic tendencies and intertextual impulses are the very lifeblood of literary change.

Beginning with a general consideration about writing histories of the novel, this study journeys southward, away from an anglocentric consideration of the novel's genealogy, toward Cervantes's *Don Quixote* by way of a work he admired greatly, Joanot Martorell and Martí Joan de Galba's *Tirant lo Blanc,* and some of that text's predecessors in Occitania and northern France. Although there could be other approaches, I have chosen a broad definition of parody as my common denominator. While parody is a ubiquitous phenomenon in medieval literature and functions differently in different genres and in the hands of different authors, it generally has the particular effect on the romance (as opposed, say, to lyric poetry) of generating a sense of narrative dynamism and a comic reflexivity that agitates for change within convention, bringing a constant sense of renewal. The romance's greatest quest is ultimately its search for itself, and a fearless—sometimes comic—striving for a center and for meaning makes it a part of the novel's illustrious genealogy.

Any flaws or sins of omission in the following pages are mine alone: the pleasure and illumination I find in these and other medieval texts come from the example of friends and teachers. I would like to acknowledge Jill Tattersall and Mike Freeman, who made the Middle Ages so lively when I was an undergraduate, and Alan D. Deyermond, whose kind erudition made me aspire to be a comparatist. The current work began in the dissertation I wrote at the University of Oregon under the patient direction of Thomas R. Hart Jr. to whom I owe much. I would also like to thank William C. Calin for his invaluable help and suggestions. I am also indebted to my colleagues and students at the University of Kansas, to the Hall Center for the Humanities, and the Camargo Foundation for their support.

Lastly, there are those good friends who make all the difference: Priscilla West, Mary Kuntz, Suzana Michel, Gina Psaki, Pamela Gordon and Harold Washington, Beth Schultz, and the incomparable Hamish. Thanks also to Peggy McCracken, who was kind enough to read an earlier draft. Finally, I always wanted Henri and Jeannette Canivez, Jean and Marianne [Pallone], Jean-Paul and Brigitte Badosa, Caty Lévêque, and Maxime Bernal to know how much they taught me about French and life: Je vous remercie profondément.

I

Rekindling the Romance
Toward and Away from the Prehistory of the Novel

Medieval romance can, of course, be regarded as a major influence on the
development of the novel—that is, if one regards reaction to romance rather than
any development from it, as an influence. . . . This discussion can be terminated by
restating what seems to be the most obvious fact of all about medieval romance,
viz. that it had little or nothing to offer narrative which had not already been
created in ancient times.

Hubert McDermott, *Novel and Romance* 104–5

Because the novel is the most protean and problematic to define of genres,
it necessarily follows that it has the most elusive of histories. In keeping
with the fundamental form it describes, any history of the novel risks being
a story itself, and the illusory nature of the novel's attempt to give a verisimilar, totalizing view of the objective world shapes our attempts to provide a convincing account of its development as a genre. The novel's lon-
gevity and vitality in Western culture since classical antiquity result from
an innate ability to adapt and survive, and consequently its myriad shapes
result in many possible histories of the genre.

Histories of the novel owe most allegiance to the narrative frame of
history. Theories of the novel are potentially freer of such temporal constraints as a structuring principle, but are confronted by the essential paradox of the novel's existence and our relation to it as pure form and style.
Most critical histories combine the two, and yet making nonfiction of
fiction is an intriguing and impossible task either way, perhaps because
constructing any factual account of the novel's rise is perforce to adopt a
novelistic stance and make a fiction of it: novels present the collective
illusion of linearity, of emergence from artistic gestation to formal maturity along a time line whose axis takes a parallel, inexorable course toward
the historical horizon and the present moment. Charting the ascendancy

of such a literary form is an act of critical retrospection, working backward from hindsight to a historical and theoretical vanishing point that we would have coincide with a presumed place of birth. Paradoxically then, our tracing the novel's rise is simultaneously a critical descent. It is a retroactive re-creation that inevitably lends artificial pedigrees to discourse and an illusive search for genealogies or hypothetical taxonomies of form that confirm or deny a preconceived intellectual or historical order. This retrospective panorama of great monuments is immediately complicated by the realization that there is no novel as such, only novels linked by a variety of common denominators that can only ever partially explain their existence and historical significance.

This is why writerly (to borrow Barthes's term from *S/Z*) or authorly histories of the novel differ so greatly from critical, historical, and readerly accounts. Rather than constructing the history of the novel and the movement toward history, their tendency is to collate the story of the novel and chart its movement away from history. The resulting *story* of the novel is bound by a double movement both toward and away from history; the imaginative power of creativity strains away from the gravitational pull of everyday reality at the same time that representing and transcending it becomes the prime objective of the genre. The history of the novel that grounds itself in history takes realistic representation and an ability to encapsulate the contemporary world as its guarantee of novelistic authenticity—an irony, since the alter-essence of the novel is its status as fiction.

Measuring realism constructs one form of literary evolution; charting the increasing sophistication with which fiction encodes its own artificiality yields another. Realism is a loaded term in every century even, perhaps, the nineteenth: Aristotle was the first to grasp that there is no such thing as complete mimetic realism in art. It is always/already a form of selective representation. This perhaps explains why, unlike those of critics, the novelist's history of the novel plays down the role of time and verisimilitude, preferring to prioritize deeper internal structures, the very things that simultaneously betray the novel's ahistoricism, artificiality, fictionality, and self-consciousness.

Such an alternative way of looking at the genesis of the novel entails examining how it struggles against history as it inevitably reflects it. Milan Kundera best expresses the double bind when he states:

> Le sens de l'histoire d'un art est opposé à celui de l'Histoire tout court. Par son caractère personnel, l'histoire d'un art est une vengeance de l'homme sur l'impersonnalité de l'histoire de l'humanité. (*L'Infini* 8)

[The meaning of the history of an art form is opposed to that of History with a capital letter. On account of its personal character, the history of an art form is an act of vengeance by man over the impersonality of the History of humanity.]

Sens here represents not just meaning, but direction and momentum, a strong textual impulse determined by friction of the individual subject against greater external forces. In Kundera's schema, the creative impulse from friction to fiction is man's act of defiance "née de la liberté" [born of liberty] in the face of—and counter to—the repressive conditions of history (8).

The novel's problematic relationship to time, space, and context leaves the ultimate question of its origins open to myriad interpretations and reworkings; as a genre it inscribes itself as a perpetual site of confrontation in which art and artist are engaged in an open present, commemorating what Georg Lukács describes as man's heroic attempt to *become* in an unstable world. Just as heroes strive to "become," so the novel is caught up in a perpetually imminent state of creation, and the literary remnants critics and authors piece together constitute

sa perpétuelle création et recréation, qui englobe toujours rétroactivement tout le passé du roman: Rabelais n'a certainement jamais appelé son *Gargantua-Pantagruel* roman. Ce *n'était pas* un roman; ce l'est *devenu* au fur et à mesure que les romanciers ultérieurs (Sterne, Diderot, Balzac, Flaubert, Vancura, Gombrowicz, Rushdie, Kis, Chamoiseau) s'en sont inspirés, s'en sont ouvertement réclamés, l'intégrant ainsi dans l'histoire du roman, plus, le reconnaissant comme la première pierre de cette histoire. (*L'Infini* 8)

[its perpetual creation and recreation, which always retroactively incorporates the whole history of the novel: Rabelais certainly never called his *Gargantua-Pantagruel* a novel. It *was not* a novel; it *became* one little by little as subsequent novelists (. . .) were inspired by it and openly quoted it as an authority, thereby integrating it into the history of the novel, acknowledging it as the first stone in that history.]

Posterity inserts works into the history of the novel: they come into being long after their literary genesis.

Kundera points to a form of literary history that transcends temporal boundaries. Rather, it charts an influential internal compositional energy that permeates the novel's subsequent development and influence, so that history becomes a series of essential textual moments echoed and rein-scribed in other works. Erich Auerbach (*Mimesis* 262–84) charts one such instance when he commemorates chapter 32 of *Pantagruel,* where Alco-fribas is swallowed by the giant and encounters a complex microcosmic universe on the way down. More than the genius of creating realistic worlds within a fantastical body itself in the body of text, what makes the episode compelling is the tangible sense of experimentalism, to the point that the narrator, the reader's controlling introit into the narrative, finds himself ingested in turn, on the threshold of becoming subject to his own creation. Always on the point of transformation, it seems as though the novel has enjoyed an existence in part autonomous of the authors who shaped it, a case of matter over the minds of authorial intent.

Exemplifying the fusion of the textual and historical, Auerbach uses a particular view of representation to locate a series of fulcra that produce a story composed of transformational instances. These are naturally a part of texts that have *become* great works through the process that Kundera de-scribes, but this process of becoming is present even in works that have not necessarily become great works in themselves. The novel has been in an ongoing process of *becoming* since antiquity. Great works and authors shape this evolution in a revolutionary way, but we can also reshape a hi/story of the novel as a kind of transformational narrative grammar cre-ated by a plurality of works and not as the result of singular events; they are part of a slower move toward generic evolution via the conduits of technique and those broader alterations—the ever-changing narrative climate.

It is not traditional to cite the medieval romance in the same breath as the illustrious line of Rabelais, Cervantes, Sterne, Fielding, Calvino, and Kundera, but however problematized its influence may be, the medieval romance provides part of the blueprint, if not a vital cornerstone, of the novel's foundation. This is not because it acted in a revolutionary way, but precisely because it did not: it evolved over time to create a horizon of literary expectation. The medieval romance gave us the bildungsroman and a central hero who tried to solve vital questions of existence and social integration, the sentimental education, the quest, and a sense of adventure. True, the romance achieves this on an often symbolic plane that eschews verisimilitude, and if realism were the sole defining criterion for the novel that it has often become, the romance's centrality to the novel would be hard to justify. It is also undeniable that in essential ways the medieval romance outlived its immediate usefulness by the time that Cervantes penned *Don Quixote* (Lukács 103). But in a more flexible, multifaceted form it continued to shape what we might consider the prehistory and the emerging history of the novel through its narrative dynamism and internal sense of renewal. *Don Quixote* has been, and remains, the touchstone of the modern novel; although critical posterity has used it as a brilliant excuse to sweep away what came before, in fact *Don Quixote* is the logical conclusion of the development of the chivalric romance that began with Chrétien de Troyes.

The clearest indicator of Cervantes's supposed radical break with tradition is the presence of generic parody, but as any medievalist of the last quarter-century will attest, such parody is often a basic feature of the medieval romance. In the great novels post-Cervantes, parody is treated as a large and visible measure of revolutionary advancement and a sign of narrative health, since critical posterity consistently measures increasing literary sophistication by a perceived ability on the novel's part to comment on itself and mock its predecessors. It is therefore no accident that so many great, seminal novelists wrote parodic works: it always has been identified as an essential part of the genre's dynamism—post-Cervantes. Why not before, in the vital centuries between late antiquity and the Renaissance, which proffer us another golden age of narrative, and not the dark age that histories of the novel fictionalize?

Parody manifests itself in all kinds of genres and is not the exclusive domain of narrative—it offers a battery of effects and techniques and works differently in different kinds of works. In the medieval lyric, for example, it establishes antigenres and renders the canon of forms more challenging and vital by creating a doubling, dissonant voice. The theater, too, uses parody as an entertaining weapon with which to lampoon man in society. In both these cases the generic attack comes from the margins, from the outside. But the particular way that parody functions in the novelistic narrative is from the inside, from the central core. Parody highlights conventions, it sets characters at odds with each other and plays texts off one another such that they resonate in comic and intertextual ways. Parody is the perfect foil for convention: like a comedy double-act, there must be a straight element in order for the deviant and subversive reaction to work.

In recent years, critics have opened and broadened the traditional definition of parody. A widely respected definition begins with the idea that the subject is as old as poetry itself, stating that "although a parasitic art, and written at times with malice, parody is as fundamental to literature as laughter is to health" (Robert P. Falk and William Beare in *The Princeton Encyclopedia* 600). Like most forms of comedy and its related subcategories of burlesque, satire, and pastiche, parody relies on a double process of

incongruity and recognition. It feeds on a perceptible genre, style, or author and then proceeds to distort what has been recognized, expressing
from within the target area what seems ludicrous without. There appear
to be as many definitions of these terms as there are critics. Referring to
The Princeton Encyclopedia once again, I agree with the author of the
entry on burlesque that "[n]o good purpose can be served by a too rigid
insistence upon nomenclature in a discussion of parody, burlesque or travesty" (88). The parodic elements of a text are necessarily burlesque in that
they are a comic exaggeration and, to an extent, travesty an original. The
degree to which they do so is perhaps more important than finding nuanced variations in the way they do it: all are literary phenomena and
operate in a similar way by displacement from one context to another.

In a wide-ranging and detailed study, Margaret Rose *(Parody: Ancient,
Modern, and Post-Modern)* emphasizes the history of parody and how it
has been theorized. In this context, and because it has already been attempted, there would be little point in sketching a history of the figure. The
purpose here is to deal with one of the subcategories of parody Rose identifies, the metafictional:

> In addition to making the target of parody a part of the parody text,
> the parodist may also choose to unmask and deflate other writers by
> using their works ironically as a temporary "word-mask" for the
> parodist. Even explicitly critical parody can make the comic discrep-
> ancy between the parodist's style and that of the target text into a
> weapon against the latter and at the same time refunction the target's
> work for a new and positive purpose within the parody in a manner
> which must make the parody's criticisms of the parodied text to
> some extent ambivalent. (51)

It is this creative and dialogic form of internal and metareferential parody
so typical of the romance that encases and reformulates narrative and adds
impetus to the novel.

The aim of this study is to re-insert the medieval chivalric romance into
a prehistory of the novel and underline an important trans-secular sense of
continuity in fiction. This modest aim, while it has no revolutionary intention or aspect, nevertheless runs counter to received ways of looking at the
romance in the context of later forms of the novel. Treating Cervantes as
the first author to make a break from the narrative past and embrace
textual modernity, most critics see the romance as everything the novel is
not. This is at least partly on account of the fact that we read the prologue
to *Don Quixote* too literally and take Cervantes's playful exordium with

less than the pinch of salt he perhaps intended. In any case, we define the romance vis-à-vis the novel, when in fact there is something to be gained by reversing that polarity. As we list the founders of the novel—Cervantes, Rabelais, Sterne, Fielding—parody is a strong part of their appeal and delineation as framers of the novel. If parody is a defining trait for them, why can it not be for the romance? There is a compelling argument for using the same parodic turn that we use to define the novel in order to scrutinize those texts that preceded these great works of the modern era. Why not look at the novel as an outgrowth of the romance and use the same yardstick to measure the romance's contribution to literary history— seeing at the least a continuity of fundamental techniques that, while they blossomed in later periods, were an inherent part of the internal develop- ment of narrative fiction. In short, literary history depicts the novel as somehow reacting to the romance, as if the novel corrects romance, and one can easily ignore the way in which the romance reacted to its own evolving narrative and consequently shaped its literary fortune as it de- regulated itself into the novel. In essence the romance contains prototypes of all the ironic, self-reflexive, and parodic properties we find so attractive in the modern novel.

Focusing on one line of novelistic development in a series of lesser- known works that predate *Don Quixote* and are related to it, and that have too long been absent from histories of the novel, I propose that these romances exemplify crucial aspects of a model for the novel. Other groups of medieval romances could and would prove equally illustrative, but the works I have chosen represent at least four degrees of separation from *Don Quixote* and a direct, if tortuous, genealogy of Cervantes's aberrant knight.

Despite its status as a genre of fiction that eschews cataloguing realistic detail, the medieval romance has much to offer critics as the prehistory of the novel if we look at its internal capacity for regeneration through parody. Because it offers no complete sense of realism, the romance is too easily ignored. Measuring its verisimilitude (or lack of it) is not sufficient grounds to limit its inclusion or even exclude it from the history of the novel. While there is no denying that medieval fiction privileges descriptive modes that veer away from recounting the minutiae of lived experience, it contributes to the history of the novel by establishing and experimenting with other literary patterns that prove to be the prime movers of fiction (the quest for self and other, trial and reward, love and loss, etc.). Impor- tant among them in romances from Chrétien to David Lodge's *Small World* or A. S. Byatt's *Possession* is the tendency from the very beginning to encode and integrate self-conscious literary parody into its narrative

workings. This expresses itself as situational irony, as the parody of character and action, and as a more convoluted process of inter-referentiality:
a playful intertextuality emerges (itself a concrete expression of ironic distancing from within a text even before we perceive its interaction with
other works) that shows the absorption, transformation, and continuity of
narrative development. The effect is such that parody—and particularly
the self-conscious literary variety—stands as a cipher for the process of
generic change and evolution. While the clever treatment of narrative elements and conventions is one manifestation of creative parody, the other
more literal kind can be found in the many lists and prominently positioned intertexts that flag the reader's attention and reveal the author's
experimental strategies and influences.

Such a topic could fill many volumes: included here are but a few representative works, chosen because they are part of an exclusive genealogy
that leads to the creation of *Don Quixote*. Chapter 2 will sketch the genesis
of the parodic tendency in Chrétien de Troyes's works, most particularly in
the *Chevalier de la Charrette*, and more generally in the Old French tradition. It is hard to say something about Chrétien that has not already been
covered by the many excellent studies devoted to his extant works, such is
his value in contemplating the French tradition. Moving on to the generation that succeeded him, many texts suggest themselves as inheritors of his
narrative mantle: the romance is not a monolithic genre, but a most elastic
form in the thirteenth century. However, chapters 3 and 4 will voyage
south and reflect on how the spirit of Old French chivalric fiction informed
the small but significant corpus of Occitan narrative. The reasons are more
than justifiable: they are too often omitted from general considerations of
the romance, and they have the advantage of being uniquely situated as a
part of the French tradition while remaining outside it. Their geographic
and political distance makes them vital reflections of the literary codes of
the day, which find themselves innately understood—and yet translated—
by Occitan authors.

The only two full-length examples of chivalric romance to have survived illustrate perfectly twin lines of parodic development: in *Jaufre* (c.
1225, the only full-length Arthurian romance, and known to Cervantes in
translation form as *Tablante de Ricamonte*), we find an inventive parody
of Chrétien's *Conte du Graal* that internalizes the mechanism of the chivalric
romance and takes its comic and parodic potential to the limits. Mean-
while, in the *Roman de Flamenca* (c. 1225–50) at the opening wedding
banquet, the reader quite literally ingests, in list form, the entire tradition
of Old French narrative. The comic conspiracy within the text and the

parodic distance between the myriad sources it satirizes are a model of narrative ingenuity and renewal. One form of parody operates on the inside, showing how the medieval romance continually "tropes" itself through convention — perhaps one could coin a term "endotropy" to describe its interior workings. The other form of parody works generically beyond the romance and could be considered both intertextual and metatextual in a similar double movement. At the same time, the word metatextual suggests lofty, ideal, and exterior heights inappropriate to the very practical working of this outward-looking generic form of intertextual parody. Perhaps it could be better considered as somehow "exotropy," which one might define as related to a form of intertextuality that goes beyond quotation or inter-referentiality, but rather sets up a dialogue not just of content, but of self-conscious form: it is a more complex generic intertextuality of pattern. Gérard Genette treats such works as hypertexts, a form of bricolage (*Palimpsestes*), that form in texts like *Don Quixote* a hypogenre.

In addition to omitting the romance, histories of the novel often forget France. Even French histories of the novel often forget the medieval romance, and those that do remember it all but forget Occitania. The contribution of the troubadours to medieval poetics has been justly rerecognized in recent decades, but acknowledgment of southern France's small but important contribution to the evolution of romance has just begun to be more fully made (Huchet, *Le Roman occitan médiéval* and Limentani, *L'Eccezione narrativa*).

Chapter 5 examines the encyclopedic Catalan romance *Tirant lo Blanc* (1490), a work much admired by Cervantes and Hispanists for its experimental blending of romance and more realistic fiction. This work manifests and generates a deeper complicity between the two strands of intertextual parody. Mario Vargas Llosa, in a much quoted eulogy, considers its main architect, Joanot Martorell, an important figure in the history of the novel: "es el primero de esa estirpe de suplantadores de Dios — Fielding, Balzac, Dickens, Flaubert, Tolstoi, Joyce, Faulkner — que pretenden crear en sus novelas una 'realidad total,' el más remoto caso de novelista todopoderoso, desinteresado, omnisciente y ubicuo" [the first of that lineage of God-supplanters — Fielding, Balzac, Dickens, Flaubert, Tolstoy, Joyce, Faulkner — who try to create in their novels an all-encompassing reality, the earliest case of an all-powerful, disinterested, omniscient, and ubiquitous novelist] ("Carta de batalla" 2–3).[1] Just as *Tirant* conveys a form of verisimilitude and veers toward historical reality, it turns away from it too by revealing a heightened parodic consciousness of its own fictionality:

Tirant absorbs brilliantly the literary patterns of Chrétien and parodies his *Lancelot* among other Old French romances, particularly *Gui de Warwic*, anticipating *Don Quixote* in an ingenious tour de force that pits realistic representation against fictional technique. Quite simply, what emerges from the reconstruction of this one line of novelistic development is one aspect of how the medieval romance continually questions and reinvents itself.

The chapters dealing with specific works take the form of focused close readings and are unashamedly selective. In order to justify them, however, it is necessary to situate the subsequent arguments in the context of the history of the novel.

The History of the Novel and the Movement Toward History

> The novel's spirit is the spirit of continuity: each work is an answer to preceding ones, each work contains all the previous experience of the novel. But the spirit of our time is firmly focused on a present that is so expansive and profuse that it shoves the past off our horizon and reduces time to the present moment only. Within this system the novel is no longer a *work* (a thing made to last, to connect the past with the future) but one current event among many, a gesture with no tomorrow.
>
> Milan Kundera, *The Art of the Novel* 18–19

Medievalists need little persuading of the intrinsic value of medieval narrative: it is an unquenchable source of innovation and interest, an intriguing, varied, complex, and enigmatic corpus so vast and diverse that its potential for interpretation seems limitless. Even canonical works find themselves contested with each critical twist, especially with the current wave of interest in gender and critical studies. While medievalists find rich veins for interpretation and would have little problem conceptualizing the romance as the distant ancestor of the novel, it is all the more surprising, then, that the same enthusiasm for the romance is not shared by historians of the novel: whatever the nature of the alterity celebrated by period specialists, medieval literature constitutes an "other" quickly dispatched as irrelevant in many accounts of the novel's genesis.

Medieval literature is treated for the most part as an inconvenient and formulaic hiatus between the classical tradition and modernity. The reasons for this treatment are many and legion, but concern the intersection of history, realism, and narrative: historians of the novel tend to erect a barrier between the Enlightenment and what preceded it. Many of the most influential theorists, on the other hand, ground their definition of the novel in nineteenth-century epistemology and redefine it according to sociocultural criteria that highlight the symbiosis between industrial society and literary production.

First and foremost, the history of the novel mostly styles itself an anglocentric category with great European ancestors, and because English medieval narrative is dominated by a few atypical great works, its role is downplayed, since on the surface it lacks the larger corpus and broader styles found in continental literature, particularly in French. At the same time, just as some of the greatest French medieval literature was written in England, by virtue of the same, some of the greatest medieval English literature was produced in French, as William Calin recently demonstrates in *The French Tradition*. In the critical xenophobia that seems to characterize the history of the novel, foreign literatures are just that, although rare works like *Don Quixote* are acknowledged as catalysts for change. The novel, as Ian Watt and Michael McKeon argue, puts down its definitive roots in the seventeenth and eighteenth centuries.[2] Other periods and works may aliment the modern novel, but it proves an unruly child that runs away from its parents and relatives and follows its own fortune by exploring the "real" world with seeming independence from its old fantasy-inspired basic model in the romance. While it disowns its forebears, it still inherits: even if the legacy is not always welcome, there are traits and mannerisms that betray a more distant past and ancestry. There is no process more easily identifiable in literary history than the famous urge to kill parents and identify with more distant literary generations: hence the dialogue between classicism and modernity was born. Cesare Segre expresses it thus: "We go back from *Don Quixote* to the twelfth-century *roman* by way of a series of oppositions which are at the same time signs of continuity. Literary history, as Shklovsky said, is the history of the successive murders of fathers, or attempts at reinstating uncles" ("What Bakhtin Left Unsaid" 25). Medieval literature becomes the estranged elderly relative whose eccentricities prove too unpredictable: once it appears troublesome, it is killed, disinherited, and pruned from the family tree. Accentuating the family ties that bind is an appropriate image when considering this modified form of genealogy, since after all, this is a quest for origins and originality.

Ian Watt highlights the crux of the matter when he discusses the change in use of the word *original*:

It is significant that the trend in favor of originality found its first powerful expression in England, and in the eighteenth century; the very word "original" took on its modern meaning at this time, by a semantic reversal which is a parallel to the change in the meaning of "realism." We have seen that, from the mediaeval belief in the reality of universals, "realism" had come to denote a belief in the individual apprehension of reality through the senses: similarly the term "original" which in the Middle Ages had meant "having existed from the first" came to mean "underived, independent, first-hand"; and by the time that Edward Young in his epoch-making *Conjectures on Original Composition* (1759) hailed Richardson as "a genius as well moral as original," the word could be used as a term of praise meaning "novel or fresh in character or style." (14)

It is vital to Watt's argument to resituate the novel's point of origin, and what better way to redefine novelistic "originality" than by delimiting it in stark contrast with the preceding stage in the evolutionary process. His claims about the special intellectual climate of the eighteenth century are entirely justified, but the redefinition of what went before is less easy to defend. He grounds the change in contemporary philosophical shifts related to realism. The medieval imagination, he argues, adhered "to a view of reality diametrically opposed to that of common usage—to the view held by the scholastic Realists of the Middle Ages that it is universals, classes or abstractions, and not the particular, concrete object of sense-perception, which are the true 'realities'" (11). Taken this way, the episte-mological reality of the Middle Ages was a universalist world of theoretical *signifiants* that held sway over the *signifiés* in the search for an originary truth always located beyond the thing-in-itself. This has obvious profound implications for the way that the subject positioned himself in relation to the sensory world. On one level, Watt argues persuasively that in the illumination of the Enlightenment, realism passes from the realm of the universal to the individual and thus to the concrete and particular. Consequently, the novel traduces a system of unmediated signifieds, back-grounding the larger universal reality. This swing in perspective simultaneously postulates a differently oriented subject whose concept of the big picture becomes radically different and conveniently creates a new authorial autonomy that makes a clean break with the past, now classed as a relatively unimaginative, stagnant tradition, concerned with large intangible categories that fail to relate to lived experience. Watt privileges realism as the prime narrative mode and measure of novelistic success, as many others have done since. This problematic concept of realism unaccountably and unevenly authenticates some works and summarily disbars others.

Watt's universal-versus-particular reasoning is original (in the modern sense) and convincing, and yet one wonders if it is possible to make such claims with real conviction beyond the realm of the theological and philosophical. Could medieval writers engaged in the composition of imaginative literature have been aware that they lived in an age of universals? Were they any more aware of writing within contemporary philosophical currents than writers now are? Is their undeniable originality not, somehow, still "original" in the later sense? After all, we live in an era of philosophical and literary postdeconstruction postmodernism, and in spite of the ubiquitousness of that ideology, many kinds of literature—particularly popular works—remain blindly insouciant of its intellectual grip. Perhaps our notion of originality is too founded on Watt's modern model and the additional cult of authorial personality. The distinct lack of medieval author figures (beyond the colossi of Chrétien de Troyes, Dante, Chaucer, Boccaccio, etc.) hinders acceptance of a more broadly conceived medieval narrative ingenuity. A perceived lack of originality might be linked to their self-effacement or strategic concealment within the works they wrote, and our distance from the author is yet another aspect of the *Verfremdungseffekt* that seems to have estranged the medieval romance from the history of the novel.

Watt follows a well-worn path determined to make literary history mirror history in orienting the medieval period as a series of absolutes or unchanging categories. He speaks of the "substantial social homogeneity of mediaeval Christendom" (61) for example, versus the teeming socioeconomic diversity of the New World of the post-Enlightenment era. Medieval Christendom embraced a vast sociotemporal, cultural, economic, and political space that was driven by more than just one philosophical abstraction. The "reality" is, surely, that medieval society conceived of itself in ways as complex as our own and not as the wrong end of a teleological journey. The imposition of a feudal political society in Europe seems to confirm the existence of a single two-dimensional model controlling the "realities" of life, but what Watt terms "the unified world picture of the Middle Ages" (31) is as much an illusion as his contrasting a "vast transformation of Western civilization since the Renaissance . . . a developing but unplanned aggregate of particular individuals having particular experiences at particular times and at particular places" (31). Such comfortable forms of periodization only work in retrospect: medieval writers cannot have had such an integrated and monolithic view of themselves, even if their literary sensibility differed tangibly from that of the eighteenth century. There can be little doubt that the literary preoccupations of medieval authors are less bound with verisimilitude and more focused on the representation of the symbolic order, but one could contest the idea that because they do not for the most part record the minutiae of daily life that they have no role to play in the history of the novel. On account of its remoteness in time, an ideological sense of closure has been conjured for the Middle Ages in part to make it the scapegoat of modernity, and it has too often been the victim of the need to create a conceptual dialectic. Such a tendency is to the fore in the postmodern era, when modernity itself has precipitated its own demise through an anticipatory use of prefixes, leaving critical thought poised intriguingly on the edge of the interpretational abyss.

The ability of the medieval period to attract sweeping and general statements is unparalleled. In his account of the novel's rise to prominence, Hubert McDermott devotes nine of some two hundred pages to the medieval contribution to the genre and begins by claiming: "It is a commonplace of literary history to describe medieval romance as the prototype of the modern novel, yet this is surely a case where the commonplace is inaccurate" (96). It is hard to find any supporters of this erstwhile commonplace who treat it in any depth, and even fewer are nonmedievalists. He describes the "utter moribundity" (96) of the English narrative in the late fifteenth and early sixteenth centuries, stating that literature "was only rescued from imminent death by the introduction of the Spanish picaresque and newly translated Greek romances" and concluding that "in spite of implications to the contrary, a study of the many histories of the English novel supports the suggestion that medieval romance played little or no part in the development of the novel" (96).

Cataloguing the negative opinions about the medieval romance as a predecessor of the novel can only compound the clouded view that it played no significant role. McDermott cites the example of Ernest Baker's *The History of the English Novel* and finds himself baffled at the number of pages devoted to cataloguing the chronological precursors of Richardson and Fielding.[3] Referring to Baker's work and his claim that Chrétien is an important modernizer of fiction and works "much in the style of the modern novelist," McDermott comments that "Baker's method is quite suspect, suggesting as it does, a teleological basis for the development of the English novel" (97). It is true that Baker does not always know what to make of the many narrative antecedents he includes, but his anthology has the virtue of recognizing a clear thread of narrative dynamism and a sense of experimentation. On McDermott's charge of unnecessary teleology, removing the medieval period and jumping straight back to antiquity merely constructs a different telos for the genre, and the notion of constructing literary history remains perforce a genealogical affair, but with more freedom to choose one's relatives.

Baker is enlightened in his ability to connect Chrétien de Troyes and romance authors pre-Cervantes as the forerunners of the novel. Indeed, this study has the same ambition: for if, as McDermott claims, the English narrative was snatched from mediocrity by *Don Quixote,* then Chrétien has earned his place among those authors deemed originators of the novel. The innovatory spirit of Cervantes goes beyond the mere reversal and overt debunking of convention. To the contrary, his genius is to have realized the full potential of the courtly romance. Cervantes crosses the boundary of the chivalric romance by setting it in an environment far from the fantasy landscape of the *roman courtois,* but the essential narrative ingredients remain the same. His ingenious gentleman is a reengineering of prior tradition—and by no means a complete break from it.

McDermott's particular objection is based on a second damaging "universalist" assumption about the Middle Ages based on historical generalities. Using Richard Southern's *The Making of the Middle Ages* as an unwitting ally, McDermott notes the generic frontier separating epic from romance as underlining a change from "localism" to "universalism" (98; Southern's terms) in the history of ideas, using a rationale much like Watt's contrasting the medieval period and the eighteenth century. Establishing this internal divide turns medieval narrative on itself in the creation of a false distinction: the line between epic or *chanson de geste* and romance is frequently blurred, and while it is true that the romance takes over a position of prominence in the high and later Middle Ages, the two are not mutually exclusive categories and continue to coexist and cross-fertilize. McDermott sees a corresponding transitional period in Greek society, but finds the medieval age inferior because it seems to last one hundred years rather than five (99). Duration need not be commensurate with lasting quality of literary change, and yet this is the implication when he finds the incubation period of the romance insufficient to produce any useful progress. Citing Friedrich Heer's *The Medieval World,* McDermott applies the notion of boundaries more generally and asserts that Heer's work "completes the picture when he speaks of the Middle Ages in terms of 'open' and 'closed' societies" (98). Heer, he states, describes the "open" societies of the twelfth century and their open borders that were later to become "iron curtains" (98; Heer's term), and he concludes that "[i]t could be argued that medieval society 'opened' much too soon from a purely literary point of view—that epic was still only developing when it was forced, by external influences, to pass prematurely into the romantic stage. Many of the defects discernible in medieval romance could possibly be attributed to this premature transformation" (99). McDermott hints at a curious collusion between politico-economic geography and literary imagination, and whereas one might have imagined openness to be a positive, modern trait, here it leads to the premature deformed birth of a paradoxically "closed" literary genre doomed from the start to unfavorable comparison with antiquity:

> The Middle Ages were not quite as "open" as the Hellenistic age, obviously: there was no such expansion in education in the Middle Ages, and no consequent development of a reading public. Huizinga describes the retention of verse in medieval romances as an indication of one of the "more primitive stages of literature," but it also indicates a correspondingly primitive stage of development in the society for which it was written. (*The Autumn of the Middle Ages* 99)

Far from contributing to the prehistory of the novel, the Middle Ages are presented as positively prehistoric. This reductive move illustrates an extreme case of the censure to which the medieval romance has been subject and goes as far as condemning the cultural context that produced it. Scholars of the troubadours and *trouvères* and of narrative poets from Marie de France to Jean Renart and Jean de Meun do not recognize the eleventh, twelfth, and thirteenth centuries as a time of primitive forms and unsophisticated literary decline.

Mcdermott treats the apotheosis of medieval romance, between 1150 and 1250, as a mere flash in the pan, after which there was no literary creativity beyond derivative "reworking old themes and materials" (99). From decline he passes to full-blown generic degradation and literal decomposition, proof of which is seen in the survival of medieval romances in chapbook form. Their indiscriminate fate is "a history of their reduction to the nursery, i.e. to become the reading matter of children" (103), so that if the *matière* had any lasting influence at all on later authors, it was through the half-remembered fantastic stories of childhood. An admission that the medieval romance might have served a useful purpose in preparing receptive terrain for the arrival of *Don Quixote* comes too late to save the genre from almost complete dismissal, especially as McDermott maintains with Robert Kellogg that medieval romances are not romances at all (101; Scholes and Kellogg 248–9). Kellogg defines romance as an autonomously generated text that differs in origin and character from one driven by "traditional" or "historical" narrative, requiring a specific concept of authorship. One necessitates the apparently spontaneous generation of plot; the other can be seen as lacking in comparison, even devoid of creativity. Kellogg's definition rejoins Watt's notion of originality: if novels, and even protonovels, are to be novel in the sense of innovatory, they must appear to distance themselves from historical ties. Accordingly, Greek romance is original in the renewed sense, and medieval romance is not. Its adherence to *mythos* and to traditional sources disbars it from the select club of literary history, and despite Kellogg's claims that "[n]o value judgement is implied" (McDermott 101), a system of literary values inevitably emerges from his analysis. The reader is meant to perceive *Daphnis and Chloé* as more innovatory than most medieval authors, and thus according to Kellogg, what makes *The Canterbury Tales* original is the framing narrative: the content reverts to traditional noninnovatory narrative. Such reasoning is problematic, as are the claims that "[a] traditional story is not 'a new thing'" (McDermott 101) and that medieval authors were not "free," but bound in the constraints of adaptation.

The tragic flaw in this schema is to assume that innovation and adaptation cannot be consonant and that the history of the novel has limited parameters that prescribe novelty and proscribe more subtle changes: that it is a question of whether we deal with prose or poetry, with tales that are fantastic or more realistic, derived from the individual imagination or from a more collective source of narrative inspiration. Rather than back-forming the medieval romance to find a product that cannot compete with our perception of what a modern narrative should be, there must be an alternative way of seeing it for what it was rather than what has been made of it with hindsight. What can be interpreted as worn tradition was part of a broader metatextual experiment in literature and was anything but hackneyed in context.[4]

Medieval narrative frequently betrays a preoccupation with lineage and genealogy, albeit in the form of a well-connected hero or a sense of continuity of *auctoritas*, which could be interpreted as a motif of exclusivity, inbreeding, or even as a potential indicator of an incestuous bankruptcy of creative topoi. Yet the fascination with genealogy also betrays a consciousness of literary pedigree—an adherence to a conceptual, coded whole that does not necessarily exclude the possibility of originality. It was more a case that medieval authors regarded the raw material of plot as the basic clay from which an original work was made. Novelty lay in the artful embellishment and polishing of fundamental structure, as Bruckner maintains in *Narrative Invention* and as C. S. Lewis demonstrates in *The Discarded Image* (198–215, esp. 210). McDermott acknowledges Lewis's famous comparison between literature and architecture, but interprets it in a more negative spirit than was probably intended.

Lewis compares the medieval author to a cathedral builder, involved in contributing to a design that he will never complete. His role is in a much larger plan, spanning a construction period substantial enough to produce different styles in different places, the general impact of which cannot be anticipated along the way. This does not mean that a distinct style is lacking: with each successive addition an accommodation is made with the existing edifice. Lewis's example is Chaucer's use of Boccaccio, "working over" material to produce a work that is neither a translation nor an original and that "cannot be ascribed to a single author" (210). This is a form of metatextual dialogism, one continually in play in the medieval act of literary creation. Here, in the creative repetition of textual models and themes, lies a positive part of the alterity, as Jauss and Haidu would have it, of the Middle Ages ("Alterity and Modernity"; "Making It [New]").

Lewis maintains that in the Middle Ages, using completely original ideas would be considered defeatist in literary terms. The point he goes on to make is crucial in assessing the degree and nature of transformation within the romance, when he says that the medieval writers' "abdication of originality" paradoxically highlights their own creativity, which is in their use of sources and convention, and how these are built on and imperceptibly modified. Medieval authors are translators, adapters, commentators, and original authors at the same stroke, and this is a sign of their polyvalency rather than a lack of ability or impetus. There is a process of transformation executed as much through convention as through consciously reacting against it as later periods seem to do. Radical progress toward the modern novel may be manifest in a revised form of "originality," but even the conservative, structured nature of medieval romance produces a slow and internal transformation that nevertheless constitutes literary evolution.

It is incontestable that medieval fiction cannot provide much that is akin to what seems so crucial in the novel's development in later centuries. As many have noted, particularly Erich Auerbach, medieval narrative is class-bound (*Mimesis* 139). Watt remarks that the casuistry of courtly love "could not itself provide the kind of connective or structural theme which the novel required . . . it belonged to an amoral world, a social vacuum where only the individual existed and where the external world . . . was completely forgotten" (136). It could be argued that love and adherence to or divergence from moral/amoral codes of behavior remain central issues in later periods of novelistic development. Moreover, beyond small pockets of insight to be found in the romance, formal realism in medieval literature is to be found most in contingent nonnovelistic genres, particularly the theater and the *fabliau,* where it is customarily consonant with crudity and anticourtliness. Watt makes a similar dialectic of love and realism, concluding that there is no realism in courtly love and no courtly love in realism. The social exclusivity of courtly romance also lends to its exclusion from the history of the novel, which although it has not always been the most democratic of genres is perceived as such, thanks to the identification that the nineteenth century makes between realism and authenticity. Beyond such binary constructs, however, there is more.

The History of the Novel and the Movement Toward Realism

Ian Watt represents the history of the novel and the sociohistorical exclusion of the romance, and Mikhail Bakhtin reflects the critical turn toward realism as a means of authenticating the form of the novel. The realism of the nineteenth century entails more than a refusal to idealize life: it seeks to give an accurate representation of life not just in verisimilar description, but also in language. As most theories of the novel emerge from the period when realistic fiction was at its height, it is no surprise that its parameters have been the novel's benchmark.

In his collection of essays, *The Dialogic Imagination,* Bakhtin seeks to define the novel and succeeds precisely because he offers a nonhistory of the genre, one which derives paradoxically from the insufficiency of critical attempts to formulate a definition of the novel: "the experts have not managed to isolate a single definite, stable characteristic of the novel—without adding a reservation, which immediately disqualifies it altogether as a generic characteristic" ("Epic and Novel" 8). The novel's one area of stability is that it constitutes "the sole genre that continues to develop, that is as yet uncompleted . . . the birth and development of the novel as a genre takes place in the full light of the historical day" (3). He establishes a dialectic between the perceived openness of modernity and the closure of antiquated literary genres, particularly that of the epic. Bakhtin constructs the novel as anticanonical and marginal, while the epic is a fixed "official" genre with a rigid sense of hierarchy expressed in a monolithic view of language.[5] The novel absorbs the real world and mimics it through the imminence and fragmentary nature of language, refracted into layers referred to by Bakhtin as polyglossia and heteroglossia.[6] Linguistic realism becomes the indicator of stability, a common denominator of form. As he explains in "Discourse in the Novel," the novelist "ventriloquates" (299) the stratified language of various social, cultural, and professional groups, rendered more complex in turn by the socioideological dimensions of individual characters, and conveys something of the verbal immediacy of daily life. He finds prose an ideal vehicle for experimentation, in contrast to poetry, which is formally as well as linguistically closed to an intricate mixing of registers. Central to the success of the narrative are the concepts of polyphony and dialogism, with their fragmentary play of ideology and ideolect.

Bakhtin's theory of language resembles Barthes's codes, as expressed in *S/Z*. Barthes's discourse analysis breaks down language into codes in order to reveal an innate plurality, a *degré zéro* of reading (to borrow from another of his titles) that allows the reader to reconstruct or rewrite a given text with an awareness of its diversity of meaning and a sense of the fragile interrelation of connotation and denotation. The network of codes he proposes (proairetic, hermeneutic, semic, cultural, and symbolic) reveal the richness and interpretive potential of the narrative (28). Although different, Barthes's codes create a sense of polyphony along alternative axes.

Both Barthes and Bakhtin find such stratifying tendencies most apparent in the nineteenth century because the intersection of realism, history, and language are most obvious. Historical and linguistic verisimilitude conspire to exclude other modes of discourse, poetry chief among them, and the more subtle interplay of registers and lexical choice. Another criterion can be found in the fact that the novel makes distinct use not just of language, but of time and space (Bakhtin, "Forms of Time and Chronotope in the Novel"). Moreover, Bakhtin argues that the novel derived its energy from an innate ability to absorb, parody, and transform and to subject itself to generic scrutiny (6), identifying the Hellenistic period, the early modern period, and the eighteenth century as times when the novel rose to prominence among other literary genres. These periods of acceleration often coincide with the resurgence of parody, since it encodes in a most visible way a process of reaction, hybridization, and experimentation with language and convention.

All but omitted from the consideration of novelistic discourse, medieval romance earns a mere parenthesis in Bakhtin's analysis of time and chronotope. Given the similarity in the way space and time create the dimensions and tone of both Greek and medieval romance, it is somewhat surprising that he champions one and omits the other; moreover, since he recognizes the significance of medieval romance as a component in *Don Quixote,* and therefore as an important factor in the development of the novel, his passing acknowledgment of most of the genre is noticeable.

After developing a dependence on specific spatial and temporal coordinates as the major defining trait of romance and the novel, Bakhtin's sin of omission raises important questions, some of which are addressed by Cesare Segre.[7] He notes that although Bakhtin mentions some romance texts, he entirely passes over mainstream northern French romance: his prime example is Wolfram von Eschenbach's *Parzival,* hardly a text representative of medieval romance as a whole. A few texts are quickly glossed over, the most notable among them the *Divine Comedy, Piers Plowman,* and *Aucassin et Nicolette* (which I will also use as an example of the positive valencies of the romance). Interestingly, Segre sees this not as the result of selective reading on Bakhtin's part, but of the parameters of his critical agenda: Bakhtin's "limited treatment" (23) of medieval romance derives from the privileging of one kind of development over another, best illustrated by his discussion of Socratic dialogue and related texts as distinct from Greek romance. The former exemplifies the innovative and experimental dialogism central to his theory of literature, the latter a more fixed set of narrative rules. Segre points out that Bakhtin's schema must perforce give more weight to the first of these elements, since his view of the novel is shaped by the modern evolution of the genre: "it would be easy to demonstrate that Bakhtin is thinking not of the novel's past but of its future; he is thinking not of its codification, but of its transformations" (24). This, Segre says, would lead him naturally to privilege the atypical works of the Middle Ages, culminating in the writings of Rabelais: indeed, of his list *Aucassin et Nicolette* represents the unique example of *chantefable,* while Dante and Langland each make a striking and distinctive use of the dream-frame and vision, and other texts, like the *Mule sans bride,* represent the more overtly parodic aspects of courtly convention.

While he is right to signal their experimental contributions to literary history, Bakhtin bypasses many key works that form part of the great chain of novelistic being and is guilty of the process of back-forming the romance, when at the same time we might analyze the ways in which it looked to its own present and future. The very dialogism of the texts he chooses as examples derives in part from their relationship to a more conventional corpus, from their struggle to emerge from a surrounding narrative context that is one side of the dialogue. In fact there are many ways in which narrative dialogism makes itself manifest, and parodic intertextuality is one particular by-product of medieval textual dynamism that seems particularly successful in establishing a plurality of voices. The plurality may not always resemble the distinct sociocultural stratification announced by Bakhtin and critiqued by Segre, but it is visible on closer inspection.

Bakhtin's divide between the Socratic dialogues and Greek romance is defined by Segre as "polyphony rather than narrative" (26). We might otherwise determine it as an opposition of content and form: as Segre writes, the former will lead to "a discontinuous, frequently interrupted series" of texts in the development of the novel, while the roman "develops, by means of its transformations, uninterruptedly and coherently to the present day" (26). Bakhtin concentrates on the former rather than the latter: polyphony, heteroglossia, and dialogism are central to Bakhtin's understanding of the novel. However, any comprehensive account of the evolution of content cannot ignore form, and Segre signals the importance of considering form as the more stable stratum beneath. In the final analysis, the two are interdependent, as are the novel and the romance. Segre also urges a redefinition of what constitutes polyphony; perhaps under the influence of the modern novel, Bakhtin seeks it only in the most obvious places. Dialogism and heteroglossia are a part of medieval literature, and of the romance, but exist in more hidden recesses.

Segre's analysis of polyphony serves the dual functions of "separating the author's voice from those of the characters" and "representing the linguistic stratification of the society being described" (26). What Segre identifies are many of the qualities we might assign to irony—implying distance and dissonance—and also parody in its narrow and broader senses. Elements of self-critique in the romance provide a doubling of central voice, a counterpoint that we might consider as polyphonic. It constitutes a simultaneous separation of language along vertical and horizontal planes: the two intersect, as Segre says, but more rarely in the Middle Ages than in other periods. The same polyphony creates a potential screen between author and subject that he can choose to preserve or remove: he can identify with his subject or critique it from a safe distance, although "this implicit polemic, which is generally linked to the social structure, is far from being exploited by all writers" (27). Segre rightly sees polyphony subtly at work in the author's strategy of distancing himself from his characters, perhaps the most striking element in Chrétien's romances.[8] At the same time there are other distances to be similarly calibrated: between author and setting and between the horizon of expectation and convention. There are strong grounds for arguing that the stratified discourses of romance also constitute a polyphonic element, but they are not cut cleanly across sociopolitical lines.

Chaucer, Langland, and Boccaccio provide examples of how this potential parodic space can be used to full effect. They also use stratified language to a greater extent than romance can—although there are notable exceptions, such as Jean de Meun's *Roman de la Rose,* where there is a very clear sense of polyphony represented in the competing discourses and points of view of characters like la Vieille, Genius, Reason, and Nature— themselves in turn the intertextual embodiment of another set of clashing worldviews, philosophies, and discourses. Among contingent genres, the fabliau strives to counter the rarified voice of the aristocratic ideal and open literature to the "real" world. Lyric genres, particularly the *pastourelle* (which Adam de la Halle dramatizes successfully in the *Jeu de Robin et Marion*), flirt with an obvious limited form of polyphony, one which satirizes courtly language through largely innocuous parody. Individual works also challenge the seeming rigidity of the romance from beyond its perimeters, but in general the obvious class rather than linguistic stratifications of the medieval canon limit or slow transformation through the introduction of new, realistic "social" registers. At the same time there are moves in the modern multivocal direction, as analysis of the works of Rutebeuf attests.

Bakhtin deals with medieval literature in a very general way. While what he says about the limited register of the roman courtois fits the schema up to a point, many texts are omitted that do make allowance for heteroglossia he wishes to find. One might consider, for example, texts that manage to deploy a mixture of languages and registers, or hybrid romances that make the most of the disjuncture between lyric and narrative. Continuations and cycles and works that recycle a familiar cast of characters in new sets of adventures are other forms of polyphony in the way that they reinscribe and dialogize the works that form their point of departure.

Bakhtin uses a simplified schema to propose that literature is obliged to evolve via one of two conduits: the first involves the "descent" into heteroglossia by some works, while others "ascend" toward the same goal ("Discourse in the Novel" 259–422; Segre 27). Change was naturally unlikely to alter dramatically the roman courtois via the ascending path from lower linguistic registers to a higher plane on account of its original social elitism and exclusivity, although, as we shall see, texts like the Occitan *Jaufre* and *Flamenca* incorporate successfully the language and conventions of more "realistic" fabliau-type narratives.

More frequently, the exclusive strata of literary language broadened from lofty beginnings to include lower levels. Segre pinpoints the locus and source of change, when it eventually comes:

> Linguistic and social tension as well as the parodic tendency, no longer limited to "carnivalized" works, are to become evident and even decisive at the exact moment when the romance widens its field of interest to a larger social milieu and opens itself up to the disinherited, the pariahs, and, above all, that bourgeois class which is soon to be the herald of innovation. (28)

It is not the dissolution of the genre, but the rise of the mercantile classes that alters the literary and linguistic rates of exchange, often by the agency of parody—or as lesser texts like *Richars li biaus* attest, through the encoding of economic discourse and overt consideration of monetary value (as opposed to the idealizations of wealth that decorate the first wave of chivalric romance). Both the Occitan *Jaufre* and Jean Renart's *Roman de la Rose* seem to confirm a revalorization of romance language in a subtle change in registers and implied audience, conveying a sense of the opening of romance to bourgeois aesthetics.

The *Roman de Flamenca* also supports Segre's assertion. Although the beginning and end of the roman are missing, the initial wedding and closing tournament place the work squarely in the realm of the conventional romance. Appearances are deceptive, since sandwiched between them lies a parody of courtly literature that finds its natural setting in the exterior world of the bourgeoisie: the inn, church, and bathhouse of the spa town of Bourbon. While the major characters remain essentially part of the aristocracy, they function in a setting that is too quotidian to allow other elements of the romance to be transplanted with them, or function successfully when they are. Gone is the component of knightly adventure: chivalry is marginal, restricted to a narrative frame, and the central adventure is an amorous one. A Chrétien-style hero evolves easily into a charming, comically devious Ovidian lover. Magic, fantasy, and the mysterious Arthurian otherworld are absent, except in the many descriptions of literary works within the text. The romance persists as a set of implied conventions just as it does in *Don Quixote*, but with essential modifications. The action of *Flamenca* is close to the model of chivalric romance, but noticeably distanced from many of its conventions. In its sensual treatment of love, as in its setting, it is simultaneously closer to realism than its model. A particular feature demonstrating its distance from, and debt to, the canon of courtly literature is the inclusion of a list of courtly works purportedly performed at the wedding banquet of the heroine and Archimbaut. Combining the transposed setting, the parodying of the conventions of *fin'amor*, and the inclusion of the literary catalogue, *Flamenca* represents a departure from convention while at the same time unmistakably remaining part of the genre: through incorporation and parody, the anonymous author effects a transformation very similar to the process of literary change through absorption, adaptation, and parody described by Bakhtin.

Taking the process a stage further, *Tirant lo Blanc* also absorbs the chivalric romance in its conventional aspect, establishing a model that Martorell then redesigns with Tirant's wide-ranging adventures. The distance such texts establish from convention, while incorporating prior tradition as part of their structure, constitutes a form of dialogism and a layering not of languages but of metatexts.

Segre highlights an important distance between author and text: it can also be argued that manifestations of this dialogic distancing are seen in the radical disjunction between characters and setting, and between generic expectations and what is found in the text. He also takes Bakhtin to task over his definition of what the action of a novel accomplishes. If the central motivation of the novel is to test the mettle of a hero beyond the rigid mold of the epic narrative, as Bakhtin maintains in "Discourse in the Novel," then Segre aptly reaffirms this as the pattern of medieval romance. Essentially, Segre's contribution to the study of the development of the novel is to realign the romance in a continuous thread of literary development, rather than to pass over it as a branchline of interest.

Segre's plea for the reinstatement of the romance makes perfect sense when we reconsider the kinds of texts foregrounded in this study. While it is true that atypical works accelerate the rate of change in a given genre and that the noncanonical forms enjoy greater potential for novelty, we should not ignore literary convention, as exhibited in the works of Chrétien, as a locus for innovation. For example, the delightful subversiveness of *Flamenca* stems from its seeming adherence to generic norms and its toying with them: the finest parodies bear the greatest resemblance to their original. Segre underlines the importance of reassessing the romance as a locus for innovation and warns against treating the corpus of the medieval romance as if it were modern: its conventionality is superficial, and subtle transformations are at work beneath the surface. As a form it is not the rigid and unremarkable genre that Bakhtin implies by his omission: it requires a different kind of analysis and a different scale of measurement. At the same time, there is a case for considering it as modern—or at the very least, we should not deem it as the very antithesis of modernity.

The Story of the Romance and the Movement Toward Parody

In suggesting the importance of parody in the broader context of the development of novelistic discourse, Bakhtin unwittingly brings out an important factor in the development of the romance and highlights one of the contributions it makes to the history of the novel:

> The novel parodies other genres (precisely in their role as genres); it exposes the conventionality of their forms and their language; it squeezes out some genres and incorporates others into its own pecu-

liar structure, reformulating and re-accentuating them. ("Epic and Novel" 5)

It becomes increasingly clear that the history of the romance is caught up in a self-critical movement toward parody, and this aspect of its generic evolution has been too long overlooked. Watt downplays its influence in Sterne for the very reason that is central to the main argument of this study and his:

> So assured, indeed, is this mastery of realistic presentation that, had it been applied to the usual purposes of the novel, Sterne would probably have been the supreme figure among eighteenth-century novelists. But, of course, *Tristram Shandy* is not so much a novel as a parody of a novel, and, with a precocious technical maturity, Sterne turns his irony against any of the narrative methods which the new genre had so lately developed. (291)

Putting aside the mysterious "usual purposes" of the novel (portraying realism, etc.), Sterne follows the medieval and Cervantine line of novelistic development very effectively. Why does the inclusion of parody in the novel make it seem the lesser, when the narrative energy of parody is at the heart of its success? Sterne illustrates the parodic continuity that constitutes the other alternative history of the novel. Citing Sterne as a forerunner of Joyce, Christopher Ricks writes:

> The innovation and the value of *Tristram Shandy* . . . [remind] us of what novelists are tempted to let us forget. That there is no such thing as a beginning, middle and end. That even in a minutely faithful novel, we cannot find out enough about people to be sure how they would behave. That all art is artifice. (24–5)

The alternate track that the history of the novel can take is not a Platonic trajectory toward modernity and authenticity, but a path that via ingeniously renewed conceits bolsters up the idea of fiction qua fiction and causes artist and reader to ponder how its limits might best be rejuvenated and exceeded—that the true destiny of imaginative fiction is to be essentially, and often comically, transgressive. In his famous essay on laughter, Henri Bergson formulates the famous equation that the comic represents "something mechanical encrusted on the living" (84). In the romance, the intrusion of parody disrupts the basic mechanism of convention and turns the reader not so much toward the real as to the "real" status of fiction—as artifice. That Cervantes is the first and greatest practitioner of the novel is beyond question, and one cannot contest Edwin Williamson's idea that

Don Quixote constitutes the "half-way house between medieval romance and the modern novel" (ix). Williamson recognizes in *Don Quixote* a point where the romance is taken beyond its limits toward something novel and novelistic; but as we shall see, the traits we find writ large in the Don's adventures are visible well before Cervantes's time.

The particular success of parody lies in the use of similarity of structure and form in order to ridicule content. This is true of *Don Quixote,* since for all that Cervantes claims to attack the chivalric romance, he uses its forms and conventions with verve and considerable pleasure. Thus, while it is undoubtedly a parody of chivalric romance, it nevertheless remains one. Similarly, it is possible to detect a literary momentum in the roman courtois that leads us directly to the techniques used by Cervantes: in the case of the medieval romance in its earliest manifestation, Chrétien de Troyes often has recourse to a constructive and dialogic form of interludic parody. In his idealized depiction of court life, the grandeur of the social model lends itself readily to self-mockery. The romance locates and encodes itself on the boundary between story and history, a fiction that swings toward and away from the historical forces that shaped it, like a pendulum alternately attracted and repelled by the competing poles of idealized fantasy and the realities of feudal society. Far from being rigid and repetitive, the forests, castles, and jousting arenas of the chivalric romance constitute a *champ experimental* for literary change and evolution. Looking closely at its outer trappings and inner workings, we can find a more problematized genre, more writerly than readerly, where competing layers of narrative struggle with one another to begin the slow but inexorable process that leads us to the modern novel. There is a form of dialogic imagination in the Middle Ages: not the same dialogue or voices, but nevertheless a true literary polyphony in an age that understood the strange beauty of the music that resulted. It is with Chrétien de Troyes that our reconsideration of courtly romance and the history of the novel continues.

2

Northern Exposure

Chivalry and Parody in the Old French Tradition

In its very elasticity the medieval romance carried the seeds of its own eventual undermining. The proliferation of romance cycles constitutes one centrifugal way that the genre came to parody itself, through a continual process of external erosion, as though an original painting were copied so often that a caricature resulted: hence *Don Quixote*. However, the romance came to parody itself in a second, centripetal way, manifest in its internal dynamics. In its essential decenteredness, the courtly world projects itself as out of kilter on many levels, subject to strange customs, idiosyncratic laws, and the whimsy of lords and kings. Its characters, situations, and settings lend themselves to extremes of behavior and emotions. Indeed, without wrongs to be righted, missing persons to be found, names to be revealed, and tournaments to be won, there is no narrative impulse. It is not a genre grounded in formulaic perfection, but in narrative attempts to achieve the illusion of wholeness that the form promises in its flawed way. Its internal striving mirrors the external experiment to push the boundaries of narrative adventure and of genre as far as they can go. The romance can also be characterized by a strong sense of genealogy and kinship, since heroes and secondary characters of the medieval romance are often related. They provide a sense of continuity akin to the narrative traits that carry over from work to work. In the later works included in this study, the influence one text has on another is manifest in the direct debt they owe in allusion and quotation: the inclusion of titles, paraphrases, and borrowed language clearly convey their interrelation. In the first wave of romances, when the patterns of romance are emerging and merging into a paradigm, such obvious borrowings, echoes, and reformulations cannot be as visible as they become later, but even among the romances of Chrétien, there is an apparent allusive and famous intertextual interconnectedness. It can be argued that the history of the novel is also a process of gradual, general bastardization—perhaps a suitable line of descent for a genre that began with an innate concern for its pedigree and legitimacy.

Simultaneously, even in its first manifestations in the works of Chrétien de Troyes, the world of romance is essentially flawed by its heroes as well as by those who threaten the court and become their adversaries. Imperfections are an obvious precondition for the motivation of the narrative, as the conflict between Méléagant and Lancelot in *Le Chevalier de la charrette* demonstrates. Romance always had a tragic dark side in need of redemption, and without the constant risk of invented perils and glamorous amorality, the genre risked losing its substance. It could set a good or bad example, and although there is little evidence of the contemporary reception of such romances, an extant account gives us one indication of their impact. Peter of Blois complains that: "Often in tragedies and other compositions of the poets or in the songs of jongleurs you will find descriptions of a man prudent, worthy, strong, amiable, and agreeable in all things. You will find also the account of the trials and injuries cruelly inflicted on him, just as actors *[histriones]* repeat certain tales about Arthur and Gangano . . . and Tristan, at which the hearts of the audience are stirred with compassion and pierced to the point of tears."[1]

Peter's description gives some indication of how courtly heroes evoked great sympathy and a sense of engagement from their receptive audience. Auerbach remarks that Peter is content to condemn the whole out of hand, finding no exemplary value in courtly virtue, merely distraction from higher contemplation.[2] We might recall other famous instances of reader-response in Dante's *Inferno* 5, where Francesca attributes her and Paolo's fall to reading a romance of Lancelot. Moral condemnation of romances persisted in Cervantes's time: having catalogued some of the serious attacks on secular literature, in "Cervantes y la caballeresca" Riquer lists some of the other charges accusing authors of ignorance, immorality, and of composing in dubious and mediocre style. Such protests also demonstrate the degree to which patterns of romance took hold in the imaginations of medieval and early modern Europe and produced dramatic effects on their audiences.

Some of the greatest romances are tragic—and the more tragic the more sublime—but the potential for tragedy in the romance has a lighter comic counterpart, exemplified by the extremely sophisticated courtly world portrayed by Chrétien and those like Jean Renart who followed. His model of chivalric virtue as embodied in Arthur's court is in constant need of secular and moral salvation and is preserved not by knightly role models, but through the agency of initially more unexpected heroes. Gauvain is an urbane paragon of chivalry (see Busby, *Gauvain in Old French Literature*), as many romances endure to prove; yet he suffers the ultimate indignity of comparison with Perceval in Chrétien's *Le Conte du graal*. Gauvain is always judged unfavorably, the suggestion being that the rustic *gallois* is worthier for all the former's polished manners and mastery of the courtly code. Likewise, Gauvain is never a match for Lancelot in the *Chevalier de la charrette*, when the better man turns out to be the one forced to ride in the ignominious cart and damage his reputation repeatedly to prove his love for Guenièvre. While there are more serious examples of his debasement, the cart endures as the best known symbol of his shame and complete submission to passion. In Chrétien's other romances neither Erec nor Yvain is an ideal courtly husband or champion, proving that the essence of many a hero lies in a capacity to be unheroic and therefore redeemable. Inability to behave according to the required standard is frequently the source of irony, if not outright comedy, and Chrétien's heroes both embody and undermine the ideal they represent.

Central to the development of the tragic or comic side of the hero are the very tenets that constitute the genre. But in order to establish these tenets it is first necessary to explore and define exactly what is meant by romance, or perhaps more accurately what is not meant by it. If defining the novel has lead to a constricting characterization of its temperament and generic boundaries, the problems in delimiting the romance prove equally great. W.T.H. Jackson points to the fundamental obscurity of the term. What began as a word distinguishing the vernacular from Latin soon came to describe "imaginative works in verse whose subject matter was felt to be fictional or non-historical."[3] Even at its outset, the definition is a broad one. As Jackson goes on to suggest, romance meant something more by the thirteenth century, when its recognizable octosyllabic rhyming couplet form acts as an umbrella for very different kinds of narrative. These cover areas of subject matter ranging from Brittany to the Orient, from heroic epics transplanted to French soil in the chansons de geste to the sophisticated, fantastic, and sentimentalized heroic ethic of the roman courtois. The romance further underwent the transition from ornate poetry to comparatively pedestrian prose, heralding the evolution from roman in the old sense to that approaching the modern. When poetic treatments had run the gamut of possibilities, prose lent new dimensions of expression, allowing for greater psychological depth, and new descriptive challenges that came with liberation from the constraints of the octosyllable. The roman of the thirteenth century became a far different, more experimental form, conjuring up such wide-ranging works as the *Roman de Tristan,* the *Roman de Renart,* the *Roman de la rose,* the *Roman de Thèbes,* the works of Chrétien, *La Queste del Saint Graal, Flamenca,* and *La Mort le Roi Artu,* each wildly different in tone and treatment.

On close inspection, generic distinctions do not appear to have the rigidity that we sometimes assign them, particularly in modern criticism outside the realm of medieval studies. In *The Art of Medieval French Romance,* Douglas Kelly makes an exhaustive survey of the inner workings of the genre and explores its extraordinary diversity and subtlety of design. Kelly claims that at its basic level "[t]he art of romance is a technique for inventing and elaborating narrative" (311), and its range and appeal derive from its ability to articulate themes, images, and stories in artfully interlaced configurations. For modern readers, he concludes:

> The problem . . . derives from the fact that the Middle Ages did not have a theoretical concept of genre; furthermore, no generally acknowledged terminological distinction was made between epic, romance, hagiography, and history in the time of the *romans d'antiquité.* . . . Beginning with Chrétien de Troyes, the elucidation of old matter and the discovery of chivalric truths in extraordinary marvels produced a kind of writing which united matter and truths in extraordinary narratives whose aristocratic heroes and heroines mirrored and exemplified prowess, love, or moral fortitude. (318)

We petrify the romance by categorizing it as being in opposition and subordinate to the novel, when in fact it manifests a similar plasticity. At least in form, the chivalric *roman d'aventure* and the saint's life had something in common with the most base fabliau in the eight-syllable line. Even when poetry gives way to prose, there is a continuity of subject matter and narrative development that unites the two forms. Also, as recent illuminating studies demonstrate, manuscript context reveals that the most disparate texts (for example, secular and religious or sacred and profane) often find themselves bound together in the same volumes, suggesting that medieval literature was more deregulated and less subject to rigid taxonomy than might be supposed. For all the encroachment of realism, the basic patterns and dynamism of the romance transcended historical determinacy and continued to shape narrative expectation long after the limited outlook of the feudal aristocratic class was forced to give way to a broader social spectrum.

The problem increases in complexity when we examine individual romances. Even the fundamental polarity between epic and courtly romance
dissolves in works like *Raoul de Cambrai* or *Huon de Bordeaux;* what
emerges in these and other like cases is a hybridization of forms bound in
a broader genus that leads us to conclude that the closer one comes to
individual texts, the more elusive their form becomes. It is essential to
remember the many guises of romance—its elasticity of form and the influence of different yet contingent genres (especially lyric poetry and shorter
narrative forms like the fabliau and the *lai*). The astounding absence of the
medieval romance from histories of the novel presumably has something
to do with the rejection of poetry as a medium for novelistic discourse, in
addition to other exclusionary factors like the degree of "realism" depicted. However, extant medieval romances provide ample proof that
while tastes evolved and changed, both media met the horizon of literary
expectation of their audience: the early history of the novel is less one of
exterior form than interior dynamic, whatever the vehicle or mode chosen.
In stretching back to the early Middle Ages to find novelistic origins, it is
useful to mention its relationship to the courtly epic, to which it is closely
linked.

The basic differences between epic and roman courtois as exemplified
by Chrétien may serve as a starting point in defining romance; these are
best summarized by Erich Auerbach in *Mimesis*. Comparing the works of
Chrétien with the *Chanson de Roland*, composed a mere seventy years
before, Auerbach notes the light, fluid narrative joined seamlessly in an
apparently casual, yet swiftly moving interlace. Gone is the weighty, rigid
form and lexicon of *Roland*; the craggy heroic landscape is transformed
into a more ethereal, yet civilized setting. Life-and-death battles are exchanged for more sophisticated and less desperate tests of endurance.
Commenting on the particular use of time in epic, Auerbach describes the
beginning of *Roland* and the plenitude of the seven years Charlemagne
spends in Spain, filled with losses and gains, as compared with the romance
Yvain, in which seven years elapse between the tale of Calogrenant and the
repetition of his adventure by the hero, and in the interim nothing has
changed. The modification in the concept of time that takes place from
epic to romance signals the removal of the epic distance and sense of history. As Paul Zumthor observes in "Genèse et évolution du genre," distance in time is replaced by exoticism of location and ambience. If the
courtly world seems artificial, it is perhaps because the epic setting had
become bankrupt as a source of poetic inspiration, as Zumthor notes:
"L'éthique implicite de l'épopée apparaît comme artificielle, sinon intol-
érable. Clercs et chevaliers instruits aspirent à une sorte de désengagement

de la parole poétique" [The implicit ethics of the epic appear artificial, if not intolerable. Clerks and educated knights aspire to a kind of disengagement from the political world] (63). Thus, the twelfth century finds a turning away from the ponderous military aesthetic of epic and chanson de geste. Courtly romance, like the epic and its updated counterpart, is a sublimation. Its setting preserves a fantasy distance from reality in which the familiar is made unusual, but identifiable, and then suspended far enough above the mundanity of everyday life to place it in the realm of the ideal. Despite the sublimation we are closer to reality in romance than in *Roland*. Romance communicates a different nostalgia for the past and reflects a narcissistic fascination with an idealized present. Auerbach famously describes the aim of the romance as a "self-portrayal of feudal mores and ideals" (*Mimesis* 131) on the part of the medieval French aristocracy. The use of fantasy coupled with the refinement of the feudal system into an elegant social code removes the romance from both the epic and the chanson de geste, with its seemingly closer ties to historiography and realpolitik.[4] For all its action, color, and movement, the world of the courtly romance is partly as static as that of the epic. The rarified rules of literary chivalry are central to its motivation: like a series of moves in a chess game they are reinforced in each use, but in their endless capacity for permutation are only ever temporarily under threat.

Northrop Frye's concept of romance is similar to that of Auerbach's; Frye considers it the attempt of the dominant social stratum to idealize itself and "the nearest of all literary forms to the wish-fulfilment dream" (186). Turning to the archetypal framework of a broader categorization of romance, Frye discerns three stages of development capable of manifesting themselves in tragic or comic mode: the first is *agon*, constituted by a journey and quest; the second is pathos or catastrophe, being a central struggle—and, in extreme cases, death—preceding the hero's rebirth or change in fortune; the third is a stage of recognition that sees the exaltation of final triumph and usually material reward.[5]

Rearranging the same elements, Zumthor, inspired by Greimas, arrives at an actantial model for the romance, in which the *destinateur* and *destinataire* (the author and reader/audience) focus on the hero's quest for success, while he is aided and hindered within the text by a series of blocking figures and adjuvants in the guise of helpful characters and powerful symbolic objects ("Genèse et évolution du genre" 67–8). The hero is thus the active intersection of an internal and external configuration of lines that make a dynamic and dramatic model of the romance form; its resemblance to dramatic comedy is evident.

Frye sees the romance setting as a Summer landscape, whose enemy is

Winter, being death and decay, and whose savior can only be vigorous Spring. The hero is no mythic being: however symbolic the landscape, he must be human, and therefore fallible. He describes dramatic comedy as the archetype of Spring and finds it exemplified in Greek New Comedy and its conventions, calling it "less a form than a formula" (163). The essential elements of such plays, particularly the appearance of blocking characters such as the aged, cantankerous parent or older, richer rival to the hero in pursuit of a love-match with the heroine, are as familiar to us from the plays of Molière and the *commedia dell'arte* as they are from Greek comedy. The twists and turns of the plot, most commonly a series of ordeals that test the lovers before they can be united in marriage, use conflict and a play on recognition as their two main motivations. While the lovers are initially subject to obstacles that prevent their integration with society, such comedies end with social approval of the lovers and the restoration of order. Repeated motifs, plots, and characters enhance our recognition and condition a comic reflex as well as a set of narrative expectations.

Chrétien's springtime courtly world is presented ostensibly as a ready-made set of paradigms whose rules are obeyed by everyone and never elaborated. Similarly, the poetry of Guillem IX, the earliest troubadour whose works are preserved, leaves the reader with the impression that lyric poetry is already highly conventional and encoded. Indeed, not only does Guillem offer us an exposition of themes and language that form the basis for the canonical poetry of *fin'amor,* but in his less refined verse he also gives the first recorded parody of the ethos he sets out. For Guillem, as for Chrétien, the rarified world of courtly love found a natural counterpart in humor and in parody. With his use of a literary world of established ethical values that he then goes on to criticize, Chrétien "deconstructs" the Arthurian court as he builds it.

Identifying how he capitalizes on this technique, Peter Haidu designates as aesthetic distance the perceived gap between Chrétien and his creations. The divide is signalled through irony:

> All the forms of irony and comedy used by Chrétien serve to inform the reader and maintain him at a certain intellectual, emotional, and moral distance from the characters in his story. . . . It is the normal experience in looking at paintings to find an optimal distance from the canvas which provides the best rapport with the work of art. (*Aesthetic Distance* 262)

The gap spans the optimum required to extract the greatest effect from Chrétien's narratives, exciting "intellectual analysis" and moral judgment.

Haidu's evaluation of the deliberate opening of interpretational space through comedy is persuasive, and while there is a moralizing advantage, there is a critical distance that permits scrutiny of the vehicle as well as the message, such that the end result is an assessment of the hero, and through him the generic model, as if the audience is far enough away from the puppet show to see the strings. In a very modern way, the eventual subject of writing becomes literature itself. Haidu explores in great detail the trope of *ironia* and shows its intricate workings at every structural level without broaching the subject of parody, perhaps because taken too literally as the takeoff of one work on another, it is too rigid a trope in its narrow sense to embrace the comic techniques he describes. His concern is focused and rhetorical, but I believe that much of what he ascribes to irony and comedy can be treated as parody in its broader sense. Parody is too often wrongly associated with a negative impact on an original model and defined too literally as blatantly intertextual; whether outward- or inward-looking, it also carries a positive valence which is creative and rejuvenating, in that the general investigation it provokes encourages the vitality of the genre by preserving it from formal stagnation. For Chrétien, the testing and refor-mulating of his heroes in a never-aging world is the best way of keeping them and the genre eternally youthful. Thus, moving outward from Haidu's perceptive analysis, I am going to call parody much of what he defines as irony.

Using *Cligès* and *Perceval* as illustrative models, Haidu analyzes rhetori-cal figures and structural irony to demonstrate Chrétien's separation from his characters.[6] Dennis Green, writing primarily about medieval German romance, sees a similar alliance between rhetorical practice and the mecha-nism of narrative irony. Moreover, because the structure and development of the romance evince a grammar of action with its own syntax of adventure, an inevitable literary tendency to convention results, what Green terms romance's "normative nature" (384):

Where there can be convention, there is room for deviation.

Put otherwise, sameness creates the space for difference. Green speculates as to the reasons for the *romanciers'* frequent aloofness from their work. He sees clerical status and training as one factor, producing a natural de-tachment and cultural distance from courtly society. However, the author simultaneously makes himself at least a temporary insider in the courtly literary environment he has chosen, but more important he uses this privi-leged position to exploit the possibilities of distancing self from fiction. Another weapon in his arsenal is the subtle use of the etiquette of language and behavior that belongs to the world of supposed social refinement: *politesse* itself is "a technique of indirection" (365) and a play on different registers that opens further ironic space in a text. In this case, the distance equals the gap between everyday language and lofty circumlocution. It operates with "an implicit discrepancy" (385).

While the operation of the many subtle rhetorical figures of ironia is difficult to schematize, the structural irony that is the outward sign of the deeper linguistic tendencies within the text is more visible, usually in the deliberate framing of the narrative in a bipartite structure. In the case of *Cligès*, Haidu places the two halves of the romance in parallel, treating the Alexander/Soredamor and Cligès/Fénice sections as complementary. The generation gap between the two sets of lovers allows a play on ideas and attitudes amplified by language and action, and the resulting relationship of model to meaning establishes itself as a complex series of oppositions expressed through humor. What manifests itself in the conveniently matching halves of the structure of *Cligès* can be applied to the similarly formed *Perceval*, in which comedy is more in evidence than in *Cligès*. The progress of Gauvain and Perceval on their separate quests produces differing views of chivalry so pronounced that the interlacing tales can practically be treated as independent romances. The diptychs offered by both texts reveal conflicting images within each romance of the courtly ethos, and while the two romances do not show the kind of dialogism Bakhtin identifies, the different treatment and style assigned to courtly themes lends itself to Segre's modified version of that same polyphonic concept. Whether one terms it dialogism or aesthetic distance, the rift between ideal and realization is a central feature in all of Chrétien's romances. As a narrative form the romance pits narrative elements and characters against each other in the same way that adversaries are destined to meet.

Haidu's methodology applies itself readily to the two texts he examines, but as he states in his conclusions, the remaining three romances present problems of interpretation: *Yvain* fits the mold of *Cligès* and *Perceval*, but not so *Erec et Enide* (263). Similarly, he affirms: "I reserve judgment on the *Lancelot*" (263). These romances offer as much if not more comic potential than the other two, and although the structural irony in these works is differently expressed, it is nevertheless abundant. In *Yvain* we are offered a before-and-after dialogic portrait of chivalric heroism and its relationship to social obligation. *Erec et Enide* involves a similar dialectic, while *Lancelot* shows an individual within whom the divergent pulls of desire and reputation create a tantalizingly unresolved rift. To summarize the romances thus is to omit unjustly their parodic qualities: particularly in

Yvain and *Lancelot* comedy highlights the dilemmas and contradictions at the heart of the literary model itself.

Noticeably downplayed in Haidu's perceptive reading of language and structure is any full consideration of parody, although irony, distance, moral judgment, and the separation between text, author, and reader surely can imply a degree of parody. As Haidu avers, referring to the presentation of Gauvain and Perceval in *Le Conte du Graal,* the comfortable viewpoint afforded by the distancing effect allows us to "enjoy their adventures, heroic and comic" (259). An important aspect of the aesthetic distance as Haidu defines it is the way the reader is forced, in this case, to regard the opposite aspects of the chivalric model to which the two knights belong. The comedy of Perceval's ingenuousness and inability to read the courtly or spiritual signs placed in front of him and of Gauvain's polished but dull progress through a conventional courtly landscape serves to show flaws in the literary model to which they belong. The structural and situational irony distances us not only from the characters and the values that they represent but also from the ethos as a whole. Chrétien's distance from his creation and the consonant gap he establishes between events in the text and the audience's involvement in them leave room not only for comedy and irony but also for a kind of generic reflection we can call at least partially parodic of a basic kind of chivalric narrative and the codes that drive it. If Chrétien institutes an ethical model it is so that he can critique it through the parodic treatment of the hero, as he also does in *Yvain* and *Lancelot.* Through the continual questioning of fin'amor and the precepts of courtly behavior, Chrétien ensures the liveliness of the model he utilizes.

In considering parody and its relation to Chrétien's romances, I would like to modify somewhat Haidu's concept of aesthetic distance and combine it with elements suggested by June Hall Martin's notion of parody in *Love's Fools.* Martin defines it as a broad comic device, having frequent recourse to incongruity, aimed largely at convention. Parody operates, she says, by being more than merely "imitative":

Some basic element must be altered so that the resulting incongruity may reveal some weakness in the original. In the case of courtly love, for example, the lofty style, the elegant manners of the courtly world, may be retained, while the characters are made base. Or an ideal character may be placed in a lowly and, hence, incongruous situation. The result is what is, indeed, a form of literary criticism which underscores some weakness or tendency toward absurdity within the convention. (15)

Didacticism and humor are the twin objectives of parody in her schema, and she applies this definition successfully to a series of courtly heroes. She observes how they juggle desire and duty, love and adventure to comic effect: "[t]he courtly lover with his blond curls, his paroxysms of weeping, and his transports of joy, was an easy target" for parody (21). How parody operates on a structural level with its multifaceted incongruity is a complex issue: however, the didactic aspect inherent in parody leads us legitimately to its literary function as a form of generic self-irony.

June Hall Martin's statements easily fit aspects of Chrétien's romances. The phenomenon of generic parody has much in common with Norris Lacy's assertion regarding lyric poetry:

> Courtly poetry, from its inception, possessed the potential for self-parody; the germ was always there. The lyric resisted such self-parody (in most cases) because the context of courtly love was entirely consonant with its sentiments. In other words, a courtly lover at a court that accepted courtly love is virtually immune to parody. But transposed to an uncourtly, incompatible context, *courtoisie* easily assumes parodic contours. ("Courtliness and Comedy" 65)

This argument recalls Green's association of the normative with the deviant: the lyric system found countergenres to absorb the parodic impulse, such as the *pastourelle,* but in addition to channeling the deviant into fabliaux, theater, and other more marginal expressions, courtly romance swallowed it whole and integrated it as a form of narrative trope. Taking the ethos of courtly love beyond the lyric form places it into an experimental setting from Chrétien onward. Green maintains that "in the first Arthurian romance [Chrétien] avails himself of the opportunity to call into question, by means of parody, the Provençal concept of love" (383). Comedy is a natural part of courtly literature and is perhaps the centerpiece of the romance, as Peter Haidu asserts: "Chrétien de Troyes, in *Cligès* and *Perceval,* is not a courtly writer in the sense that he propagandizes the ideals of courtly love, but only in using them as literary subjects toward which he suggests an attitude that is primarily ironic" (*Aesthetic Distance* 262). I would agree with his conclusion that Chrétien uses the romance as a vehicle and a source for comedy. The two elements are interdependent: the romance produces comedy as a by-product of its manipulation of convention, and the possibility of exploring departures from the unspoken literary norm of the roman courtois is a prime mover in choosing it as a vehicle. Green correctly believes that humor inoculates the romance against outside contamination:

[M]edieval irony, unlike the admittedly often nihilistic corrosiveness of modern irony, still has a positive function in strengthening the ideal, rather than necessarily weakening it, just as any irony, particularly if employed at the narrator's expense, can be a device to protect and not destroy the illusion created in the story. (393)

Irony seems synonymous with parody here, and the parodic commentary does not only reinforce the model; it *is* the model, integrating and enacting a natural form of self-defense.

Lancelot illustrates vividly the way that Chrétien uses the chivalric romance as a double paradigm.[7] The plot is typically simple and tortuous: at Ascensiontide, Méléagant comes to Arthur's court and carries off the queen. Gauvain follows, and in the forest he meets an unknown knight (later revealed as Lancelot) engaged in hot pursuit. They both seek Guenièvre, and Lancelot agrees to climb onto the shameful cart in order to obtain vital clues to the quest. United on a single mission, the two knights head in the same direction toward the land of Gorre and have marvelous adventures before learning they must traverse the watery boundary to that world via separate bridges; Gauvain takes the slower route across the paradoxical bridge under troubled waters, while Lancelot tackles the Sword Bridge that will exact a painful toll on his martyred hands and feet. Lancelot encounters a staged rape and a field of courtly games before a surreal cemetery reveals his purpose as the savior of exiled people of Logres, who are trapped by Méléagant's tyranny and a set of repressive customs. Lancelot negotiates a stony passage, a revolt, and a tough combat before he crosses the bridge. Although a clash of arms with Méléagant is repeatedly postponed, Lancelot eventually fights him in combat in front of the queen, who reveals Lancelot's identity and gives him a cold reception afterward. Lancelot goes off to search for Gauvain, and his absence provokes the softening of Guenièvre's heart as she laments what she is sure is his death and almost dies herself. On Lancelot's return the lovers finally enjoy a night of bliss, but the mood soon changes when the next morning the injured Keu is accused of having consorted with the queen. As a result, Lancelot has a second postponed combat with Méléagant, goes to search for Gauvain again, falls for a trap, and is captured by Méléagant's seneschal. Tricked by a false message, Keu, the queen, and the liberated prisoners leave Gorre and the missing Lancelot for Logres, where a tournament at Noauz is announced. Lancelot charms his way out of prison, enters the tournament in disguise, and performs badly or bravely according to the controlling whim of Guenièvre. Victorious, he surrenders himself to prison again and is walled up until he is liberated by Méléagant's

sister, and he can finally avenge himself by polishing off his adversary.
Chrétien refers to his hero as "le chevalier de la charrete" in line 24 and
does not name him until line 3660. In the meantime the reader follows his
adventures seeing him as a paradoxical combination of *courtois* and *vilain*,
since knight and cart are at obvious opposite ends of a value spectrum.[8]
The collocation of noble and base in Lancelot's pseudonym reflects his
lofty chivalric virtue and his ignoble subjection to the passion he feels for
Guenièvre and constitutes the fundamental dialectic in which he operates.
His attachment to the cart represents his detachment from chivalric society, since the latter embodies the antithesis of the former's codes.

The decor of Arthur's court furnishes a stable paradigm of meaning, in
which Keu suggests the lowest value and Gauvain the highest. Keu loses
the queen through his egoism and incompetence. Gauvain shows his courtly
polish and valor, but fails to arrive at the needed time. Only Lancelot has
the depth of human strength and weakness to merit testing in the magical
assault-course that comprises his environment. The medieval romance is
often centered on the notion of "making a name" for the hero, and Lancelot must first "unmake" the epithet coined for him: its mission is to assign
value and continually reevaluate it and what it represents. Similarly, Perceval must lose the tag *gallois*, and Yvain must earn the right to have his
identity restored through the redemption that comes with his association
with the lion. In *Aucassin et Nicolette* when Aucassin's reputation precedes
him in the land surrounding his father's estate, he parodies the spread of
Lancelot's fame, already a parody in itself, since everyone encountered by
the shamed knight readily associates him with the cart, even in distant
Gorre. The designation Lancelot carries with him removes him from the
surrounding world of value, while his intrinsic merit makes those around
him seem comparatively shallow and vacuous. The lame and the somewhat disappointing ending supplied by Godefroi de Leigni leaves the
reader wondering whether Lancelot and Guenièvre manage to be reintegrated into courtly society as it is portrayed at the beginning, and, if so,
how. In the intensity of their passion Lancelot and Guenièvre no longer
belong to the stylized, ritual form of *amor de lonh* favored at Arthur's
court. Leslie Topsfield associates the portrayal of love in the romance with
the inspiration of the troubadours, particularly Bernart de Ventadorn
(*Chrétien de Troyes* 108).

Lancelot, who reveals himself a forebear of Aucassin, exaggerates
many of the characteristics of a poet-lover. In his meditation over
Guenièvre he forgets everything, including his own existence:

et cil de la charrete panse
con cil qui force ne deffanse
n'a vers Amors qui le justise;
et ses pansers est de tel guise
que lui meïsmes en oblie,
ne set s'il est, ou s'il n'est mie,
ne ne li manbre de son non,
ne set s'il est armez ou non,
ne set ou va, ne set don vient;
de rien nule ne li sovient
fors d'une seule, et por celi
a mis les autres en obli.
(ll. 711–22)

[And the man in the cart is lost in thought like one who has no strength or defence against Love, who holds sway over him, and his musing is of such a kind that he forgets himself, nor is he aware of where he is, or isn't—nor does he remember his name, or if he is armed or not, he has no idea where he is going, or where he came from; he is mindful of nothing except that one thing, and for her he consigns everything into oblivion.]

Bringing knightly self-effacement to a new high, this passage reveals an ironic range of paradoxes: thinking equals forgetting, being is nothing, and the knight is no longer a symbol of the active individual but a passive and defenseless victim of an unseen aggressor. The multiple negatives underscore the counteractive force of his love for Guenièvre: Lancelot is at a point of virtual nonexistence that would be tragic were not bathos imminent in the person of the defender of the ford, who quite literally treats him to a cold shower, sending him in an undignified fashion into the water and thereby snatching him from his reverie. To add insult to injury, Lancelot has to rescue his knightly accoutrements as they float off downstream. Lyric poetry provides the conventional inspiration for the love-meditation, but the comic potential of romance banalizes its realization.

The notion of the religion of love is also exaggerated beyond its lyric confines when transposed to romance as Lancelot examines Guenièvre's comb, the most mundane of objects that Lancelot transforms into a reliquary (l. 1384).[9] Lancelot loves her more than Piramus loved Thisbe (l. 3803), and to prove this he bends the bars of the prison that separate him from Guenièvre at the court of Bademagu. Death and rumor of death prompt a ludicrous suicide attempt (l. 4295), soon forgotten in transports of joy when he finds he had no reason to give way to despair. After a long conventional and woeful monologue on death and love, Lancelot wants to put an end to his sufferings. However, on discovering that the queen still lives, his gloom is dispelled with a simple and comic "Tantost Lanceloz se conforte" (l. 4402), and his martyrdom for his beloved is quickly forgotten. Perhaps we should imagine audiences like those observed by Peter of Blois following along with the emotional charge of Chrétien's verses—but such techniques of narrative exaggeration carry with them a parodic charge too.

Lancelot's self-abasement continues with his imprisonment by the unscrupulous Méléagant (l. 5248) and his submission to the will of the queen at the closing tournament by fighting badly "au noauz" (l. 5645) before triumphing over his adversary. Godefroi's ending serves to intensify the sense of shallowness that emanates from Arthur's court. In the same way that later romances subsume and parody other romances, Chrétien's heroes absorb and parody the values that coexist with them. Lancelot portrays the conflict of love and adventure as insoluble, which may be one reason why Chrétien left the completion of the story to another poet.[10]

The negative irony of *Lancelot* and its parody of the courtly lover is matched with what Edwin Williamson terms "positive irony" (16) in *Yvain;* here love and adventure manage to coexist, but not until the courtly model has undergone comic scrutiny. In a reverse of the use of the name topos in *Lancelot,* Yvain begins with a reputation and a name that he loses through his neglect of social obligation by leaving Laudine to attend tournaments with Gauvain. The irony is that in its first half the hero achieves the happy ending that concludes most other romances: he redeems the family honor by finishing the adventure begun by Calogrenant, he woos and wins the widow of a knight he has killed, and he gains fame and fortune at a stroke. Only the ideal of chivalry that promises wish-fulfillment keeps him from bliss, as Gauvain tells him, "Honiz soit de sainte Marie, / Qui por anpirier se marie" [May he be shamed, by Saint Marie, he who gets married only to go downhill] (ll. 2487–88). Contained in Calogrenant's attempt to challenge Esclados and Yvain's successful completion of the adventure is the making of a romance in itself.[11] True to the courtly experiment that Chrétien conducts in each romance, what would seem a fitting conclusion is only the beginning. Yet it is not just a question of setting an ideal social order, represented by Laudine's kingdom, against a selfish model of chivalry concerned with tournaments (Topsfield, *Chrétien de Troyes* 176). While Gauvain's selfish logic in enticing Yvain away from domestic contentment is faulty, the egotistical reasoning behind Laudine's acceptance of Yvain as a husband is, after all, even more ridiculous (ll. 1589–2048). In a perceptive analysis Charles Muscatine argues that "[n]o scene in French romance equals in brilliance and virtuosity of style the sequence in *Yvain* that leads to the marriage of Laudine to the slayer of her husband" (*Chaucer and the French Tradition* 47). The rationale behind accepting Yvain's suit is that it will restore the social stability of the estate: this, of course, would be unnecessary if Esclados were alive. As the result of Laudine's elegant capitulation, the fundamental social order emerges as faintly ridiculous and as a rationalization rather than a rationale. Arthur's removal of the entire court to assist at the adventure of the fountain provides another ironic implication of the comic social model of the roman courtois, since the court is so bereft of meaningful activity that it displaces itself for what seems a trivial adventure initially related as an after-dinner anecdote.

Ultimately, the defense of the spring at the root of all the adventures is meaningless, a fact perhaps reflected in the disturbance of nature when the adventure begins with the pouring of water onto a stone: the violent, indiscriminate tempest leads to sudden and bloody combat for no apparent reason and seems merely to validate the ritualized games enacted around it. While the storm focuses narrative attention on nature, human nature, and the combative nature of medieval society, it strikes a note of magical absurdity. A calm follows the storm, foreshadowing the extremes Yvain will endure before he arrives at his point of departure at Laudine's castle.

When Calogrenant relates his tale, it gives all the indications of being a conventional courtly adventure: he passes from the forest into the welcoming household of a hospitable noble with a daughter. From there, however, he encounters an uncouth and hideous *bouvier* (l. 289) who first directs him to the spring. Like the rustics in the later *Aucassin,* the herdsman is unimpressed by Calogrenant's searching for adventure, as it is beyond his ken: "D'aventure ne sai je rien'" [I know nothing about adventure] (l. 368). He knows nothing except the essential information about the fountain and its defender: being a vilain he is excluded, but at the same time the incident is a measure of the fact that beyond a paradigm of assigned value, the concept and importance of chivalric games is fairly meaningless. This is one instance where the artificiality of convention manifests itself in a distancing clash of registers, rather like the dissonance of the pastourelle. Its effect is to suggest a generic irony, a moment of comic literary reflection when worldviews find themselves at counterpoint.

The parodic play of *Yvain* generates a picturesque cavalcade of adventures as the hero redeems himself, and thereby the somewhat tongue-in-cheek chivalric ethos. His meeting with the lion and their subsequent friendship after Yvain's wild wanderings in the forest have provoked much comment. The lion's ennobling symbolic freight is as clear as that of the cart in *Lancelot:* the lion is noble, valorous, virtuous, providential, and loyal. When it tries to kill itself, it is also extremely comic, such that, like the cart, it underscores the existence of a doubling of meaning, one tending toward a normative reading and another toward a comic, self-reflexive interpretation. Thus aided by an external symbol of his return to noble nature, Yvain defends the right, liberates the damsels who slave for a pittance in the castle of *Pesme Aventure,* defeats the giant Harpin, and rescues Lunete (whose *ami* Gauvain is of little assistance when the chips are down) from certain disaster. Yvain's reward is to reclaim Laudine, and Leslie Topsfield finds the ending unsatisfactory: "Chrétien's commonplace references to the mutual joy and peace without end of Yvain and Laudine, leave some doubt whether he did not see in this conclusion the patching together of a story which on its higher level of meaning had transcended its narrative framework" (*Chrétien de Troyes* 205).

Given the light-hearted social model at the heart of the romance, the transcendent level of meaning was always in jeopardy. In the second half, Yvain nevertheless rehearses redressing the imbalances of society through his adventures: stabilizing the economy, preserving justice and the status quo, ensuring the circulation of goods and inheritances, and maintaining the primacy of the fighting class (exemplified by its lone entrepreneur, the knight). Each of these adventures appear as an extreme mutation of a basic root of aristocratic evil. The transcendency of the message is something we intuit rather than see instantly. To find balance and social integration, the knight must conquer his own nature, submit himself to the nature of society, and combat its natural excesses and by-products: tyranny, greed, and selfishness.

The trite ending of *Yvain* points to the flaws in the model Chrétien exploits: in the prologue he laments the old days and adopts a critical stance toward the lovers of his time. The nostalgia is short-lived, however, as the court also has its imperfections, and he gently lampoons lovers of former times as well as of his own. At Arthur's court, because he is tired and apparently bored, the king absents himself from the assembled company and stays overlong in the queen's chamber, much to the general astonishment of the knights and ladies. As entertainment, Calogrenant relates his shameful tale and his ignominious return, horseless and bereft of the weapons that symbolize his status. Yvain's eager departure to gain the glory for himself, even with the weak excuse of family honor, shows the desire for adventure and the scarcity of it at court.

In *Yvain*, the twin themes of love and chivalry are parodied in a different way than in *Lancelot*. In both cases the Arthurian court provides a flawed ideal from which the heroes detach themselves through self-exile or rejection. Their attempts to accommodate love and chivalry lead to comic reflections on their characters, but more important bring us to an assessment of the literary convention that they defy and redeem. To account for the enduring popularity of Chrétien is to acknowledge his ambidextrous skill at forging a convention while he balances its inflexibility with novel heroes. To him, the romance is a mutable genre that seems continually in transformation.[12] Those who came after him are offered a pattern with the potential of being a conventional paradigm, a backdrop for literary reflection, and a vehicle for more radical narrative experimentation.

In *Aucassin et Nicolette*, one of the works Martin chooses for detailed analysis, the anonymous author employs a battery of parodic techniques summarized *en gros* by Omer Jodogne as "le jeu permanent du contrepied, l'exagération et la bouffonerie" [the continual game of the unexpected, exaggeration, and buffoonery], of which the net effect is the destabilizing of convention.[13] Although its form represents the unique extant example of the *chantefable, Aucassin* is an appropriate point of departure for an analysis of the tendency toward parody in Chrétien's works and more generally in chivalric romance, since it shows in caricature form many of the comic aspects of the romance as utilized by Chrétien. Moreover, although classified as a chantefable, it is a clear variant of the romance in content and form. Quite simply, the lyric and narrative elements have been separated and thrown more clearly into relief.

Barbara Nelson Sargent asserts that *Aucassin* "appears to be a sort of thirteenth-century anti-novel, without the bitter and destructive quality that frequently marks the corresponding modern phenomenon" ("Parody in *Aucassin*" 605). Its uniqueness of form is only matched by the intensity of its sustained attack on the themes of courtly literature. Rudy Spraycar defines the chantefable form as "literary license" (115): its deviation from the form of the romance allows for a privileged vantage point from which to view convention and constitutes another form of generic distance from the body of texts it comically reflects. In fact *Aucassin* follows the process Bakhtin describes as the development of the novel, when having established a position beyond the canon, a text absorbs and parodies prior models to produce a new hybrid.

Although *Aucassin* relates a simple tale of separated lovers, the multiplicity of the literary genres on which it draws lends it great subcutaneous complexity. This unique text is certain, says the narrator in the opening lines, to cheer any downcast listener. The hilariously named Bougars de Valence besieges Aucassin's father at Beaucaire, but Aucassin, who should be the great hope of the town, is too moonstruck with love to do anything about it. As the heroine Nicolette is not his social equal, she is put in prison out of the way—much to Aucassin's plaintive chagrin. Stirred by the promise of reuniting with his love, Aucassin captures Bougars, but is thwarted in his quest to regain Nicolette. Aucassin rebels against his father and is put in prison, where he languishes while Nicolette escapes, disguises herself, and goes off into the forest. Reunited after Aucassin has accomplished a swift intelligence test, the lovers journey to Torelore, a strange inverted feudal world where the queen fights and the king suffers sympathetic pregnancy pains in bed. Armed with picnic comestibles, the two armies battle it out, greatly aided by Aucassin, who wields a real sword to heroic effect. Saracens capture Torelore, and Aucassin and Nicolette are taken off in different ships. By luck, Aucassin is driven by sea currents back to Beaucaire, where his parents have conveniently died and left him everything. Nicolette arrives in Carthage and remembers conveniently that she is a princess of the city. When events make it likely that she will marry a rich, pagan king, she puts on blackface and travels as a minstrel back to Provence, finds Aucassin, and marries him.

The text is a wonderful juxtaposition of prose and poetry, with many lyric genres embedded and parodied in the intercalated sections. It is a highly effective pantomime send-up of chivalric convention and courtly refinement and makes a habit of confounding our expectations. Its deep triviality should not allow us to lose sight of the fact that it exhibits detailed knowledge of a variety of genres: the lyric *alba* (chap. 15), pastoral poetry (chaps. 19 and 26), the *sotte chanson*, and the *chanson religieuse*. Registral clashes abound: the chanson de geste vies with romance topoi, the lyric with the prosaic, and the high with the low. The banality of love poetry, a constant target, is parodied in the short lyric sung by Guillem in chapter 25, and heavy use is made of the amorous monologue, a convention used both in the romance and in troubadour and trouvère *planh*-style lyrics. It is a clear example of narrative polyphony of the kind that Segre would have us recast.

It is not just the comic treatment given literary genres that adds to the impression of the "aesthetic distance" between them, but also the clever assimilation and subversion of them that has taken place. Critical opinions diverge on interpreting the text. Most critics agree that the text is a parody.

Tony Hunt finds that *Aucassin* "s'apparente évidemment plus au conte populaire (Märchen) qu'à la parodie littéraire" [is evidently related to the folktale more than to the literary parody] ("La parodie médiévale" 375), and he downplays the parodic role he sees overplayed in most analyses. It is an interesting thesis, but the unlikelihood that the text had its origins on the margins or even beyond a charmed compositional circle makes its learned origin and parodic character even more probable and stronger.

Mariantonia Liborio represents a moderate voice when she affirms that while *Aucassin* holds up a distorting mirror to the courtly world, the integrity of the reflection is restored by the uniting of the lovers in marriage at the end of the story: "La parodia è allora solo sovrastruttura. . . . Il sistema ha resistito all'assalto" [Parody is at that point only superstructure. . . . The system has resisted the attack] (71). Whether restoring the upturned conventions and genres necessarily entails reapproval of the basic form is open to question, since the intended effect has already been accomplished. In a romance like Heldris de Cornouailles's *Roman de Silence,* after a highly unconventional series of adventures, when the world and gender-role normativity returns, the effect is of self-righting the values of the courtly world and making what has gone before seem like an intriguing experiment.

In another way we could interpret Silence's marriage to King Ebain as conventional protection for the events that have led up to it. However, in the case of *Aucassin et Nicolette* the consistent burlesquing of literary conventions is hard to undo by bringing the tale to a conventional close: the ending is insufficient and too late to restore the original integrity of the model. Indeed, the perfunctory and stereotypical union of *Aucassin et Nicolette* is perhaps the high point of the comic treatment of courtly love:

> Andex ses bras li tendi,
> Doucement le recoulli,
> Les eus li baisse et le vis.
> La nuit le laissent ensi,
> Tresqu'au demain par matin
> Que l'espousa Aucassins;
> Dame de Biaucaire en fist.
> (Chap. 41, ll. 13–19)

[He stretched both arms toward her, gently enfolded her, and kissed her eyes and face. The night leaves them thus, until the following morning when Aucassin wed her; he made her Lady of Beaucaire.]

The discreet withdrawal of the narrator as the scene closes on the lovers is as clichéd a summation as any to be found in medieval romances: the tale ends with a stereotypical fanfare that reinforces rather than nullifies the parody of romance and other genres enclosed in it. Liborio concludes that what has occurred is "un gioco ottico . . . un *divertissement* estetico" [a game of mirrors . . . an aesthetic entertainment] (71) that undermines the literary mask of courtly society without penetrating further. But *Aucassin* is no less a sardonic reevaluation of the artificial conventions of literature because of its happy resolution. The audience cannot retract the laughter it has already enjoyed at Aucassin's expense, in spite of the clichéd tableau that closes his adventures.

As one might expect, the prose sections of *Aucassin* are more comic than the lyric interludes: the verse sections give the noble characters a vehicle for lofty sentiment and lyrical effusions, while the more pedestrian narrative brings the protagonists into contact with less courtly characters in a group of shepherds (chap. 18), a bouvier (chap. 24) of the kind found in *Yvain*, and the king of Torelore (chap. 29), whose outrageous behavior places him firmly in the world of the fabliau. The meeting of Nicolette and then Aucassin with the rustics has led Jill Tattersall to treat the work as a social comedy and a parody of feudal society ("Social Observation and Comment in *Aucassin et Nicolette*"): beyond the surface of literary parody lies a rudimentary form of estate satire and a sardonic commentary on war and the status of women.

The contrast of vilain and courtois in the rustic scene is reminiscent of the collision of registers exploited for comic purposes by Adam de la Halle in *Le Jeu de Robin et Marion*. The protagonists' encounters in the prose section have the effect of juxtaposing them with other noncourtly registers and thereby deflating their courtly rhetoric. When Aucassin meets the bouvier, his vulgar interlocutor inquires why he is crying, since if the bouvier were rich he would have no cause to weep. Aucassin, who has lost Nicolette, replies that he has lost "un blanc levrier, le plus bel del siecle" [a white greyhound, the most beautiful in the world] (chap. 24). The herdsman, who tells a woeful tale of a lost cow and attendant social deprivation sufficiently moving to extract money from Aucassin, upbraids the noble youth for deploring the loss of a mere "cien de longaigne" [stinking dog] (l. 61), to which Aucassin replies in his typically inane way, "certes tu es de bon confort, biax frere" [indeed, you are a great comfort, fair brother] (l. 63). Neither party escapes caricature in the encounter: Aucassin appears insipid and vacuous, while the herdsman emerges as a square-headed oaf. At the same time, the confrontation between the two registers produces an ironic reflection on courtly values: the homespun philosophy of the bouvier, like the voice of the *bergère* in the pastourelle, is a form of criticism against courtly convention.

The parody of courtly values is also in evidence in the scene just prior to Aucassin's meeting with the bouvier, when the shepherds that Nicolette has charged with relaying her message use a courtly tone to deliver their information:

> Sire nos estiiens orains ci, entre prime et tierce, si mangiëns no pain a ceste fontaine, ausi con nos faisons ore; et une pucele vint ici, li plus bele riens du monde, si que nos quidames que ce fust une fée, et que tos cis bos en esclarci. (Chap. 22, ll. 32–36)

> [Sir, we were here a short while ago, between prime and tierce, eating our bread at this fountain, just as we do now; and a young lady came here, the most beautiful creature in the world, so much so we thought she was a fairy, and the whole wood was lit up by her!]

The real, mundane world of the shepherds, at odds with their capacity for more flowery language, is momentarily exchanged for a comic rehash of the magic otherworld of the romance, conjuring an illusion soon dispelled by the discussion of the practical details of the hunt Aucassin is to take in the forest.

Later, the sublime becomes ridiculous once again when Aucassin unexpectedly springs into action in a most uncourtly way on surprising the king of Torelore *en couvade:*

> Quant Aucassins oï ensi le roi parler, il prist tox les dras qui sor lui estoient si les houla aval le canbre. Il vit deriere lui un baston; il le prist, si torne, si fiert, si le bati tant que mort le dut avoir.
>
> Ha! biax sire, fait li rois, que me demandés vos? Avés vos le sens dervé, qui en ma maison me batés?—Par le cuer Diu! fait Aucassins, malvais fix a putain, je vos ocirai se vos ne m'afiés que jamais hom en vo tere d'enfant ne gerra! (Chap. 30, ll. 1–10)

> [When Aucassin heard the king talking that way, he took all the covers off him and threw them on the chamber floor. He saw a stick behind him; he grasped it, turned, struck, and beat him within an inch of his life. "Ha! Fair sir," he said, "What do you want from me? Are you out of your mind, beating me up in my own house?" "By God's heart!" replied Aucassin, "you evil son of a bitch, I'll kill you

unless you swear that no man in your kingdom will ever lie in
childbed!"]

Aucassin behaves as if he were a character from a fabliau. As usual, he
is most masculinely aggressive when he is in no danger. The earthy language and action completely debase the ethereal lyricism of his poetic
excursions, as he unwittingly fuses the pathetic and the bathetic. The juxtaposition of the clichéd lyric sections with the less than courtly prose
opens a stylistic rift that produces a further comic dimension.

Not surprisingly, the plurality of languages has drawn critical attention.
Eugene Vance goes so far as to consider the lovers as "icons of discourse"
(60) above all else, and here too it is not hard to identify a plurality of
worldviews. The coexistence and superimposition of literary languages
leads to the undermining of all the levels of narrative involved: at risk is the
conceptual framework of courtly literature, to the extent that Barbara
Nelson Sargent's labelling of the work as an antinovel is not inappropriate;
more than in exact replications of different genres, the success of the text
lies in its intricate use of literary clichés and courtly vocabulary in order to
attack the artificiality of literature. The dissonance of languages can also
be interpreted as a form of polyphony, as a generic dialogism that reveals
the text as both a proto- and an antinovel. Nathaniel Smith terms the
rhetorical excess of *Aucassin* "stylistic overkill" (486), and what is true
of the language of the text is matched by a hyperbole of character and
setting: the uncourtly behavior of Aucassin's father and his enemy Bougars is a magnification of the kind of treachery found in the courtly
romance. Smith's exposé follows the repetition of language and structure
and the inherent "density and enumeration" that betray a high concentra-
tion of convention.

Most of all, the religion of love so prized by medieval poets finds unusually comic distortion in the speech delivered by Aucassin on the relative
merits of heaven and hell. Heaven is unappealing: full of old priests,
marginals, and unfortunates, while to the warmer regions go "li bel clerc,
et li bel cavalier" [beautiful clerks and knights] (l. 33), accompanied by
noble ladies, aristocrats, and entertainers. Aucassin's heretical description
calls to mind Guillem in *Flamenca* and some of Chaucer's creations.

On the surface Aucassin and Nicolette appear to reverse roles, since
Nicolette plays the active, heroic part, while Aucassin is most frequently
presented as weak, in despair, and without resolve. The sufferings of the
lovers recall those of Floire and Blanchefleur, Piramus and Thisbe, and
countless other couples.[14] Aucassin, who is as conventionally beautiful as

Nicolette, is a vain, love-struck youth, for whom everything is of secondary importance next to his passion. He meditates on love to such an extent that he is oblivious to the outside world.[15] Erec, Cligès, Yvain, Lancelot, and Perceval share with Aucassin an Ovidian tendency toward the pale, mooning, amorous trance, but few match the latter for ludicrous expression of its conventions—except, perhaps, for Lancelot at the ford. Imitating the model, when riding into the forest to seek Nicolette, Aucassin is so deep in reverie that he falls off his horse and dislocates his shoulder. Undeterred by his incapacity, he stumbles into the bower Nicolette has built, where she pops his shoulder into place before he can wax lyrical as he gazes into the stars and sing a ditty of all the formal sophistication and sentiment of "Twinkle, twinkle little star" [Estoilete, je te voi] (chap. 25). His feebleness as a hero makes him a caricature of the less than ideal romance hero as Chrétien portrays him. Going into battle against Bougars de Valence, it is only the thought of losing his head and never seeing his beloved again that makes Aucassin attempt to save his threatened inheritance (chap. 10), and separation from Nicolette often causes him to weep. When he is imprisoned, it is Nicolette who assumes the risk of escaping from her own captivity, just as at the end it is she who disguises herself as a *jongleur* in order to find him again (chap. 38). She responds with ingenuity to every challenge, while her paramour languishes apathetically. However, in essence their roles are not reversed, but only exaggerated: Aucassin carries the characteristics of the courtly lover to an extreme, but his is not a role reversal in comparison with the king of Torelore. Similarly, Nicolette closely resembles the resourceful Lunete and the stubborn Laudine in Chrétien's *Yvain*, and represents the active strain of headstrong heroines already well attested in Fénice, Enide, and Guenièvre.

The only real inversion in *Aucassin* is found in the kingdom of Torelore, a peculiar distortion of feudal society in which war is waged continuously with no casualties. It is also an unusual instance of gender reversal, with the undomestic queen sent into battle with weapons like cheese and mushrooms, as if to point out the chaos that would ensue if any lasting change in roles were to occur. Again, like *Roman de Silence, Aucassin* turns out to be a normalizing parody in terms of gender, returning characters to their "rightful" places, but the unusual treatment of the central characters leaves its mark on the development of courtly narrative. A classic example of *mundus inversus*, the inverted reality of Torelore is a *mise-en-abyme* of the twisted courtly romance the reader has already observed: like Gorre in Chrétien's *Lancelot*, Torelore heightens the contrast in behavior between the two protagonists that we have already observed in their original environment. Perhaps the greatest irony is that only in an exaggerated non-sense world does Aucassin show signs of becoming an assertive character. When the couple return via different routes to their point of departure, it is once again Nicolette who must go in search of her lover.

The protagonists' adventures are a collection of literary topoi strung together in a humorous attack on convention, using the displacement of genre, inversion, exaggeration, and, above all, the caricature of the hero as major devices. Not just genre, but even the mode of discourse is displaced, as the radical disjuncture between poetry and prose in the text suggests.

In a text that deliberately appeals to the audience's recognition of literary models, we measure Aucassin against an ideal behavior drawn from a horizon of expectation conditioned by familiarity with the roman courtois and a host of other genres. As Anne Cobby observes:

> In *Aucassin et Nicolette,* the parodic references to the romance, and to a lesser extent to the *chanson de geste,* are fundamental. In those *fabliaux* which make use of parody . . . it adds a further dimension to a simply humorous story. In *Aucassin et Nicolette* it is parody which makes the story humorous; such comedy as it would otherwise have is very slight, and would be such as to direct laughter at the author for producing poorly motivated events and a ridiculous hero. (80)

The structure and literariness of *Aucassin* also inform us about the audience of the chivalric romance and courtly literature in general. The anonymous author attributes to his audience both a sophisticated critical faculty and a sensitivity to subtle literary play. The hero is a deliberate exaggeration of a stereotypical hero of the Floire, Yvain, or Perceval type: what, then, does Aucassin teach us? Does he make redundant the romance model after which he is patterned? Jill Tattersall speculates that the "author consciously set out to create a *jeu d'esprit* which would disconcert and disorientate *[sic],* as well as amuse, its public," and that in order to do so "he resorts to a kind of 'scrambling' procedure" ("Shifting Perspectives and the Illusion of Reality" 257–58). I agree with Tattersall that Aucassin never reaches the heights of an antihero and that he is an "occasional hero" (262). As such, however, Aucassin is not an exception to the courtly rule, but a rather extreme example of a tendency already inherent in the genre.

Aucassin et Nicolette is unique not only in form but also in the scope and range of its treatment of language, theme, and genre. It constitutes a humorous rebellion against all forms of convention pertaining to action, language, and sentiment. In addition, its singularity of form sets it at an unusual cartoonlike distance from the models upon which it draws and affords a unique view of their infrastructure, heightened by its formal detachment. Formal analysis of most all chivalric romances would reveal a comic kernel that had a parodic effect on literary convention: the point here is to underscore the importance of this lampooning tendency as what makes the romance "tick."

From the outset the French courtly tradition developed paradigms of convention that provided both a structure and a point of departure. The yardstick of normative chivalric and courtly behavior sets up a model that encourages deviation from those same norms, such that there is a strong sense of generic parody inherent in clashing characters, registers, and episodes. Few would deny their comedy, but some would argue that the provocative dissonance is not parodic, unless a broader definition is given to it. The high degree of inter-referentiality apparent in the works of Chrétien corresponds in great measure to what Genette refers to as the kind of hypertextuality that creates a hypogenre within the romance. While comedy and parody are not necessarily consonant, they often are: not in the limited sense of direct quotation, but in the way that characters and situations seem to exist in dialogic relationship to one another. The prologues of Chrétien are remarkable for the much-discussed way in which he inter-relates his own works and pays homage to his *auctor* Ovid: from the outset there is a tangible sense of connection between romances, and between medieval authors and prior models of discourse. In later works, the degree of comic and parodic collusion between intertexts is more apparent in the direct reference and allusions encoded in them. But these, as we will see, are the outward sign of a more deep and innovative parody of the conventions that shaped them as the heart of the matter.

3

Going South

Courtliness and Comedy
in the Occitan Tradition

On the native soil where it grew and flourished, the roman courtois developed into a complex, playful system of literary rules applied to a symbolic
game of love and heroism played out in a concatenation of exemplary adventures. Designed to instruct and entertain, the most three-dimensional courtly
heroes succeed in their very failure to live up to an ideal; in short, they are at
their paradoxical best when they are least perfect. The art of the romance
was to provide a steady diet of courtly adventure without lapsing into mere
repetition. Maintaining the vitality of the romance meant exploiting its conventions as a source of experimentalism, whether by hybridization with the
lyric, by prose adaptation, or by using the inbuilt, dialogic creative space that
discordant heroes, settings, and adventures provided. At this juncture, there
are many potential directions to take in mapping out the contributions made
by the medieval romance to the novel.

Within the northern tradition there are rich and varied examples of
artful recrafting of the basic genre. However, to journey south to Occitania
provides a relevant example of the trajectory that the romance hero took
in the second wave of literary activity post-Chrétien. Occitania, with its
two remarkable full-length romances *Jaufre* and *Flamenca*, provides a limited but crucial corpus that is too often excised from consideration of the
French and European tradition. In the last decades it seems that the troubadours have finally come into their own in critical terms, and the influence they exerted on the north and beyond now receives its due attention.
With such an important flow of ideas, genres, and concepts from the troubadours to the trouvères, it would be illogical to suppose that the reverse

osmosis did not occur from north to south, although for political reasons it is easy to imagine why there may have been particular kinds of resistance to the importation of French literary models. The lyric works of the trouvères suggest the embracing of principles applied to a simpler set of lyric genres and the cultivation of a less ornate style. The same is not true of the way that the south reworked the model for the romance. The paucity of extant examples suggests that romances either remained in the original French or never achieved the kind of popularity enjoyed elsewhere. At the same time, there is an unusual richness in the Occitan corpus that contains a greater contribution to the development of the romance—and therefore to the early history of the novel—than has often been acknowledged.

Flamenca is the pièce de résistance of the surviving works, and it will be examined in chapter 4. *Jaufre,* the other substantial surviving romance and the only specifically Arthurian one, dates from the first quarter of the thirteenth century.[1] Arthur is also tangentially connected to the shorter récit *Blandin de Cornoalha* (mid-fourteenth century), a work of somewhat disputed quality and geographical origin. *Blandin,* as Keith Busby has pointed out in *"Blandin de Cornoalha* and Romance Tradition," has often been treated as a parody of Arthurian romance, although its connection to the matière is almost circumstantial, and certainly not deep. In tracing the forebears of *Don Quixote, Jaufre* proves an unexpected link in the chain, since in a Spanish version the romance was known to Cervantes, as *La corónica de los nobles caualleros Tablante de Ricamonte y de Don Jofré hijo del Conde Donasón* (Toledo, 1513). He cites it in part 1, chapter 16 of *Don Quixote* when the narrator praises the author of the romance for the minute detail in which he relates the knights' adventures. The passage, undoubtedly strongly ironic, suggests that the reworked text was a paragon of prolixity.[2]

Jaufre tells of the hero's arrival at court, where his father had previously served the king. Immediately on his recognition and knighting he leaves in pursuit of Taulat de Rougemont, who affronts the king by killing a dinner guest and swears to do the same every year on the same day. Just as there is parallelism between the magical happenings at the opening and closing of this romance, one cannot help but see an internal reflection in the choice of Taulat as the sworn enemy of the *Taula redonda* (Round Table). While searching for Taulat, Jaufre encounters many adventures. He defeats Estout de Verfeuil, hangs a recalcitrant dwarf, frees twenty-five prisoners held by a sergeant, battles two villainous lepers, and finds the mysterious palace of Monbrun, where he falls in love with its beautiful ruler, Brunissen.

The surrounding countryside is oppressed by sadness for reasons that Jaufre is unable to discover with his questions, as he finds when he lodges with Augier d'Essart.³ He solves the mystery when he discovers a worthy knight subjected to horrible tortures at the order of Taulat. Waiting for his adversary, Jaufre defeats the Black Knight, and saves Augier's daughter from a giant (related to the lepers defeated earlier) before returning to force Taulat into submission and to restore Augier's daughter to her father. Not wishing to delay his return to Arthur's court and Brunissen, Jaufre leaves, rejoins his lady, becomes engaged to her with the blessing of her feudal lord Mélian (the wounded knight), and then sets out for Arthur's blessing at the court of Cardueil. However, his adventures are not at an end, and after having fallen into an enchanted fountain and entered the kingdom of Guibaldac, ruled by the Fée de Gibel, Jaufre defeats Fellon d'Auberue. Finally, he returns to wed Brunissen, receives supernatural gifts from the mysterious Fée, and arrives crowned with glory and success at Monbrun.

No author's name is mentioned in *Jaufre,* but in the closing lines there is an exhortation to God to forgive "cel quel romantz comenset" and "aquel que l'acabet" [he who began the romance and he who finished it]. Precisely who is responsible for the alpha and omega of the tale is unclear: however, given the unity and continuity within the romance, one author is more likely than two. The split poetic subject is intriguing. One might recall C. S. Lewis's analogy (*The Discarded Image* 198–215) of a medieval author to a builder who completes and develops a design that has already been in the making for some time. *Jaufre* has the blueprint of a northern French romance, but the construction is executed in a southern French style. Thus, one might say that in a sense Chrétien began it and the anonymous poet completed it. We will probably never solve the mystery, but one thing is certain: the narrative from beginning to end points to elaborate comic invention on the author's (or authors') part. In his discussion of the opening scenes of *Jaufre* ("Le Roman à nu"), Jean-Charles Huchet highlights their remarkable and quite literal baring of chivalric convention, lending them a unique status in the annals of chivalric romance.

In the opening scenes, Arthur rides off to the forest in search of predinner adventure with his knights, whom he subsequently leaves to go off alone. He hears a woman crying and finds her in the doorway of a nearby windmill, wherein a ferocious beast is eating her corn. The monster owes something to the bouvier in Yvain: a shaggy, rustic beast, but with the addition of fearsome horns and teeth. At first, Arthur is unimpressed with his seemingly vegetarian adversary and smites the monster on the rump with the flat of his sword. In an act of rash bravado, the king sheathes his weapon and takes the beast by the horns, soon to be caught on those of a dilemma as he is stuck and helpless as a result of his actions. The king undergoes a full range of extreme emotions, while the beast remains placid and guileless. The monster is in the process of carrying Arthur off when Gauvain discovers what is happening and summons the most famous companions of the Round Table. Because the beast is passive and unconcerned by the incident, the king exhorts his nephew not to attack. The monster wanders onto a high rock, such that Arthur dangles into oblivion: for lack of any better solution, and after some lateral thinking, the assembled company strips off and makes a pile of clothing that will serve as a cushion for the king's fall. The creature turns out to be a knight of Arthur's own court with a magician's power who fabricates the adventure to amuse and occupy the assembled company before dinner.

The adventure is anything but dramatic: it is ridiculous, a quite literal fall from the sublime. To begin with, the setting for it is low-class—rather than a damsel in distress we find a miller's wife or daughter, who is not threatened with actual bodily harm, only loss of corn. The king proceeds to have a nonbattle with the beast and winds up in an undignified position because of his own actions. It is hard to see his predicament as anything more than a burlesquing of the notion of suspense. The anti-adventure underscores in a highly parodic way a systematic demystification of romance trumpery.

At the end of the romance, a magical bird of the same magical origin as the beast abducts Arthur (l. 9902) and causes an uproar. Once more, it is an artificial diversion. More interesting is the fact that once the prologue has set the scene it is left to the *encantador* to provide the narrative frame for subsequent events, a reminder of the literary illusion of the romance, something akin to Segre's notion of "fictionality." This self-conscious artificiality finds most blatant expression in works that flaunt their status as fiction; in Renaut de Beaujeu's famous *Le Bel Inconnu,* for example, the narrator breaks off and swears not to continue and have Guinglain reunited with his *amie* until his own lady, an audience to the story, relents. This extratextual factor renders the narrative blatantly artificial (unlike all those texts that claim to be true) and also flatters his lady by suggesting that his professed love for her makes their relationship like the idealized *amour courtois* of romance, demystifying fiction and fictionalizing reality at a stroke.

In a different way, the narrative frame of *Jaufre* achieves the same ends. Huchet proposes the magician as a metaphor for the author, who through his literary wizardry renews a tired Arthurian universe. So hackneyed has the ritual court opening become in the eyes of the poet that the opening of the romance finds Arthur's companions waiting around for an adventure as a condition to be fulfilled before they can sit down to dinner. Arthur is no more than an *amuse-gueule,* and the prestidigitation that opens and closes *Jaufre* suggests that southern French poets had a detached and ironic attitude toward the northern French tradition; this also appears to be the case in *Flamenca.* Adventures beginning at a banquet are conventional, but in *Jaufre* the fantastic adventure that materializes is not generated in the mysterious Celtic otherworld outside the court, but within. The poet of *Jaufre* creates a knight-magician as the instigator of symbolic adventures. Huchet singles out the first of the magician's feats as particularly significant as "les fictions arthuriennes ne sauraient prétendre incarner la Loi du roman sans subir, au pays d'Oc, une mise à nu" [Arthurian fictions could not even begin to embody the Law of the roman without undergoing an undressing in the *pays d'Oc*] ("Le Roman à nu" 93). Culturally and linguistically, the south profits from the distance between established convention and transposed literary reformulation: it encodes in a vital and refreshing way the basic grammar of adventure. Chrétien and his successors commonly represent Arthur as an aged *justicier* who, while he preserves his intellectual powers, is in a form of virtual decline. Just how the south received the northern French Arthurian romances in general is hard to judge, since *Jaufre* is the only extant example: the lack of other examples suggests a commentary in itself.

The treatment of Arthur in *Jaufre* turns him into a figure of parody. Huchet detects a symbolic *dévoilement* in the disrobing of Arthur's court:

> On sait, depuis Macrobe (Ve siècle), que le vêtement . . . est métaphore du texte, notamment chez un Chrétien de Troyes . . . Dévêtir Gauvain, Yvain et Tristan . . . , c'est dénuder les fictions qui les animent; c'est déshabiller le roman arthurien. ("Le Roman à nu" 95)

> [We know, since Macrobius (5th century), that clothing is a metaphor for text, particularly in the works of Chrétien. . . . To unclothe Gauvain, Yvain, and Tristan. . . is to denude the fictions that animate them; it is to undress the Arthurian romance.]

The stripping of an old guise prepares for a renovation, in this case the donning of "les habits neuf de la fiction" [the new clothes of fiction]:

> Rêve d'un roman occitan qui parviendrait à se débarrasser de la tunique de Nessus des fictions arthuriennes et du roman d'Oïl, et trouverait sa matière et sa manière, en harmonie avec l'héritage des troubadours. (99)

[The dream of an Occitan romance that would manage to cast off
the tunic of Nessus of Arthurian fiction and the northern romance,
and which would find its own matter and way of treating it in harmony with the heritage of the troubadours.]

Huchet is justified in seeing a rejection and reworking of the Arthurian
model. He rightly insists on the association of text, texture, and the *retis-
sage* (99) of the warp and weft of chivalric fiction; the development of
Jaufre supports the conclusions Huchet draws from his analysis about the
reformulation and transformation of the Arthurian world.

Arthur undergoes a process of acclimatization in the south, a transition
requiring a divestiture of established convention. Huchet's point about a
renewal of fiction is reinforced by the identity of those involved in the
undignified act of breaking the king's fall.[4] In lines 101–12 we find well-
known members of the Taula redonda:

Aqi fon moseiner Galvain,
Lancelot del Lac e Tristan
El pros Yvans, lo natural
Erec e Quexs lo senescal,
Persaval e Calogremans,
Clige, us cavalier prezans,
E Coedis l'aperseubutz,
E foi lo Bels Desconogutz
E Caraduis ab lu bras cort,
Tug aquist fon a la cort.
E ac n'i mais d'autres ganre
Q'ieu vos dic, car no m'en sove.

[Sir Gauvain was there, Lancelot of the Lake and Tristan, brave
Yvain, noble Erec, and Keu the seneschal, Perceval and Calogrenant,
Cliges, the worthy knight, and Coedis the Shrewd. You could see the
Fair Unknown there, and Caraduis Short-Arm: all those knights
were then at that court. There were many more others than I am
telling, because I don't remember their names anymore.]

The poet shows a notably selective memory, including only names drawn
from famous romances; the list constitutes a digest of the northern French
tradition.[5] Ten of the *douze pairs* are easily recognizable, as are five of Chrétien's principal heroes. The company assembled to witness the magician's
handiwork is a representative delegation from the northern French tradition, a literary genealogy. And since the knights endure debasement far

worse than Lancelot's in Chrétien's romance, the effect is one of demys-tification. Chrétien is the first to exploit the potential of the courtly model, and the *Jaufre* poet is illustrative of the way in which poets who followed used similar devices and strategies to distance the knights even farther from the basic conventions that shaped their development.

The *Jaufre* poet uses cultural as well as geographical separation to re-move them from home territory. The knights that witness Arthur's indig-nity serve the same function as the list of works read at the wedding of Archimbaut and Flamenca. The intention of including the knights in *Jaufre* is clearly parodic: however, the *Jaufre* poet does not go nearly as far as the author of *Flamenca* in debunking courtly mythology, in particular the ethos of northern French romance. Through reflection, incorporation, and parody, the tone of the northern romance is irrevocably changed, and the *mise à nu* described by Huchet becomes a mise-en-abyme for the fate of the northern romance outside its context. François Pirot has catalogued refer-ences to King Arthur in troubadour verse and concludes that an often sardonic tone accompanies them. Citing examples from Bernart de Venta-dour, Guilhem de Berguedan, Peire Vidal, Gaucelm Faudit, and Elias de Fonsalada, Pirot notes that expressions such as "wait like the Bretons" or "hope like a Breton" were synonymous with useless expectation (441–3).

Some critics have read the opening of *Jaufre* as more deeply symbolic. Hans-Robert Jauss asserts that if courtly values are undermined, it is in order to replace them with higher ones, with a new, religious knightly ideal seen in the dedication to the *noveltz cavaliers* of the worthy king of Aragon mentioned in line 69 ("Le sens de l'aventure dans le roman de *Jaufré*" 28–33). *Jaufre* can readily be interpreted as belonging to a new order of chiv-alry, but not in as spiritual a way as the one suggested by Jauss: the hero is no Perceval, for all that he seeks to cure a mysteriously wounded lord and restore a model courtly society. His ambitions are worldly, and it is signifi-cant that although the beginning and the end of the romance find Jaufre seeking approval at court, he finally leaves to find real fulfillment at Mont-brun.

At the end of *Jaufre,* the enigmatic Fée de Gibel has replaced Arthur's court as the focus of the hero's attention. Jaufre is a new, renewed ex-emplary knight, imitating and parodying Chrétien's Perceval, with the dif-ference that his questions lead to no spiritual development or self-improve-ment. Instead, his questions are a source of humor, provoking the most unlikely and unknightly reactions in his interlocutors in the form of verbal or physical abuse unworthy of even the most unsophisticated gallois, as here:

"Aram digatz, fe qe.m devetz,
Veritat, se far o sabetz,
Per qe cridun aquestas jens
La nuit ni.l jorn ta feramens,
Ni per qe menon tan gran dol.
Faun o forsat o ab lur vol?"
El cavaler a escridat:
"En bastartz, plen de malvestat,
Vostra mort avetz demandada!"
(ll. 4667–75)

["Now," said Jaufre, "by the faith that you owe me, tell me truly, if you are able, why these people cry so wildly night and day, and why they mourn so? Do they do it by choice, or are they forced?" And the knight replied: "Lord Bastard, full of evil, you have asked for death!"]

An early interrogation earns Jaufre the title of *en vila, fil d'avol pajes* [Lord Villain, son of a vile bumpkin] (l. 4415). The model here is clearly Chrétien: Perceval's fault is that he fails to ask the right question and thereby elicit the correct answer, whereas Jaufre asks the pertinent question, but receives the most violent and evasive responses. Perceval is destined to unlock a spiritual mystery, and while Jaufre also redeems courtly society through a process of question and answer, the potential spiritually redemptive aspect is missing. Jaufre's scenes of interrogation provide moments of ridicule for the hero, when the courtly and the noncourtly are juxtaposed in a fine registral clash of styles. However comic Perceval might be, his questions provoke a more serious and profound response, and his innocence and naivety provide a source of comedy for Chrétien, who sets his hero's lack of polish against the worldly Gauvain, and whose want of a renewed chivalric ideal keeps him from meaningful adventures. Huchet sees in the *Jaufre* poet a careful reader of Chrétien's text and one who goes on to exceed the base model of the quest narrative:

Non seulement, l'auteur de *Jaufré* a lu *le Conte du Graal*, mais il l'a médité en profondeur pour sortir des impasses que lui imposait son modèle. Il a réduit le Graal à son essence, à une question dont l'altérité doit être apprivoisée, maîtrisée par d'innombrables métamorphoses afin qu'un homme d'oc puisse faire sienne une parole venue d'oïl et y trouver, en marge du rituel lyrique, le moyen d'une interrogation de l'aventure subjective et de l'expérience littéraire. ("*Jaufre* et le Graal" 173)

[Not only has the author of *Jaufre* read the *Conte du graal,* but he has meditated deeply on it in order to find a way out of the narrative impasses that the model imposed on him. He has reduced the Grail to its essence, to a question whose alterity must be tamed, mastered by innumerable metamorphoses so that a man from the pays d'Oc can make his own a word originating in the north, and find there, in the margins of the lyric ritual, the means of interrogating the notion of subjective adventure and literary experience.]

On a formal and conceptual level Huchet identifies a deliberate southern plot to solve the riddle of the Grail, but rather than proposing an answer, *Jaufre* reformulates the question.

In *Jaufre* comedy derives from the lapses from courtly virtue manifest in many of the hero's adversaries. Man's baser instincts and his capacity for antisocial behavior instigate most conflicts, and there is a vulgarity in many of Jaufre's combats that is absent from Chrétien's romance. That Jaufre's fights are baser and more comic than Perceval's is particularly evident when he encounters the leper who has carried off a child. As an opening salvo, the leper gesticulates at Jaufre:

El li fes la figa denant:
"Tenetz," dis el, "en vostra gola!"
E no l'en fes jes une sola,
Ans l'en a faitas mais de tres.
(ll. 2278–81)

[And he made the sign of the fig right in front of him. "Shove that in your mouth!" he said. And he didn't do it just the once, but on the contrary did it more than three times.]

The amusing vulgarity of the leper's gesticulatory retort exceeds even the conventionally exaggerated distinction between cortois and vilain, apparent for example in Calogrenant's and Yvain's encounters with the herdsman. In this instance the obscenity debases Jaufre's chivalric intentions and throws them into comic relief, and what finally seals the parodic effect more than the gesture is the narrative description of its occurring not on one occasion, but *mais de tres.* The vilain from a mysterious otherworld is transposed to a more realistic plane and makes Jaufre's idealism temporarily anachronistic, rather in the same way that the mule-drivers encountered by Don Quixote show up his chivalric pretensions on the occasion of his vigil of arms (part 1, chap. 3). The hero's excursion takes us beyond the normal boundaries of romance and into the baser realm of the fabliau—a comic registral descent hinted at in Chrétien's works, yet never fully developed.

Moreover, as Suzanne Fleischman in *"Jaufré* or Chivalry Askew" observes, there are few grounds for assuming with Jauss that *Jaufre* represents the refinement of a previous courtly model. His behavior as a champion is not ideal: for example, when he is temporarily stunned from his combat with the leper, Jaufre mistakenly crowns the lady he is supposed to be serving in slapstick fashion:

E ela non o a tardat,
Mais vai coren per l'aiga clara,
E a l'en gitat per la cara.
Es el leva sus per poder,
E cujet l'espasa tener,
E a donat a la donzela
Tal un colp apres l'aureila,
Qe si tenges l'espasa nua,
Agra la ben per mig fendua.
(ll. 463–71)

[And she did not waste time, but goes running to get clear water, and she threw it in his face. He gets up with all the force he can muster, and thinking he has his sword in his hand, gives the maiden such a blow around the ear that, if he had held a naked sword, he would have split her in two.]

The scene echoes the battle-aftermath scenes in the *Chanson de Roland,* as the hero, Turpin, and Olivier stagger around in their death throes. Rather than administering the last rites, the maiden delivers a slapstick cold shower that brings a parodic mock-epic response. Jaufre is much more a vehicle for comedy than his northern French counterparts, and it is only logical to conclude with Fleischman that Jaufre both deliberately resembles and lampoons his Arthurian brothers-in-arms.

In both *Flamenca* and *Jaufre* the conventions of Arthurian romance are superseded by southern literary inventions. In the case of *Jaufre,* the code of chivalry as exemplified by Chrétien's heroes has been undermined and replaced not with a renewed spiritual code of honor as Jauss argues, but with a different literary system and a sophisticated consciousness of the romance as a locus for intertextual games. On all narrative levels, the construction of *Jaufre* points to the systematic debunking of the very mechanism of courtly adventure, and its banalization. This is reflected on a subtle level even in the choice of names coined by the Occitan poet. The familiar names of the opening list add a recognizable pedigree, but those that are part of the internal logic of Jaufre's adventures share an unusually generic quality even by romance standards, suggesting a "system" on the part of the author. The issue of proper names in the text does not arise in the Foerster/Breuer edition. Brunel states that aside from the Arthurian contingent "les personnages portent d'ordinaire des noms banals, sans doute empruntés à la poésie épique" [characters ordinarily have banal names, doubtlessly borrowed from epic poetry] (xxxix-xl), citing Robert, Simon, Doson, and Augier as examples and noting Jaufre and Brunissen as Germanic in origin. Of the non-Arthurian place-names, he claims that the Arab Gibel/Guibaldac could have come through chansons de geste and that Rogimont, Vertfueil, and Monbrun are suggested by actual sites in southern France. Unknown are Albarua, Monmelior, and Dinsaure/Siraure. René Lavaud and René Nelli cover much the same ground as Brunel and add that in general the names "n'ont rien de spécifiquement méridional" [have nothing specifically southern about them] (*Les Troubadours: Jaufre, Flamenca, Barlaam et Josaphat* 31). It is possible that Melian has no association with the Midi, but the combination of Melian with Monmelior recalls Monmélian near Chambéry. Fellon d'Albarua has an obviously negative adjective as a first name, and the second part of Augier d'Eissart's name evokes the word for clearing (*essart*) (32). They also note the singularity of the form Guilalmier for Guenièvre and concur with Rita Lejeune concerning the predominance of color references in Monbrun, Vertfueil, Albarua, and Rogimon ("La date du *roman de Jaufre*" 273n. 45). She associates brown with sadness, green with treachery *(la couleur musulmane)*, and red with stealth as well as badness. The *Jaufre* poet is surely ingenious enough for this, although it is perhaps more likely that since colors are such a frequent occurrence in toponyms, the convenient paradigm of names could also be a part of the banalization of the grammar of adventure and romance.

Of the immediate association between Jaufre's main adversary Taulat de Rogimon, and the word for table, *taula* or *taulat*, which Lavaud and Nelli say "fait peut-être songer l'auditeur à une vaste corpulence" [perhaps makes the reader imagine a vast corpulence] (*Les Troubadours: Jaufre, Flamenca, Barlaam et Josaphat* 32). Taulat is the key figure here, and rather than indicating his stoutness, it is clear that his name is a further indication of his function in the narrative, which is to embody the very antithesis of the Taula redonda (l. 33), over which an undignified and disempowered Arthur presides. Taulat, or variants of it, appears as a name in northern French romances, mentioned briefly in *Erec et Enide,* where he appears after Gilflez (of which Jaufre is a variant), and it is said that "onques d'armes ne fu las" [he never tired of arms] (l. 1697), while in Chrétien's *Lancelot* (l. 5814) he appears as Taulas de la Deserte at the tournament at Noauz. Fernand Flutre's index cites many more examples.[6] The collective references made to Taulat and its variants in various romances suggests the generic quality of a largely positive minor character, and in romances predating *Jaufre* there is little to suggest his future development as an important adversarial figure. It is evident that careful strategy governs the choice of names made by any romancier: he might draw on regional place-names with a certain resonance, include references suggestive of historical figures or events, or include items for purely euphonic reasons. In addition, incorporating characters from other texts ensures another important metatextual, literary continuity. The *Jaufre* author avails himself of all the above possibilities and also aligns his choice of names with the overall design of the romance to create a series of models and antimodels.

In the crucial case of Taulat, if the Round Table proper represents virtue, then Taulat is its dark side: the connection between the two presents itself at the outset, when Taulat slays his first victim at the table (ll. 577–91). Emmanuèle Baumgartner compares Taulat's challenge to that of the *Chevalier Vermeil* in Chrétien's *Perceval* ("Le défi du chevalier rouge dans *Perceval*" 239–54). This chivalric *acte gratuit* is in keeping with the artificial opening of *Jaufre,* designed to present a deliberate tabula rasa of the very concept of chivalry itself. There are so many instances of the doubling of names in medieval narrative, the two Yseuts in the *Tristan* romances being chief among them (Eufeme and Eufemie in the *Roman de Silence* are another example of linked names that express opposite qualities), that although comparing a character with an inanimate object is undoubtedly rarer, the *Jaufre* poet could have alighted on the name Taulat precisely because of its homophonic qualities and resonance. At the risk of pushing the association too far, Taulat's challenge literally and figuratively turns the tables on Arthur.

The bulk of Jaufre's subsequent trials occur when he searches for Taulat, who has cast a blight over the land through his persecution of Melian. Taulat's influence pervades the landscape and the mechanism of feudal life portrayed in it, and the path leading to him is an appropriate trail of destruction, strewn with dead, wounded, or captive knights and blocked by obstacle-figures that share a common motif. When Jaufre eventually confronts Taulat, their long-anticipated combat is short and lackluster and justifiably termed by Suzanne Fleischman as "singularly anti-climactic" and "an undercut version of what promised to be the quest in its highest form" ("*Jaufré* or Chivalry Askew" 115, 116). In addition to being part of the parodic plan, the final confrontation exists as it does because Jaufre has fought fragmentary aspects of Taulat's character all along and will fight him in the central combat of the narrative in the transposed and surreal form of Fellon: he is not so much an individual as the personification of moral and social disorder, an "anti-Table."

As for the knights that stand for the values of this anticourtly universe, their collective quality is summarized by the name of Estout de Vertfueil, from the adjective meaning haughty or prideful. His other name, "Green-leaf" may allude to his jealous nature. He has so humiliated a group of aristocratic prisoners that they are reduced to the level of cooks, the ultimate knightly disgrace as outlined in texts from the *Chanson de Roland* onward. On defeating Estout, Jaufre restores the symbols of their rank when he gives them back weapons and mounts. As Marc-René Jung states, "[t]out est signe dans *Jaufre,* mais rarement ce signe est expliqué par l'auteur, ou par un de ses personnages" [everything in *Jaufre* is about signs, but rarely is the sign explained by the author, or by one of his characters] ("Lecture de *Jaufre*" 429).[7]

On a basic level, the semiotics of these first adventures are bound up with the feudal/chivalric values expressed in Chrétien's works and the devaluation of the code, be it in a loss of dignity or equipment. The episode of *lo brun de la lança* (ll. 1332–1657) reinforces this idea, when Jaufre's adversary proposes the following alternative to being hanged to those defeated by him:

> Qe jamais a sa vida
> Non calvages, ni non tolges
> Cabels ni onglas qe ages,
> Ni manjes pan de froment,
> Ni beges vin, ni vestiment
> Non portes si el no.l teisía.
> (ll. 1444–49)

[For the rest of his life he can never ride a horse, trim his nails or hair, nor eat white bread or drink wine, or wear clothes he hasn't woven himself.]

Estout's alternative represents nothing short of reduction to the status of a peasant. In a comic retort, Jaufre rejoins that to learn all those skills would be too difficult (ll. 1451–2), to which the knight replies that he could teach him "[a]ns qe sion passatz .vij. ans" [before seven years had elapsed] (l.

1464). The monolithic block of seven years appears on several occasions in the text, and represents the classic measure of epic time as it does in the *Chanson de Roland*, where it is never associated with the domestic arts.

To juxtapose the heroic/militaristic ethos with the exacting demands of the basest servitude and the notion that Jaufre spend the same amount of time perfecting his tailoring skills as Charlemagne took conquering Spain is to cite but one instance of the author's sly humor. Knighthood is in need of redemption, as in most courtly romances, but the nature and the threat menacing it are configured in singular style in *Jaufre*. This is supported by the number of narratorial asides devoted to bemoaning the social decline provoked by social climbing and the promotion of the wealthy but ignoble to the ranks of the aristocracy (for example, ll. 2565–630), suggesting that the enemy of true nobility is not only without but also within. Veronica Fraser is by no means alone in seeing a strongly satirical streak in *Jaufre* ("Humour and Satire in the Romance of *Jaufre*").

The risk of losing rank to inferiors is a common motif, but is unusually persistent as a theme in Jaufre's adventures. It is also prevalent in the episode involving the *sergent* who exacts the toll for allowing travellers through his mountain pass of having them abandon arms and horse. As previously, he has many prisoners who have submitted to his challenge and endured debasement, and they are grateful for the liberation Jaufre provides—rather like the prisoners in Gorre who find rescue with Lancelot's arrival. As in Chrétien's romance, we expect some magical or mystical custom. But the mundanity of nonpayment of tolls is a comic treatment of the strange custom: it banalizes and parodies such incidents. They constitute a part of the ethos of antichivalry created by Taulat, whose dominion over the realm beyond Arthur's court is as firm as Arthur's over his bored subjects, collectively unable to cultivate adventure in a landscape brimming with iniquities.

If Taulat threatens the honor of knighthood, the anonymous lepers represent another kind of plague on society: the danger of brutality directed against women and children. And the diabolic Black Knight personifies the moral turpitude of those denatured by having given in to the dark side of unrepressed violence. Later, Fellon d'Albarua, Taulat and Estout's otherworld double, is a final personification of a twisted antimodel of chivalry—and apparent as much from his name as from the detailed description of his moral and physical malformation (ll. 8760–90).

In *Jaufre* there are many instances where we see the world upside down, beginning with Arthur's court. Brunissen's castle and the surrounding landscape seem similarly disordered, and even in the reflective mirror-world of the *fada de Gibel*, the distorted model is another replication of the feudal chaos on the surface of the romance. Although its underground, underwater depths add an enchanted dimension to the romance, there is little real magic in the sunken kingdom. If anything, the location conveys the real depth of feudal corruption and disorder and the level to which contemporary knighthood has sunk in the form of Fellon, who is the final in a series of generic or symbolic adversaries.

The named figures in Jaufre's quest are few, belonging either to the Taula redonda or to Jaufre's adversaries and the endangered group of nobles in need of redemption that occupy the middle ground of the romance. Augier recalls the comic Audigier and the spirit of epic. And Brunissen, whose name has more resonance to it than Germanic derivation, suggests what Rita Lejeune sees as a connection with the verb *brunezir:* "s'obscurcir, s'attrister" [darken, sadden], making Brunissen literally "l'attristée, celle qui souffre" [the saddened lady, she who suffers] ("La date du *Roman de Jaufre*" 273 n. 45; also Nelli and Lavaud 32). Augier and Brunissen represent the dynastic future of feudalism, with its promise of economic and social stability.

A third figure has been as overlooked as Taulat in the analysis of names: Melian de Monmelior. Rather than any specific geographic connection, we should perhaps seek something more emblematic in his name and a probable connection with, or verbal echo of, *melhor* (better), *melhs* (best), or the verb *melhorar* (improve). Melian, the good, crippled knight, and the best that the chivalric code can hope or strive for, is a less cryptic and spiritual version of the wounded Fisher-King, personifying feudal ideals besieged by the destructive Taulat. In Melian's existential punishment we can read a transposed form of that undergone by Sisyphus: his test of endurance represents the vicious circle of violence inherent in the feudal system and the circularity of the chivalric narrative like some *machine infernale* that mirrors it. Melian's torture could thus also be interpreted as the futility of the romance genre as a whole: like the initial scenes with the magician, it reveals the relative emptiness of the self-perpetuating cycle of adventure. The final notable act that brings closure to the romance is Melian's releasing of Taulat from his sentence for a month, bringing a temporary peace to the perpetual and familiar conflict between good and evil that provides the narrative impetus.

Two other possible meanings of *taula* may be useful in exploring Taulat's role and significance: *taula/s* also designates a gaming table, and thus contains a ludic dimension suitable for the adversarial game of pursuit and strategy expressed in the moves and countermoves of adventure.[8] Lastly, *taulas* can also refer to writing desks, and thus encloses the literal space on which texts take shape: this final meaning underpins the reader's sense that this ingenious text is also about writing itself. It is always dangerous to argue that an author encumbers a word with all its possible meanings when using it. However, the closer the analysis of courtly narrative, and Occitan narrative in particular, the less gratuitous even small details seem and the more suggestive they become: the Round Table represents circular fiction, and is surely a ludic model of writing. In *Jaufre* we find a text that conveys a sense of literal and figurative iconoclasm, as well as a deep awareness of the courtly romance as a faintly ludicrous game, exposing its inner self-reflexivity and doubly artificial strategy of narrative regeneration. To modern eyes, so many medieval texts send the reader back to the underlying theme of artistic creativity and writing about writing, and in this regard *Jaufre* is no exception with its construction of polished and elegantly distorting mirrors of chivalry.

Everything in Taulat's character, and in the various guises of Jaufre's obstacles to success, encodes a crisis in, and reinscription of, the concept of chivalry—both the self-referential literary kind and the extratextual historic kind. An ineffectual court is the gateway to a sterile landscape, redeemed only by an original and unconventionally conventional hero whose agency originates beyond the boundaries of chivalric tradition. The *Jaufre* poet is as much an outsider as his hero, and he takes pains to distance himself from the tradition he exploits and critiques. Dedicating his work to *lo rei d'Aragon* (l. 61), using the medium of a native language that of historical necessity establishes a barrier between it and the original northern ethos, and claiming that the tale he is about to relate was told to him by a *cavalier estrain* [foreign, unknown knight] (l. 87), are all devices that estrange the reader from the Arthurian matter in hand, or at least create an objective distance from it. *Estrain* is a synonym for French, and the name of the narrative ruse in this particular case is to strip chivalric convention of its nostalgic northern luster and restore its tarnished image in a changed and renewed narrative landscape. In his cultural resistance to northern French tradition, Jaufre perhaps has something in common with the other great southern knight of literature, Cyrano de Bergerac, whose enemies, like Jaufre's, were the mediocre personifications of the qualities lacking in a true lyric knight. Jaufre is as comic as Cyrano is comi-tragic, but they both define themselves much as Occitan culture has always done in relation to it close neighbor: in strongly individualistic opposition and in competition. Poetry may or may not be overtly political, but the history of fiction proves beyond a doubt that there is no keeping out political consciousness.

Why are there not more Occitan romances? Even given the strong probability that some texts have been lost, the significantly different treatment given the form by southern writers points to other factors. The predominance of lyric poetry is one such factor to be considered, since the flourishing of the troubadours coincides with the sparse production of narrative texts. It may perhaps have to do with the appropriateness of language to literary genre, as Raimon Vidal suggests: "La parladura francesca val mais et [es] plus avinenz a far romanz et pasturellas, mas cella de Lemosin val mais per far vers et cansons et serventes" [The French language is more worthy and beautiful for composing romances and *pastorelas,* but that of the Limousin is better for composing *vers,* songs, and *cansos*] (*Marshall* 6). The only differentiating trait in the list Raimon gives is length, in the case of the romance, and the importance of dialogue in the pastourelle when compared with other genres. It is surprising that he finds the pastorela less fitting in Occitan, given its success as a genre and of the other longer debate poem, the *tenso.*

Raimon's allusion to the pastorela begs further investigation. Other grammarians and literary commentators do not share his appraisal: in the anonymous *De doctrina de compendre dictats* (Marshall 95–98), the pastorela is fully incorporated into the range of lyric genres, and the author recommends that for variation you change her name from shepherdess to swineherd, goatherd, or some other according to the animals she tends (ll. 45–49), rather than altering the narrative. This treatise is claimed by Marshall to be by Jofre de Foixà, author of the *Regles de trobar* (c. 1286–91), since the short *Doctrina* is appended to it. Most intriguing is the possible underlying suggestion that French is more aesthetically suited to the longer narrative and Occitan to lyric genres, the romance belonging more to the *pays d'Oïl* than to the *pays d'Oc.* Agility and subtlety over the short distance of lyric genres is perhaps contrasted in this instance with the long-distance stamina required for more narrative works. Here a sustained and consistent approach to language and structure is essential.

Troubadour lyrics were in circulation in the north and were very influential, yet the hermetic style of *trobar clus* is not practiced to the same degree in *trouvère* lyrics, where the simplicity of *trobar leu* is much more in evidence. In the domain of romance, exposition is all, and the *sens* and *conjointure* at the heart of the conceptual plan of Chrétien's romances require qualities opposed to those needed to produce complex courtly lyrics. The external logic and need for thematic development in the romance contrasts with the compositional intricacy of poetry.

It is more likely that Raimon's separation of the two languages is the result of his Catalonian origin, and of his writing at a time when the maintenance of the purity of the literary language was an important issue. He may not even have been thinking about literary criticism, but his remark may reflect a contributing factor to the lack of romances in Occitan. The fact that he describes French as *plus avinenz* for romances may suggest that some texts were available for comparison before the date of composition of *Jaufre* and *Flamenca,* and that therefore more romances than have come down to us may have existed. This is speculation: the important fact that remains is that those romances that have survived are characterized by a parodic treatment of the conventional northern French material. It is also likely that we see a case of cultural resistance in the refusal to adopt the roman: given the dates of the Albigensian crusades and the political upheaval it produced, it is not unreasonable to suspect that writers in the south identified the genre strongly with the domestic policy of the north.

That the Occitans were familiar with the characters and plots of Arthurian romance is shown by the nature of the parody in *Jaufre* and in the catalogue of works recited during the banquet scene of *Flamenca*. François Pirot's research into the literary allusions made by the troubadours shows an early familiarity with the *matière de Bretagne* (435–525). The paucity of surviving romances in the south attests either to the mild reception accorded Occitan romances on home ground, or to the comparatively greater success of their French counterparts. It must be added that French romances would have been more easily disseminated to southern audiences than Occitan texts to northern ones. This is not entirely because of language difficulties, since Occitan and French were readily understood outside the boundaries of their home territories. At the same time it was (and is) easier for a southern speaker of Occitan to understand French from a northerner than vice versa. The farther north a text travelled, the farther it was removed from its natural linguistic environment. It is more a question of genre: romances with their sustained plots are more accessible in the south, whereas decontextualized courtly poetry designed for an elite audience and composed in a deliberately arcane style would have been more difficult to understand for those in the north. And yet ease of comprehension could well have been offset by other kinds of cultural resistance to the importation of a feudal worldview that was potentially at odds with the Occitanian one.

The *vida* of Elias Fonsalada, although dating from a later period, provides further clues about the production of narrative texts:

N'Elias Fonssalada si fo de Bargairac, de l'evesquat de Peiregors. Bels hom fo molt de la persona. E fo fils d'un borges que se fez joglars, e.n Elias fo joglars atressi. No bons trobaire mas noellaire fo, e saup ben estar entre la gen. (Boutière and Schutz 235)

[Lord Elias Fonsalada was from Bergerac, in the bishopric of Péri-gord. He was a good-looking man. And he was the son of a burgher who became a performer, and Lord Elias became a performer also. He was not a good poet, but was rather a narrative writer, and knew how to get on with people.]

Noellaire, to date, occurs only here, and contrasts with *trobaire*, suggest-ing that the professional activity of one differed from the other. The word has been variously translated by critics: Boutière and Schutz summarize critical differences of opinion when they hesitate between defining it as the author of a particular genre, or "tout simplement un beau parleur" [quite simply a good talker] (235). Given the context of the vida's deliberate contrast of the two terms, the second definition seems less likely than the first: the final clause tells us of Elias's social ease, and given the economy of the vida it is unlikely that his eloquence would require more than one citation. Moreover, we are told that Elias's father was a *joglar*, which would make the definition of *noellaire* as a contrasting professional activ-ity more likely.

Manfred Raupach has dated the work of Elias Fonsalada to the closing years of the twelfth and first quarter of the thirteenth century, a period which coincides with the flourishing of the troubadours and the produc-tion of those few extant narrative works referred to as *novas*. He bases his dating on references made to Fonsalada and other troubadours who are more easy to pinpoint chronologically, thereby dating Elias's two surviving cansos to the end of the reign of Peter II of Aragon (d. 1213). Given the existence of such works as a genre, it is not unreasonable to translate noellaire as "composer of novas." If so, this vida is unique and intriguing in that it mentions a narrative genre: moreover, the inference here is that he wrote narrative poetry because of, or in spite of, the fact that he was not a good composer of lyric poetry. Were his talents too modest to enable him to be a successful troubadour? If so, was being a noellaire second choice, and if this is the case, what does this tell us about the reception of romances written in Occitan and contemporary attitudes toward their composers? The answer might support Raimon Vidal's assertion that Occitan was more appropriate for poetry and not as fitting for romances.

To speculate is problematic, since the views of the vida writer might derive from the later literary aesthetic of Italy. Even allowing for the intervening time period, however, the description of Fonsalada is the exception to the conventional troubadour portrait. We might regret that while two of his poetic works remain, nothing of his production as an author of narrative endures, if indeed he wrote anything. Although it only leads to speculation, the existence of the word *noellaire* (like the intriguing *trobairitz* of *Flamenca*) provides a trace of narrative activity at the height of the flourishing poetic culture of the south and begs the question as to why there is so little narrative activity as opposed to lyric, when there is clearly motive, means, and opportunity. It is clear that Occitan narrative tradition did not develop as the northern French did, showing a movement from epic to chanson de geste to courtly romance. The delicate subject of lost Occitan epic and the development of chanson de geste are beyond the scope of this study: it is important to note the late character of the Occitan romance and its thematic dependence on the north. Moreover, the treatment given the conventional material is different: accounting for the ironic distance between the two competing views poses problems.

Analyzing the tone and treatment of chivalric romance in *Jaufre*, Suzanne Fleischman considers the reasons for the parody of northern French romance and speculates that it might be due to a differing concept of chivalry. At the same time she signals the impossibility of proving such a hypothesis, while appropriately demonstrating the need to read *Jaufre* as a parody — not as a parody of chivalry per se, but of the language and worldview that created it and was expressed through it. That the *matière de Bretagne* seems to belong outside the *langue d'oc* is confirmed by its rejection as a positive narrative model by the author of *Jaufre*. It is as though the southern writers could not use the chivalric conventions of the romance as they had been established in northern France.

Perhaps Raimon's Catalonian perspective provides an outside view of the way in which French and Occitan were viewed not just as different languages but as different literary systems requiring a modification in order to accommodate them on foreign ground. What we see in *Jaufre* is not just the rejection of a form of chivalry, but the reappropriation of a symbolic system of language and convention. Alberto Limentani discerns

un primo notevole cedimento della fiducia nell'ideale eroico che aveva presieduto alla storia del genere romanesco, e specie arturiano: e forse non si può andare molto più in là, almeno coi fatti di cui disponiamo, specie se si ricordi che al di sotto dell'umorismo c'è sempre un fondo amaro, pessimistico, che conduce più a un rifiuto di termini dati che a un'affirmativa proposta di nuove idealità. (101)

[a first notable lapse of faith in the heroic ideal that had been at the forefront of the romance genre, especially the Arthurian romance: and perhaps one cannot go much further than that, at least not with the facts at our disposition, particularly if one recalls that beneath the humor there is always a layer of bitterness and pessimism, which leads more to a rejection of given boundaries than the affirmative setting out of a new ideal.]

If the author of *Jaufre* adopts the conventions of courtly romance, it is in order to transgress them. Limentani points to a dark undercurrent of resistance to imported convention and to the heroic ideal beneath the surface parody of the text. What, then, does the "rifiuto" suggest?

It is clear that both *Jaufre* and *Flamenca* represent uses of, and departures from, the form of romance, and that the transposition from north to south brought new treatment to the conventional content of romance. The use of the word *novas* to describe the story to be told is significant. Emile Levy describes it as being equivalent to "nouvelles," "conte," or "récit" (262). The author of *Flamenca* refers to his tale as *mas novas* (l. 250), and since we lack the prologue and epilogue, this remains our only indication of how the author viewed his text. We have more nuanced information about *Jaufre,* since in the opening line the author calls his poem *un cumte de bona maniera* [a well-made tale] and in the closing lines terms it a *romant* (l. 10949).

While there is nothing exceptional about this nomenclature, the context in which it occurs is intriguing: "Car om nun deu comprar ni vendre / Ni l'us a l'autre conselar / Can au bunas novas comtar" [Because one should never buy and sell, nor should one counsel another when one hears a good story told] (ll. 14–16). The use of the verbs *comprar* and *vendre* is all but unthinkable in most conventional courtly romances in the north before those of Jean Renart. The most striking exception is Chrétien's *Yvain* (ll. 5107–5346), in which the maidens held prisoner in *Le chastel del Pesme Avanture* are forced to labor in squalid conditions for low pay. The way that Maxime Chevalier describes the importance of chivalric romance to the aristocratic readers of Spain in *Lectura y lectores en la Espana de los siglos XVI y XVII* seems to apply here: in the opening lines of *Jaufre* the narrator calls for the suspension of urban, mercantile activity, to which the antidote is the nostalgic landscape of the romance. Buying and selling are not approved social activities in a literary setting that sought to trade the present for an otherworld, and the specific reference made to the marketplace perhaps informs us as to the broader audience enjoyed by the Occitan *novas*.

Linda Paterson suggests that in the social fabric of the south there existed a more urban, mercantile class of knight, unlike in the north (41). Such knights might have been part of the intended audience of the novas, and it is not unreasonable to speculate that this and other differences in the forms of knighthood practiced in the south influenced the forms of courtly/ chivalric literature that sprang up in the Midi. Raimon Vidal, in the opening of the *Razos de Trobar,* speaks of the universality of poetry and of audience:

> Primerament sapies que totas gens, christians, iuheus, sarrahins, senyor, emperador, rey, princep, duch, comte, vezcomte, comdor, vezcondor, cavaller, clerch, burgues, vila, o home pauch e gran, menon [tot] dia trobar e xantar. (Marshall 3)

> [First, know that all people, Christians, Jews, Saracens, lords, emperors, kings, princes, dukes, counts, viscounts, marquises, barons, knights, clerks, burghers, villains, or men great and small take part each day in composing and singing.]

Those exhorted to stop buying and selling in *Jaufre* undoubtedly belong to the *borgues* end of the hierarchy, associated in more traditional criticism with the fabliau than with the romance. More recent investigations into the fabliaux, however, establish that these bawdy tales enjoyed popularity across the spectrum of the social classes.[9]

What is true for the audience of fabliaux may well be true for the courtly romance: there was certainly a more mixed audience for the northern French romance than that implied by the elitist setting and orientation of Arthurian literature. In the south, as for the more hybrid *romans réalistes* like *Guillaume de Dole* in the north, there seems to be a move toward verisimilitude and the debunking of cares, thus away from rarified idealism, toward a setting more consonant with a broader social orientation toward the town rather than the castle. Perhaps it is fairer to say that we find ourselves much further removed from fantasy in a textual economy that owes much more to the ethos of buying and selling. In effect, there are two sets of measurements under consideration, relative to distance from an earlier model and proximity to what we can term a limited verisimilitude, or at the least a more realistic discourse. Limentani comments on the different literary development of the south, saying that there is nothing comparable with *Roland, Renard,* the *Roman de la Rose,* or with the fabliaux, owing to "la peculiarità individuale" [the particular individuality] (5) of the *pays d'Oc* and the literary rivalry within the area as well as the influence from without.

While it has a complex network of lyric forms, one reason that the south has few narrative forms that can be compartmentalized into recognized genres may be that by the time *Jaufre, Flamenca,* and the novas appear, the essential elements of narrative genres had already been subsumed and rearticulated in different form. In *Jaufre,* for example, two northern works are at the heart of the narrative: Marie de France's *Les Dous Amanz* and *Le Conte du Graal. Les Dous Amanz* is read aloud to *Jaufre* and his companions (l. 4460) and recurs as an echo in the episode of the wounded knight, who Sisyphus-like must carry a great burden (in this case a stone) to the top of the hill, just as Marie de France's hero carries his beloved up a steep slope and dies in the attempt. This is one of her most ironic lais, one that openly lampoons the conceits of love and motifs like the love potion and lover's test. Perhaps only Marie's *Le Chaitivel* does more to burlesque the rarified tenets of courtly love. Moments of bathos abound in *Les Dous Amantz,* such as the instance when, to help her lover make ready to carry her up the mountain, the doomed girl goes on a diet to supplement the strength training and magic potion that already figure in the preparations. Marie's narrative has great pathos but is also remarkable for its parodic edge.

Le Conte du Graal is first and foremost among *Jaufre*'s intertexts. While critics debate over whether *Jaufre* influenced Chrétien or vice versa, most favor the latter solution, both because the northern romancier appears to be much more influential and widely read and because *Jaufre* suggests a parody of the Grail theme of Chrétien's work. It is far more likely that the *Jaufre* poet found material to parody than that Chrétien found a comic theme to treat more seriously: that is quite simply not the path that literary development takes. It does not introvert a text or set of conventions and thereby turn the comic into serious matter, but rather extroverts them, and turns the original into something more lighthearted. *Perceval* is already a partial critique of the Arthurian world, designed to show its bankruptcy as an endless source of adventures. In this it resembles *Jaufre,* but with an important difference: just as Chrétien uses Gauvain as a deliberate counterweight to Perceval, so Perceval in turn provides a foil for more weighty issues. *Jaufre* represents a parody both of Gauvain and Perceval, addressed to an audience already familiar with the vagaries of northern chivalry and its literary manifestations.

We may speculate that the author of *Jaufre* directed his novas to a broader audience, one both urban and urbane, sophisticated enough to pick out the literary allusions. At the same time we may imagine a southern audience politically and culturally opposed to the north, particularly in the years of the first quarter of the thirteenth century. Such an audience might indeed anticipate a reaction against literary conventions from outside, and that a novel use might be made of them. It may also be that issues of genre and audience concealed beneath the surface in northern France are more in evidence in the small but suggestive narrative corpus of the south. In the case of *Flamenca*, we might find equal support for a broader audience in the choice of central characters and location; although the beginning and end of the work find the protagonists at court, the central action takes place in the church, inn, and bathhouse at Bourbon. Noncourtly characters, such as Pierre Guy the innkeeper, his wife, the bathhouse proprietor, the priest, and Flamenca's maids (much more in keeping with the spirit of Molière's servants than with the noble Lunete of *Yvain*) are essential agents in the unfolding of the plot. The action takes place not in a gauzy, heroic past, but in a more or less contemporary setting. An extremely practical kind of courtly love is at the center of the narrative, with the problems involved in effecting the *liaison dangereuse* between Guillem and Flamenca dealt with in detail: we find plotting, bribing, digging and tunnelling, disguising, and cuckolding described with extravagance. Both *Flamenca* and *Jaufre* are influenced by elements of the shorter novas form that takes the place occupied by the lai and fabliau in the north.

In one respect *Flamenca* shares a particularly common theme with other shorter novas. Indeed, the cuckolded husband punished by his wife is as frequent to Occitan literature as it is to the northern French fabliau; two other surviving novas, Raimon Vidal's *Castìa-gilos* and Arnaut de Carcassès's *Novas del Papegai* share a similar theme.[10] Both are short, 450 and 339 lines respectively, which in itself raises problems of generic definition. Their germane property is found in the reinforcement of the system of courtly love while parodying it: the novas, as comic amplification of the more serious themes of courtly love, provide the twist in the tale of *Flamenca*.

The issue of the origin of the novella is obscure: the surviving Occitan examples show all the features of style and tone associated with the heyday of the form. Although clearly an established literary genre in the south, the word *nouvelle* as a genre in French belongs to the Renaissance, having been by all accounts borrowed from the Italian, and modelled on Boccaccio.[11] However, in the Middle Ages short narrative forms abound in the vernacular and in Latin, any of which (or more likely a combination) contribute to the evolution of the genre. Marie-Louise Ollier describes the short narrative as being as "protean" as the romance, once certain defining criteria are established (78). Not surprisingly, there are similarities in terms of narrative structure between the lai, fabliau, novas, and novella. One of the important defining characteristics is that these genres are always historically and culturally specific, and the most intriguing area of exploration lies in determining what the forms meant in their milieu.

The Occitan novas date from a particular setting and time. They provide an interesting case for analysis, since the few surviving examples suggest that the form was defined by content and not by length (see Huchet, *"Jaufre* et *Flamenca"*). Although content defining form is frequent in lyric genres, it is interesting that it should be the case with the novas, since the variance in length is so marked in the surviving examples, equivalent to seeing the modern short story and the novel as essentially no different. Even given the elasticity of the roman, the novas is indeed a most elastic form, since both *Jaufre* (10956 lines) and *Flamenca* (8096 lines) call themselves novas along with two much shorter works. The two short works are linked in tone and presentation to their longer counterparts and are closely joined thematically to *Flamenca*. Writing on Marie de France, Marie-Louise Ollier points out the historical specificity of each manifestation of the short narrative form: what she claims for the lai in northern France can easily be applied to the novas of the south.

Raimon Vidal's *Castía-gilos* dates from around 1214 and tells of the love of Bascol for Alvira in spite of her watchful and jealous husband. She is chaste and will not give in to Bascol's advances. However, her husband is persuaded by malevolent advisors that the amorous courtier is her lover ante facto and tries to test her by disguising himself as Bascol. During a nocturnal tryst she hits her disguised husband as hard as she can and locks him in her chamber, where he remains stunned but happily convinced of her innocence. She then visits Bascol and stays the night in order to teach her spouse a lesson. An analogous story, significantly perhaps set in Paris on fabliau territory, is to be found in *Decameron* 7.7, in the tale of Lodovico and his love Beatrice, and her husband Egano. The moral of the story blames the husband and calls jealousy a "laia malautía" [an ugly sickness] to be avoided at all costs: adultery is portrayed as a legitimate aristocratic recreation, and stopping it only leads to the undignified ridicule of the injured party. Alphonse is closely related to Archimbaut in *Flamenca,* who, if anything, is much more of a caricature, and bears a close resemblance to the cuckolded husbands of the fabliau tradition.

The *Novas del Papagai*, dating from the first half of the thirteenth century according to Nelli and Lavaud, is an appealing tale of fin'amor concerning the lovers Antiphanor and an anonymous married lady, united by the agency of his eloquent and talented parrot. The lovers organize a meeting in the locus amoenus of the castle garden, and while the parrot sets fire to the tower of the castle to provide a distraction, they embrace. The literal and symbolic fires having been extinguished, the lady makes Antiphanor promise to go forth and do as many good deeds as he can. When the lady dismisses her lover at the garden gate, we are reminded of Flamenca's instructions to Guillem after their affair has progressed: when her cure is complete, she too sends her lover out into the world to prove himself. Arnaut concludes his poem by instructing husbands not to restrict their wives too much: the approval of the lady's actions implicit in the narrative suggests that the author is trying to portray the affair as socially productive.

The parrot uses the argument that it is a lady's duty to encourage those who would die for her, citing the precedents of Blancheflor, Iseut, and Thisbé (ll. 84–6). In the latter two examples we find no positive model to encourage a lady to embark on an extramarital affair, since, amusingly, their trysts lead to an early grave. As for the *Roman de Floire et Blancheflor*, the heroine of this widely disseminated tale represents the epitome of youthful, innocent passion in a sinful, lustful world, in which, in the spirit of Greek romance, she is sold as a slave into an emir's harem. This being said, there is an almost alarming undercurrent of narcissism, not to mention incest, in the story. She and her lover resemble each other so much that it is difficult to tell them apart. The more tragic cases of Tristan and Iseut and Pyramus and Thisbe similarly stress the nobility and intensity of courtly love.

All three tales present archetypal obstacles to the union of the lovers, be they in the form of kings, husbands, or parents. Taken together, they demonstrate the virtues of love, its grandeur and sublimity in the face of overwhelming odds; the treatment allotted to these themes in the *Novas del Papegai* seems intentionally parodic, and the sublime has been rendered charmingly mundane. The wide-ranging and exotic adventures of Floire and Blancheflor are reduced to one amorous adventure in a garden. Antiphanor, a somewhat weak figure without his skilled, feathered rhetorician, is no Tristan or Pyramus. Empires are not at stake; the husband poses no threat to the union of the lovers, except in the degree to which he influences the lady's initial moral resolve. Human desire supplants the lover's draught, and the tomb that separates the doomed lovers of the Pyramus and Thisbe legend is transformed into the garden gate that is overcome with no opposition. Even a passing reference to these works adds an element of informed literary parody to the intrigue of Arnaut's tale, in addition to the inherent comedy of the situation. In a tale where the flames of passion are kindled by a parrot with a bucket, it is not hard to see creative ways in which Occitan authors put a damper on the artificial refinement of fin'amors.

Raimon Vidal's *Castía-gilos* deploys no such subtle intertextual references, but has a more overt and farcical form of comedy, in the form of the jealous husband who receives the humiliating punishment he would have meted out to Elvire's innamorato, the ineffectual Bascol (Lavaud and Nelli, *Les Troubadours* v. 2, 210–14). However, his attempt to trap the lovers has a more serious precedent in King Mark in *Tristan et Iseut*. For all its aristocratic setting, Raimon's text is in the spirit of the fabliau, as here when Alfonse visits Bascol's room in which the lovers have enjoyed undisturbed bliss, "la fenestra clauza" [the closed window] (l. 392) shielded from the gaze of watchmen and spies. In the spirit of comic misinformation, Alfonse, who now believes our hero innocent, treats the locus amoenus as a sickbed—when in fact a different kind of sexual healing is more to the point.

To consider unfulfilled love as a sickness is a commonplace in courtly poetry: the illustration of physical debilitation post facto belongs much more to the fabliau or to the lyric genre of the *gap*, or poems of sexual boasting, of which Guillem IX was an exponent when he was not writing more courtly lyrics. Limentani points out that the pragmatic philosophy underlying the reasoning of the novas is found in the work of the first recorded troubadour (73). For example, Guillem's obscene "Companho, tant ai agutz d'avols conres" [Comrades, I have had so much bad equipment] (P-C 183.5) concludes:

E quan lo bocx es taillatz, nais plus espes,
E.l senher no.n pert son comte ni sos ses;
A revers planh hom la tala,
si.l dampnatges no.i es ges.
(Bond 12–13)

[And when the wood is cut down, it grows even thicker. And the lord does not lose his revenue or his income from it; the devastation is wrongly lamented if there is no damage at all.]

Good husbandry evidently involves the management of complex natural resources. Love casuistry is reduced to forest management, or a choice of horses to mount.

And then, of course, there is the cat poem, "Farai un vers pos mi sonelh" [I'll compose a poem, since I'm falling asleep] (P-C 183.12), in which a heroic knight errant encounters two women in a forest. The horizon of expectation is that these women will be shepherdesses, but they are noble women in search of a discreet lover. They greet the knight (who replies as one of Boccaccio's most famous heroes will) with unintelligible babble. The delighted women take him off for a tryst, feed him, have him remove his clothes, and bring out their red house-cat to use as an instrument of torture and to test the hero's mettle. The narrator treats this episode as an act of supreme bravery, for which he is rewarded by being able to enjoy a week of happy congress with the women: hardly the stuff of amor de lonh.

A clearer example of the earthy, direct tone of some troubadour lyrics is found in the less risqué "Compaigno, non pus mudar qu'eu no m'effrei" [Comrades, I cannot help being upset] (P-C 183.4), in which the speaker, borrowing from Ovid's *Ars Amatoria*, addresses his audience and complains of the way in which a lady is guarded, warning of the consequences:

> Qu'eu anc non vi nulla domn'ab tan gran fei
> Qui non vol prendre son plait on sap mercei,
> S'om la loigna de proessa, que ab malvestatz non plaidei.
> (Bond 6, ll. 12–15)

> [For I never saw a lady with such fidelity, who would not take her case where she knows she can find clemency. So that, if she is separated from Worthiness, she makes an accord with Baseness.]

The basic pattern for the novas also derives from the earliest troubadour lyrics and from Ovid: if a woman is mistreated or kept from society, trouble results. The most satisfactory way we can account for the production of obscene lyrics of courtly origin, like those of Guillem IX, is to see them as part of what Leonard Forster calls an array of "conventional safety valves" (chap. 3). Such lyrics are a natural by-product of the ethereal system of fin'amor used by the troubadours. However, their function is not as protection for high ideals, as C. S. Lewis describes the purpose of humor in the romance. Guillem's poetry serves as a reminder that irony is a fundamental part of the troubadour worldview, deliberately calculated to decenter the courtliness otherwise at its core. The novas reveal a common thread of parody and provide an antidote and complement to the refinement of troubadour love-lyrics, and Limentani's reminder of the close alliance between lyric and narrative in the south is appropriate. The novas, and especially *Flamenca*, are formed of an alliance between the more risqué comic love of the troubadours and the sensual realism of the fabliau-like form.

When the romance ventured south it could not stay the same. With a separation in time and in culture, it grew differently, and in parodic soil. In the case of *Jaufre*, there is a clear delight in, and resistance to, the conventions of northern chivalry. This derives from political considerations, and from the pre- and coexistence of a strand of realism in short fiction that blended the sophistication and atmosphere of courtly narrative with the down-to-earth comedy reserved for the fabliau. The evidence of *Jaufre* shows the author to be a careful student of Chrétien: his romance is a parodic reencoding of the ethos of northern chivalry filtered through a playful ambiguity and energy derived from the troubadours. The result is a renewed sense of adventure and an engagement with narrative that in turn lends a dynamism to the reencoding of the romance.

4

The Uses of Literacy
Parodic Fusion in the *Roman de Flamenca*

If *Jaufre* shows one parodic path that the chivalric romance took as it went south, *Flamenca* demonstrates another. If the *Jaufre* poet introduces the elegant earthiness of the novas to the roman d'aventure, the *Flamenca* poet mixes its courtly love triangle with an elegant send-up of troubadouresque fin'amor and the conventions of romance. The central theme of the jealous husband is also popular in northern France, treated in the fabliau and in a more refined (sometimes tragic) fashion in the lais of Marie de France.[1] In the former the result is comedy consonant with Bakhtin's *bas corporel* *(Rabelais and His World),* while in Marie's most poignant lai, *Laüstic,* the pure love of a married lady and her courtly neighbor is symbolized by a nightingale, subsequently trapped and killed by the husband. The lady sends the dead bird to her sweetheart, who enshrines it in a jewelled box, intended as a reliquary for the martyred innocence of love. While the cruel husband who wrings the nightingale's neck in Marie's poem bears a resemblance to Archimbaut in *Flamenca,* the treatment given the theme of the *jaloux* and the courtly lovers is more refined: in the spirit of tragedy, they cannot be united, and their amor de lonh finds its perfection in unfulfillment. In *Flamenca* there is a comic and more earthly *jouissance.* The celebrated troubadour vida of Guillem de Cabestanh recounts the same myth as Marie's *Laüstic* in more graphic fashion, with the lover's heart served up for the unsuspecting lady to eat (Boutière and Schutz 530). There is heart-trouble in *Flamenca,* too, but of a lesser order.

Transposed into a different key in *Flamenca,* the clandestine affairs of the châtelaines and their admirers become comic and serve up a different dish quite as peppery, but more farcical, than the one in the vida. Much more akin to the shorter novas, the romance has an Ovidian moral to its story:

Baboins es e folz e nescis,
s'era plus savis que Boecis,
maritz ques, on despendre cuja
sa mullier ad amic estuja.
(ll. 7685–88)

[Weak-headed, idiotic, and stupid is the husband who—even if he is otherwise as sage as Boethius—thinks he can spend what his wife reserves for her lover.]

Taking *Jaufre, Flamenca,* and the two shorter works together, length is not a defining criteria for the novas: we must look instead to the treatment of themes as a defining characteristic rather than length. All except *Jaufre*—and there, too, it is arguable that courtly love finds exaggerated and comic treatment, such as Jaufre and Brunissen's first meeting, which is treated with the playfulness that Chrétien reserves for Laudine and Yvain. All the texts share a strong element of parody as well as a lightness of tone and sharp descriptive focus. No narrative tradition springs fully formed, or in a pure and univocal state, but the combinations made of such elements can be innovatory, and in *Flamenca,* as in Chaucer's work, the friction between the courtly and the more realistic bourgeois element constitutes what Bakhtin would term heteroglossia. The mixing of the ethos of the fabliau and the aristocratic romance results in the satire and parody evident throughout *The Canterbury Tales.* Chaucer's treatment of the ménage à trois in the *Merchant's Tale* exemplifies this when the wily May lectures her elderly, cuckolded husband Januarie after he has interrupted her and her lover Damyan enjoying forbidden fruit in a pear tree. Januarie, whose sight is suddenly restored by Pluto, sees all, but is talked out of punishment by his wife:

"Ful many a man weneth to seen a thyng,
And it is al another than it semeth.
He that misconceyveth, he mysdemeth."
And with that word she leep down fro the tree.
This Januarie, who is glad but he?
(ll. 2408–12)

Once more the noble husband is never right: his blindness and clear vision prove no help to him. It is appropriate that this comic tale of courtly love, an analogue of Boccaccio's *Decameron* 7.9, be told by the merchant and offer the same parodic view of courtly love that we find in the Occitan novas.

Muscatine sees a naturalistic style at work in Chaucer's reworking of fabliau and courtly themes, and his definition of naturalism is relevant to the discussion of Occitan literature and *Flamenca:*

> I use the terms realistic and naturalistic, then, loosely—for lack of better ones—to indicate that for the Middle Ages, and particularly in contrast to the courtly tradition, this literature has a remarkable preoccupation with the animal facts of life. It takes, in the ordinary sense, a realistic view of things. It finds its easiest subject in low life, but with high or low it is impartially impolite—and often vulgar and obscene. (*Chaucer and the French Tradition* 59)

What he claims for Chaucer in terms of realism and a lusty disrespect for the niceties of fin'amor, we can apply to the Occitan novas and especially to *Flamenca*, since however courtly the subject matter and setting may be, we confront a more down-to-earth treatment of human affairs. Muscatine believes that Chaucer's style derives from his reading of the French literature of the thirteenth century, and that this, rather than any source English, Latin, or Italian, constitutes his "literary matrix" (5). Combining the influence of the fabliau, the romance, the *Roman de la Rose,* and what Muscatine calls "the Renart poets and their brothers of the naturalistic tradition" (5), Chaucer produces a hybrid collection of tales that are parodies of their predecessors. He ventures further, saying that Chrétien's *Yvain* and *Flamenca* show "stylistic promise" (70) that finds its perfection in *The Canterbury Tales.*

Muscatine's deterministic aim is, of course, to highlight Chaucer's originality: his reading of Chaucer's French inheritance is as enlightening as it is *raisonné.* However, it is significant that he stops short of allowing some of Chaucer's predecessors full credit for the modernity of their literary creations: the *Flamenca* poet "is not a critic of courtly sentiment" (57) and his humor "hardly shades off into satire" (57). Chrétien tries "to illuminate courtly romance from the direction of comic realism," and the same tendency leads courtly convention to be "pushed to the limit" in the Occitan text (131), so that *Flamenca* represents romance in "its terminal form as such" (57). Muscatine does not allow full transgression before Chaucer's time of what he sees as the boundaries established in courtly romance, but rightly identifies *Flamenca* as an important stop along the way.

In the Occitan narrative tradition, which seems colored by a more extreme form of parody from the outset, *Flamenca* does indeed prove to be highly conspiratory in its comedy: it not only criticizes courtly sentiment, it is a deliberate parody of the courtly world. *Flamenca* does not represent a genre under ultimate strain, but one that has already been transformed by the very sensual, vulgar, and subversive laughter C. S. Lewis hopes some romances ward off with their internal defense mechanisms.

In the closing pages of *Epic and Romance,* W. P. Ker traces the development of medieval secular literature as far as Chaucer, arriving at the same conclusion as Muscatine regarding Chaucer's genius, but via a different route. In Ker's view, Chrétien raises the romance to its noblest stature and foreshadows more sophisticated literary developments. He shows great foresight in dubbing the *Flamenca* poet one of Chrétien's "cleverest pupils" (359) and defines the text as "a work in which the form of the novel is completely disengaged from the unnecessary accidents of romance, and reaches a kind of positive and modern clearness very much at variance in some respects with the popular ideas of what is medieval" (359). Ker is exactly right; essential to the comic structure of *Flamenca* is the principal that the *aventure* of earlier works is replaced by a carefully orchestrated series of meetings following a detailed church calendar. The precision timing of the meeting of the lovers seems to be a deliberate parody of the apparent randomness of the roman courtois. According to Ker, *Flamenca* represents "one of the highest and most distinctive points" in the medieval romance, moving close to what he defines as the aim of the genre since its inception, namely "the expression in an elegant manner of the ideas of the Art of Love, as understood in the polite society of those times" (359). A combination of classical literary influences and sophisticated contemporary narrative, *Flamenca* would have been a worthy "representative masterpiece" (360) of medieval literature, but for its breaking with convention. He goes on to term it "the perfection and completion of medieval romance in one kind and one direction" (361), that of the expression of courtly sentiment.

Ker highlights important issues and innovations in the text, but his discussion omits highlighting parody, and his tendency is to read it as an uncanonical but straight romance. Like Muscatine, Ker takes *Flamenca* as sailing close to the edge of a literary new world, but stops it at the limits. In Ker's opinion, the threshold from medieval to modern is crossed with Chaucer's *Troilus and Criseyde,* since it is:

> the poem in which medieval romance passes out of itself into the form of the modern novel. What Cervantes and what Fielding did was first done by Chaucer; and this was the invention of a kind of

story in which life might be represented no longer in a conventional or abstract manner, or with sentiment and pathos instead of drama, but with characters adapting themselves to different circumstances, no longer obviously breathed upon by the master of the show to convey his own ideas, but moving freely and talking like men and women. (367–8)

It is clear that to both Ker and Muscatine, *Flamenca* is enigmatic: conventional, yet unconventional, a romance, but at the same time a high point and a limit within the genre, a transgression to something else as yet undefined. Such critical appraisals would doubtless have delighted the anonymous author, particularly since his work is deliberate literary mischief, being both a parody of literary creation and creations, and of reading as well as writing. Reading and the interpretation of literature are at the heart of *Flamenca,* and it is with this notion that we begin a closer analysis of those elements which foreground the "fictionality" of the text and its subversive and polyphonic use of intertexts.

After centuries of neglect, MS34 of the Bibliothèque Municipale in Carcassonne was rediscovered and sent to François Raynouard in 1834. Describing and commenting on this find in 1838, Raynouard first brought to light the contents of what he called *Le Roman de Flamenca.* Since both its beginning and end are missing, we cannot know if the text did in fact assign itself another title, or one at all. The poem tells of the marriage of the heroine, Flamenca, to the rich and wholly eligible Lord Archimbaut. Conventional appearances soon prove deceptive, since following their wedding he quickly turns from a paragon of chivalry into a comically grotesque and cruel jailer, keeping his innocent wife imprisoned in a tower of his castle in the spa town of Bourbon, with only her two maids for companions. His extraordinary behavior makes him notorious in the surrounding areas, and soon Guillem de Nevers, intrigued by the challenge of the situation, deliberately conceives a troubadouresque amor de lonh for Flamenca and vows to win her at any cost. The idea of love from afar in its most familiar exposition is parodied in *Flamenca,* since Guillem is not content to adore from afar and uses his considerable talents to satisfy his desires. Aided by books, his natural cunning and wisdom, and with the help of dream-visitations from Amor and Flamenca, Guillem transforms himself from knight to cleric and begins to put a two-pronged strategy into effect. As an acolyte he capitalizes on his privileged position to contrive an intermittent exchange with Flamenca during mass on Sundays and feast days, subverting the liturgy with his willing interlocutor and showing his devotion to the religion of love.

At night Guillem tunnels under his lodgings (through the conveniently soft limestone, as the narrator realistically points out) to the bathhouse where Flamenca is to take a cure for "heart trouble." This is because in reply to her husband's inquiry as to what ails her, Flamenca claims: "Sener, al cor ai una gota / que m'auci e m'afolla tota / e cug que d'aquest [mal] morrai / si conseill de mege non ai" [Lord, I have a gouty heart, which kills and drives me mad, and I think I will die of it, if I don't have a doctor's help] (ll. 5671–74, 168).

The waters of Bourbon drew *curistes* from all over France according to lines 3797–800. Charles Grimm notes the testimony of the Duc de Monpensier, given to Jean Aubéry and published in 1604, as to the particular efficacy of the waters in matters sexual:

Tout de mesme apprins-tu que tant de Lits steriles,
Dedans ces tiedes Bains plus feconds devenus,
Ne laissant les baizers de l'Hymen infertiles,
Monstrant qu'en l'Eau salée a peu naistre Venus.

[All the same, learn that so many sterile beds were made fertile, not leaving the kisses of Hymen infertile, showing that Venus could be born in salt water].[2]

The association of the baths with curing infertility is particularly appropriate here. Love is both the malady and the doctor: Guillem and Flamenca are eventually united and enjoy a blissful liaison, until Flamenca realizes that they can no longer hope to continue the deception, so complete is her cure. Taking her husband to task, she swears an oath (undoubtedly of the same sort as Iseut's oath to Mark, were it extant) and brings about a transformation in Archimbaut, who promises to return to his old ways and to liberate her from prison, as well as to organize a splendid tournament in a year's time. Flamenca sends Guillem to perform deeds of chivalry (like Antiphanor in the *Novas del Papegai*), and when the allotted time has elapsed, husband and lover return as brothers-in-arms.

Guillem even goes so far as to make Archimbaut an unwitting go-between by having him deliver a formal lyric *salut d'amour* to Flamenca. This is one of the many embedded lyrics in the work, and unfortunately its text is missing. One might speculate that it was removed and put in a poetic anthology, as was the fate of the only known outside reference to the text, described by Stefano Asperti (*"Flamenca* e dintorni"). In the late fourteenth- or early fifteenth-century Catalan codex of Estanislau Aguiló, now in Palma, Mallorca, and referred to as MS E, there is a fragment corre-

sponding to lines 2713–20 of *Flamenca*, in which Guillem makes a plead-
ing speech to the allegorical figures of Amor and Merce. As Asperti says,
this could mean that the Occitan poet borrowed this text to use in his own.
However, the other possibility is more probable, that the romance was
known outside Occitania to some Catalan readers and that this is an ex-
cerpt from the text of *Flamenca*. This would also seem to be in keeping
with the tendency of the romance to diffuse southward.

Asperti makes the excellent point that in the Occitan text, the beginning
of this particular section is marked off by a decorated and enlarged initial,
which may have made it stand out as a passage of relative autonomy in the
text. While the text does not seem to have a consistent strategy for the
distribution of capitals, Asperti's point is a relevant one: particularly since
Guillem's salut d'amour (ll. 7101–13) missing from the manuscript of
Flamenca is an autonomous unit described within the text as having a
decorated miniature (ll. 7100–12). The text describes the salut as having a
portrait of the two lovers, together with Love as an angel, recognized by
Flamenca as likenesses of Guillem and herself. The actual text of *Flamenca*
is plain and workmanlike, having no miniatures: however, the passage
does constitute an independent section within the text and could have had
a decorated initial, and its removal because of this cannot be ruled out. It
also provides an interesting clue as to one way in which the romance may
have been read, proof that sophisticated recognition of poetic forms was
shared by the audience of *Flamenca*. Within the text, Flamenca recognizes
herself and Guillem in the manuscript illumination of the text he sends as
well as in the content of the verse, in which she has the mysterious designation *la bella de Belmont*, a troubadouresque *senhal* (a commonplace
device that conceals the identity of the addressee). His choice of name is
perhaps both erotic and humorous: *Belmont* can easily be interpreted as
the *bel mont* or the *mons Veneris*. Grimm, more innocently, identifies Belmont with the picturesque castle of Bourbon-Larchambaud, set on a hill
(107–8). His interpretation adds the appealing dimension that Flamenca is
hidden beneath an obvious designation, since her association with Bourbon-
Larchambaud is obvious—and yet in a work so characterized by subterranean desire, it is tempting to play up the more hidden, erotic possibilities.

The lovers meet again, and when the text breaks off, feats of chivalry are
being performed at Archimbaut's tournament. The stage is set for a spec-
tacular finish when the manuscript breaks off, leaving the reader in suspense.

The date of the work is still a subject of debate: one of the many unusual
features of the narrative is a detailed church calendar so accurate that only

three years can be candidates for the period in which the events take place in the text: 1139, 1223, and 1234.³ Clearly, we are dealing with a late romance, one that subsumes and incorporates an extensive previous tradition, as the long list of known courtly works included in the text indicates. The problem of dating the work is allied to the difficulties of defining its genre: the critics who have tried to ally the characters depicted with historical figures treat it primarily as a *roman historique*. While it is true that the *Flamenca* poet abandons the more traditional Arthurian framework in favor of an equally courtly but less obviously idealized setting closer to contemporary reality, the valiant attempts made by Grimm and particularly Rita Lejeune to identify the main protagonists with documented contemporaries have proved intriguing but inconclusive.

While we know of a Bourbon Archimbaut VIII (ll. 1216–42), we know little about him; nothing links him to mistreatment of his spouse and to the character portrayed in *Flamenca*. The names give a semblance of history, but stop short of allowing any definite historical interpretation. Moreover, as Merton Hubert and Marion Porter suggest, it would have been dangerous to lampoon a powerful political contemporary: "So, calling his protagonists by familiar names, but carefully leaving them unidentifiable, Bernadet once more indulges in a *geinh*, a bit of craftiness which permitted him to give an air of reality to his romance and to taunt his contemporaries a bit without leaving himself open to reprisals by them."⁴ The king and queen of France who appear in the text are not named: the names of other nobles are suggestive, but elusive.

Attempts to identify the author are equally futile. In lines 1732–37 he appears to name himself, when referring to "Bernadet" and a certain *seners d'Alga* (l. 1723): it is unclear from the text exactly who they are and what their connection is, although a relationship of patron to poet seems most likely.⁵ As this is the glimpse of an author, it is significant that "he" chooses to portray himself as embedded in the text: whether he also announces his identity in the prologue or epilogue we cannot know, but his presence at this particular juncture in the warp and weft of the narrative leaves room for speculation. The *geinh* apparent elsewhere in the text suggests that Bernadet's presence could be interpreted as an instance of literary hide-and-seek, and there are strong grounds for doubting the sincerity of his playful self-identification.

In line 1564 the hero, Guillem de Nevers, is introduced for the first time, and we are given a lengthy portrait of his gifts and attributes, both physical and intellectual. We learn that his Parisian education in the liberal arts exceeds any cleric's, and that his poetic training makes him the equal of the finest jongleur:

Chansons e lais, descortz e vers,
serventes et autres cantars
sabia plus que nuls joglars,
neis Daniel que saup ganren
no.s pogr'ab lui penre ren.
(ll. 1706–10)

[Songs and lais, *descortz* and poems, *sirventes* and other songs he
knew better than any jongleur; even Daniel, who knew a lot, could
not hold a candle to him.]

The Daniel referred to is possibly Arnaut Daniel, although it is strange that
the surname rather than the Christian name should be used to identify him.
Comparison with such a literary lion is excessive praise for the urbane but
innocent Guillem. The portrait of the hero is intended to exceed all other
stylized descriptions of moral and physical perfection to be found in
romances: he is aristocratic, skilled in warfare and the arts of tournament, a generous administrator, a patron of the arts, an almsgiver, and a
court diplomat. The excessive description is parodic, particularly since
the description of beauty ascribed to Guillem is more suited to a woman.
Bartolozzi-Bustini interestingly suggests that because he is the object of
so much detailed and somewhat lascivious description, the romance is
oriented toward women, with Guillem as the ultimate ideal lover (69–70).

The passage above is by no means the only instance of exaggeration: it
is a deliberate strategy as well as a recurring feature of the narrative.[6] The
lines that sketch him are so hyperbolic that they exceed caricature: lover,
intellectual, knight, cleric, and troubadour, Guillem is an impossible blend
of courtly, ecclesiastic, and scholarly virtues.[7] He represents both the conventional romance hero of the northern French tradition and the sophisticated literary lover of the south, embodying what Limentani sees as proof
of a cultural rapprochement between north and south (286). In essence,
Guillem indeed represents the fusion of two literary traditions. While he is
northern in form, he is distinctly southern in content, the unstoppable
enfant terrible of both traditions.

For all his naïveté in the arts of love (although not in the *Ars Amatoria*)
the description we have signals his fitting background for the comic test
that awaits him, as he becomes engaged in a game at which he instantly
proves a master. His relationship to "Bernadet" is one of literary conceit in
both senses of the term, as one is the narcissistic double of the other: it is
appropriate that the "author" of *Flamenca* should insert himself (l. 1732)
alongside his creation, as if to stress that his hero was made in his own
image. Many have speculated as to the character, if not the identity, of the

Flamenca poet, and this passage gives weight to the arguments of those who would have him *cavalliers et clercs* (l. 1800) like the hero.

Guillem is the personification of literary artifice and the perfect instrument to parody the various literary conventions and genres that come into play in *Flamenca*. He has never experienced love:

> Ancar d'amor no s'entremes
> Per so que per ver en saupes;
> Per dir saup ben que fon amors.
> Cant legit ac totz los auctors
> Que d'amor parlon si feinon
> Consi amador si capteinon.
> (ll. 1761–6)

> [He was still unversed in love, as far as knowing the truth about it; in theory he knew what love was, having read all those authors who talk about love and invent how lovers behave.]

This passage clearly recalls the *Ars Amatoria* and its many medieval adaptors and imitators, with their humorous expositions of the art of seduction. Guillem's familiarity with *totz los auctors* (l. 1765), particularly Ovid, reveals him as the embodiment of a collection of literary ideas that can be seen through the many texts quoted in the body of the poem. There is an element of play and guile in the way that the poet uses his literary skill and varied sources. *Flamenca* targets the genre of romance in a critical and theoretical way: one of the central grounds for this interpretation is found in the list of works cited early on in the story (ll. 583–709) at the wedding banquet of Archimbaut and Flamenca. In charting how this romance might contribute to the prehistory of the novel, there are many possible directions to take: but this romance exemplifies such a particular kind of sophisticated intertextual parody, that what follows will concentrate on how other works and genres are encoded. The plethora of works embedded in *Flamenca* is an expression of textual polyphony that adds an element of postmodern sampling to the work, placing it squarely among those innovative works that deserve to be considered in the line of novelistic development.

While enumeration and listing is a feature of medieval literature, the way in which the list of works performed at the heroine's wedding is presented is the first sign of a novel use made of a narrative convention, since its extent and playful extravagance reveal it to have as much in common with Rabelais as with contemporary sources.[8] Such lists are found in some fabliaux. Examining *Du con*, Keith Busby notes that the beginning of the text presents a cavalcade of heroes and then places itself in the same lofty tradition before revealing the real subject of the tale.[9] The bathetic distance between proposed literary model and the actual narrative provide an obvious example of the kind of technique employed by the *Flamenca* poet, who carefully measures the distance between expectation and actual content and its comic potential, a descent from the sublime to the ridiculous. Busby calls the ploy comic deception, and the result is parodic, since as he says, the best audience to appreciate the trick is the one versed in the subtleties of the romance and chanson de geste. Busby shows a passage where author Gautier de Leu echoes lines of Chrétien's *Yvain*, as well as other instances in which the fabliaux deliberately play on the courtly register for their effect. As it appears in *Flamenca*, the list of literary works functions similarly, and as a mise-en-abyme or a parodic aegis of the work as a whole.

The wedding scene is described in detail, with particular attention given to the literary works recited by various jongleurs and minstrels:

Apres si levon li juglar;
Cascus se volc faire auzir.
Adonc auziras retentir
cordas de manta temperadura.
Qui saup novella violadura,
ni canzo ni descort ni lais,
al plus que poc avan si trais.
(ll. 592–98)

[Afterward the jongleurs got up; each wanted to be heard. Then you would have heard instrument strings tuned all kinds of ways. Whoever knew a new viol tune, a song, descort, or lai stood up to perform as soon as he could.]

The formulaic listing of canso, descort, and lai foreshadows Guillem's repertoire (l. 1706) and the panoply of lyric genres that spread the news of Archimbaut's departure from reasonable behavior (ll. 1171–78).

Additional embedded genres are found later, as on leaving church, Guillem hears strains of popular song:

Las tosetas agron ja trachas
las maias que.l sera.s son fachas
e lur devinolas canteron.
Tot dreit davan Guillem passeron
cantan una kalenda maia.
(ll. 3231–5)

[The young girls had already taken up the may branches that had been planted the night before, and were singing their love-riddles. They passed right in front of Guillem singing a *kalenda maia*.]

Their song wishes joy to the lady who takes a knight as her lover without making him wait for her favors, and manifests her affections in spite of her jealous husband. In this wish-fulfillment fantasy, the cuckolded husband goes away and leaves the lovers in peace at the slightest reprimand from his wife. Guillem, quite understandably, prays for the realization of this particular maidens' prayer. The blending of sacred and secular is the essential feature of the central section of the romance, one that sends up the religious register of courtly love and sets it at a dissonant distance from the slapstick of the action.

In the introduction to the banquet scene the simultaneous musical performances amplify the variety and layering of poetic genres, in turn expressed in the wide range of instruments (ll. 603–16).[10] Acrobats and jugglers supplement an already considerable cast of extras. The wedding banquet is a riot of music and color and provides a vivid entrance into a labyrinth of intertexts. Noting the influence of Chrétien and other French sources, Limentani (200–41) points to the description in *Erec et Enide* (ll. 1989–2001), which appropriately occurs at Erec's wedding feast.[11] The references to musical richness, combined with the opulence of scene and setting in the northern French romances, are transposed into *Flamenca*, but with a difference. No fleeting attention is paid to the poetic accompaniment: the poet describes with relish the literary digest complementing the musical performance. There is a further fragmentation into genre and individual works, constituting a layering of narrative voices. The centerpiece of the celebration is a catalogue of medieval literature: here we encounter what Limentani terms the "dimensione eccezionale" of this particular work, its "grandeur rappresentativa" (200). Like the poet's description of his hero's attributes, this is a deliberate exercise in exaggeration and a remarkable example even given the tendency for accumulation and intertextuality in medieval romance; the extensive list given in *Flamenca* goes beyond the boundaries of conventional description and attempts to encapsulate entire literary traditions.

The many well-known texts cited could not possibly be performed in a week, let alone during the banquet, so that we must look elsewhere for the reason for their inclusion. The poet provides a literary tour de force to show off his literary pedigree. He also targets a sophisticated and well-versed courtly audience, familiar not just with the content of stories, but with poetic form and generic expectations of convention. Most important, he underscores the fictionality and conditions the reception of what follows, since the conventions suggested by the quoted works create expectations on the part of the audience of the subsequent narrative. Thus, in the poet's exposition we not only find a reading of literary history but also the key to his parodic strategy, as he conditions the audience's response to his own romance and by implication sets his own text at the end of the list. The subsequent tale surrounds and engulfs the cited works and supersedes the condensed works contained within it.

Commenting on this catalogue, Ker says that the poet "does his best to cover the whole ground" (384), and he reads the passage as an unusually thorough attempt to distill the essence of the medieval romance, implying that the *Flamenca* poet's approach magnifies the more parodic accumulation of references in works like Chaucer's *Sir Thopas*. The association of these two texts is an appropriate one, because of their similarity of approach and shared generic target for parody. Although *Sir Thopas* does not attract the critical attention of other tales, it is an important passage not least because it is the story that Chaucer the architect of *The Canterbury Tales* assigns Chaucer the narrator, suggesting an emphasis on its subject matter and transforming it into a mise-en-abyme of the whole text. The subject in this case, as in *Don Quixote,* is pointing out a worn narrative model that pales next to the originality of the other tales. The narrator tells his host that he knows no other story to tell the assembled company except "a ryme I lerned longe agoon" (l. 709). What follows is a pastiche of an amusingly anachronistic form of courtly romance. In the first section of the tale, we find a formulaic description of the hero and his prowess and "love-longynge" (l. 772) and follow his excursion into the land of Fairye where he meets a giant and prepares to do battle. While making ready he finds literary inspiration:

> "Do come," he seyde, "my mynstrales,
> And geestours for to tellen tales,
> Anon in myn armynge,
> Of romances that been roiales,
> Of popes and of cardinales,
> And eek of love-likynge."
> (ll. 845–50)

Sir Thopas is a tongue-in-cheek invention, a clichéd accumulation of romance conventions, and Derek Pearsall views this tale rather in the same way that Charles Muscatine assesses *Flamenca,* stating that "[t]he genre of *Thopas* seems to be rather that of burlesque, which can perhaps be distinguished from parody by the glee with which it absorbs all the business of satirical puncturing and deflating into the joyful celebration of the ridiculous" (Pearsall 162).

Pearsall contrasts his view with that of Arthur Moore ("Sir Thopas as Criticism of Fourteenth-Century Minstrelsy"), who claims that *Sir Thopas* is a biting satire of the medieval romance. The dilemma over the issue of parody, satire, and burlesque is identical to the central issue of interpretation in *Flamenca:* in essence Pearsall and Moore make the same assessment of the tale, but measure differently the degree of surreptitious pleasure that Chaucer enjoys in his recounting. In the final analysis blurred terminology produces false distinctions, and just as *Sir Thopas* is burlesque, it is also parodic: the "glee" expressed in the comic use of conventional material distinguishes the parody rather than negates it, or contrasts it with another form. Something burlesque must also by definition be in part parodic: there can be little compromise, since both involve a travesty of recognized sources. *Sir Thopas* crosses the line of parody as clearly as *Flamenca* does, even if we conjecture that the poet has a fondness for the genre he is lampooning. Exactly how we demarcate the line of transgression, or attempt to measure it, is more difficult to determine.

E. Talbot Donaldson attempts a practical solution by looking at Chaucer's use of poetic language drawn from the "conventional vocabulary of popular poetry" ("Idiom of Popular Poetry in *The Miller's Tale*"). Changes in poetic language can be seen, he says, through a process of comparison with contemporary or previous literature. Trying to situate a particular author, especially one as unique as Chaucer, is fraught with danger. This is due to the frequent impossibility of gauging the proximity or distance from prior poetic models and the problems of quantifying the different values assigned to language in a new context. This is also the source of literary interest and intrigue in *Flamenca.*

Donaldson concentrates on the internal logic of *Sir Thopas* and *The Miller's Tale,* and he looks at the special use made of a few borrowings given special emphasis by their sparing use and significant context. He is more resistant in his assessment of Chaucer's "continental" culture. He claims that "Chaucer . . . may not have been very much aware of the literary tradition from which he is presumably in revolt; and this means that anyone who, in search of comparison with Chaucer's diction, goes to the most prolific of the vernacular literary traditions, the romance . . . must consider himself in danger of wasting his time" (13). It is hard to imagine that someone of Chaucer's talent, imagination, and wit could not have been familiar with the ethos of the continental tradition, whether in direct or in bastardized form. The very nature of *Sir Thopas* suggests comic contempt bred from familiarity. It provides a suitable point of departure because it has the advantage of providing "a criticism of vernacular conventions of every sort" (15) from the action of the tale down to the use of certain words.

Both Absolon in *The Miller's Tale* and Sir Thopas share a somewhat unusual description of their handsome features: Donaldson says that they have "fallen across the fine line which in medieval poetry separated feminine beauty from that of beardless youths" (21). Sir Thopas's shapeliness is more typical of Aucassin, or an Ovidian-inspired French romance hero (or indeed a romance heroine) than a bold knight: both he and Absolon are described with a bland androgyny that recalls in exaggerated fashion the idealized perfection of the stereotypical romance, typified by the lovers in *Floire et Blanchefleur,* or in the romances of Chrétien. At this point we might recall the fulsome description of Guillem in *Flamenca:* he takes the inherent comedy in most courtly heroes to a new level, what Donaldson calls in connection with Chaucer the "use—or abuse—of conventional idiom" (27).

More revealing examples of the misuse of courtly terms are found in *The Miller's Tale.* According to Donaldson, the epithet *hende* found in association with Nicholas undergoes a change of signification typical of the devaluation of the genre of courtly romance in this tale. From being a common word in Middle English romance to describe the nobility and worthiness of the hero, hende reverts to its other less exclusive meaning of handy or skillful. Chaucer implies through his use of the word that Donaldson says it has become "so déclassé and shopworn as to be ineligible for employment in serious poetry" (18). He goes on to say that hende becomes associated with Nicholas's proficiency in love—a particular kind of love that manifests itself in a comic, earthy, and secret passion. Nicholas's skill as a clerk and lover, and his association with stereotypical romance heroes make the obscene and fabliau-like climax of the tale a demystification and devaluation of the literature of courtly love.

Like Guillem, Nicholas stands out because of his learning and wisdom in all areas. One passage in particular recalls the Occitan hero:

His Almageste, and bookes grete and smale,
His astrelabie, longynge for his art,
His augrym stones layen faire apart,
On shelves couched at his beddes heed;
His presse ycovered with a faldyng reed;

And al above ther lay a gay sautrie,
On which he made a nyghtes melodie
So swetely that all the chambre rong;
And Angelus ad virginem he song.
(ll. 3208–16)

Here we see Nicholas as the same mixture of secular scholar, poet, and cleric. His subversion of the sacred parallels Guillem's: John the carpenter is made into a cuckolded Joseph, when Nicholas as Gabriel brings his own particular annunciation to Alison. The psalm *Dilexi quoniam* appears in line 2294 of *Flamenca,* and on finding this line as he opens the psalter, Guillem responds "ben sap ar Dieus que voliam" [now God knows what we want], a secular vernacular variation on the actual line "exaudiet Dominus vocem orationis meae," since the answer to Guillem's prayer is as earthly and tangible as Nicholas's "Mary." To further the connection, we might recall the illumination on the salut d'amour written by Guillem and sent to his lady. Love is disguised as a messenger angel, kneeling before the lady with flowers issuing from his mouth linking the verses beneath, a pose clearly meant to echo the Annunciation scenes stylized in books of Hours. Once again, sacred and religious mingle to comic effect.[12]

Similarly, the clandestine nature of Nicholas's passion for Alison, described by the adjective *derne,* comes to parody the private rendezvous of fin'amor just as Guillem and Flamenca enjoy more comic trysts in the inn and bathhouse. Although in *Flamenca* we find ourselves closer to, but not entirely in, the setting of the fabliau, there are parallels to be made between the style and tone of *The Miller's Tale* and the Occitan romance—and also in the systematic deflation of courtly values.

With his foppery and French oaths, Sir Thopas resembles his tale: superficial and representative of a parodic exercise in which form is devoid of any worthwhile content, as the host makes clear with his mordant analysis of the literary merit of the tale:

"By God," quod he, "for pleynly, at a word,
thy drasty ryming is nat worth a toord!
Thou doost noght elles but despendest tyme.
Sire, at o word, thou shalt no lenger ryme."
(ll. 929–32)

The ethereal and hyperconventional courtly romance comes face to face with the vocabulary of the fabliau, from doughty to "drasty" at a single stroke of inevitable descent. Whereas conventions are the target of the first section, alluding to other romances is the central feature of the second:

Men speken of romances of prys,
Of Horn child and of Ypotys,
Of Beves and sir Gy,
Of sir Lybeux and Pleyndamour,
But sir Thopas, he bereth the flour
Of roial chivalry!
(ll. 897–902)

The superficial list of names, particularly the mock-French Sir Lybeux (another Fair Unknown, perhaps?) and Pleyndamour, indicts the absurdity and artificiality of the genre of medieval romance. Sir Thopas, rather than representing the culminating point in the development of the hero, becomes the top-heavy sum total of his literary predecessors, and the most trite example of fictional knighthood. By using convention and allusion, Chaucer conspires to parody the romance in a manner that closely resembles that of the *Flamenca* poet. Donaldson's association of *Sir Thopas* with *The Miller's Tale* is appropriate since they show the two main ways in which the romance can be parodied, through the reduction of language and action. *Flamenca* achieves both, as first becomes apparent when the catalogue is examined in more detail.

Grimm notes the list of works in *Flamenca* and says that it not only is an indication of the lateness of the romance but, more important, provides evidence of the poet's literary preference for the north. One might conjecture that the poet's relationship to the matière of the north was much like that of Cervantes to the romance tradition. The first thing to note about the repertoire is that it manipulates another existing poetic genre of the south, the *sirventes-ensenhamen*.[13] There are many kinds of didactic poetry in the corpus of the troubadours, but three works are usually classified together as a specific branch within that general classification. Guerau de Cabrera, Giraut de Calanson, and Bertrand de Paris en Rouergue each wrote a sirventes aimed specifically at jongleurs, and as Pirot summarizes, they share the same features:

Le poète reproche à un exécutant la minceur de son repertoire littéraire et la faiblesse de ses aptitudes musicales et jongleuresques. Du même fait, le poète énumère, sur le mode négatif, le bagage idéal d'un exécutant. (40)

[The poet criticizes a performer for the slimness of his literary repertoire and the weakness of his musical and performing skills. As part of it, the poet lists, in a negative tone, the ideal baggage for a performer.]

Such poems are characterized by sardonic rhetorical excess, consisting of lists of characters and stories jumbled together into a catalogue of references designed to show off the literary pyrotechnics of the speaker. Their disparaging tone has led critics to categorize them as a form of *gap*, or boasting poem. While it is true that a single jongleur is the implied audience of the sirventes-ensenhamen, and many troubadours and jongleurs take part in the banquet entertainment in *Flamenca*, the list of works they relate bears a striking resemblance to the works contained in the three Occitan poems.

Taking the references in the three poems together, most are found in *Flamenca*. Of the some sixty-three items in the catalogue, half are found in one or more of the three sirventes-ensenhamens. The *Flamenca* poet differs in that his list displays a detailed knowledge of Arthurian material, a departure from troubadour convention that is significant in the assessment of *Flamenca* as a particularly parodic romance. In the tour de force of the lyric poems the aim is to highlight what the jongleur does not know: in *Flamenca* the negative list is made positive, signalling not what the poet does not know, but what he does, and what he has incorporated into the narrative. It is almost as if the *Flamenca* poet has tried to weave every possible allusion into his text in the determined way that Arnaut Daniel reworks assorted items of vocabulary into a sestina. Occitan poetry favors sophisticated literary exercises, and *Flamenca* is another example of the same tendency, but on a generic level. The author demonstrates his knowledge of the troubadour repertoire and mastery of Chrétien and the northern French tradition. Just as the intrigue of *Flamenca* forms a unique romance while recalling the Occitan novas, the courtly catalogue also refers back to southern literary tradition and makes subversive use of a genre already a parody itself. Even before we begin to explore the possible literary significance of the cited works, they already belong to an established genre of courtly parody designed to highlight the artificiality of courtly literature by a process of devaluation and *reductio ad absurdum*.

Even within the tradition of sirventes-ensenhamens *Flamenca* is exceptional: first because the references fall into a semblance of chronological literary history, and second because, although the works are a parody of form, their content is often revealing if we read the list as the humorous lampooning and encoding of courtly convention it appears to be. The first group cited are Breton lais:

L'uns viola [.l]lais del Cabrefoil,
e l'autre cel de Tintagoil;

l'us cantet dels Fins Amantz,
e l'autre cel que fes Ivans.
(ll. 599–602)

[One played the *lai du Chèvrefeuille,* and another that of Tintagel,
one sang about the Noble Lovers, and another the one composed by
Yvain.]

All these references suggest the Tristan legend. Gschwind notes that *Cabre-foil* does not necessarily indicate Marie de France's composition, and that it
does not help with dating the text: "Il est peu probable, selon M[eyer], que
le poète fasse allusion à ce lai, les lais de Marie de France étant destinés à la
lecture ou à la récitation, tandis que dans *Flamenca,* il s'agit de petits textes
chantés et accompagnés par quelque instrument" [It is unlikely, according to
Meyer, that the poet is alluding to that specific lai, the lais of Marie de France
being destined to be read or recited, whereas in *Flamenca* it is a case of short
sung texts accompanied by some instrument] (note to l. 601).

Gschwind's explanation is somewhat unconvincing. This passage marks
the excursus of a literary fantasy, and it is illogical to use what we consider
as real performance criteria as justification for excluding what seems otherwise to be a reasonable interpretation. The list in *Flamenca* has been
taken both too literally and not literally enough: it is a polyphonic ca-
cophony of works designed not to give the impression that they were
performed in real time, or reflected historical accuracy in terms of performance style, but rather to be emblematically encyclopedic, to create a sense
of self-conscious polyphony.

And why not Marie's *Chievrefoil?* For the work concludes by revealing
that Tristan's skill as a harpist led him to compose his lai, suggesting that
musical accompaniment for such a narrative was perhaps not unusual, and
was implied in the text, if not outside it. At the end of *Chievrefoil* Marie
adds:

Pur les paroles remembrer,
Tristram, ki bien saveit harper,
En aveit fet un nuvel lai.
(ll. 111–13)

[In order to remember the words, Tristan, who knew how to harp
well, had made a new lai of them.]

The performativity of this lai within a lai is evident, and the figure of the
ingenious lover-poet fits Guillem as well as his more tragic predecessor.

Moreover, in a typical sleight-of-hand, referring to the poet within the text makes Tristan a suitable double for the enigmatic author of the romance. While it is true that the *Flamenca* poet uses the verbs *cantar* and *violar* in this section, even if Marie's lais were destined for unaccompanied reading, does this necessarily preclude us from considering the reference to be to her? It could refer to Marie's tale of an illicit encounter between lovers, since the unfolding of events in *Flamenca* could easily be read as a parody of the tale.

In Marie's version Tristan defies his banishment to Wales in order to return to Cornwall, where he remains incognito in the forest to discover news of the queen. On hearing of the imminent arrival of Arthur's court he hides along their planned route, splits a hazel twig, carves his name, and binds it with honeysuckle as a sign to the queen. Iseut sees it, manages to slip away, and enjoys a meeting with her lover. Flamenca and Guillem are equally dependent on secret communication, both in the fragmented discussion in church (ll. 3947–5721) and when Guillem sends the salut d'amour as proof of his return and continued interest in their liaison. Both episodes employ the poetry of fin'amor in humorous fashion; the first appropriates a stanza from a canso of Peire Rogier, and in the second instance the poem arrives via her husband and the courtly sublime is reduced to a farcical situation. There is a further parallel between Tristan and Guillem, since both are poets. Marie's reference to Tristan makes the disputed emendation of Ivans (l. 602) to Tristans (see Gschwind) plausible. The author of *Jaufre* knew the *les Dous Amanz* well enough to make it a component of his romance, and it is possible that the author of *Flamenca* also makes conscious use of other of Marie's lais. The mention of the *Fins Amanz* could be a similar reference to the "Dous Amanz." In the final analysis, it matters little whether reference is made to actual works, since in the space of four lines the author of *Flamenca* conjures an image of the poetic universe of the Breton *lais,* and the allusion to their performance merely inscribes their literary space as generic intertexts.

If the lai of the *Fins Amanz* is obscure, so is the lai concerning Tintagel and "cel que fes Ivans," save that once again Tristan and Iseut are the figured pair. Commenting on this passage, Jean-Charles Huchet perceptively concludes that the references to lais: "fixent un modèle amoureux exemplaire . . . auquel les amants des novas auront à coeur de s'identifier, avant de le surpasser, suivant un mode de fonctionnement qui paraît non seulement constituer le principe de l'écriture de *Flamenca,* mais de l'écriture médiévale en général" [fix an exemplary lovers' model . . . with which the lovers in the novas will strive to identify, before surpassing it, following a working model which appears not only to embody the principle of writing in *Flamenca* but also that of medieval writing in general] ("'Trouver' contre le livre" 34).

The inclusion of Tristan and Iseut foreshadows the clandestine relationship of Guillem and Flamenca and arouses expectation on our part, since the audience at this point is unaware that the heroine will love anyone but her husband: the illicit liaison will be as great in stature, but in achieving success they will surpass and parody their more serious courtly predecessors.

When the narrative requires precision for effect, the author uses it; but while he gives scrupulous attention to the church calendar within the text, complete accuracy regarding literary sources and the realistic possibility of their recital is unimportant. Fitting to the poet's purpose is to convey the idea of a complete tradition, in this case the *matière de Bretagne,* for the express purpose of parodying it later. However, taking *Chievrefoil* as the likely source for the reference allows us to conjecture about a possible and more devious strategy on the part of the poet: to set out exemplary works of courtly literature that color our interpretation of what follows. Secret communication is a motif central to *Flamenca:* as further proof of this, Huchet reminds us of the passage in lines 6808–22, in which as the lovers part, their tears write on their fingers what is written in their hearts:

[Et] aitals era l'escriptura
don cascus som par assegura
"Bel amics, sovenga.us de me."
(ll. 6817–19)

[And such was the writing by which each gives the other assurance,
"Fair friend, let it remind you of me."]

The echo of Tristan's words to Iseut at the end of *Chievrefoil* seems clear.

A second block of texts (ll. 617–60) deals with classical and biblical material. First we find stories relating to Troy:

quar l'us comtet de Priamus,
e l'autre diz de Piramus;
l'us comtet de la bell'Elena
com Paris l'enquer, pois l'anmena;
l'autres comtava d'Ulixes,
e l'autre d'Ector e d'Achilles.
(ll. 621–26)

[One sang about Priam, another about Piramus; one told the story of Hélène, how Paris won her and carried her off; one told of Ulysses and another of Hector and Achilles.]

Gschwind notes that the poet probably drew on a version of Benoît de Sainte-Maure's *La Destruction de Troie la grant* for his material. This passage sets the narrative style of the list: *comtet* and *diz* alternate with *comtava,* suggesting that the works are not recited individually but simultaneously, the many speakers telling parts of the same story, adding to the effect that an entire literary history is being given pell-mell in a vast rich intertextual symphony—with inbuilt elements of discord. We move from one name to the next, and the effect of running them consecutively is similar to that achieved by Chaucer in *Sir Thopas* and Rabelais in his lists: reduced to a superficial collection of names, the enumeration becomes ridiculous. The inclusion of Piramus, an odd man out, is a good example of the humor generated by the list. Stuck without Thisbe, in the immediate context he is an exception, since references to Ovid are found further on (ll. 643–49). His value here is chiefly euphonic, being only a slight variation on Priamus: at the same time, however, he provides another example of a lover who must resort to secret communication. On the surface, the poet's general concern here is sound, rather than content, and conveying the impression of Greekness. Hector, Ulysses, and Achilles (the latter two forming another convenient rhyme) represent epic heroism: later in the text (l. 1575) the latter two, with Paris, are used as examples of *sen, valor,* and *beutat* to be outshone by Guillem in the extensive and exaggerated description of his talents that follows. The reechoing of names in the text is one more indication of the fact that the literary catalogue has no gratuitous inclusions, and that what appears here will return later, woven into the story of the comic lovers.

The center of this short section focuses on Helen and Paris. According to Gschwind, references to the three heroes are rare in the Middle Ages, and we can infer that the poet's use of them reveals his unusually rich background in classical literature. Leslie Topsfield ("Intention and Ideas in *Flamenca*") reminds us of a connection between the mention of Hercules and Guillem. In line 1635, we learn that our hero is seven feet tall, the same as the classical hero. Once again, we find a tongue-in-cheek connection between the catalogue of works and the text that follows. Just as the key to *Chievrefoil* is secret communication, so stealing away a wife is at the center of the Troy section. Archimbaut is no Menelaus, but the notion of Flamenca and Guillem as a comic Paris and Helen is appealing.

In keeping with chronology, we then move from Greece to Rome, where material drawn from the *roman d'Eneas* is the central focus. Aeneas is not depicted as the conquering hero, but as a lover entangled with two women, the unhappy Dido whom he leaves "dolenta e mesquina" [grieving and miserable] (l. 629) and the courtly Lavinia (l. 630). The brief reference focuses on her, "con fes lo breu el cairel traire / a la gaita de l'auzor caire" [how she had a letter thrown attached to a tile via the watchman of the highest tower] (ll. 631–2). Prevented by her parents from seeing Eneas, she has a secret message sent to her lover, again underscoring the thematics of secret communication. The figure of Eneas is not portrayed as a hero or an empire builder: the focus is on his role as a courtly lover who must overcome the hostile figure of Lavinia's father, which could be interpreted as a foreshadowing of the triangle formed by Guillem and Flamenca and the obstacle of her husband.

Following the mention of Rome, we move to Thebes and Byzantium, and beyond: another trio of exemplary heroes paralleling the Greeks is found in Pollinices, Tideu, and Etïocles (ll. 633–4), suggesting familiarity with the body of material making up the *roman de Thèbes*. Apollonius of Tyre, Alexander, Hero and Leander, and Cadmus follow in rapid succession, providing another absurd mix of founders of cities, kings, and lovers. Hero drowns herself on hearing that her lover Leander has drowned. This is the first in a trio of images dealing with drowned lovers, culminating in Narcissus. In the second, Jason and Hercules make way for Phillis, the princess who dies for love of her husband Demophon whom she believes drowned. And in line 646 we arrive at the third drowning story, that of Narcissus. This links thematically with both Hero and Phillis, but the themes of the Narcissus story connect much more readily with the melodramatic tale of Piramus and Thisbe. Drowning in a bath does not feature among these tragic narratives, but it is tempting to see the watery setting for Flamenca's trysts with Guillem as a distant echo.

Both Narcissus and Piramus and Thisbe were popular poetic subjects in the Middle Ages, an important aspect of the revival of interest in antique literature manifest in the classical references above. That Ovid provided the foundation for much courtly literature from around 1150 onward is evident: the debt Chrétien owes his auctor is apparent in the prologue to *Cligès*, where he describes himself as: "Cil que fist d'Erec et d'Enide, / Et les comandemanz d'Ovide / Et l'art d'amors an romans mist" [he who wrote of Erec and Enide, and translated the Art of Love and the commandments of Ovid] (ll. 1–3). The tales of Narcissus and Piramus in particular incorporate many of the Ovidian themes dearest to courtly audiences and authors.

These two tales are worth consideration here, since they shape the character of the development of *Flamenca* and force us to consider the extent and influence of Ovid on the text. Piramus, as we have seen, appears early in the list; the famous story of *Metamorphoses* 4 concerns the ill-fated lovers who converse through a crack in a wall and provides the central source of comedy in *Aucassin et Nicolette*. The Babylonian lovers furnish an archetypal story of love in the face of overwhelming odds: in the context of *Flamenca*, as in the *Novas del Papegai*, there is a distinctly parodic treatment of aspects of the tale, particularly in the use of the prison walls that keep the lovers apart, and the motif of the secret conversation that creates a sense of complicity between them. Clearly the story of Piramus and Thisbe appealed to a courtly audience with an appetite for refined and spiritual love, insurmountable obstacles, and the opportunity for the individual characters to wax lyrical in emotional monologues.

The expression of courtly love in sensual language as the narrative focus is exemplified in an important version of the story dating from around the mid-twelfth century (Cormier, *Three Ovidian Tales of Love* 3–82). Guillem and Flamenca are comic reflections of Piramus and Thisbe, since they are subject to separation because of her imprisonment: indeed, it is a precondition for the eroticism of the story as it is for the Babylonian lovers, since the attraction of Flamenca is her unattainability. She and Guillem spend much time in withdrawn contemplation of love and its pangs, and while this in itself is not overtly parodic, the practical steps undertaken to remedy their lovesickness, and thereby resolve their plight, turn the tragic to comic and the sublime to the ridiculous.

Narcissus also leads us to speculate about further meaning for his inclusion. The *Flamenca* poet briefly alludes to the myth: "l'us dis com neguet en la fon / lo belz Narcis quan s'i miret" [one told of how Narcissus drowned in the spring when he looked at himself] (ll. 646–7). This reference to *Metamorphoses* 3 depicts the well-known tragedy of self-obsessed youth celebrated by myriad authors and troubadours, notably Bernart de Ventadorn. However, that more could be read into this tale and adapted to the problems of courtly love is apparent in another version of the story circulating from Chrétien's time onward, a reworking that might add to our interpretation, and is worth including by virtue of its ingenuity (Cormier 87–191 dates it to c. 1165–75). Its relevance to *Flamenca* will soon become apparent.

In this version, the legend of Echo and Narcissus is conflated with elements from the Danaë and Zeus myth: Dané is imprisoned in a tower by her father, and one day she sees a perfect youth riding by. So struck is she, that she falls in love with the image. Dané subsequently steals away from captivity and offers herself to Narcissus, who refuses her. He later sees his reflection, becomes aware of his self-love, and dies of grief at the thought of life without the comfort to be gained by loving another. Finding him, Dané dies embracing him and lamenting her lost love, and the anonymous poet concludes with a warning: "Or s'i gardent tuit autre amant / Qu'il ne muirent en itel sanblant" [Now, let all other lovers be careful that they don't die in the same way] (ll. 1001–2). The highly polished surface of this text reflects the self-absorption of courtly love: Dané is seduced by the image of another as much as Narcissus is smitten with his own.

Jean de Meun makes detailed and devious use of the Narcissus tale as one of the framing tales of the *Roman de la Rose,* along with Pygmalion, but in *Flamenca* the classical myth becomes a lower-key courtly fable, one that examines the inner workings of human passion in a sophisticated way. The lovers die of mental anguish, having realized the fatal attraction of beauty in self and other. In essence, the myth has been reinscribed with a troubadour aesthetic as a tribute to amor de lonh. It is appropriate that the final word of the poem is *sanblant,* warning about the danger of appearances.

Bernart de Ventadorn's distinctive use of the Narcissus myth appears in "Quan vei la lauzeta mover" (P-C 70.43):

Miralhs, pus me mirei en te,
m'an mort li sospir de preon,
c'aissi.m perdei com perdet se
lo bels Narcisus en el fon.
(ll. 21–4, Martín de Riquer, *Los Trovadores* 1:385)

[Mirror, since I beheld myself in you, my beseeching sighs have killed me, thus I lost myself just as fair Narcissus lost himself in the spring.]

The mirror is the eyes of the lady, but here again is the notion that the ultimate degree of love for another is reflected by the most complete love of Narcissus for himself.

Similarly, in the *Roman de la Rose* the fountain is a perilous mirror of love (l. 1571) in which Cupid has used all "ses engins" [his ruses] (l. 1592) to trap unsuspecting men and women. The mythological decor of Ovid, with its gods, showers of golden rain, nymphs, and supernatural transformations, is readily translated into the vernacular and into a contemporary setting, seen in the northern French text in the castle and tower in which Dané, like Flamenca, is a prisoner. She longs for an idealized escape as much as the *malmariée.* Dané's love, like Flamenca's, is a product of her imagination, and its strength grows proportionately to her isolation. Without suggesting that the Occitan poet knew either of the northern French

Ovidian tales, his malmariée heroine is a humorous distortion of both Thisbe and Dané.

Narcissus is a product of imagination and desire, and Guillem likewise represents the fulfillment of an equally artificial, literary fantasy. Narcissus embodies the tragic love of the *Metamorphoses,* while Guillem personifies the comic side of Ovid's *Ars Amatoria* that prevails in *Flamenca:* indeed, Nelli considers the work to be an Occitan Art of Love (Nelli and Lavaud, "Examen du *roman de Flamenca*"). Both he and Limentani (chap. 3) highlight the direct parallels between the romance and Ovid's text: in *Flamenca* we find the arrows of love striking Guillem (l. 2713) and the heroine (l. 5631), and both suffer physical and mental anguish that can only be cured by the ministrations of the other. That they find a cure at a spa, without the aid of the waters, is one more indication of the parody that pervades the text.

Just as in the *Roman de la Rose,* the lover is the servant and mercenary of Love: however, in *Flamenca* Love is a woman, since the word love is feminine in Occitan: "E si con Ovidis declina / Amors es domna e reïna" [And just as Ovid describes, Love is sovereign lady and queen] (ll. 5569–70). In the *Ars Amatoria* Love is lord and master, not mistress and queen. In *Flamenca* she is a combination of Venus, Boethian consolation, and *senoressa* (l. 5577) to Guillem, who is her vassal and prisoner. René Nelli cites this as one of the many instances of a southern use of Ovidian themes. Many of these he sees as commonplaces reworked by the troubadours: love as a feudal relationship, a sickness, a paradoxical state of being ill and well, sad and happy, and suffering delicious wounds. However, he ends:

> [P]our conclure, ce qui appartient à Ovide dans l'art d'aimer de Flamenca semble bien peu de chose. Le romancier occitan a beaucoup pratiqué certes, le poète latin, il s'est inspiré de son art et de sa connaissance du coeur humain; il lui a fait mille emprunts précis. . . . Mais sur tous les points essentiels, il a développé exactement le contraire de ce que pensait Ovide. (82)

> [In conclusion, what belongs to Ovid in the art of love of *Flamenca* seems very little. The Occitan romancier is certainly well acquainted with the Latin poet, he has been inspired by his art and knowledge of the human heart; has made a thousand precise borrowings from him. . . . But on all these essential points he has developed exactly the contrary to what Ovid thought.]

In keeping with his tendency to privilege the independent originality of the south, Nelli claims much of the treatment of love in *Flamenca* as particular to the *langue d'oc*. This is because he considers the fundamental tenets of fin'amor as being opposed to those set out in the *Ars Amatoria*. In book 1 of Ovid's poem, the speaker gives advice to a young man as to how to capture his lady. In a cynical tone, the narrator suggests the most expedient means to achieve success as a lover, with as little effort and financial outlay as possible. Love examines the tactics of wooing in detail and sets them out for a would-be lover: contrive a meeting in a public place, choose a sweetheart (married or not, but as in courtly love married women are desirable because one cannot have lasting obligation to them), surreptitiously show your favor, send letters, gain the confidence of the lady's maid, and perhaps seduce the maid into the bargain as well (as long as it is done after the seduction of the mistress), and await a moment propitiously chosen by the lady (perhaps coinciding with the calendar), for the final seduction.

Guillem is not far from Ovid's model: Flamenca is chosen as a target, and the seduction is undertaken with subtle skill and much dissembling. Timing is crucial, as is the complicity of the maids. Without doubt, Ovid and the transposed figure of Amor provide both the strategies and the justification for indulging in illicit passions:

Aissi con Ovidis retrai,
tems sera que cil c'aras fai
parer de son amic no.l vueilla,
jaira sola e freja e viella.
(ll. 6275–8)[14]

[Just as Ovid describes, there will come a time when she who makes a show of not wanting her lover now will sleep alone, cold and old.]

The moral of the story is profit now and carpe diem, at any cost. For Guillem this includes giving expensive gifts to the innkeeper and his wife, Na Bellapila. Such materialistic considerations not only reflect the increasingly bourgeois character of the times but also the materiality that we find in the *Ars Amatoria*.

Ovid is omnipresent in *Flamenca*: how he is used is a more complex issue. René Nelli states that the references to Ovid seen in the list of works at the wedding banquet are there only for decoration and represent indirect borrowings from the Latin poet (20): the essential *art d'aimer* of the text is provided by troubadour aesthetics. For Nelli, fin'amor is not the misogynistic phenomenon it is in Ovid, and he posits the essential notion of *service d'amour* to the lady that results in a sincere expression of emotion. In Nelli's assessment Ovid's text embraces a different worldview, arguing passionately about the difference between the Ovidian and troubadouresque views of love, a divergence that rests on the intentions and sincerity of the narrative voice.

It is here, I think, that Nelli's approach fails to convince, mostly because it relies on a serious, un-ironic reading of both the troubadours and *Flamenca*. After all, the troubadours manipulate a series of conventions and strategies as artificial as Ovid's, and because of the variation found in the uses made of the same conventions, one cannot make claims for the troubadours as a group. What Nelli claims for Ovid can be said of Guillem IX, whose fictitious biography tells us that he was at the same time "uns dels majors cortes del mon e dels majors trichadors de dompnas" [one of the most noble men in the world and one of the greatest seducers of women] (Boutière and Schutz 7). He also expresses courtly sentiment in love poetry—but what we can gauge of his sincerity is strongly in doubt in most of his works.

The coexistence of courtly and anticourtly genres undermines the view that there existed a unified and coherent treatment of love in Occitan lyric. These "conventional safety valves," to borrow Forster's term (*The Icy Fire*), provide a counter to a poetic system that was recognized as fundamentally unrealistic in its treatment of human affairs. The generation of parodically anticourtly poems comes as a confession that behind the exquisite rhetoric of courtly love, seduction of the desired object was the aim of the speaker, a distortion of reality and a dissemblance worthy of Ovid's sly techniques of wooing. The self-interest of the *Ars Amatoria* is not so much suppressed by the troubadours as it is often plastered over with sentiment and channelled into lyric refinement: the canso directed to the lady as a plea for mercy is, after all, a form of lyric *chantage*.

The *Flamenca* poet is as familiar with Ovid as he is with his troubadour contemporaries: it is not a question of deciding whether he is under the influence of either Ovid or the troubadours, or whether he wholly embraces or rejects the system of courtly love. Rather, we see the *Flamenca* poet deliberately play one against the other, dialogically. His task, in essence, is to accentuate the Ovidian nature of refined courtly love: from the courtly beginning of the poem we are drawn in the central section to an increasingly naturalistic setting that provides a locus amoenus for sensual, earthly passion. If the troubadours did indeed adapt Ovid to higher purposes, the *Flamenca* poet restores the comic luster of his strategies of seduction. The difference from Ovid, of course, is in the compliance and complicity of the desired lady: Guillem and Flamenca are very much the well-matched equals that Andreas Capellanus describes as the ideal for courtly love (*De Amore* 80–110).

An analysis of Guillem's strategy in winning Flamenca reveals that his behavior does not differ greatly from that of Ovid's pupil. He learns of Flamenca from hearsay (ll. 1774–9) contained in the unflattering popular songs about Archimbaut:

Ja sabon tut per lo païs
qu'en Archimbautz es gelos fins;
per tot Alverg[n]'en fan cansos
e serventes, coblas e sos,
o estribot o retroencha
d'en Archimbaut con ten Flamenca.
(ll. 1171–6)

[Everyone in the area already knows that Archimbaut is the perfect jealous husband. All over the Auvergne they make up songs and sirventes, couplets and ditties, satirical songs, or *retroenchas,* about Archimbaut and how he treats Flamenca.]

Both Guillem's rival and his love are parodic lyric creations. Encouraged by Amor, he makes his conscious decision to love her because she represents a paragon of beauty and the ultimate *avantura* (l. 1786) because of her elusiveness and inaccessibility. Practical steps in executing his plan ensue, measures that are successful because of the qualities he inherently possesses, as Amor tells him:

Fort l'o presica e.l salmona
e mostra li: "Ben es artos
e sobre totz homes ginos."
(ll. 1788–90)

[She preaches him earnestly and lectures him, and points out, "You are artful and the most crafty of men."]

Artos refers us directly back to the *Ars Amatoria.* This adjective only occurs once in the text and clearly echoes Ovid, who always uses *ars* as a pivotal, loaded term. In addition, making Guillem *ginos* perhaps points to the way in which he represents a fusion of the courtly *trichador* and Ovidian hero. He is not only ginos by temperament, he even looks the part, as his mouth is described as "bella e ginnosa / et en tot quan diz amorosa" [beautiful and clever, and in all speech, amorous] (ll. 1599–1600).

Here we arrive at the most important aspect of Ovid in the text: his essential contribution to the education of the lovers. The superficial references to Ovidian material in the list of works read at the banquet may be ornamentation as Nelli suggests, but it is more likely, given the guile of the poet, that they carry more significance. Ovid imparts a crucial body of knowledge to Guillem, who combines the student of the *magister amoris* with Guillaume de Lorris's adaptation of Ovid's ideas in the figure of the Amant.

Nelli highlights one of the most important tenets for the prospective lover in the *Ars Amatoria*, regarding the capital importance of education (31):

> Disce bonas artes, moneo, Romanus juventus . . .
> Non tantum trepidos ut tueare reos;
> Quam populus judexque gravis lectusque senatus,
> Tam dabit eloquatio victa puella manus.
> (Mozley 44; bk. 1, ll. 457–60)

> [Learn noble arts, I counsel you, young men of Rome, not only that you may defend trembling clients: a woman, no less the populace will surrender, defeated, to eloquence.]

One cannot help recalling the insistence of the *Flamenca* poet that Guillem has also studied *las .VII.artz* (l. 1623) to the extent that he could teach anywhere. His eloquence, good judgment, and skilled rhetoric are praised throughout the subsequent description. Educational accomplishments are of paramount importance to the would-be love, male or female. Flamenca's maid Alis says that Guillem's principal attractions are his eloquence and culture, and that a rich man without learning is not worth bread or salt (ll. 4793–4838). Education is an asset to men, but also for Alis's mistress reading has been a life preserver:

> Ara digas, fe que.m deves,
> si non saupes tan con sabes
> ques agras fag ar a dos anz
> qu'aves durat aquestz afanz?
> Morta foras e cruciada!
> Mais non seres ja tan irada,
> quan leges, que.l ira no.s fonda.
> (ll. 4813–19)

> [Now tell me lady, by the faith you owe me, if you had not known as much as you know, what would you have done these two years that you have suffered such torment? You would have been dead and tortured! But you will never be so angry that your ire will not melt away when you read.]

Isolated after her marriage from courtly society, Flamenca's education consists of reading. Her tutor is the same as Guillem's: we learn that Amor teaches Flamenca "son joc" [her game] (l. 1413) when the moment is appropriate, so that later the goddess "la ten ad escola" [schools her] (l. 4766). The Ovidian nature of her education is echoed in a reference to the only book the audience is told she possesses, *lo romanz de Blancaflor* (l. 4477). This provides one more instance of the secular replacing the religious, as Flamenca calls for the book to be used as a replacement for the breviary she kisses in church. In the A version of this text, the hero and heroine's education consists of learning about love:

Livres lisoient paienors
u ooient parler d'amors.
En çou forment se delitoient,
es engiens d'amor qu'il trovoient.
(ll. 231–4)

[They read pagan books where they heard talk of love. And they delighted much in the strategies (*engiens*) of love they found there.]

Guillem and Flamenca constitute a more mature, but nevertheless similar couple.[15] The cruel emir, who keeps his wives for only a year before beheading them, is replaced in *Flamenca* by the unkempt and cruel Archimbaut: both imprison their ladies in a tower.[16] The emir has his wives guarded, with strict instructions: "[n]e veut que clerc ni chevalier / ait la feme qu'il a eüe" [he does not wish any knight or cleric to have the woman he has had] (l. 1971). This also seems to be reechoed in *Flamenca*, in which the hero is a fusion of the two. Thus the Old French romance is appropriate reading material for Flamenca as she dreams of rescue. Her reading this text, and the playful use she makes of it in her *joc d'amor*, points to a particularly humorous and subversive use of another work.

This excursus on Ovid began with the brief references to Narcissus and Piramus, and their inclusion signals a deeper significance. Few items on the list read aloud are gratuitous: the works constitute a series of clues, or perhaps more accurately a paper-chase through literary history. In the case of Ovid, the superficial references to the creator of myth conceal Ovid the ultimate authority on Love, who hides in the text as Amor, and whose ideas are made flesh in Guillem.

The final reference to Ovid in the banquet list relates how Orpheus loses his wife, stolen by Pluto (ll. 648–9, referring to *Metamorphoses* 10). Just as with the reference to *Eneas*, the story is told from an unusual viewpoint: the *Flamenca* poet includes it as a tale of wife-kidnapping. It becomes even more parodic when we consider that in the myth as told by Ovid, Eurydice is bitten by a snake and dies: the well-known instance of kidnapping to the underworld involves Pluto and Persephone, and it appears that the two legends have been conflated to form yet another love triangle consisting of Orpheus, Eurydice, and Pluto paralleling Dido, Eneas, and Lavinia. We might interpret this in one of two ways; that Guillem is a comic Pluto, who steals Flamenca underground away from her husband and becomes her lover, and where instead of dying as a result of her kidnapping, Flamenca comes to life. Alternatively we might interpret the reference to Pluto as a foreshadowing of the fierce and grim guardian that Archimbaut becomes after the wedding, while his wife pines in solitude parted from her courtly lover-poet. The *Flamenca* poet's use of the myth reflects a contemporary reworking of Ovid, and provides a narrative thread that is picked up later in the intrigue of the romance.

Given that Guillem is an astute, noble poet and warrior who triumphs against overwhelming odds, the figure of David defeating Goliath is an appropriate model for the courtly hero: "l'autre comtet del Philisteu / Golias, consi fon aucis / ab tres peiras que.l trais Davis; / l'us diz de Samson con dormi, / quan Dalilan liet la cri" [another told of how the Philistine Goliath was killed by three stones that David threw; another told about how Dalila dressed Samson's hair while he slept] (ll. 650–54). The poet overcomes the giant, and the woman the warrior. This motif recurs twice in the subsequent narrative, first when Archimbaut threatens to cut Flamenca's hair (ll. 1120–34) in order to keep suitors away, and second when Guillem prepares to be tonsured (ll. 3547–53) to the sorrow of the assembled company, since he has such fine hair.

Jean-Charles Huchet comments that this incident reveals the motive behind some of the references in the catalogue. In essence their inclusion is to provide a list of narrative models, "fournir des schèmes qui vont être réécrits afin de narrativiser une réflexion sur les chances de l'écriture" [to provide schemas which will be reinscribed so as to put into a narrative a reflection on the fate of writing] ("'Trouver' contre le livre" 31). His analysis of the role of the list as a deliberate exercise is justified: it is also transgressive. The echoes set up in the unfolding of the story send us back to the list and make us read it in a new light of complicity. They are a complex and scheming form of allusion that reminds the audience of the story it already knows: the comedy lies in the distance established between the original and the caricature. Guillem does not have his head shaved by a woman, but for one.

The trio of biblical heroes is completed by Judas Maccabeus, whose main function is to provide a contrast with Julius Caesar: "l'us comtet de Juli Cesar / com passet tot solet la mar, / e no i preguet Nostre Senor, / que no.us cujes agues paor" [one told of Julius Caesar, how he crossed the sea all alone, and did not pray to Our Lord] (ll. 657–60). He resembles Ulysses in Dante's *Inferno* 26, an example of pagan endeavor to the limits of the known world. The poet's pious distinction between pagan and Christian is a mockery, given the irreligious tone of the rest of the poem.

The latter half of the *Flamenca* list returns to chronology and the *matière de Bretagne*, with a small excursion into the *matière de France* (ll. 688–97). The references to all five of Chrétien's romances, the Bel Inconnu, and Tristan are of capital importance, since their recital at the banquet lulls the audience into the false sense that they are about to embark on another series of adventures in the nebulous Celtic twilight:

L'us diz de la Taula Redonda,
que no i venc homs que no.il responda
le reis segon sa conoissensa;
anc nuil jorn no i failli valensa;
l'autre comtava de Galvain
e del leo que fon compain
del cavallier qu'estors Luneta;
l'us diz de la piucella breta
con tenc Lancelot en preiso
cant de s'amor li dis de no;
l'autre comtet de Persaval
co venc a la cort a caval;
l'us comtet d'Erec e d'Enida.
(ll. 661–73)

[One told of the Round Table, to which no man came to whom the king did not reply according to his wisdom, for never was worth lacking there; one told the story of Gauvain, and of the lion who accompanied the knight who rescued Lunete; one told of the Breton maid who held Lancelot in prison when he refused her love; one told of Perceval, when he came to court on horseback; one told of Erec and Enide.]

Arthur presides in his customary role as *justicier* over the Round Table, and as so often in Chrétien, Gauvain is first among knights. Four of Chrétien's heroes follow; Yvain is referred to obliquely as the owner of a lion and rescuer of Lunette; Lancelot as the knight imprisoned for with-

holding his love (not, interestingly, as the queen's lover); Perceval is remembered for his gallois-like arrival at court; and finally the fourth hero
is introduced in *Erec*. Like the Arthurian knights assembled at the beginning of *Jaufre*, and like the lesser assortment that closes the Arthurian
section (Governail, Tristan, Fénice, the *Bel Desconogut*, Keu, Mordred,
the Fisher-King, and Merlin), they are invoked in encyclopedic fashion to
conjure the spirit of literary chivalry and a model that will soon be superseded in the unfolding of the narrative. An appended short excursus lists
and compartmentalizes epic and historical heroes like Charlemagne, Pépin,
Clovis, Gui de Nanteuil, and Olivier.

The final group of references have been read as extremely significant:
"l'us diz lo vers de Marcabru, / l'autre comtet con Dedalus / saup ben volar,
e d'Icarus / con neguet en sa leujaria" [one recited the poems of Marcabru,
another told how Dedalus knew well how to fly, and of Icarus, and how he
drowned because of his frivolity] (ll. 702–5). Huchet has proposed a link
between these references: Lucifer (l. 699) and Julius Caesar. As unlikely a
combination as this may seem, Huchet's argument is quite convincing. In
his view all are transgressors of various kinds: Lucifer is an obvious example of Christian hubris (his position in between the Merovingians Clo-
doveu and Pepi [l. 696] and heroes of chansons de geste may be intentionally humorous), while Dedalus and Icarus and Caesar have the same value,
but are transgressors of pagan law. With Caesar we find the sixth of the
Nine Worthies in the text also, the others being David, Judas Maccabeus,
Hector, Alexander, Arthur, and Charlemagne—only Joshua and Godefroy
de Bouillon are missing—completing yet another embedded catalogue in
the romance.

Marcabru is the apparent exception, and is the only troubadour named
in *Flamenca* apart form the possible reference to Arnaut Daniel (l. 1709).
Charles Stebbins sees Daniel as a logical choice for inclusion in the text,
concluding that as one of the most adept exponents of *trobar clus*, he is a
natural complement to the complex intrigue of courtly love orchestrated
by Guillem and Flamenca, and because the twin themes of nostalgia for the
past and criticism of the present found in his poetry are prominent in the
romance too.[17] While Marcabru exploits the notion of literary *ubi sunt*,
there is another, and perhaps more satisfactory explanation for his appearance as the only troubadour on the list. One of his two extant vidas informs
us that he was remembered above all as a misogynist and critic of courtly
love, "[d]e caitivetz vers e de caitivetz serventes fez e dis mal de las femnas
e d'amor" [he wrote bad songs and bad sirvetes, and spoke ill of women
and of love] (Boutière and Schutz 10–11), and that this was because he

possessed a particular view of love, "saup d'amor cum degruna" [knew how love turns out] (l. 3), and never loved, nor was loved.

In "Dirai vos en mon lati" [I will tell you in my own language] (P-C 293.17), Marcabru criticizes the loose morals of his time and in "Dirai vos senes duptansa" [I will tell you without a doubt] (P-C 293.18), the poem from which the strophe in his biographical vida is drawn, the speaker berates women as the root cause of problems with love. A sardonic misogyny pervades other texts: perhaps the best example is his tenso with Ug Catola. In "Amics Marcabru, car digam" [Now I will tell you, friend Marcabru] (P-C 451.1), Catola calls Marcabru to task for his scathing views on love. Marcabru denounces *faus'amistat* (l. 6), particularly the way in which wives betray husbands, using the example of Samson. As support for his mistrust of women, Marcabru calls on Solomon, David, and Ovid as authorities, and calls love a game with loaded dice.

Of all the troubadours that the *Flamenca* poet might have chosen to conclude a wedding banquet, Marcabru is an unusual choice, but an appropriate one as what follows is a parodic view of the courtly world and of the love that poets claim as its prime mover. Assessing Marcabru's work, Martín de Riquer states that in general his tone is bitter, ironic, sarcastic, and often vulgar: the poet declares himself a particular enemy of married women who take lovers. Marcabru also criticizes his fellow poets for promoting Amar rather than Amor. Moreover, Suzanne Fleischman remarks in a footnote that "the Bourbon bathhouse is a far cry from the cleansing *lavador* of Marcabru's crusading song 'Pax in nomine Domini'" ("Dialectic Structures in *Flamenca*" 233). Riquer's description of Marcabru's "irresistible e intencionada necesidad de ironizar o parodiar" [irresistible and deliberate necessity to ironize and parody] (*Los Trovadores* 1:175) makes him a fitting conclusion to the repertory of courtly works and heralds what Huchet terms, "l'insolence libertine avec laquelle sont dévoilés les arcanes de la fin'amor" [the libertine insolence with which the arcana of fin'amor are demystified] ("'Trouver' contre le livre" 19).

The catalogue of works recited at the banquet, then, fulfills several functions. It demonstrates the virtuosity of the poet, who reveals his ability to blend classical, northern French, and troubadour culture to form a unique whole. He borrows and exaggerates the many banquet scenes found in medieval romances: the scene is intended to outdo all previous descriptions and reveals a taste for hyperbole found elsewhere in *Flamenca*, notably in Guillem's description, but also in the excessive behavior of Archimbaut and the meticulous detail of the church calendar. The visual and verbal excess of the banquet descriptions familiar in northern romance fuses with a distinctly southern literary tradition of the sirventes-ensenhamen. The style of enumeration drawn from this parodic genre lends a further dimension of absurdity to the proceedings and turns the feast into a literary banquet.

Huchet finds a tinge of nostalgia in all this: "Forme douce de la mélan-colie qui, elle ne consent jamais au deuil de l'objet, elle découvre qu'il faut perdre pour retrouver. . . . Le projet de *Flamenca* est mélancolique" [A sweet form of nostalgia that never consents to grieving for the object, it discovers that one must lose in order to find. . . . The *Flamenca* project is melancholic] (*L'Etreinte des mots* 39). But there is a comic side too. On one level, the juxtaposition of so many references can be read as absurd; how-ever, the content of the references may allude to a further level of meaning and a collection of courtly metatexts that include the audience in a literary game of hide-and-seek. The difference between the surviving sirventes-ensenhamens and *Flamenca* is the inclusion in the latter of so many refer-ences to Arthurian material, adding to the notion that this is to be the object of literary games that have as their end more than the urge to resur-rect a bygone literary ethos. Writing on the language play in *Flamenca*, Helen Solterer ("*Sermo* and *juglar*") comments that the presence of the works in the catalogue results in the different literary languages being subtly present: not only are they present, but absorbed and parodied, and they play off one another in a creative, comic, and dialogic way.

Many of the included items appear to have an exemplary value: the love of Tristan and Iseut and the many famous pairs of tragic lovers drawn from classical literature offer a grand model of amorous intensity to the newly-weds. However, the list begins with sublime courtly love and ends with the name of Marcabru, one of its well-known detractors, and the perfect foil to the lais of Marie de France. As Huchet maintains, Marcabru's presence suggests the inclusion of a transgressor of the rules of courtly love (*L'Etreinte des mots*). As a critic of courtly sentiment, Marcabru is as remarkable as the absence of other troubadours, who are virtually eclipsed by his pres-ence. The fantasy of the breton lai finds itself opposed by the realistic view of fin'amor as *Amar*, playing on the duality of love and bitterness: the erotic tension of amor de lonh expressed in the protracted dialogue during the mass is broken and counterbalanced by the more earthy consumma-tion of passion enjoyed by the protagonists. Guillem and Flamenca as courtly lovers owe much to their literary predecessors, but the sensuality and humor of their union distances them from previous literary models, leading Phillip Damon to comment that while early scholars deemed them "the ideal embodiments of the code" of fin'amor, this amounts to "calling

Don Quixote the perfect knight or the embodiment of chivalry—true in a way, but hardly adequate as an account of the author's complicated treatment of the ideal in question" (608).

The chivalric romance has pride of place in the catalogue, but in the subsequent unfolding of the narrative finds itself marginalized to provide a frame for the real narrative model of the text, the more naturalistic castía-gilos. The poet is conscious of the interplay of the two treatments of love. He intrudes on one scene in which the lovers meet to comment:

> Un petit fan plus que non devon,
> mais amoretas son corals
> don [non] gostan vilan ni fals
> domnejador outracujat;
> e pesa mi car n'ai parlat,
> mais tan n'i a que non puesc mais
> si.n parle, mas abtan m'en lais.
> (ll. 6010–16)

[They do a little more than they should, but such are love affairs, of the kind that base or insincere seducers, who try too hard, never enjoy. I'm sorry I spoke of them, but they are so numerous that I cannot ever not mention them, but with that I leave the subject.]

This presents itself as a more serious aside: however, courtly love in a bathhouse and in Guillem's room at the inn somewhat deflates the model of elegant sensuality and makes the message a little less self-righteous.

The more open treatment of earthly passion foreshadows later treatments and the presentation of love in *Tirant lo Blanc*. Toward the end of *Flamenca*, the lovers are reunited during the tournament, through the agency of her husband. There follows an explicit description of their meeting, and the morning after we learn that the dawn rises crimson, as if blushing (ll. 7689–90). The customary object of the chivalric quest, gaining the lady, is the focus of the narrative, but the extraneous exhibitions of prowess and magical encounters common to the romance are missing. Indeed, one of the only instances of enchantment occurs in line 6445, when Guillem's squires Otto and Clari fall under the real and alluring spell of Alis and Margarida. The attraction is not their magical charm or inaccessibility, but their real presence and their tangibility: reality in this romance is more appealing than any illusion. While I cannot agree with Gordon Shedd's characterization of this scene as a "rather unpleasantly comic spectacle of communal copulation" (64), he is nevertheless justified in considering *Flamenca* as a comic treatment of courtly love, although not a "withering satire" (43). Hermann Weigand perceptively comments that love is "no longer the ideal stimulus but the pleasure principle" (149).

When the lovers first meet and exchange stories, Flamenca declares that she knows Guillem to be highborn and worthy, otherwise he would never have sought her. It is as if she is rescued by an errant knight; however, it is not Guillem's mission to save her honor. While she might be impressed with his ingenuity, she has little proof of his heroism. He has not stormed the forbidding tower, but dug underneath the bathhouse. He adjusts his elegant dress accordingly:

Un capell lini ben cosut
ab seda, e moscat menut,
ac en son cap, non per celar
la corona, mais per garar
sos pels de la cauz qu'es el trauc.
(ll. 5835–39)

[He wore a linen hat, well sewn with silk, and finely ruffled on the crown, not to hide his tonsure, but to protect his hair from the chalk in the tunnel.]

Comically descriptive excess predominates: in informing us that the hat does not cover his tonsure, the poet deliberately reminds us that Guillem is disguised as a priest, a fact we might have forgotten in the richness of his courtly costume. In addition, the hat prevents chalk falling on his head, prompting us to recall the undignified way in which he reaches his lady. In more conventional romances, attention would be paid to the quality of arms and preparation for a joust. Lightly dusted, like a clown, Guillem loses his heroic luster. He has not wandered from castle to castle enjoying the hospitality of noble lords, but has come on hearsay and bribed the innkeeper and priest (who replace the traditional petty noble and hermit encountered by wandering knights) as necessary to accomplish his plan. His chivalric reputation, mentioned in the initial description of his attributes, is never put to the test until the final tournament. The *aventure* he undertakes is a calculated game of love: indeed, Flamenca refers to it as a game for equals, a *joc par* (l. 6512), and at the height of their affair the verb *jugar* plays an important role, occurring as a verb or noun eight times in the space of forty-two lines (ll. 6491–533). The primacy of the notion of play in the exchange between Guillem and Flamenca quashes any serious view of romance: what should be serious is rendered comic, although the charm and sensuality of the genre is preserved.[18]

The opening catalogue is a fanfare that paves the way for the ludic unravelling of the plot: it foreshadows the suggestive, subterranean way in which the romance will quite literally undermine itself through the lovers' adventures. It also gives us a summary of literary history, and Huchet rightly maintains that it is a parody of medieval literature:

Le fonctionnement du catalogue constitue donc une invite à transgresser, à traverser la surface du récit, à franchir avec César la narration, à plonger avec Icare ou à sombrer avec Lucifer dans les abîmes du texte pour s'y perdre. ("'Trouver' contre le livre" 33)

[The functioning of the catalogue thus constitutes an invitation to transgress, to traverse the surface of the tale, to cross the narrative with Caesar, to plunge with Icarus or fall into the darkness with Lucifer into the abyss of text, in order to lose oneself there.]

What he finds at the bottom of the text, glimpsed through the catalogue, is a disjuncture between lyric and narrative, a "tension" (20). In any case, it is a form of collusion between the two literary discourses: the catalogue of clues and intertexts sends us underground with Guillem. The erudite surface, showing familiarity with numerous northern narratives, conceals a troubadouresque conspiracy beneath. The text, like Guillem, is a romance in disguise: after his tonsure he claims that he will no longer live a life of pleasure of court. The narrator then comments:

Aissi presica N'Aengris,
Mais, sil capellas fos devis,
Ben pogra dir si con Rainartz
"Gart si Belis de totas partz!"
(ll. 3687–90)

[Thus preaches Sir Isengrin. but if the priest had foresight, he could well say like Renart: "Let Bélin watch out on all sides!"]

Gschwind, citing Leslie Topsfield and René Lavaud, links this passage to a sirventes of Peire Cardenal, in which he attacks hypocritical priests as Isengrins.[19] Guillem is a knight disguised as a cleric, and a troubadour disguised as a romance hero. The catalogue, like the hero an amalgam of literary sources, is a subversive rearrangement of literary expectations disguised as a statement of convention.

Whether one views *Flamenca* as a parody or not depends in part on how the list is read, on assuming that there is more to it than a conventional enumeration. However, even if it is read as a straight literary history, there is an element of play, since the cited works are embedded in yet another text: they represent works that have, in the sense that Mikhail Bakhtin describes the development of novelistic prose, been swallowed and digested. As such they constitute a mise-en-abyme of the process of literary creation, a conscious play on the wilful literariness of romance and the artificiality of its conventions. The fictionality of the catalogue signals an awareness on behalf of the audience that a subtle game of allusion is in process. This is signalled in the inherent exaggeration in its presentation, termed an "orgia nominalistica" [a nominalistic orgy] by Limentani (246), and its deliberate summation of previous tradition—the very particular tradition of northern French literature. The collective references have also completed the third stage in Bakhtin's formulation of the development of novelistic discourse, that they have become a parody of the works and genres that they represent.

The function of the list comes closer to what Pierre Bec *(Burlesque et obscenité)* describes as the aim of the *contre-texte,* of which there are many kinds, in troubadour lyric. He deals specifically with the openly erotic, obscene, and mordantly satirical: many of the texts he highlights are parodies of courtly love, and he once more demonstrates the interdependency that we already see in the poetry of Guillem IX of the parodic on the conventional:

> Car s'il est bien évident que l'on écrit toujours avec sa culture, on écrit spontanément contre elle . . . en conformité avec un code littéraire donné mais aussi en rupture avec lui: toute idéologie dominante ne supportant la subversion de l'écrit que dans la mesure où, par contre-coup, elle la sert et la confirme. (8)

> [Because if it is obvious that one always writes *with* one's culture, one writes spontaneously *against* it . . . in conformity to a given literary code, but also at odds with it: any dominant ideology not tolerating the subversion of the written, except inasmuch as, as a result, it serves and validates it.] (my italics)

Flamenca presents us with this basic duality: the rupture may be on a more subtle level, but it is there nevertheless. The literary code is that of the northern French romance, and the breaking away from its conventions derives from the poet's collusion with his own southern culture: the parodic lyrics of the troubadours and the conventional plotline of the novas permit a quiet revolt against the ethos of northern French romance. What Haidu terms aesthetic distance when he speaks of *Cligès* and *Perceval* might reasonably be reformulated, redefined, and applied to *Flamenca,* when the poet plays on the distance between the literary systems of north and south *(Aesthetic Distance).* His brand of parody, examining one convention through the subterranean workings of another, neither serves the interests of, nor reinforces, the conventions of the romance: they are subverted and transformed. As such, the poet finds a novel solution to an important question of quotation defined thus by Sarah Kay:

> Le roman de Flamenca affronte le problème du déjà-dit sur le terrain occitan. Le caractère archi-littéraire de ce roman de génie a été de tout temps reconnu. . . . Personne ne conteste que *Flamenca* est l'oeuvre par excellence du déjà-dit, du déjà-écrit, et du déjà-chanté. (41)

> [The *roman de Flamenca* confronts the problem of the *déjà-dit* on Occitan soil. The supremely literary character of this brilliant romance has always been recognized. . . . No one contests that *Flamenca* is the work par excellence of the *déjà-dit, déjà-écrit, déjà-chanté.*]

As Donaldson shows in his provocative analysis of *Sir Thopas* and *The Miller's Tale,* repeating the same conventions does not necessarily entail the conveyance of the original message. Transposing chivalry and courtly love into another key, as in *Don Quixote* and in *Tirant lo Blanc,* produces different results. Kay observes that Guillem is the perfect spokesman for the ethos of his time and place, and as such he is the ideal candidate to subvert the literary influences on the list because he is a product of them.

Guillem's particular form of literary transgression, outside the many exaggerated components forming his character, concerns his use of the liturgy and courtly lyric. The general influence of the troubadours is concealed beneath the surface of the text in what Limentani calls "una miriade di tessere—lessico, sintagmi e locuzioni, segmenti e sequenze ritmiche, ecc.—derivate da un inesausto assorbimento ad opera del poeto del linguaggio trobadoresco" [myriad fragments—lexicon, syntagmas and phrases, segments and rhythmic sequences, etc.—derived from an inexhaustible absorption of troubadour language into the work of the poet] (255). Like Guillem's underground passage, the poet's troubadour culture lies beneath the surface of the romance and tunnels subversively beneath its narrative conventions. Conversely, the narrative elements disrupt and recontextualize the integrity of the lyrics spun into them. If the courtly romance provides the form for *Flamenca* and the fabliau-style novas the content, the

language of the troubadours and fin'amor provide a third point of departure for literary play.

Noteworthy in this respect is the use of Peire Rogier's canso "Ges non
puesc en bon vers fallir" [I cannot fail in providing good verses] (P-C 356.4),
which constitutes the central dialogue between Guillem and Flamenca.
Riquer assumes, with Jeanroy, that Rogier was active c. 1160–80. In his
poem, the anguished aristocratic male speaker expresses with conventional imagery his supposed inner turmoil in love:

> Ai las !—Que plangz?—Ja tem morir.
> —Que as?—Am.—E trop?—Ieu hoc, tan
> que.n muer.—Mors?—Oc.—Non potz guerir?
> —Ieu no.—E cum?—Tan suy iratz.
> (*Los Trovadores* 1:269–71, ll.41–44)

> [—Alas! What ails you?—I'm afraid I'm dying.—What is wrong?—
> I am in love.—Too much?—Yes, so much, I fear, that I am dying of
> it—Dying?—Yes.—Can you not recover?—Me? No.—And why
> not?—I am in such turmoil.]

The strophe seemingly borrowed and modified by the *Flamenca* poet
shows the speaker engaged in inner debate expressed appropriately by
coblas tornadas and destined to be read before his lady, disguised by the
senhal "Tort N'avetz" [Lady Wrong], so that she will understand his feelings. The *Flamenca* poet transposes the sequence as a secret dialogue between lovers taking place not in court but at mass:

> —Hai las! (l. 3949)—Que plains? (l. 4344)—Mor mi. (l. 4503)—
> De que? (l. 4761)
> —D'amor. (l. 4878)—Per cui? (l. 4940)—Per vos. (l. 4968)—
> Qu'en pucs? (l. 5039)
> —Garir. (l. 5096)—Consi? (l. 5155)—Per gein. (l. 5204)—Pren l'i.
> (ll. 5217, 5230)
> —Pres l'ai.(l. 5309)—E cal? (l. 5458)—Iretz. (l. 5460)—Es on?
> (l. 5465)
> —Als banz. (l. 5467)—Cora? (l. 5483)—Jorn breu. (l. 5499)—Plas
> mi. (l. 5721)

> [Alas!—What ails you?—I am dying.—Of what?—Of love.—For
> whom?—For you.—What can I do?—Provide a cure.—How?—By
> crafty resolution.—Take it.—I have.—And what is it?—You will
> go.—Where?—To the baths.—When?—Someday soon.]

Here another subtle literary parody is at play, a ludic, disjunctive hide-and-seek well analyzed by Roger Dragonetti *(Le gai savoir)*. Peire D'Alvernha's well-known "Cantarai d'aqestz trobadors" [I shall sing of those poets] (P-C 323.11), composed c. 1165–73, lampoons many of his fellow writers. As a poet of love, d'Alvernha suggests that Rogier would be more at home in a more spiritual setting, "valgra li mais us sautiers / en la glieis'o us candeliers / tener ab gran candel'arden" [a psalter would suit him more, or holding a big, burning candle in church] (334), which is exactly what happens to Guillem, who speaks of love while holding the psalter Flamenca is to kiss, a move she has already practiced in a secular setting using *lo romanz de Blancaflor* (l. 4477) as a substitute.

Peire Rogier's later vida tells that the poet left the canonry in order to become a jongleur and travel from court to court (Boutière and Schutz 267). His changing of roles makes him a fitting model for the transformations undergone by Guillem in the comic service of love. The fragmented recasting of Rogier's simple strophe occupies over 1700 lines (3949–5721), which would be comic in itself, since short dramatic monologue becomes long banal dialogue. The rhythm of the exchange is dictated by the visits made to church by the heroine, who comically announces the final liberating *plas mi* (l. 5721) that leads to the subsequent chain of events on the feast of St. Peter in vincula—a highly suitable feast for those about to be sprung from their confining torment.

The lyric pastiche becomes the most important part of the mass for the lovers. While it is a matter of some gravity to them, it is described comically to us. Guillem, as a troubadour and unusually well-educated cleric, has little trouble improvising his side of the dialogue. For Flamenca, supplying her part requires planning and consultation. Indeed, the lone occurrence of the word *trobairitz* is found in *Flamenca,* and its use parodies the kind of poetic compositions written by the troubadours. Flamenca contemplates her next reply with Margarida and Alis. Baffled at the prospect of composing the *mots justes* herself, Flamenca enlists Margarida's help, who after reviewing the lovers' exchange to date, adds her contribution:

De que?—Deu! Hoc, domna, bos es?
—Margarida, trop ben t'es pres,
E ja iest bona trobairis.
—O eu, domna, mellor non vist,
Daus vos e daus Alis en fora.
(ll. 4575–79)

[Of what?—God! Lady, is that good?—Margarida, you've outdone yourself, you are already a good trobairitz.—Oh lady, a better one was never seen, except you and Alis.]

The use of the word *trobairitz* here is delightfully ironic: it is meant to stand out, and even within the context of a romance that parodies courtly literature, the scene offers a particularly comic view of poetic production. The pronouncement of the stunningly ordinary "De que" deflates the entire courtly ethos. In context the words are not composed by a learned nobleman, but by a servant, and a woman. This literary commentary constitutes more than a sly dig at the troubadours and their poetic clichés—it provides a hint of misogyny. Margarida's words are hardly original and decidedly lacking in literary imagination: praise of Margarida's skill by Alis and Flamenca is anything but sincere, as we quite literally move from the sublime to the ridiculous. The lifted dialogue is so highly unmemorable that the effect is to parody clichéd love-lyrics and the troubadours that write them. In context, it is not impossible that there is a sly misogynistic dig at Margarida, Alis, and Flamenca, since a lot of concerted intellectual effort goes in to producing relatively little.

As has often also been observed, parody, which is at the heart of this particular text, cannot function without the complicity of the audience or reader. Parody suggests but does not always imply rejection, and this is the case in *Flamenca*. The references embedded in the list of intertexts and the narrative that surrounds it point to a model of recognition between poet, text, and audience. Literary parody is both form and content in this romance: as readers we are conscious of a wide range of models and their fictional status. Naming genres or quoting works en masse distances us from the illusion of fiction: to borrow and extend Tilde Sankovitch's metaphor for the relationship between author and text as that of puppeteer and play, we are constantly made aware of the strings ("Romance of Flamenca"). Using a process of superimposition, the poet layers fictional models and finishes off his creation with a veneer of convention. Strictly speaking, *Flamenca* is a chivalric romance: not one in its ultimate form, but in its most hybrid. Taking his cue from the already inherent sense of play and parody in Chrétien, the *Flamenca* poet restores the potential of romance by shedding its commonplaces and conventions at the beginning during the banquet ceremony. By the time Archimbaut lapses into his uncourtly state, the sum total of courtly literature has paraded past; the courtly entertainment prepares the way for the novas, in which, as the use of the liturgy proves, nothing is sacred.

The *Flamenca* poet is indeed a critic of courtly sentiment, and his work is deliberately and overtly satirical. He not only crosses the boundaries of romance but also dismantles the walls of its inner sanctum from the outside. It is not merely that *Flamenca,* as a late romance, is at the end of a tradition: it would be more correct to concur with those who claim it as at the forefront of another more modern and novelistic trend.

Flamenca's particular form of comedy makes it a parody of the northern French tradition, through a double process of exaggerating comic strategies developed by Chrétien and fusing them with elements drawn from a small corpus of parodic narratives of the southern tradition. In essence, *Flamenca* is a distinctly southern parody of northern romance, and a northern-style parody of southern lyricism: its provenance and, to put Haidu's term to a new use, its aesthetic as well as geographical distance from the northern French tradition, are strong factors contributing to its success as a systematic attack on the tenets of fin'amor *(Aesthetic Distance).*

The group of texts Ménard *(Le Rire et le sourire)* includes in his summation is noteworthy, particularly as it ends with *Flamenca*—so often treated as an important text in the development of the roman, and so often ignored. Charles Muscatine comments on the same texts as Ménard and sees *Flamenca* as the culmination in a line of development of the courtly romance *(Chaucer and the French Tradition).*

Deciding what constitutes parody, satire, and burlesque, and where the line is drawn between them, is a problem that perplexes even the most helpful and insightful commentators on comedy in courtly literature. Muscatine examines the fine line between satire and outright parody and sees Chrétien's use of what he calls the "parodic-realistic excursion" of *Yvain* during the episode in which he becomes betrothed to Laudine as "a device, or at most a temporary vagrancy" (54). He speaks of *Yvain* on the whole as "on the edge of humor, if not satire" (47), and claims that *Aucassin et Nicolette* "can be read as a delicate but consistent parody of courtly tradition" (55). But Muscatine asserts that *Flamenca* is "the finest and most striking example of all," as he explains:

Its unfailing lightness of touch marks it off from the tradition. Its author is so much at home in courtly literature and society that he can afford a certain amount of disrespect, even to the king and queen of France. Compared to the Arthur and Guenivere of earlier romance, the former is something of a playboy, and the latter a jealous, troublemaking shrew. The poet is so much a master of the courtly style and situation that he can play with them, to produce a romance to end all romances. The central action is a single dialogue, so

quintessential of the difficulties and stratagems of courtly love that
it trembles on the edge of burlesque. (55)

Flamenca indeed holds a unique position, but it is not its originality or
"lightness of touch" that separates it from the rest, and particularly from
the northern French tradition; after all, Chrétien's style begs similar claims.
Part of *Flamenca*'s singularity derives from being produced in the south. In
addition, while it may appear sui generis as a romance, *Flamenca* illustrates themes and ideas drawn from the small but distinct corpus of narrative literature from the pays d'oc. This geographical and aesthetic detachment contributes to, and perhaps accounts for, the poet's ability to hold a
healthy disrespect for the king and queen of France. The anonymous poet
has complete mastery of his material and betrays an encyclopedic knowledge of the medieval romance. In essence, he produces a romance not to
end, but to reflect all romances, to incorporate an entire tradition as T. S.
Eliot describes, with an added satirical slant that results from his privileged position outside the northern French tradition. This text not only
"trembles on the edge" of satire, it also crosses the line with its parodic
treatment of courtly themes.

Muscatine claims that the *Flamenca* poet "is not a critic of courtly
sentiment" and that his humor "hardly shades off into satire" (57). He
asserts that we are dealing with a romance in "its terminal form as such"
(57), describing the poet's use of courtly convention and love poetry as
"pushed to the limit" (57 and 131). *Flamenca* cannot flirt with the burlesque without being burlesque, and at so many junctures it crosses the
line. Muscatine highlights a central problem when he states that while
remaining a romance, *Flamenca* refuses to conform to generic expectation.
A similar dilemma involving the picaresque and its earlier model causes
Ulrich Wicks to comment that "the picaresque embodies the romance at
the same time it inverts it" (46), and that consequently the picaresque emits
two sets of signals, one that preserves a normative sense of convention and
another that contradicts it. So it is with *Flamenca,* a romance in which the
normative courtly and deviant parodic find themselves in collusive alliance
and not in opposition. In expanding the inherent potential of the romance,
the southern poet effects a significant transformation within the genre.

Muscatine and Ménard treat *Flamenca* as if it were an integral part of
the courtly tradition. Hence, perhaps, their unwillingness to see *Flamenca*
as an outright parody. But *Flamenca* is not a romance in its terminal form,
nor is it merely at the limits of the tolerance of courtly convention. Rather,
it assumes the disguise of a courtly romance and dismantles the courtly
edifice of convention in order to rebuild it into a modified form, one that

follows and exemplifies the process of absorption and parody that Bakhtin finds central to the development of the novel. *Flamenca* reflects a new phase in the development of the romance and of the novel, one that finds common ground with *Tirant lo Blanc* and ultimately *Don Quixote:* in all three of these texts the medieval romance is treated as an outmoded and unrealistic model for action, and therefore the perfect backdrop for parodic heroes, who highlight the artificiality of the model and of literature itself.

Muscatine's solution to the problems raised by the parodic elements in the works of Chrétien, *Aucassin,* and *Flamenca* is to say that these works "testify further to the possibilities of stylistic and ideological alterations within the tradition" (55). The first two works on his list attest to this, but to *Flamenca* the added distinction of its dialogic position outside and within the tradition must be added. However, Muscatine judiciously implies that the adaptability of the romance form can be measured by its capacity to parody itself. Once this element of parody is present, it is the sign of change or reflection within the basic form: while Chrétien's romans conform to variations on a recognizable theme, they manage to break the mold in original ways. While the *Flamenca* text retains the outward appearance of a roman courtois, its narrative techniques reveal a profound self-consciousness of genre and convention revealed as an inner awareness of the courtly mechanism and an exterior defrocking of its codes.

Its position beyond the geographical boundaries of northern France alone might lead to reassessing Muscatine's definition of *Flamenca* as the "romance to end all romances." *Flamenca* is a romance to parody and absorb all romances—and thus to effect a plurivocal transformation of the basic model and mark a stage of evolution toward the modern novel. Flamenca presents us with this basic duality and a double textual movement: the rupture may be on a more subtle level, but it is there nevertheless. The literary code is that of the northern French romance, and the breaking away from its conventions derives from the poet's collusion with his own southern culture: no more nor less than a quiet revolt against the ethos of northern French romance.

5

Romance into Novel

Tirant Lo Blanc

We have already seen how travelling south away from the epicenter of the romance of chivalry lent an important generic distance. Continuing further in time and geography, the romance holds its parodic, reflexive trajectory in another vital example of this regenerative process, the Catalan romance *Tirant lo Blanc* (1490), whose main architect is Joan Martorell (c. 1414–68), with additions by Martí Joan de Galba. The exact nature of Galba's contribution to the work is uncertain. It is possible that he added revisions throughout, or added original material at various junctures, or supplied the last section of the romance.[1] Most critics focus on the opening and middle sections of the work and therefore treat *Tirant* as if Martorell were its main author.

Like *Flamenca, Tirant* absorbs, parodies, and transforms the courtly romance, linking the ideal world of chivalry with the more realistic or naturalistic setting of the modern novel; Cervantes was the first to recognize the importance of *Tirant* in the history of the novel, and there can be little doubt that Martorell merits his place in the genre's pantheon. Also in common with *Flamenca,* which exists in only one manuscript, *Tirant* appears to have had a limited circulation and therefore probably had a limited popularity in its time. Thomas Hart notes that the 1490 edition of *Tirant* was reprinted in 1497 and not again until the nineteenth century ("Comedy and Chivalry in *Tirant lo Blanc*" 64). Cervantes knew a 1511 translation into Castilian, of which a single copy still exists, leading Hart to conclude logically that "[f]ew readers of *Don Quixote* would have been in a position to follow the priest's exhortation to the barber to take it home and read it." According to Hart, the priest's enthusiasm for *Tirant,* and presumably Cervantes's, derives from the same phenomena that probably made the work less than popular at the time of its writing, namely the unconventional way that Martorell treats the conventions of chivalric romance by anchoring them firmly in reality in order to lampoon them. However poorly received in its own time, *Tirant*'s strong sense of innovation and blend of fictional model and naturalistic treatment makes it an appropriate influence on Cervantes, marking another point at which the romance once again transgresses its limits in the interests of its own evolution. Cervantes identifies in *Tirant* that authorly strand of narrative experimentalism that accelerates the novel in its movement toward and away from history and its unmistakable, dynamic "coming into being."

In his book on *Don Quixote* and romance, Edwin Williamson leaps from the romances of Chrétien to *Amadís de Gaul* as forerunners of Cervantes. Treating developments of the thirteenth century, Williamson concentrates briefly on the birth of the vast proliferating cycles that sprang up after Chrétien and particularly on the development of spiritual knighthood in the Grail romances, leading to moral condemnation of secular romance and the subsequent destruction of the Arthurian world. These provide the material Cervantes exploits to the full in *Don Quixote*, a masterpiece that, Williamson says, provides "a readily accessible half-way house, from where the modern reader can contemplate the heroic age that has been left behind" (214). However, the same assessment could be made of Homer and Virgil, and Williamson's statement raises serious questions about the way in which we view literary history and at what point a radical reevaluation of heroism begins. In Martorell's Valencia, the age of literary heroism survives as it does a century later for Cervantes. It is not so much that the heroic age has been left behind, but that it has been transformed, just as the code of chivalry had been in contemporary society.

Williamson sees Chrétien primarily as a Christian Platonist, who uses the romance to "contain its powerfully subversive, pagan ironies within an orthodox Christian explanation of the world" (28). An excessively moral tone in this pagan world, characterized by its incestuousness, later killed one line of literary progress of the courtly romance in *La Mort le Roi Artu*, and a succession of blander continuations of lively originals similarly stripped the chivalric hero of his appeal and dulled the luster of his armor and his sword's literary edge. What is missing in this late work is the protective generic self-irony of Chrétien's romances, the very sine qua non of the genre: the parodic elements in Chrétien's romances inadvertently make way for the kind of literary expansion taken up by the *Flamenca* poet, among others. The internal function for laughter and self-parody is as a generative force for transformation, as well as a purely protective element. The writers who went on to treat the *matière de Bretagne* in endless serious continuations excised a vital source of energy and began a process of degeneration that made many literary heroes appear rigid and absurd, hence *Amadís* and eventually *Don Quixote.*

If Cervantes turns the full force of satire on this aspect of the medieval romance, he also takes stock of another self-ironic branch of development in the romance, one not taken into account by Williamson; ironically, the flaw in his argument is the idealism with which he views romance. Just as he credits Chrétien with an essential Platonism, so he perceives the voyage of chivalry from the earliest days to *Don Quixote* as a linear progress from perfect model to total parody in measured stages. Dubbing Cervantes as representing a halfway house to modern fiction is chronologically convenient, if we measure the distance from Chrétien's time to our own and pinpoint the early seventeenth century as a rough boundary, but there are other stops along the way: indeed, not only is the road more tortuous but also there is an alternative route that exploits the inherent self-parody of romance at a much earlier date. Martorell incorporates the courtly romance into the first section of his work: his references to chivalric romance at the beginning of *Tirant* serve as a metatext and as an artificial frame for a much more realistic, or rather naturalistic, work. The distance between the ideal of knighthood and its portrayal is the source of irony, humor, and the unexpected. If we are to identify a "half-way house of fiction," we must look back at least as far as *Tirant,* to a stage where as in *Flamenca,* the romance is absorbed as a genre and embedded in a different kind of narrative that adopts a stance outside, and to some extent, against the model it imitates.

The regenerative power of parody in the courtly romance is well represented by *Flamenca* and *Jaufre,* which take up the parodic treatment of courtly convention where Chrétien left off, and by *Tirant lo Blanc.* Chrétien, the *Flamenca* poet, and Joan Martorell set fundamentally human protagonists into a seemingly conventional literary background that is nevertheless anchored in elements of comparative realism. Similarly, on being asked to aid the emperor of Constantinople, Martorell's hero declares to the Greek emperor: "senyor, jo no puc fer sinó tant com un home" [Sire, I can only do it as a man].[2] Martorell proves his point by making Tirant die before enjoying the glory that should be his as a reward for saving the Greek Empire from pagan invasion and converting vast numbers to Christianity during his tour of North Africa. Tirant's psychological weakness as a lover, physical strength as a hero, and innate cunning as a military strategist make him both a surprisingly human hero and a complex blend of previous literary models and contemporary historical counterparts. He is a protean, but mortal hero who wanders not in a limited landscape, but over most of the known world. At the beginning of the romance, Tirant meets a hermit—who turns out to be William of Warwick—and gets knightly training in England. He then travels around establishing his prowess in strategy and combat. Over the course of 487 chapters, we see him all over the Mediterranean: in Sicily and Rhodes, on a campaign with the king of France in Cyprus and Tunis, and at many other exotic ports of call. He aids the Emperor Frederic, falls in love with his daughter Carmesina, and ranges all over the Greek Empire, before undergoing another series of elaborate adventures in North Africa. It is an incredible tour de force—and often a tour de farce.

With *Tirant* we encounter romance on an exaggerated and outrageous epic scale: his grandiose agenda to save Christendom and rise through the ranks to become the emperor's right-hand knight contrasts with the most demanding siege he must endure in his private battle to overcome Princess Carmesina's virtue, which he eventually does by force in chapter 436, after lengthy meanderings that make Odysseus's homecoming look like an afternoon excursion. When Tirant consummates his love for Carmesina, we also see the final union of the vocabularies of war and love that find themselves in comic opposition throughout the romance: indeed, the familiar knightly oscillation between desire and duty fuels the unravelling of Martorell's tale. As Cervantes has the priest declare, *Tirant* is a work in which knights die in their beds, as well as on the battlefield. In fact, the protagonists of *Tirant lo Blanc* divide their time between the battlefield and the bedroom, which in itself constitutes a parody of medieval romance: while the twin themes of military prowess and wooing dominate the roman courtois, the physicality and open eroticism with which the two are blended in *Tirant lo Blanc* are unthinkable in medieval romance, although hinted at in *Flamenca*.

Tirant's wavering between roles typifies the extreme oppositions that shape the work: in addition, the alternately passionate and chaste moods of the tormented princess and the public virtue and private lust of her comically named nurse and confidante, the Viuda Reposada [the Easygoing Widow], evoke a fluctuating universe that has much in common with the world of romance, though it has become more overtly sensual and completely amoral. Again, in analyzing the complex and comic layers of the work, there are many possible directions to take: but what interests me here is the same phenomenon that we find in *Flamenca*. As in *Flamenca*, the vaporous and symbolic otherworld of medieval romance disappears in the main body of *Tirant:* its heroes and heroines and the ideals they represent are replaced by a series of courtly entertainments, or pictures on tapestries that provide tacit narrative accompaniments to some scenes.

This tendency to reduce the sum of chivalric romance to decor, however sumptuous, achieves the same kind of generic distancing achieved by the *Flamenca* poet with his list, and as coincidence would have it, a similar canon of courtly predecessors recurs. For example, when Venus's arrow first strikes Tirant as he gazes on the beautiful Carmesina, the assembled company enter a sumptuously decorated room "tota a l'entorn hestoriada de les següents amors: de Floris e de Blanxesflors, de Tisbe e de Píramus, d'Eneas e de Dido, de Tristany e d'Isolda, e de la reina Ginebra e de Lançalot, e de molts altres, que totes llurs amors de molt sobtil e artificial pintura eren divisades" [illustrated all around with the following love stories: Florice and Blanchfleur, Pyramus and Thisbe, Aeneas and Dido, Tristan and Isolde, Queen Guinevere and Lancelot, and many others, whose affairs were set out in very subtle and artificial painting] (chap. 118, 374). As well-executed as the images are, the narrator stresses their status as fictions, and they function just as the banquet list in *Flamenca* does. This literary and pictorial excursus announces the nascent passion of the hero for Carmesina, while at the same time foreshadowing the parodic treatment to be given to the theme of fin'amor and its most famous lovers. The juxtaposition of so many famous models in a catalogue verges on the absurd and paradoxically distances Tirant from the ideals with which he identifies by recalling their artificiality in a form of stylistic overkill.

In the same short chapter, Tirant apes and exceeds his love-struck courtly predecessors by having to go and lie down to rest because he is overcome by his passion. He claims to be the victim of seasickness, a familiar play on *lo meu mal és de mar* (chap. 119, 381; also in *mal . . . de l'aire de la mar,* chap. 118, 375) and *mal d'amar.* Unable to distinguish between nausea and love, Tirant's exaggerated and debilitating queasiness puts him in the company of Aucassin, Guillem, and countless courtly lovers, especially since, as Martín de Riquer recalls (*Història* 686), this particular play on words is found both in Gottfried von Strassburg's *Tristan* (via a lost part of Thomas's version of the story) and more important in *Cligés* (ll. 537–44). Tirant's stereotypical behavior, magnified by allusions to an excessive number of intertextual models and courtly discourses, is clearly comic. There are myriad examples of conventional overkill.

Much later we find another excessive and comic incident, this time literal as well as figurative. Tirant displays Roland-like heroism as he swings his axe and cleaves the head of an unfortunate Saracen: "Ne cres jamés pus bel colp haguessen fet los magnànims cavallers passats, ço es, Hèrcules ni Anxilles, Tròiol, Hèctor, ni lo bon Paris, Samsó, ni Judes Macabeu, Galvany, Lançalot, ni Tristany ni l'ardit Teseu" [I do not think that the noteworthy knights of days gone by ever struck a better blow, which is to say Hercules, Achilles, Troilus, Hector, Paris, Samson, Judas Maccabaeus, Gawain, Lancelot, Tristan, or ardent Theseus] (chap. 344, 940).

To reinforce this notion, when in the following chapter (119, 377–8) Diafebus interviews Carmesina on Tirant's behalf, they find themselves in "una gran sala molt meravellosa, tota obrada de maçoneria per art de molt subtil artifici" [a large and very marvellous hall, all worked in masonry in techniques of the most subtle artifice] (377) decorated with a contrasting and much more spiritual set of literary clichés more in keeping with Carmesina's idealized view of courtly virtue: "Les imatges de les parets divisaven diverses històries de Boors e de Perceval e de Galeàs com complí l'aventura del Siti perillós, e tota la conquesta del Sant Greal" [The images on the walls depicted different stories of Boors and Perceval and of Galahad, how he accomplished the adventure of the Perilous Chair, and the whole conquest of the Holy Grail] (378). The precedent of historiated rooms of this kind is, of course, Chrétien's *Lancelot,* and the *Prose Lancelot* that extended and completed it (on this last text see Rafael Ramos).

Martorell's descriptions fulfill a similar narrative and aesthetic function: they also constitute a mise-en-abyme of the two strands of chivalry at odds in the character of Tirant, as well. While the hero sees Carmesina through the images of refined passion, the reader and Diafebus view Tirant's beloved surrounded by images of chivalric purity, as if Martorell uses well-worn convention to express a visual, shorthand form of intertextuality. The tapestries, friezes, and mosaics decorate a more realistic and ambivalent world that will soon see the hero seem to mock the two themes of love and chivalry, when he attends a tournament sporting a jewel-encrusted stocking on his left leg to commemorate his having placed that limb between the knees of his beloved, and therefore within range of Carmesina's virtue. On his head he wears a helmet supporting a Holy Grail bearing Carmesina's comb (chap. 189, 621), again reminiscent of Lancelot's trancelike contemplation of Guenièvre's hair strands in Chrétien's romance. Tirant may be confident of his sincerity, but at every turn the reader doubts Martorell's: his artful reading of courtly romance exaggerates and distends the inherent self-parody of romance until it pushes the limits of the genre.

Typical of the princess's behavioral double standard, later in the same chapter she promises the hero that he will soon have the opportunity to wear a companion stocking: the boundary between the sacred and profane branches of chivalry is no longer significant in *Tirant*, and courtly love is acknowledged as an erotic and artificial narrative game.

The status of the figures depicted on the tapestries and mosaics as literary fiction, set against the novel, mutable, and vivid frame that Martorell constructs around them and his hero, shows once more how the chivalric romance has been subsumed, absorbed, and parodied. In the development of the courtly love theme the conflicting demands of desire and duty find different and more "modern" expression in the intrigue of this vast work. Its characters are as unstable as the political universe they inhabit: the trials and tribulations of the hero, the structure of the work, and its continuation by another hand lend an air of experimentation to *Tirant lo Blanc*.

It would be easy to describe the work as an outright parody of chivalric romance were it not for the historical importance given chivalry as a social order and as the ultimate guarantee of good government in Martorell's Valencia. Tirant's struggle with the Turks and then the North Africans reflects a serious concern on Martorell's, and then Galba's, part, particularly if we recall that the fall of Constantinople in 1453 was in living memory for Martorell, who died in 1468. Maintaining a political and religious balance in Europe was thus a more than pertinent issue. Martorell treats chivalry as a martial code with the utmost gravity, so that sometimes it becomes—perhaps sometimes almost unintentionally—a self-parody. Its pomposity is counterbalanced by the scrupulous lack of morality applied to the social side of the chivalric code as it relates to lovers.

Aside from the broader political importance of knighthood, there is also the question of the contemporary importance of chivalry as a private code of justice. Martorell, born around 1414, seems to have led a life almost as colorful as Tirant's, judging by his surviving *cartas de batalla*.[3] The *cartas* are challenges to duel and constitute a literary exercise that exceeds their real, more practical purpose to seek redress in disputes. Martorell's letters are grandiose, rhetorical set-pieces dealing with what the author views as serious affronts to his family honor. However, as Riquer (*Història* 635 and *El Combate* 13) comments on the exchange between Martorell and Joan de Monpalau, irony and a certain wry humor accompany the seriousness of the letters. The florid, baroque style is often injected with deflating insults, and the clashing juxtaposition of the two styles produces a darkly comic effect.

In one of the letters, Joan de Monpalau counters the accusation that he has breached his promise to wed Martorell's sister Damiata. After an elaborate and flowery opening salvo full of legal and chivalric rhetoric, he declares that Martorell accuses him "pensant tan poch en vostra honor e mentint per vostra gola" [thinking so little of your honor and lying through your big mouth] (*El Combate* 45). In the midst of legal formulae and formality, the expression *mentint per vostra gola* is at odds with the calculated civility of the rest of the letter. The change in registers reveals a comic bathos designed to ridicule the reader as it inflates the speaker.

Martorell makes frequent use of the serious and comic registers present in the cartas to enhance his novel, particularly in connection with combat or seduction. A fine example of this is found in chapter 226, when Plaer-demavida encourages the princess to love Tirant in a rousing rhetorical speech, which she ends by uncharitably wishing to see the Viuda punished for her evil tongue: "No tinc altre desig en aquest món sinó que la ves assotar per vila nua ab lleus de vaca que li donassen per los costats, per los ulls e per la cara" [I have no other desire than to see her paraded naked through the town as they beat her ribs, eyes, and face with cow's lungs] (685). Such sentiments are scarcely sporting, and irrevocably interrupt the delicate courtly register one might more easily associate with aristocratic women in romances.

Just because the code of chivalry had a serious and expedient role to play in solving such legal impasses as the cartas relate does not mean that chivalry per se was perceived entirely seriously. Literary ritual enhanced the aristocratic illusion of chivalric reality in Martorell's Valencia: he clearly views it as one of the privileges of rank. At the same time there is an element of parody in the inflation of self and deflation of the potential opponent. The effect of the letters is to raise the duel to a fictional level: the reality of chivalry relies on a literary ideal to preserve its status and dignity, perhaps suggesting a symbiosis between literature and life paralleling—yet not resembling—that which emerges from thirteenth-century France when the roman courtois is at its height. Many such letters appear in *Tirant lo Blanc:* the first from the comically named Kyrieleison de Muntalbà, whose bold challenge proves a pathetic letdown, since he dies before he can even take the field. In the imaginary as in the real cartas de batalla, words speak louder than actions, since not all challenges were accepted or probably intended to lead to a fight. Kyrieleison's initial letter to Tirant illustrates the rhetoric of fiction contained in the cartas. He calls Tirant "més cruel que lleó famejant, falsificador i escampador de la sang real" [more cruel than a famished lion, a falsifier and usurper of royal blood] (chap. 77, 263), to which our hero replies that his taunting words "són eixides d'aqueixa falsa boca" [came out of that false, big mouth] (chap. 79, 267). The letters contained in the novel are almost as extraordinary as their real-life counterparts. The ornate language expresses the intensity of the insult, and the rhetorical force promises, and perhaps replaces and displaces, actual violence. Consciousness of dissonant registers is apparent, for example, after Kyrieleison's death, when his giant brother Tomàs arrives to fight in his stead. He issues a verbal challenge that Tirant requests "sens dir tantes rondalles" [without speaking in a roundabout way] (chap. 91, 270), thereby showing his scorn of the elaborate rhetoric of the chivalric code.

Edwin Williamson notes the parodic aspects of *Tirant* and likens the work to *Orlando Furioso,* but distances them both from *Don Quixote* since "for all their misgivings about the idealized world of chivalry, Ariosto and Martorell are ultimately trapped by the genre: the conventions of romance determine the structure of their narratives and shape the experience of their characters" (81). And yet just as for Cervantes, the constraints of convention provide a liberating vehicle for textual play. For all that *Tirant* follows the pattern of the romance, it surely does not share its traditional itinerary.

The romance provides a boundless source of possibilities for Martorell and Galba as it will later for Ariosto. Rather than trapping them in an anachronistic, restricted fantasy world, the romance offers an idealized aristocratic model not too far removed from a representation of a more realistic one. Contiguity with aspects of the real world has already brought about one transformation of the genre, one that permits the full range of chivalric conventions and yet does not limit the possibilities for transforming a ready-made literary blueprint into something more experimental. On the fusion of fiction and life, Martín de Riquer justifiably remarks: "En su novela, Martorell fundió en una sola realidad las antinomias vivir y representar, ser y parecer. En *Tirant lo Blanc* vivir es representar, ser y parecer" [In his novel Martorell melded in one single reality the conflicting notions of living and representing, being and seeming] (*El Combate* 26).

Recognition of this kind of paradox leads Mario Vargas Llosa to a much-quoted view in which he sees Martorell as a God-supplanter, creating a sense of "realidad total" so convincing that we should treat his work as a modern fiction rather than as an archaeological rarity ("Carta de batalla" 4–5). Dámaso Alonso identifies a "realismo vitalista" in the work generated by its verve in describing life and particularly sex, which he says is portrayed immorally (243). Considering the greater verisimilitude in *Tirant* however, we might regard the open sensuality of the text as immoral only if we expect perfect behavior of the Christian knights and princesses:

Martorell's world, like that of Ariosto, is more morally ambivalent and closer to "reality" than to a literary ideal. While Tirant's cause is noble, we do not expect him to behave like Sir Galahad off the battlefield. This is not only the province of the male characters: Carmesina is almost literally the last bastion of courtly virtue, while other female characters share the same amoral code of behavior as the men and have ceded theirs long since. Alonso finds the confluence of "positivismo diario" and chivalric idealism an ideal source for *Don Quixote* (241).

Cervantes recognized the encyclopedic nature of Martorell's text, which included "estas cosas de que todos los demás libros deste genero carecen" [those things that all the other books of this kind keep hidden] (part 1, chap. 6, 118). In the same chapter where the priest praises *Tirant* as the best book of its kind and a mine of recreation (117), he lists the incidents that make the work memorable to him, selecting for special mention the characters Don Kyrieleison of Muntalbà and his brother Tomàs, and also Tirant's fight with the Prince of Wales's mastiff, the amusing repartee of Plaerdemavida [Pleasure-of-my-life—not so much a troubadouresque senhal as an advertisement] and the Viuda Reposada, and finally the love of the empress for the squire Hipòlit. None of these makes *Tirant* the best chivalric romance, but all contribute to making *Tirant* perhaps the most parodic. Edward Aylward compares the episodes quoted by Cervantes with the tone, treatment, and themes of *Orlando Furioso* (199). He makes an interesting comparison, but gives no concrete examples, except to compare Ariosto's Polinesso with the devious and vindictive Viuda Reposada.

The exception in Aylward's comparison is the knight Fontseca. Aylward cites Riquer in speculating that Cervantes chose the name because it happened to be at the bottom of a page of the edition to which Cervantes undoubtedly had access. However, like Plaerdemavida and the Viuda, Fontseca has a comic, semi-allegorical name that suggests a lampooning of the romance. Fontseca makes a brief appearance in chapter 132 as the emperor's standard bearer, after which he disappears. Many chivalric romances, including Chrétien's *Yvain*, feature knights whose job it is to protect a spring, a sign of plenty and not of sterility as Fontseca's name of "dry-spring" suggests. In *Don Quixote* (part 1, chap. 6, 118) throwing French romances into a dry well is deemed a suitable punishment for works barren of interest. Fontseca's role in *Tirant* is to carry the emperor's banner, featuring the Tower of Babel (a curiously catastrophic device for a monarch saving Christendom). It bears the inscription "Mia és la ventura" [mine is the venture], perhaps a foreshadowing of the ironic and comic demise of the emperor. A cursory look at the incidents cited bears out this assumption.

Kyrieleison of Muntalbà makes a brief appearance (chaps. 76–80) to challenge Tirant by letter and then in person in order to avenge the death of the king of Frisia. Upon seeing the arms of his lord and his companions hanging beneath Tirant's in St. George's Chapel in Windsor Castle, the distressed knight strikes his head repeatedly against the shields and drops dead, overcome with his own bile and anger. As his ridiculous name suggests, Kyrieleison is more a caricature than a character. His bland provenance "Muntalbà" recalls the generic color-coded place-names of *Jaufre*. Of the other incidents mentioned by Cervantes, two categories emerge: Tirant's fight with the dog represents the combative side of the chivalric code and its conventions, while Plaerdemavida, the Viuda Reposada, and the empress's liaison with Hipòlit show the exposition of the various themes of courtly love as they are subverted into a more boisterous register—and a descent into Bakhtinian heteroglossia.

Tirant's animal combat occurs during his stay in England. Embodying the implied surly and uncouth traits of his master, the Prince of Wales's dog attacks Tirant unprovoked. A struggle ensues in which the hero throws aside his sword in favor of equal weapons, using his teeth to dispatch the coup de grâce. Sylvia Roubaud treats this incident seriously; she traces the combat to marvellous battles between man and beast in Celtic mythology and Arthurian romance and links these to a kind of popular contemporary combat between a knight armed with a stick and the dog of a slain knight ("Chevalier contre chien"). Her remarks may inadvertently shed light on the obscene cat lyric of Guillem IX, "Farai un vers, pos mi sonelh" (P-C 183.12) in which the two lascivious noblewomen trap a knight they believe mute, for their pleasure. After his feline ordeal and the obscene conclusion of the revels, the speaker boasts of his courage in withstanding his foe. If this and Tirant's combat hark back to a prototype in Celtic myth, they do so parodically. As Roubaud admits, the match is not perfect, since Tirant does not have a stick and the dog's master is alive. In addition, it does not conform to the Arthurian pattern, since a London street has little in common with the Celtic otherworld. Dismounting from his horse to face the foe, Tirant exclaims: "Je no sé si est diable o cosa encantada" [I don't know if it is a devil or an enchanted being] (chap. 88, 235). In the context, enchantment is unlikely, and the reality is that it is just a mad dog. Furthermore, there are many comic combats with animals in the annals of courtly literature. It is a motif that lends itself easily to debasement. Beside the popular *Renart* cycle, there are comic romances like *Audigier*, in which the hero's father Turgibus makes his reputation by overcoming a butterfly, before being outnumbered in a surprise combat with assorted bats, dung-beetles, and flies (Davis, "*Audigier* and the Poetics of Scatology"). She justifiably identifies this late-twelfth-century text as a precursor of the parodic type of chivalry manifest in *Don Quixote* (237).

Roubaud's conclusions about the mastiff combat are ingenious, but their exclusion of any humor that might be attached to the incident makes the serious interpretation unappealing. Despite the nobility of the animal (or alternatively the baseness of the Prince of Wales), Tirant still kills him by rolling around in the street-dirt for a half hour and biting the dog. In *Mimesis* (41–2) Erich Auerbach explores the potentially ennobling power of ignominy in literature, using Peter's denial of Christ and then the Passion as his example; through powerful narrative shifts there emerges a sense of dignity. This might, of course, have some bearing on Tirant's fight with the mastiff: however, the emotive context of the New Testament is far removed from the setting of *Tirant*. Does Tirant accrue a sense of dignity from the fight? Probably not, since his dignity is compromised in the first place and is restored only after the judges have conferred on the worth of the combat.

For all the attachment to a code of chivalry, the irony is that the dog is part of the real world. The priest in *Don Quixote* mentions this combat as a highlight: of all the encounters that take place throughout the text, the dogfight is perhaps the most ridiculous, and the furthest from the idealized world of romance contained in the first 39 chapters of the work, in which Martorell relates the story of Guillem de Varoic. Like Jaufre's encounter with the lepers and Lancelot's emblematic journey in a lowly cart, Tirant's combat belongs to a paradigm of adventures that compromise the dignity of chivalry and the hero.

The Guillem episode that frames Tirant's career is significant on several levels. Guillem distinguishes himself as a Christian knight by saving England from the Saracens and leading a virtuous existence with his wife in a small, remote hermitage. The action takes place in an idealized setting, "la fèrtil, rica e delitosa illa d'Angleterra" [the fertile, rich, and delightful island of England] (chap. 2, 118), a place that seems far removed from the urban setting of the wedding Tirant is to attend. Guillem's exemplary conduct reflects the perfection of thirteenth-century French chivalry and the literary ideal of romance: he belongs to an era long since past, but that validates the present as it is described for Tirant. He is a chivalric fiction restored to life, a combination of military and especially moral perfection. While Tirant wishes to emulate him, he can only do so in England by becoming the kind of knight created by Chrétien: the errant noble in search of his fortune in courtly society. Tirant's adventures at court and in London are banal, valorous, and occasionally ridiculous. He and the hermit portray the two faces of literary chivalry: the perfect Christian knight and the earthly, social knight of the kind we see in the works of Chrétien.

There is a clear demarcation between the forest clearing and chapel, where Tirant encounters the ancient Guillem, and the more worldly setting of London, where Tirant attends the king's wedding. The difference between them is hard to define, since they coexist: however, one is an ideal world, and the other is concerned with more practical issues. Between them lies an important disjuncture. Speaking of the swift scene shifts of the Greek romance, Mikhail Bakhtin characterizes "a subtle and highly developed type of adventure-time" ("Forms of Time and Chronotope in the Novel"). This is one of Bakhtin's "chronotopes" and also typical of the medieval romance and the way it orchestrates space and time so that many things seem to happen without time passing. Bakhtin labels the setting of chivalric romance as "a miraculous world in adventure-time" (154) that later disintegrates with the increasing transition from poetry to prose. Bakhtin sets this unworldly time against the novelistic trend to subsume historical time, or what we might term real time.

One of the differences between the romance and the picaresque is that the latter transposes a similar pattern into a different configuration of time and space. This is, of course, to oversimplify the picaresque. However, a work like Cervantes's *Rinconete y Cortadillo* exemplifies the difference. Rinconete and Cortadillo find themselves in a situation not unlike that of budding errant knights, as they wander in search of fortune and adventure until they come to Seville. They join an exclusive society, with a strict code of honor, and enter the service of Monipodio as if he were a feudal noble. Monipodio's champions and damsels are tough thieves and prostitutes, among whom he dispenses justice like a down-at-heel King Arthur.

Although there is much more to this exemplary tale than a transposition of chivalric conventions, the comedy of the heroes' mock-courtliness derives from their existence in a time, milieu, and place inappropriate to the conventions associated with them. As Bakhtin recognizes, when Cervantes combines another space and time with a different use of the chivalric romance, the result is *Don Quixote*. *Tirant lo Blanc* shows the same features: Guillem's exploits belong to a finished past, whereas Tirant's belong to an open present much closer to everyday life, a form of time that runs counter to the episodic and elastic measuring of days in the romance.

After having met Guillem, Tirant returns after the festivities in order to recount his first chivalrous deeds, including the slaying of the dog, and to get the hermit's seal of approval. Tirant rewards him for his spiritual nourishment with food and supplies before he leaves, after which "no es fa més menció de l'ermita" [no further mention is made of the hermit] (chap. 97, 293). In this final scene, the hermit conveniently disappears into a forest closely resembling the timeless otherworld of chivalric romance, having handed down the title of most virtuous knight to Tirant. The self-contained episode at the beginning of the work gives a particular treatment to the serious side of romance and provides a contrasting model to the rest of the work.

Martín de Riquer notes the existence of another work known to be by Martorell, bearing the title *Guillem de Varoic* (BL MS. Old Royal 15 E VI, *Història* 646–52). Riquer notes that the manuscript was a gift from John Talbot to Margaret of Anjou on the occasion of either her wedding to Henry VI in 1444 or her coronation in 1445. The unfinished story closely resembles the intrigue of the opening chapters of *Tirant* and appears drawn from a prose romance in a manuscript preserved in London. The same manuscript contains a French translation of the Order of the Garter statutes that feature prominently in chapters 85–97 of *Tirant,* and also a version of Honoré Bouvet's *Arbre des Batailles,* mentioned first in chapter 28 of *Tirant* as the book the hermit reads, and with which he instructs Tirant in the ways of chivalry (chaps. 28–39).

Many critics have noted that the chapters read aloud by the hermit are inspired by the *Libre de l'orde de cavalleria* of Ramon Llull (1232?–1313), although the text of *Tirant* states that he is reading from the *Arbre de batailles.* This could be the result of confusion on Martorell's part, or perhaps keeping the matière of the section in the French spirit by referring to Bouvet's late-fourteenth-century work instead of Llull. While, as Riquer says, it is not possible to make a direct link between this manuscript and the dates of Martorell's visits made to England, it seems extremely suggestive that so much relevant material should exist in one place. There is also speculation that Martorell may have had access to a version of the Guy of Warwick legend on a known visit to England in 1439, a date coinciding with the death of one of Guy's descendants, Richard de Beauchamp, who according to Riquer (*Història* 649–50) led a colorful life embellished by efforts to preserve the romance of the romance of chivalry: during one tournament he jousted on consecutive days as the Green Knight, the Waiting Knight, and lastly as himself. One might imagine why such a flamboyant character would have appealed to Martorell.

Speaking of Ariosto's use of literary sources for *Orlando Furioso,* Thomas Hart (*Cervantes and Ariosto* 56–7) uses Erasmus's notion of *aemulatio*, a form of incorporating texts that Hart describes as a use of material with the intention of associating with it and then surpassing it. While *Flamenca* and *Tirant* predate Erasmus, this is clearly the procedure followed by their respective authors: Guillem de Varoic's main function is to deliver the chivalric code to Tirant and to represent an idealized aspect of it. When he has done so, he disappears, along with the classic chivalric romance in its French form, which has effectively been subsumed into Martorell's narrative. Henceforth, when we encounter the conventions and heroes of the medieval romance, it is in a different, more parodic context rendered all the more so since the William of Warwick episode establishes a literary and intertextual horizon of expectation. Tirant's function is to save Christianity, but he does so in a world far removed from that depicted in the hermit episode: balanced with Guillem's perfection as a knight is his appreciation of chastity, a quality not considered as important by Tirant.

Guillem gives a history of chivalry similar to Chrétien's account of the transfer of the code of chivalry from one country to another in the prologue of *Cligès*. In chapter 37, Martorell's hermit mentions biblical heroes, the epic heroes of ancient Greece and Rome, and then Joseph of Arimathea and the Grail knights of La Queste del Saint Graal. Of these Galaad is the most memorable "per virtut de cavalleria e per sa virginitat" [by virtue of his chivalry and on account of his virginity] (182). Galaad's qualities mirror Guillem's, but not Tirant's. In his enumeration of model knights, the hermit bridges the gap between the heyday of literary chivalry and Martorell's time by mentioning *lo duc d'Atzètera* and *Joan Stuart*, both knights of the first half of the fifteenth century. Similarly, the inclusion of the founding of the Order of the Garter in chapter 38 puts us into the fourteenth century. The founding is said to have taken place in the reign of Edward III, c. 1344–51; the blending of suggestive fact and fiction, as in *Flamenca*, creates a different atmosphere in the romance.

In addition, virtually every critic underlines the similarities between Tirant and more contemporary historical figures, particularly Roger de Flor and the Hungarian general János Hunyadi.[4] Although Tirant's existence is firmly rooted in the real world and perhaps in historical circumstance, Martorell has Tirant trace his lineage back to King Arthur. Tirant reveals his Breton origin to the hermit: "A mi dien Tirant lo Blanc, per ço com mon pare fon senyor de la Marca Tirània, la qual per la mar confronta ab Anglaterra, e ma mare fon filla del duc de Bretanya e ha nom Blanca" [I am called Tirant lo Blanc because my father was lord of the Tiranian

March, which faces England by the sea, and my mother was the daughter of the duke of Brittany, and was called Blanca] (chap. 29, 170).

It is as well he justifies his title, since the notion of a "white tyrant" presents a contradiction in terms from a different perspective. Dominique de Courcelles has yet another, perhaps even more fanciful derivation for Tirant, seeing it as "soit tiré, tendu, soit dur, c'est à dire pas encore mûr" [either drawn, tense, or hard, which is to say not yet ripe] or even "tout objet qui sert à éviter la séparation de deux choses" [any object that serves to impede the separation of two things] (113). Later, a Turkish sailor questioned by Tirant informs him that the Turks regard him as a French devil (chap. 163), and that his deeds are evil since, after all, his name means tyrant. Thus there appears to be some ambivalence regarding the hero's name: ironically Tirant is neither a tyrant, nor is he entirely "white" in the sense of purity. While not suggesting that Tirant is a mixture of vice and virtue, the potential contradiction in his name leaves room for speculation about his ambivalence as a character.

This is part of what Alan Yates has termed the "creative ambiguity" of *Tirant*, and he interprets this as a deliberate strategy on the part of Martorell, since "whatever degree of artistic improvisation or intuition might have originated it, [it] is neither sporadic nor uncoordinated in its effects" (186). As evidence Yates cites the subtle way that Tirant's motivations for heroism as a mercenary appear in the central section of the novel, where the hero saves the Greek Empire. The treacherous duke of Macedonia, whose character seems to be an amalgam of Ganelon in the *Chanson de Roland* and Keu in Arthurian romance, continually raises doubts about Tirant's character and his reasons for seeking glory. Rightly fearing that his influence with the emperor wanes as Tirant's grows, the duke sends a letter to the emperor voicing his mistrust of Tirant because the latter is a foreigner, and therefore dangerous (chap. 141, 459–60). Yates also notes that some of Carmesina's reservations about succumbing to Tirant's charms are founded on his being a foreigner (187).

Yates also perceptively comments (186) that the misgivings of some characters are amplified by the hero himself when, for example, Tirant declares to his men that if they win their battle, "tot l'Emperi serà nostre" [all the Empire will be ours] (chap. 156, 528–9). Similarly, Tirant refuses immediate rewards for his victories by stating openly that he will not accept any title except that of emperor (chap. 161, 556) and, as Yates says, Tirant thinks first of his proximity to the throne when he celebrates his secret marriage with Carmesina (chap. 272, 784). Consequently, the reader is forced to question Tirant's altruism. Yates's "suggestive ambiguity" (188) creates a distance between an ideal of chivalric behavior that we expect because of prior models, notably the inclusion of the carefully orchestrated Guillem de Varoic episode at the beginning of the romance, and the reality of a politically astute general who exhibits patent self-interest.

The suggestion that Tirant may be more complex and less reliable than he appears contributes to our image of him as a more modern hero. Arthur Terry rightly says of the author: "Yet what is really impressive in Martorell's achievement, one could argue, is that his most original effects are obtained largely by exploiting the existing possibilities of medieval narrative" ("Character and Role in *Tirant lo Blanc*" 185). Martorell indeed proves that this is not realized by destroying a model in confrontation with the real world, but by subtly accommodating it in a modified setting that opens a distance between generic expectation and the events in the narrative. The "existing possibilities" are the conventions of medieval romance.

Tirant follows a classic blueprint for development, learning about the chivalric code from an old, valiant knight, and then going forth into the world to prove his valor and gain fame and fortune through service d'amour to a noble lady. Humor and the parody of courtly love that appears in the central section of the novel distance him from the potentially flat reiteration of banal adventures. The ironic distance between knight and lover is also an existing possibility, since Chrétien draws heavily upon it for his comic effect. Martorell fuses the medieval and the modern in his hero by making him a direct descendant of King Arthur. More detail of Tirant's genealogy emerges later, when the origin of the line of Roca Salada is described (chap. 223, 677), about how Uterpandragó cheats his brother out of a wife by using false letters of credence. In the French Arthurian tradition, the seduction of Ygerne and the begetting of Arthur are achieved through disguise and not forgery; the displacement of this motif is significant in that it provides yet another example of the unreliability of the written word within Martorell's narrative, a further playful example proving that all is not what it seems. The king of France, the outraged father, lays siege to the usurper's castle for over a year before a settlement is reached. This links Tirant with King Arthur, although not entirely honorably: Tirant is not a blood relative, but a symbolic and loosely related pretender, a bastardization of the pure bloodline, which in turn reflects the novel's relationship to the French chivalric corpus.

The inclusion of the Order of the Garter fuses the literary ideal of the Round Table with historical reality. The trivial origin of the garter, passing from the leg of a flirtatious court lady to that of the king, is much more in keeping with the playfulness of Tirant's chivalric code. The fusion between old chivalry and new is revealed in the story of the motto. In chapter 96 we find the impossible story of the hunting of a white stag with a collar sewn under its skin bearing the device adopted for the garter, placed there by Julius Caesar. Neither Diafebus, who narrates the implausible story, nor the hermit can account for the beast. It is one of the few magical occurrences in the work, and one that draws on the conventions of romance, where literal and symbolic white stag hunts abound. Outside the context of the hermit's dwelling, the magic world is an illusion. The transition between the model of romance and the more naturalistic, modernistic section of the work occurs during Tirant's stay in England when he is no longer with the hermit. In London and Windsor he plays the knight errant: he defeats the champion Muntalt in the tournament following the wedding, defends himself against Agnès's suitor Vilasermes (chap. 61), fights the dog (chap. 68), defeats the four kings (chaps. 78–84), and accepts a challenge from the Scottish knight Vilafermosa (chap. 84) before gaining victory over Tomàs de Muntalbà. Even their names, "Nicetown" and "Nastytown" suggest Sir Thopas-like banality. To round off the conventional succession of individual challenges and duels, Tomàs is expelled from the order of chivalry in the way already described by the hermit (chap. 36), and Tirant is inducted into the noble Order of the Garter.

By the time he leaves for Rhodes, via his native Brittany, Tirant has exhausted the conventional paradigm of knightly adventures: he has been instructed, knighted, proven in combat, and has defended a lady's honor. Even the gamut of exotic settings associated with the chivalric romance has been run: the hermit's forest, the magic stag hunt, a wedding, a tournament, and a mysterious castle. This latter incident comically reinforces the artificiality of the courtly romance in the work.

After the wedding, the party encounters a rock made of wood in the middle of a field, on top of which there is a castle defended by soldiers (chap. 53). A noble combat follows, using pretend weapons: the intruders believe it is a real battle until their lack of injuries makes them realize that it is *una burla* (200), which turns out to be presided over by the "God of Love." This favorite allegorical figure of courtly romance, and educator in dreams of countless heros, becomes part of a burlesque entertainment, in which outlandish furnishings of occasionally doubtful taste are a prominent feature. The king's apartment has a silver statue of a lady with wrinkled breasts from which water spurts into a crystal basin. The queen's apartment has a gold statue of a woman with wine pouring from her genitalia. Another has oil pouring from a bishop's mitre, and a fourth a crowned lion with honey gushing from its mouth. The central courtyard finds a dwarf at the center of a fountain, with wine spouting from his navel, and a silver statue of an old man, whose hunchback provides an endless supply of bread. While decorative excess and elaborate ritual were certainly the order of the day, historical veracity does not preclude seeing humor here. The descriptive excess of the scene and its travesty of romance commonplaces like the dwarf, beautiful maidens, and an enchanted castle is unmistakable. The opulence of the trappings only serves to enhance the aesthetic incongruity of the subjects represented in fountain form.

In describing the castle to the hermit, Tirant is clear to point out that the special effects are not achieved by magic, but by artifice (p. 203). This is also the case later, when King Arthur and Morgan le Fay arrive at a court entertainment for the Greek emperor (chaps. 190–202). The king lectures the assembled company on good government, honor, the duties of a knight, and the nobility, covering much of the same material as the hermit. The company is impressed by the artifice, particularly by the king's barge: "e estaven admirats del que havien vist, que paria que tot fos fet per encantament" [they were full of admiration for what they had seen, that it seemed as though everything was done by enchantment] (chap. 642). But there is no magic: there is even a comic touch when Martorell says that even "la mala pudor de la sentina" [the bad smell of the bilge] (642) at the dockside is replaced by pleasing perfume. This hyperrealistic detail, like the mundanity of the street in which Tirant fights the mastiff, is doubly deflating, and a further indication of the artificiality of the entertainment. In addition, there is the curious encounter of Espèrcius with the Senyora de les Illes (chaps. 410–13) in a curious excursus from the main narrative.

The story of the senyora's transformation into a treasure-guarding dragon is magic: its inclusion in the narrative is obtrusive and proves an exception to the general rule. However, even here there is deflation in the way the incident is described, as the shepherd's lively narration reveals. The youth who finds her is dazzled by her beauty, and yet: "Lo jove se pensà que fos qualque folla fembra o comuna qui estigués aquí per fer bona companyia als hòmes qui passaven" [the young man thought her some mad woman, or a common trollop who was there to keep company with the men who passed by] (1044). The comic tone deflates what would otherwise be a straight courtly narrative, in a similar way that elevating Dulcinea to the status of a courtly lady does not work when the same deflatory technique reappears in Don Quixote. The incident also provides another intertext for Tirant lo Blanc, since it is largely drawn from Sir John Mandeville's Travels.

Once outside the geographical area of the matière de Bretagne, Tirant no longer behaves like an individual knight errant, but like a career soldier. His stay in England corresponds to the bildungsroman stage of many chivalric romances. His real adventures begin with Rhodes, and then the Greek Empire, and while his subsequent adventures still follow the general outline of the romance, they take place in a transformed setting and in a more "historical" time. When Cervantes cites Tirant's fight with the mastiff as an example of Tirant's chivalric prowess, he is surely injecting a note of irony. However serious Martorell makes the battle by having judges and the assembled company declare that the combat is equivalent to fighting a knight, to Cervantes's more modern eyes, as to ours, there is potential comedy in the encounter. It is the least of Tirant's victories—and one that parodies the perfect model of chivalry of the opening chapters. The slight transposition from the forest to the street devalues any symbolic interpretation the reader might assign it.

The wedding procession, in which the king, his knights, and retinue are held up by a confrontation between the blacksmiths' and weavers' guilds, already heralds the deflation of the perfect courtly model and the encroachment of the modern world. The king solves the dispute by hanging the lawyers assigned to solve the conflict, to the joy of the onlookers. The procession resumes with entertainers taking precedence over the clergy, young nobles, great lords, nuns, and soldiers, with the gaily dressed prostitutes and their procurers completing the parading of the estates. The pomp and solemnity of the proceedings is ruined by the entertainment provided by the lower orders. The excess of the description matches the ceremonies, festivities, and tournaments: although the contemporary existence of elaborate public events and displays of wealth might lead us to avoid assigning extraordinary significance or humor to them when they appear in *Tirant,* this is perhaps denying a comic dimension to some descriptions.

Rabelais has a similar fondness for pageantry and vivid description reflecting a side of sixteenth-century reality—the existence within the realm of the possible does not preclude comic description. For example, the war between the cake bakers and shepherds in Rabelais's *Gargantua* resembles the petty dispute between the guilds in *Tirant.* No one would think to consider incidents in Rabelais as lacking humor because they were historically accurate, since his parodic intention is clear. The seriousness with which Martorell treats chivalry, and the attention he gives to portraying rituals and ceremonies makes his humor less obvious, but already in the first section, and even more so in the central parts of the novel, we see the emergence of a parodist.

Tirant's adventures in England introduce, reinforce, and gently parody chivalry as a perfect system by transferring it from an idealized twilight to a well-lit present. Even though the theme of preserving the Christian Empire remains serious, Martorell undermines the credibility of his hero and parodies him, and the courtly romance, through his treatment of fin'amor. Cervantes identifies this second area of appeal in the priest's description in his references to Plaerdemavida, the Viuda Reposada, and the empress.

When Plaerdemavida encourages Estefania to secretly marry Diafebus, she upbraids her for holding out too long against her impatient suitor:

> Quin mal és lo besar? Que ells en França no en fan més menció que si es donaven la mà. E si a vós volia besar, ho deuríeu consentir, e encara si us posaven les mans davall les faldes, en aquest temps de gran necessitat. E aprés que siau en tranquille pau, fer del vici virtut. (Chap. 146, 492)

> [What harm is there in kissing him? In France they make no more mention of it than if they clapped hands with someone. In this time of great necessity, if he wanted to kiss you, or even put his hands in your petticoats, you ought to say yes. And then after calm peace is restored, you can make a virtue out of vice.]

With France once again a comic model, courtly virtue, it seems, is all in the mind, and an ideal that has little in common with actual circumstances. The *gran necessitat* is especially comic in the circumstances, since the Christian world is under siege: sacrificing chastity, the driving force behind Guillem de Varoic's concept of Christian society, is an ironic heroic sacrifice on the part of the ladies of the Greek court. And yet within the ethical system established in the work, there seems nothing wrong with this: Plaerdemavida's attitude typifies the amorality of the novel.

E. C. Riley termed *Tirant* "one of the most disconcertingly ambiguous novels of chivalry ever written" (24) on account of the way in which the courtly lover in Tirant makes the Christian hero an absurdity. He asks how we can take Tirant seriously "after he has been bundled under the bedclothes, sat on by the Princess Carmesina, and narrowly escaped being sat on by the Empress? How could anyone in the Counter-Reformation take this lascivious hero for the paragon of virtues the author obviously intended?" (24).

Chrétien similarly takes pleasure in placing his heroes in social and moral dilemmas. In *Yvain* the hero hides out in Laudine's chambers and falls in love with the widow of the knight he has just slain, encouraged by her maidservant Lunete. Her logic in persuading her mistress that Yvain is the right match for her especially because he has killed Laudine's first husband is as questionable as that which sees the gran necessitat in sacrificing virtue. Indeed, in Chrétien's schema for the romance the fundamental reason for creating a certain kind of chivalric heroism is often to undermine and contradict it in a domestic setting. The accommodation of the martial and the social is part of Chrétien's comic strategy, and Tirant is the exaggerated conclusion of a scenario already well-developed in the late twelfth century.

One logical answer to Riley's question about Martorell's hero is that we are not meant to take Tirant entirely seriously. What Martorell intended we shall certainly never know, but what he wrote suggests an ambivalent attitude toward his hero. Riley suggests the presence of a "confusion" of literary approaches and that the "fumbling comic irony is at variance with the otherwise serious and elevated tone of the book" (25). The divergent poles are exaggerated and confuse the reader as they do the hero. For Riley, those who view the work as either serious or parodic are only half-right, and he suggests that neither is a complete view, but that determining a third option is problematic because of the "absurdities" (i.e., obscenities) apparent in the treatment of courtly love. If we view *Tirant* wholly seriously, we cannot account for Tirant's domestic campaign at the court of the Greek emperor. Similarly, if we regard the novel as parodic, the Christian militant loses his luster.

Tirant's mission to save the Christian world is further undermined by the nature of the people he is saving. At the end of the novel, one tragedy after another befalls the imperial household. Carmesina dies, having broken her nose against Tirant's corpse in the violence of her grief, adding bathos to an otherwise tragic moment, shortly to be followed in death by her father. Scenes of women's grief abound in romances, where dead lovers and husbands are frequent. Most notably, one thinks of Chrétien's Yvain falling in love with Laudine as she laments over her husband's dead body, pulling out her hair and tearing at her flesh with her fingernails. In an instance of voyeurism, Yvain watches her unseen and is smitten. Chrétien patently delights in the paradoxical joy that comes from grief. Carmesina's violent self-inflicted death has a kind of slapstick pathos that elicits a comic response as well as sympathy.

Seeing her family disappear one by one, the reader might expect the empress to join them, but instead she orders her youthful lover Hipòlit to organize the funeral arrangements expediently, "perquè aprés se puixa complir lo desig vostre e meu" [because afterward our mutual desire can fulfill itself] (chap. 479, 1170). His name reflects an incestuous overtone in their relationship, as it recalls the obsession of the seductive and rapacious Phaedra. The empress addresses him as "Mon fill e senyor" [my son and lord] (1171), and cannot wait to legalize the affair that began long before (chap. 248, 734). Although the empress is justified in marrying in haste by the request of the nobles that she do so in order to restore political stability, as in *Yvain* and *Jaufre*, the chivalric marriage for the common good is parodied here by the empress's age and sterility, and by the suggested sexual irregularity of the union. Hipòlit is a perfect courtly lover, but at the same time politically minded; he does not grieve excessively at Tirant's death because he realizes that he can become emperor. The narrator remains impartial and does not overtly judge the union; however, the displacement of Tirant and Carmesina as an idealized chivalric couple by the aging empress and her overly youthful consort is a departure from the literary norm and a humorous modification of one of the fundamental patterns of chivalric romance.

The night the lovers consummate their passion is typical of the comic treatment of love in the novel. The empress does not hesitate long before surrendering herself with comic haste to Hipòlit: "La tua molta virtut e condició afable me força passar los límits de castedat" [your great virtue and weakened condition compel me to cross the boundaries of chastity] (chap. 260, 750). Preparing for her rendezvous, she has Carmesina keep the emperor occupied while she makes ready, and the empress lies to her maid Eliseu by saying that the preparations are for the emperor. She then feigns illness to ensure her privacy: "Prestament vengueren los metges e tocaren-li lo pols e trobaren-lo-hi molt mogut per lo moviment que tenia, que s'esperava entrar en lliça de camp clos ab cavaller jove, e dubtava la perillosa batalla" [The doctors came quickly, felt her pulse, and found it high on account of her agitation, she who hoped to enter the lists of the tournament field with a young knight, and she was nervous about the dangerous battle] (chap. 260, 752).

Here the narrator uses the same imagery of erotic combat that we later find used for Carmesina and Tirant on their chaste wedding night (chap. 280, 796) and on the occasion of their reunion (chap. 436, 1089). The notion of love as a war, fought with weapons and devious strategy, is already well-developed in Ovid and then in the *Roman de la Rose*. Particularly in Guillaume de Lorris's section of the roman, the military service endured by the lover in order to conquer the rose forms a lively and picturesque euphemism for the underlying eroticism of the tale. In *Tirant* the same matrix of vocabulary points to more explicit and real assaults. The clichéd terminology of courtly love does not mask, but rather intensifies what is being described.

In the case of the empress and Hipòlit, the amorous joust of love occasionally becomes an obscene farce, before the sensual consummation takes place in the unconventional setting of the palace roof (754). Love as a sickness and love as combat are the two most common metaphors for courtly love. The third is the religion of love, exploited by the *Flamenca* poet as he literally superimposes religious devotion on earthly desire to the extent that it interferes with the mass. In a similar conflation of secular and sacred, the empress awaits the propitious moment to allow Hipòlit into her chamber, when Eliseu surprises her as she opens the door leading onto the roof. The empress excuses herself by saying that she forgot to say her evening prayers, which she then goes on to describe to the maid. The empress says that she prays to the Magi to intercede with Christ and Mary and to beg forgiveness and protection from disgrace just as they escaped harm at the hands of King Herod.

This *devoció* (753) is particularly appropriate, since she prays to a spiritual mother and son, of which she and Hipòlit are the earthly counterparts, for protection from an earthly king and from an unspecified "vergonya e infàmia" [shame and infamy] (753), which in this case is discovery of her affair. The following morning, when the emperor arrives, the empress reacts as if some cruel tyrant has arrived to slay her firstborn. This fits in with the constant identification between her and the aptly named Hipòlit as her offspring, reinforced by the compromising posture in which she and her lover are discovered. She fears that he will be treated as a heretic "com tu es enamorat de ta mare" [as you are in love with your mother] (755). The comic note of perversion surrounding the affair is added by the empress herself, who carries her identification of Hipòlit as her son to its ultimate degree by recasting the previous night's encounter to the emperor and doctors as a prophetic dream in which her dead son appears leading Hipòlit by the hand, begging her to receive him as she would her own offspring. The dream-frame is, of course, a common feature of medieval romances. Its significance is completely reversed in *Tirant*. The empress relies on the fact that the rest of the household will give the dream its literal interpretation, as an indication of hidden truth on another level of reality. However, in the realistic world of Martorell's romance, dreams cloak reality. This is true of the other "dream" in *Tirant*, in which Plaerdemavida voyeuristically recounts the encounter she has actually witnessed between Tirant and the princess (chap. 163).

The empress's story elicits the sympathy of her immediate audience and laughter from the reader. At dinner she eats heartily "com a persona cansada de molt caminar" [like a person weary from having walked all day] (chap. 262, 762) and proceeds to keep Hipòlit in the alcove of her room for a week until he shows signs of weariness, recalling Guilhem IX's obscene cat poem and the conclusion in which the narrator enjoys a week's ribald solace in the two women's company. The fin'amor of the troubadours and courtly romances thrives on the joy of the chase and the exhilaration of being perpetually close to the object of desire. In *Tirant,* courtly love is similarly treated in an unusual, unrestrained, and realistic way. Frank Pierce asserts that the treatment of sex in the text fits the general pattern of the novel "to describe things factually and fully" (297) and that it represents an area of a broader courtly life described by Martorell. This explicit treatment of human affairs makes *Tirant* unique: Arthur Terry remarks that "[m]any episodes in the book would be merely pornographic, were it not for the humour and naturalness with which they are presented" (*A Literary History of Spain* 51). The frankness with which the love interest is presented parodies the conventions of courtly love: the episode with the empress and Hipòlit shows how the generic expectations of the courtly romance have been absorbed, emulated, and surpassed with a novel and vivid approach.

The only female character who even resembles a conventionally virtuous woman, or the heroine of an Arthurian romance, is Carmesina. While it is politically necessary for her to behave in an exemplary fashion because she is the emperor's daughter and heiress to the Greek Empire, her adherence to an old-fashioned code of conduct under pressure from the more amoral characters around her occasions frequent humor. Her zealous purity is not, after all, inherited from the empress. Her conflict of duty and desire are manifest from her first meeting with Diafebus, who makes her blush by assuring her of Tirant's admiration. She is typically divided in her emotions: "car amor d'una part la combatia, e vergonya d'altra part la'n retraïa. Amor l'encenia en voler lo que no devia, mas vergonya lo hi vedava per temor de confusió" [because love on the one hand pressed her, and shame on the other held her back. Love compelled her to want what she should not, and shame threw her into confused fear] (chap. 119, 379).

This is the pattern of their subsequent bipolar courtship. The courtly beginning to their romance soon turns to comedy, as the following day Tirant wears a pearl-studded cloak with sheaves of corn embroidered with the motto "Una val mill e mill no valen una" [one is worth a thousand, and a thousand are not worth one] (380–1), and Carmesina inadvertently dons a jewel-encrusted gown embroidered with *amorval* (love-in-a-mist) bearing the legend "Mas no a mi" [But not to me] (381). The mottos are humorously complementary and suggest a sardonic view of courtly sentiment. Opulent fashion brings the lovers together in other ways, as Diafebus's comic and gallant gesture shows, when he rips Tirant's gold-and-pearl-studded cloak from his back and places it on Carmesina's shoulders, using the excuse that it matches her dress perfectly (383). Diafebus plays an Ovidian cupid, slyly acting as go-between rather in the way that Tirant fulfills the same office for Felip and Ricomana, persuading the reluctant princess that her suitor is worthy of her attention.

Tirant's passion for Carmesina grows incrementally with his timidity. His lack of resolve is compounded with Carmesina's ever-increasing obsession with her virtue. Her coyness, in turn, is matched by Estefania's lack of scruples in her own involvement with Diafebus and in Estefania's advice to the princess:

> Per què Déu no em féu a mi filla de l'Emperador, e que vós fósseu Estefania e jo Carmesina? Jo us assegur, res que fos en la mia persona no lí fóra denegat, e si ell m'alçava la falda del meu brial, jo li alçaria la mia camisa que ell o ves, e el contentaria en gran part. . . . Aquest és lo que vostre altesa ha mester, que us sàpia guardar de mal a vós e tot l'Imperi, e el sàpia defendre e augmentar així com fa. Aquest és aquell qui us farà cercar tots los racons de la cambra, adés tota nua, adés en camisa. (Chap. 138, 450)

> [Why didn't God make me the emperor's daughter and you Estefania? I assure you that no part of my person would be denied him, and if he lifted my skirt, I would take off my blouse and would content him a good deal. . . . This is the man your highness needs, who will know how to keep you and the whole Empire safe, and will know how to defend and keep it just as it should be. This is the man who will play hide-and-seek with you in all the crannies of your chamber, sometimes naked, sometimes in your shift.]

Carmesina, although amused by Estefania's remarks, does not share her pragmatism. Estefania and Diafebus, like Plaerdemavida, the empress, and Hipòlit, are both driven by desire.

Even the Viuda Reposada is driven by self-interest and her love for Tirant. She goes to elaborate lengths to convince Tirant that Carmesina is unfaithful to him by dressing as a Moorish gardener and playing lewd games with Carmesina (chap. 283, 804–5). The Viuda's risqué behavior is completely opposed to her otherwise prudish manner when she urges the princess not to sacrifice her honor, and tries to persuade Tirant that he wastes his ardor on a wanton woman in Carmesina. Her chastity is ultimately as self-seeking as the liberality of Estefania or Plaerdemavida, both of whom end the novel with fame, status, and fortune.

Just as the character of Tirant plays on the gap between a literary ideal and the social norm, so the reader of *Tirant* enters the central section of the novel with expectations of the treatment of the courtly love theme that are replaced with the unexpected. The descriptions of lovemaking are not parodic, but the way in which they are orchestrated often is, as on Estefania's wedding night, when Plaerdemavida leaves five kittens in the newlyweds' bedroom (chap. 220, 669). The sensual passion of the protagonists is framed by a series of practical jokes and lewd innuendos that add vitality, while undermining the ethos of fin'amor.

In the following chapter, the friar delivers a speech about ideal behavior (chap. 221, 671–4). He sets out eighteen points of good conduct for men, and then he points out the virtues of women, with the disclaimer that "E açò és tot lo que elles deurien tenir, e és tot lo contrari" [And that is all that they should do, and it is completely to the contrary] (chap. 221, 673). Thus he affirms what the reader already suspects, that ideals rarely manifest themselves in the real world, and that courtly love in particular has undergone a comic transformation. During his hilarious sermon, the friar reveals the main source for his observations regarding love and society: "Diu Ovidi que lo major bé d'aquest món és amor, e la Sancta Escriptura ho conferma" [Ovid declares that the greatest good in this world is love, and the Scriptures confirm it] (673). The friar comically confuses *eros* and *agape*, and as in *Flamenca*, the friar's speech confirms the pervasive influence of the ethically ambiguous *Ars Amatoria* throughout *Tirant*. Strategy in love is as important as tactics in battle. Events on the battlefield are serious, but courtly campaigns are as comic as they are dangerous, as Tirant finds to his cost.

In a scene that Frank Pierce describes as one of "advanced sensuality" (296), Tirant finds himself in bed with Carmesina, with Plaerdemavida present in the room as go-between (chap. 233, 702). After he has plucked up the courage to take on the adventure, Plaerdemavida having left him alone in the dark "en camisa e decalç" [in his shirt, and trouserless] (702), his rapture is soon interrupted by Carmesina's and the Viuda's cries of alarm. In a scene worthy of farce he drops from the end of an escape rope and breaks his leg, at which point the narrative also breaks off, leaving him on the ground, and returns to the bedlam in the princess's bedroom, where the ladies explain that a rat has caused the disturbance. The following chapter finds Tirant groaning like a woman, to the extent that Hipòlit cannot recognize him. The injury Tirant sustains subsequently prevents him from leading the Christian forces, giving a comic demonstration of how desire and duty conflict in the novel.

The setting and characters are those we would expect in a roman courtois, but the world and our expectations have changed, as Diafebus makes clear when he acts as messenger to Carmesina and is sent to his master bearing three hairs from her head as reply:

> —No em vala Déu—dix Hipòlit—si jo los prenc, si ja no em dieu la significança per què són estats més tres que quatre, que deu o vint. E com, senyora, pensa vostra altesa que siam en lo temps antic, que usaven les gents llei de gràcia? Car la donzella, com tenia algun enamorat e l'amava en extrem grau, dava-li un ramellet de flors ben perfumat, o un cabell o dos del seu cap, e aquell se tenia per molt benventurat. No, senyora, no, que aqueix temps ja és passat. Lo que mon senyor Tirant desija bé ho sé jo: que us pogués tenir en un llit nua o en camisa. (Chap. 251, 738)

> [May God find me unworthy—said Hipòlit—if I take them, if you do not tell me the meaning of why they are three rather than four, or ten, or twenty. Lady, does your Highness think we are in the good old days, when people followed the laws of grace? For a maiden, when she was very much in love with someone, would give him a posy of fragrant flowers, or a hair or two from her head, and he counted himself highly favored. No, Lady, no—those days are long gone. What my Lord Tirant wants I know very well: that he might hold you in bed, naked or in your shift.]

Glossing this passage, Alan Yates says: "The controlling point-of-view, though, in this aspect as in the case of the treatment of chivalry, is richer and more complex than sheer iconoclasm. The satirical and burlesque effects should not obscure the seriousness of the author's involvement with his subject. The demythification of the courtly ethos is set in a framework which *realistically* shows the potency and security of the myth" (190).

There is undoubtedly an element of iconoclasm in Diafebus's speech. While the courtly spirit still prevails in public politeness, its values as a private system of behavior have undergone an adjustment in the real world and are shown to be as artificial as the tapestries on the wall. Things are not what they once were, as is demonstrated by the empress and Hipòlit's inheritance of the empire, rather than the restoration of courtly society by

a young and vigorous hero. Terry is justified in finding more than iconoclasm: Martorell alters the fundamental pattern of the chivalric romance.
Finally, Tirant's wish comes true, and shortly afterward he dies after a brief
illness, making his will and dying in his bed, just as Cervantes's priest
relates. His elaborate peregrinations, unheroic death, short marriage, and
lack of reward for his deeds run counter to our expectation of the genre.
Indeed, there is dark humor in his ending, and a realistic reminder of the
absurdity of life and the human condition. In Martorell's original hero,
mortality and literary ideal meet, and do so in a landscape that no longer
makes provision for the symbolic, the fantastic, or the ideal. As the emperor laments over Tirant's corpse, he unwittingly provides a final comic
key to interpreting his character when he declares: "Muira jo, e iré als
regnes de Plutó, de tanta dolor portant ambaixada; faré que Ovidi del meu
Tirant digníssims versos esmalte" [Would that I might die and bear my
affliction to Pluto's realm, there to make Ovid forge verses for our cham-
pion] (chap. 472, 1153; Rosenthal 608). We might wonder why the emperor chooses Ovid as a potential eulogist, since he is not best remembered
as a recorder of history, heroism, and virtue, but as a celebrator of fantasy,
love, transformation, and satire. The contrast of military strategist and
Ovidian lover is pronounced, and the extremism it represents is a source of
comedy—and puts Tirant in the doughty lineage of Guillem, Jaufre, and
Chrétien's heros. While the code of chivalry remains a serious issue, its
application to every aspect of life does not.

    The unfolding of Tirant's adventures makes us look back over the work,
particularly to the first section with the hermit, and to the prologue. Like
Don Quixote, Tirant has an opening that declares the author's stance toward his subject. Cervantes hides his parody behind weighty and witty
claims about his condemnation of the romances of chivalry and their danger, while Martorell in his dedication extols the order, the knights of old,
and Tirant as the best knight that ever was. To add to the weight of his
work, Martorell goes on to state that his work will provide a beacon of
morality, furnish a good example of correct knightly behavior, and attack
vice ("Pròleg" 114). Given the comic adventures and slapstick comedy,
one can only imagine that the prologue has more than a hint of irony—not
to mention parody—in it. Tirant may be a reworked Mirror of Chivalry,
but the reflection is quite distorted.

    Both Aylward and Riquer (31; Història 75), among others, signal the
incorporation of other texts by Martorell in his dedication. Much of
Martorell's text is apparently drawn from a dedicatory letter by Enrique de

Villena for the *Doze trabajos de Hércules.* Tirant as a latter-day Hercules adds a comic dimension to some aspects of his character—particularly given the contrast between his labors on the battlefield and off. He remains an exemplary knight, but as for the private behavior that contrasts and undermines his military heroism, one could hardly call him a perfect hero, even though Martorell avoids judging his behavior—remaining at an ironic distance from his creation. In the prologue we encounter a catalogue of figures classical and biblical, all renowned for their heroism. Tirant is the last of these, and in the first section with the hermit it appears that he really is going to follow in the hallowed footsteps. The model, literary beginning changes our perspective of what follows. By the time Tirant dies our view of him has evolved from that of a potentially timeless literary hero to an amusingly flawed, mortal general in a world that juxtaposes the farcical and the serious and that confounds any ethical system. With *Tirant* the chivalric romance is transformed by the evolution of Martorell's central character. Mario Vargas Llosa says of the work that it is "Una novela total. Novela de caballería, fantástica, histórica, militar, social, erótica, psicológica: todas esas cosas a la vez y ninguna de ellas exclusivamente, ni más ni meno que la realidad" [A totalizing novel. A novel of chivalry, fantastic, heroic, military, social, erotic, psychological: all these things at once, and no one thing exclusively, no more or less than reality] ("Carta" 15). With its encyclopedic incorporation of previous literary tradition, a broad social spectrum, and wide-ranging setting, *Tirant* does not exceed the boundaries we would ascribe to the courtly romance. Rather, Martorell creates a hybrid form that incorporates the outside world with all its levels of experience while retaining the shape of the original model.

At the end of his study of *Tirant,* Arthur Terry recalls Huizinga's affirmation that "the hero worship of the declining Middle Ages finds its literary expression in the biography of the perfect knight" (194). What, then, should we make of this imperfect knight? Yates reminds us of the necessity of placing Tirant in his specific sociohistoric context and not measuring him by using a "Cervantine yardstick" (194). Instead we should, perhaps, measure *Tirant*'s distance from Chrétien as a proximity to the parodic aspects of romances of chivalry and as a result find a different, earlier foundation for the "half-way house of fiction." Tirant is an important step in the development of chivalric fiction. His French roots are clearly discernable, as is his pedigree. He is the creative and irreverent scion of Arthur and the collective inspiration of the Round Table, and he exemplifies the way in which, as the chivalric romance moved south and found their formal maturity, their plastic potential was realized in comic mode. The genius of *Tirant* is to take a small, seemingly closed society and open it to the known limits of the world, using well-established conventions to find ever-inventive twists in the tale. While *Tirant* breaks away from the chivalric past and updates the form, its energy confirms the vitality of the basic model and sends it spinning in novel directions.

6

Conclusion

Familiarity Breeds Content

Llenósele la fantasía de todo aquello que leía en los libros, así de
encantamentos como de pendencias, batallas, desafíos, heridas, requiebros, amores,
tormentas y disparates imposibles; y asentósele de tal modo en la imaginación
que era verdad toda aquella máquina de aquellas sonadas
invenciones que leía, que para él no había otra historia
más cierta en el mundo.

[His imagination was stuffed with all he read in his books about enchantments, quar-
rels, battles, challenges, sounds, wooings, loves, agonies, and all sorts of impossible
nonsense. It became so firmly planted in his mind that the whole fabric of invention
and fantasy was true, that to him no history in the world was better substantiated.][1]

Don Quixote, Book I, Chapter I

Don Quixote is perhaps the best-known, if least critical reader of late
romance, and has been used as a model of the rejection of that genre from
serious consideration as a precursor of the modern novel; indeed, the romance seems to constitute its very antithesis. The description of the salient
features of the books Don Quixote reads is a catalogue of clichéd generic
conventions, and for Cervantes, the world of romance is a distant and
absurd one; it projects a literary artifice animated by impossible logic and
imposing a skewed reality in which interminable adventures drag on ad
infinitum in a landscape set beyond the pale of credibility, yet within the
realms of reality, populated by two-dimensional paragons of chivalry and
overly idealized courtly heroines.

Don Quixote is a brilliant condemnation in the early seventeenth century of a genre that seemed ludicrously anachronistic: it is evidently still
popular, euphuistic, and an easy target for ridicule, not least because of the
vast top-heavy cycles of stories circulating in Spain concerning such heroes
as Amadís de Gaul and Palmerín, who in turn took their cue from the

proliferation of chivalric romances that had their genesis in twelfth-century France. Conversing with the prologue writer, the "amigo . . . bien entendido" [well-intentioned friend] (56) reveals Cervantes's avowed intention of attacking books of chivalry that do not seem to belong to the august lineage of works having the *actoritas* "de quien nunca se acordó Aristóteles, ni dijo nada San Basilio, ni alcanzó Cicerón" [of which Aristotle never dreamed or St. Basil said a word or Cicero had any knowledge] (Ormsby 13; 62). Juxtaposing authoritative sources drawn from ancient philosophy, patristics, and classical rhetoric with the popular romance foregrounds both the superficial, nonauthoritative character of the genre on the one hand, and the pomposity of contemporary exegesis and literary criticism on the other. It is as though in lampooning the romance Cervantes satirizes writing itself: scholastic works, poetry, and in particular that other popular genre, the pastoral, are also consistent objects of parody.

Nor is the narrator immune to self-parody, and even readers too are subject to criticism; romance as a genre and the romance-reading public are the prime targets, the former on account of its mechanistic naivety and the latter because of a collective gullibility in continually embracing such an escapist fantasy. And yet still there is a Cyrano de Bergerac touch of panache and bravado about Don Quixote and his efforts not to be mundane in a world that encourages imperfection, mediocrity, and life without codes to which to aspire: the Don's embrace of an ethic and aesthetic, and his refusal to sink to the quotidian level in the face of the gravitational pull of the "real," lend him a kind of shabby heroism, and it is perhaps not so surprising that at certain points in history the work was read more seriously and less iconoclastically.

With the condemnation of the romance genre also comes a critique of certain aspects of contemporary life, suggested in the expression of moral and political decline and in the existence of a genteel, impoverished, and sometimes errant knightly class in the recent past, explored by J. H. Elliott ("Self-Perception and Decline in Early Seventeenth-Century Spain"). This appears to be true of elements in society at the time of Cervantes, as Thomas R. Hart suggests when he accounts for at least one reason for the enduring appeal of the eccentric hero: "Don Quixote's situation as a member of this class [the nostalgic aristocracy] goes a long way toward explaining the powerful attraction exercised upon him by the romances of chivalry" (*Cervantes and Ariosto* 49). Hart goes on to cite Maxime Chevalier on the charm of the romance setting for Cervantes's contemporaries: "Un público aristocrático debía gustar del mundo puro e irreal de los *Amadises,* mundo que no admitía al mercader, en el cual el dinero no tenía ninguna importancia, en el cual el ciudad, sitio de las actividades económicas de la burguesía, no aparecía nunca" [The aristocratic public tasted the pure and unreal world of the *Amadís* romances, a world which did not admit trading, in which money held no importance whatsoever, in which the city, the site of bourgeois economic activity, does not appear at all] (*Lectura y lectores en la Espana de los siglos XVI y XVII* 98).

The appeal of the romances lies not only in what they include but also in what they exclude: the social homogeneity of romances lends a patina of nobility and an illusion of importance to a class on the point of being eclipsed by a rapidly expanding urban middle class. A perceived degentrification and embourgeoisement of society, and its descent toward commerce, heteroglossia, and the modern world would undoubtedly have lent potency to the chivalric myth and opened new levels in it. While the focus of many a romance centers on the acquisition of wealth and social status, objectives dear to the bourgeois as well as aristocratic heart, the collective aristocratic fantasy of love and chivalry permits social fulfillment without admitting the mundane practicalities of a monetaristic society of exchange. The evidence Chevalier has collected regarding editions, prices, and readership points to a well-off and well-to-do audience for the genre in the sixteenth century. This does not exclude the less affluent bourgeoisie or other classes from the audience of chivalric romances, but yields important information about which stratum of society was capable of purchasing them, and presumably most considered the works worth owning. Of the popular taste for romances of chivalry among classes who could not own them there can be little doubt, as the seventeenth-century French Bibliothèque bleue attests, with its many abridgments and compilations of texts devoted to knightly exploits. While this argues for their descent into a more popularizing register, it also testifies to the enduring appeal of the genre and to the continuing appeal of its patterns, values, and capacity to engage the reader.

Daniel Eisenberg analyzes the readership of romance in Cervantes's time using evidence taken from dedications of individual texts, information about editions, and internal evidence from the *Quixote,* concluding quite reasonably that only the upper classes and the bourgeoisie were able to indulge the expensive habit of purchasing romances ("Who Read the Romances of Chivalry?"). Eisenberg dismisses the idea that the peasantry or nonaristocratic strata of society read romances despite the internal evidence of the *Quixote:* Don Quixote's deranged view of the romance does not exclude a realistic depiction of a wider readership—or more correctly, audience (part 1, chap. 32, Juan Palomeque). Eisenberg's rejection of a wider audience for aristocratic literature on account of Palomeque's class, semi-illiteracy, and faulty memory serve to preserve boundaries of influence and reception may be too limited on a broader level: medieval studies are currently profiting from the dismantling of artificial distinctions made between audiences and genres, high and low culture, such that the class/readership dichotomy might be worth revisiting. Once we admit that ethereal love poetry and obscene lyrics often issued from the same pen, and that fabliaux were not restricted to vulgar audiences (in both senses of the word), then our view of subsequent texts and the mixing of styles, as well as the notion of reception, must evolve. It is probable that a wider social band in the Middle Ages intimately knew the mechanics of the romance than could own them. Possession may be nine-tenths of the law, but it is not necessarily consonant with familiarity with the works.

The appeal of a *Don Quixote* derives not just from its undoubted iconoclasm, but on account of its form—its attraction is precisely that it *is* a romance, albeit one that purports to kill off the genre that lends it a distorted, yet recognizable shape. Just so, it is the endurance of the patterns of romance, and not their destruction, that is at the heart of Cervantes's work. There is no denying the onset of a more "realistic" world—this turn toward history is apparent even in the thirteenth century with its patina of mercantilism: and yet what Cervantes illustrates par excellence is the way that his creation turns toward its literary roots, toward the very tenets of romance. Cervantes labors his point about romance in the prologue at the beginning of part 1 and has Don Quixote disavow such works as a harmful illusion when he is on his deathbed at the conclusion of part 2.

Given historical factors, Cervantes makes Don Quixote less of an anachronism than might at first seem apparent: Don Quixote's status as a misguided reader of romance makes him as much a parody of a kind of contemporary reader as he is the most ludicrous representative of an outmoded literary genre. His madness appears in a modified light, since his confusion about literary reality and the real world stems from a second perceptual problem linked to generic definition. He is clear about the features of romance, but as Martín de Riquer ("Cervantes y la caballleresca") suggests, his inability to distinguish fact from fiction is also the result of contemporary confusion surrounding chronicles, biographical books of chivalric feats concerning contemporary knights, and fictional novels of chivalry.

Such genres deliberately blurred the boundaries between fact and fiction, and between story, history, and legend. Chronicles concern themselves with the elaboration and fictionalization of supposed historical fact, the biographies enumerate the exploits of contemporary knights, and the historical novels invent the adventures of a literary figure. Fiction idealized history, which in turn drew on imaginative literature to embellish its heroes. It is easy to imagine how in creating *Don Quixote* Cervantes might mischievously blur still further the boundary between fact and fiction by conflating history and imaginative literature as his contemporaries did. Given that all three types of literature were popular and that all might relate tales as incredible as Don Quixote's, perhaps his derangement has a degree of historic verisimilitude and is less of a departure from normalcy than we might suppose, and rather than confounding a model, he is merely following several simultaneously in an exaggerated fashion.

It is obvious that even before Cervantes parodied the romance, romance had in a sense already superseded itself in the endless replication of a limited number of settings and basic plotlines; the line of romance that took itself seriously was destined to implode along with the Arthurian world. Its social pedigree worn thin with time, the coinage of romance had become so debased by Cervantes's time that his presentation of the aristocratic genre portrays it as destined for the entertainment of laborers, priests, and barbers in country inns. Juan Palomeque (part 1, chap. 32) says that he keeps several books of chivalry at hand to be enjoyed by the workers after a long, hard day at harvesttime. As the aberrant knight polishes up his old armor and modifies his helmet with pasteboard (which he naturally expects to perform like steel, so great is his belief in artifice), Cervantes undertakes a deliberate, relentless, and humorous demolition of the infrastructure of romance, beginning with its tarnished exterior forms. But as he does so, he follows a long succession of writers who did the same thing: he reinvents the romance and turns it loose on an unsuspecting contemporary world and shares it with a less refined, yet broader constituency.

Imitating the baroque language of contemporary successors to the threadbare mantle once worn by Chrétien, Don Quixote sets out with Rocinante, immortalizing his own adventures in mediocre, overly ornate poetic language before he has even begun them in earnest:

Apenas había el rubicondo Apolo tendido por la faz de la ancha y espaciosa tierra las doradas hebras de sus hermosos cabellos, y apenas los pequenos y pintados pajarillos con sus harpadas lenguas habían saludado con dulce e meliflua armonía la venida de la rosada aurora, que, dejando la blanda cama del celoso marido, por las puertas y balcones del manchego horizonte a los mortales se mostraba, cuando el famoso caballero Don Quixote de la Mancha, dejando los ociosas plumas, subío sobre su famoso caballo Rocinante, y comenzó a caminar por el antiguo y conocido campo del Montiel.

[Scarce had the rubicund Apollo spread o'er the face of the broad spacious earth the golden threads of this bright hair, scarce had the little birds of painted plumage attuned heir notes to hail with dulcet and mellifluous harmony the coming of the rosy Dawn, that, deserting the soft couch of her jealous spouse, was appearing to mortals at the gates and balconies of the Manchegan horizon, when the renowned knight Don Quixote de la Mancha, quitting the lazy down, mounted his celebrated steed Rocinante and began to traverse the ancient and famous fields of Montiel.] (trans. Ormsby 30; part 1, chap. 2, 84)

Don Quixote's mastery of the language of courtly epic is as impressive as the knight's attempt to apply the chivalric code in a setting that has no tolerance for it is humorous, with the resulting gulf between theory and praxis. His departure heralds the comic clash of rigid form with the plastic possibilities of content, pitting a pattern of literary idealism on a realistic landscape that in no way fits the heroic mold.

But the prologue to the illustrious adventures upon which he then embarks reminds the reader that *Don Quixote* is more than a parody of literary form and chivalric adventure. This is apparent in the selection of tongue-in-cheek preliminary verses Cervantes inserts after the prologue; the authors of the dedicatory poems purport to be characters from other romances, and they speak more or less admiringly of the knight. Like the banquet list of *Flamenca* and the knightly directory of *Jaufre,* Cervantes's lyric exordium establishes a line of pedigree and of parody. Orlando Furioso, for example, claims:

Non puedi ser tu egual; que est decoro
se debe a tus proezas y a tu fama,
puesto que, como yo, perdiste el seso.
(Ormsby 19)

[I cannot be a rival for thy fame. And prowess rise above all rivalry, albeit both bereft of wits we go.]

Both Ariosto and Cervantes reconfigure the notion of *proeza* in astounding ways. Likewise, Amadís and characters drawn from related romances eulogize Don Quixote in high and prolix style before he has even set off.

Cervantes's famous parody is successful not because it upsets the traditional form of the romance, but because the essential features of the genre remain discernible, while its conventions are subject to a process of exaggeration and distortion.

The fundamental mechanism, a courtly machine of perpetual narrative motion, functions as it usually does; the essential service d'amour is directed at the peasant Dulcinea, and on Don Quixote's first adventure the conventional hospitable castle becomes an inn. In addition, the vigil of arms is moved from chapel to stable, the avuncular figure who initiates the knight into the ways of chivalry is an innkeeper instead of a noble, the horse trough serves as the perilous fountain in need of a courtly defender, adversaries abound in the ignoble form of vulgar mule-drivers, and available damsels are neither particularly virtuous nor in apparent distress. The famous giants Don Quixote fabricates from windmills are mere distortions of the real world, as is the invading flock of sheep that seems an army to the confused hero.

However, Cervantes's parody works both ways: while he highlights the world of chivalry as a contorted form of reality, he similarly portrays the "real" world as a comic and shabby place that at times seems tragically lacking in idealism of any kind. The realistic world appears more so on account of the knight's persistent fantasy, and his derangement strikes the reader as all the more tragicomic because of the inability of his surroundings to transcend mundanity and embrace the realm of the symbolic. The gulf between the two is indeed a dialogic space for narrative renewal: the knightly adventure is no more nor less than the novel's decentered quest for self.

It is not that Don Quixote's world is upside down, but that the inverted reality of courtly romance has been juxtaposed to something resembling the everyday world. As Thomas R. Hart has suggested, comparing the same opposites in connection with *Don Quixote* and his distant Italian relative: "The pattern of art is in both cases formed by the conventions of chivalric romance, just as nature is the pattern of life in an early modern Europe still breaking away from its medieval past. Both *Orlando Furioso* and *Don Quixote* examine the disparity between life as we experience it and life as it is depicted in books" (*Cervantes and Ariosto* 39). Hart cites the "often quoted statement" (39) of Harry Levin in which Levin calls the same disparity in *Don Quixote* "the pattern of art embarrassed by the confrontation with nature" ("The Example of Cervantes" 79). For Levin, parody and imitation form a natural alliance in the history of the novel, and he reminds us of Malraux's remark that "every artist begins with a pastiche" (96), before giving us his own definition of the growth of an author:

The novelist must begin by playing the sedulous ape, assimilating the craft of his predecessors; but he does not master his own form until he has somehow exposed and surpassed them, passing from the imitation of art through parody to the imitation of nature. (96)

The essential stage in development is signalled in parody, which stands on the boundary between emulation, imitation, and originality. Literary parody functions by exploding the infrastructure of a satirized text and making visible its salient features in magnified form. It is a seditious act of homage, an inventive and original form of mimicry that has been a constant driving force in the development of the novel, as well as the pressures of history. In general terms, parody brings us closer to the workings of a genre by distancing us from it, remaining paradoxically intimate with its interior life while dismantling it from outside the walls of its own premises. In this dislocating double movement the comic potential of both original and copy fulfills itself, and in the case of *Don Quixote,* we see the symbiosis between two evolving forms, one at the end of its literary life span, and one closer to its destination on a long journey toward modernity: rather than competing forms, we see them sewn together with a comically visible join.

Parody is a simple process that nevertheless makes sophisticated demands on the reader, since it presumes a position outside the frame of reference of the original object and an inside knowledge of convention, and Cervantes wrote for readers of romance as well as for critics of it. In the prologue to part 1, the author declares in no uncertain terms that he will wage war against the romance; once inside the text, however, author and narrator revel in its absurdities and details in what can be viewed as an affectionate caricature in spite of its avowed intention to destroy what it imitates. His initial stance regarding the romance must be seen in the context of his amigo's other exhortation, namely that he make his tale as amusing as possible. The enthusiasm of the second statement makes us doubt the absolute sincerity of the first, or at least introduces a note of sardonic ambiguity to the proceedings, since the second aim runs almost counter to the first.

Destruction and amusement provide Cervantes with a particular kind of literary recreation not unlike that enjoyed by Rabelais in the prologue and narrative of *Gargantua* (*Oeuvres complètes* 38–41). Rabelais's prologue encourages readers to look beneath the surface of the *boîte de Silène* he fashions and to probe his narrative as the dog does his marrow bone in order to interpret the work meaningfully. However, if we learn not to trust appearances, what are we to make of the final Utopia in the *abbaye de Thélème?* Another result might be to encourage the reader to be skeptical even of prologues, since this is where authorial sleight of hand perhaps reveals itself the most, because this is where the reader expects to find the extradiegetic truth. While it is certainly not parodic in intention, the prologue to *Manon Lescaut,* in the tradition of risqué novels, declares that it will describe shocking examples of vice in order to help readers avoid moral pitfalls, as Laclos does in the *Liaisons dangereuses:* a weak excuse for the pleasure of recounting a story of amorality far more fascinating than virtue ever could be.

Prologues may well set out literary strategies, but it is almost always a case of caveat emptor, for appearances are all too often playfully deceptive, and so it is with Cervantes. He shares a sense of exordial playfulness with the heirs of Rabelais, such that the reader should not take the declaration of war on the romance entirely seriously. Cervantes gives a clear illustration of the positive use of literary parody in his exploration of medieval romance in a reformed landscape: the disjunction between Don Quixote and the world he inhabits is obvious, one in which, as in the works of Chrétien de Troyes before him, convention and comedy are in creative collusion.

To examine how the parodic displacement of convention conspires in the evolution of the novel, it is useful to refer to the work of Elder Olson, who raises many germane issues in his discussion of dramatic comedy. While the elements of tragedy are easily discernible, the comic is much harder to analyze and define. Using Aristotle's *Poetics* as a general frame, Olson breaks the comic into three constituent parts: what is laughed at, who laughs, and what the relationship is between the two (12). This final category is the most problematic, but in simple terms the minimal requirements are a particular kind of object of humor, a distinct frame of mind on the part of the observer, and grounds for causing the reaction. Applying this schema to Cervantes's novel, Don Quixote is the object of laughter, and Cervantes and his readers are the subject: their relationship is one of necessary complicity, since Cervantes's successful use of convention depends on conditioning a predictable response.

In analyzing the plays of George Bernard Shaw, Olson points to his "suspension of form," what he calls "a systematic attack upon all the conventional . . . responses of the audience" in order to replace them with a new set (123). Shaw targets dramatic expectation with a particularly

skilled use of convention allied with comic reversal; Cervantes also sus-
pends form and uses literary convention to create novel effects in both
senses of the term. In a romance of the type Cervantes criticizes, each
fantastic episode in an impossible concatenation leads the reader into an
increasingly unreal world: in Cervantes's comic reversal, each incident
brings a greater sense of realism through the same process. The parody he
uses is a type of substitution exemplified in Olson's exposition by Aris-
tophanes's *Peace,* in which Bellerophon and Pegasus (drawn from Eurip-
ides's *Bellerophon*) are replaced by a farmer and an enormous dung beetle.
The success of the model depends on familiarity with the original: the
essential "grounds" are those of deflated expectation and the perceptible
descent from high to low in an inventive reductio ad absurdum.

The attack on the absurdity of romances in the "real" world in Cervantes's prologue is followed by a further direct assault on individual
works in part 1, chapter 6, when Don Quixote's library is subject to a
veritable inquisition; as a consequence most of its holdings are condemned,
and yet again we find an intertextual list that is both pedigree and parody,
and a case of familiarity breeding content as well as form.

Just as in *Flamenca* and *Jaufre,* there is an attempt to subsume and
subvert previous literary tradition by providing a list that serves as a literary lineage and a parodic enfolding of prior models: *Amadís,* as the long-
winded primogenitor of peninsular romance, is spared, but his many ill-
conceived offspring are condemned. The *Mirror of Chivalry* is spared
because of its connection to Boiardo and Ariosto, while all works pertaining to "French matters" (50) are consigned to the purgatory of a dry well.
The only work to emerge with its reputation almost untarnished is *Tirant
lo Blanc,* hailed by the priest as "un tesoro de contento y una mina de
pasatiempos" [a treasure of contentment and a mine of pastimes] (117).
The priest adds that "por su estilo, es éste el mejor libro del mundo: aquí
comen los caballeros, y duermen y muermen en sus camas, y hacen testa-
mento antes de su muerte, con estas cosas de que todos los demás libros
deste genero carecen" [for its style it is the best book in the world: here
knights eat, sleep, and die in their beds, and make wills before their death,
along with those things that all the other books of this kind omit] (118).
The accolades accorded *Tirant* are not without reservation: "Con todo eso,
os digo que merecía el que le compuso, pues no hizo tantas necedades de
industria, que le echaran a galeras por todos los días de su vida" [Neverthe-
less, I say that he who wrote it, for deliberately composing such fooleries,
deserves to be sent to the galleys for life] (Ormsby 52; part 1, chap. 6, 118).
Acknowledged as an obscure passage by many, the implication of this

statement is assessed in two ways; first, that being sent to the galleys implies punishment, second that for an author to be sent to the galleys means that his work is destined for reprint. Opinion is divided, but set within the context of the priest's praise of the work as a whole, the condemnation seems less than serious and to constitute one more instance where playful ambiguity opens horizons of interpretation and points to a code of conspiracy beneath the surface of the text.

The only work spared from the dry well, *Tirant* is the one that paradoxically most embodies and least resembles the fruits of medieval chivalric romance. That knights "eat, sleep, and make their wills" already implies an increased degree of realism and a setting in which the world ages instead of remaining eternally in its youthful, courtly prime. Chivalry as an ethical code on the battlefield or in a tournament persists with rigid conventions, but a new sensual pursuit of self-gratification replaces the code of love inseparable from valor in earlier courtly romance. In terms of the development of the novel, the parodic distance between literary expectation and narrative reality creates a space that is both conventional and experimental, lending comic tension that does not diminish in the 487 chapters that conclude, appropriately, with a simple *Deo gratias*. The many encoded intertextual references to the French tradition, and in particular to the works of Chrétien and Grail texts, show the extent to which the august lineage has been digested and reworked into a novel form. Tirant's defense of the Christian world has a high moral tone; however, his equally persistent sallying of Carmesina's virtue seems comically at odds with his knightly mission. Chivalry is not dead, but altruistic heroes are few by Martorell's time in either fact or fiction, and yet they still bear the indelible imprint of their self-ironic forebears.

For Martorell, as later for Cervantes, parody is the central source of energy in the development of the narrative: in *Tirant* he undoes the conventional chivalric romance, exploiting the courtly hero's capacity for self-interest in a way reminiscent of the many later picaresque heroes, who perform their exploits in a more cynical and less readily rewarding world. If Tirant saves empires and cities, it seems almost incidental to his pursuit of self-gratification. He combines the epic line descended from Roland, the more unscrupulous collection of chanson de geste heroes (such as Raoul de Cambrai), the chivalric knight as portrayed in the works of Chrétien, and the Ovidian pleasure-seekers related to Guillaume de Lorris's Amant and Jaufre. As such, Tirant is a perfect synthesis, and an encyclopedic depiction of knighthood, placed in a setting far different from those of his earlier counterparts, one in which conventional action becomes radically experimental.

Considering *Tirant lo Blanc* and its place in the history of the novel, Mario Vargas Llosa states:

Martorell es el primero de esa estirpe de suplantadores de Dios — Fielding, Balzac, Dickens, Flaubert, Tolstoi, Joyce, Faulkner — que pretenden crear en sus novelas una "realidad total," el más remoto caso de novelista todopoderoso, desinteresado, omnisciente y ubicuo. ("Carta de batalla" 2–3)

[Martorell is the first in that line of God-supplanters . . . who try to create in their novels a complete sense of reality, the earliest case of an all-powerful, disinterested, omniscient, and ubiquitous novelist.]

Encyclopedic realism is not a term we would usually apply to romance, but it undoubtedly applies to *Tirant*. That Vargas Llosa describes the transformed settings of Martorell and Cervantes by referring to their realism is undeniably problematic, since the term "realism" immediately recalls a particular literary configuration of the nineteenth century. In a reconfigured, more relative form of realism, description of setting or characters is measured in two ways: first, in proximity to an unidealized world resembling daily life, and second, in a distance from a perceptible model of literary fantasy. In *Tirant* and *Don Quixote*, the calibration of these two factors differs, their adherence to an evolving generic model becomes clearer, and they are not so much destroyers of past tradition — they are innovators in a renewed literary landscape. Martorell places his characters in a world resembling that of the chivalric romance, where all the characters are more or less noble, inhabit castles, frequent noble ladies, and fight honorable battles. However, the comparatively limited world of the feudal romance has been enlarged to encompass the whole Mediterranean area and an expanded political and social reality.

If we give *Tirant lo Blanc* its due as a realistic chivalric romance, it is no surprise that Cervantes found much to admire in Martorell's achievement. Both authors demystify the genre, while rejuvenating and transforming the genre through their flagrant misuse and transformation of its conventions. *Tirant* and *Don Quixote* free the romance from the restrictive social setting of the court and reliance on the absurd magic landscape of the otherworld by restoring its spirit of experiment and renewed adventure. Martorell drew his cue from a familiarity with French romance, identifying in it a capacity for experimental regeneration and limitless horizons. Assessing the novelty and importance of *Don Quixote*, Mikhail Bakhtin observes: "Characteristic . . . is the hybridization of the 'alien, miraculous world' chronotope of chivalric romances, with the 'high road winding through one's native land' chronotope that is typical of the picaresque novel" ("Forms of Time and Chronotope" 165). In a paradoxical way the romance's potential is revived, and the plasticity of form that led to the flowering of the chivalric romance in twelfth- and thirteenth-century France finds itself rejuvenated rather than superseded in fifteenth-century Catalonia and in early-seventeenth-century Spain.

Seen in this light, distant works appear to be more closely related on inspection: Cervantes and Martorell do not "kill off" their literary forebears, but reinstate them in a modified form. Literary history can, and should, trace a line of continuity between the medieval and Renaissance romance, a process of "reinstating uncles" that links Chrétien and Martorell and subsequently Cervantes. If we identify Martorell as a precursor of the modern novel—and surely we would also have to include both Rabelais and Cervantes in that pantheon of "God-supplanters" who have shaped this most protean of genres—there are serious critical implications. The defining criteria for inclusion on Vargas Llosa's list appear to be a combination of transformed comic convention with realism, which seems appropriate as a working definition of significant literary change. It would be tempting, but too easy, to label Martorell as first in line: we would have to go back further in time, to classical antiquity and to Petronius's *Satyricon*. To reexamine the evolutionary forces that forged *Tirant lo Blanc* is to locate the generic change that was perhaps already well underway in the heyday of the courtly romance, but in the medieval period we find the first expression in the modern era of the novel's most fundamental dynamism. As paradigmatic readers, we have a tendency to treat the conventions of chivalric romance as static, while the genre is anything but monolithic. Just as lyric poetry constantly reevaluates the concept of love, so the romance insistently reexamines its own ethical raison d'être in the codes of love and war and modifies its shape accordingly, in a fashion that resembles the contested, dialogic sites of Bakhtin and the polyphonic reconfigured codes of Barthes.

For Chrétien, the vitality of the romance lies in its capacity for internal renewal. Courtly convention is part of a two-pronged strategy that combines with self-irony to produce a comic reflection that is restorative, and not destructive, of the courtly model. The presence of comedy does not fulfill an external function in protecting the romance from outside attack, but satisfies an internal need for narrative regeneration. Rather than being a rigid, codified genre, the chivalric romance shares a suppleness and expansivity with other branches of the same poetic form, and its possibilities are as endless as the capacity to produce new heroes and place them in novel settings. Chrétien provides a new, flexible literary stereotype; the knight-errant of the roman courtois is a far cry from the unbending heroes of epic and chanson de geste. In most of the works treated in this study, lists and a particular kind of reflexive literary parody have been the focus, since they constitute the *signes extérieurs* of the evolutionary process that the romance undergoes. Chrétien does not have enough of a prior tradition to produce such a list, but the number of references he makes in his works to his other texts, and to Ovid, show him to be the precursor of romanciers like the *Flamenca* and *Jaufre* poets, and of Martorell and Cervantes.

Chrétien is in collusion with the conventions he stabilizes, and his success can be gauged by his many imitators. The author of *Aucassin* reveals an acute sense of "literarity" and employs a sophisticated range of generic pyrotechnics to parody the notion of courtly literature in general. The unique form of this poem sets it at a particularly pronounced "aesthetic distance" from the models its author uses. The comic mechanism of *Aucassin* is a perfect example of the process Mikhail Bakhtin sees at work in the development of novelistic discourse: *Aucassin* consumes and subverts pre-existing genres and then parodies them and forges an original hybrid form. What is apparent in *Aucassin* is less obtrusively present in Chrétien, but is nevertheless a defining feature of the genre. Even if he probably did not have an extensive written tradition upon which to draw, parody and literary renewal of a distinct literary code are present in his works. His establishment and re-use of a paradigm of courtly characters with predetermined values acts as a form of intertextuality: this self-referential literary grid extends to the frequent references he makes to his own works, particularly in *Cligés* and *Yvain*.

As Segre notes, a more subtle form of dialogism is in play in the seemingly more conventional romance, one that establishes multilevelled and multivalent perspectives and different forms of distance. For Segre, the most important gap lies between author and text. I have sought to explore other narrative divides, particularly that which separates the reader from generic expectations. In the case of Chrétien, there is a comic distance between the hero and his setting, amplified in the use of incongruous elements and a magic otherworld. The use of parody in later works is not an innovation or, necessarily, an outside attack on the romance as a genre, but a force of renewal applied on a comic stage already cleared for internal change.

The *roman de Flamenca* makes particular use of the concept of "aesthetic distance" and literary parody through allusion to, and reincorporation of, other works. Already one step removed from the northern French tradition by its later date and southern origin, this text engages in a play on the "artificiality" of literature, and especially the romance as exemplified by the works of Chrétien, quite literally digesting an entire tradition in the banquet scene. The comic traits of the northern French romance become more exaggerated when reflected in the distorting mirror of the southern poet's work. It constitutes a parodic odyssey through literary history that simultaneously distances and absorbs the conventions that the references represent. The ensuing exploding of courtly myth and citing of comic pre-cedents has a liberating effect on the subsequent narrative.

The inclusion of a list for comic effect is an important element of the other extant Occitan romance *Jaufré*, where it fulfills a similar function to that of *Flamenca*. Part tour de force and part act of resistance, these works illustrate playful familiarity, joyous experimentalism, and comic contempt for what has gone before. Chaucer's *Sir Thopas,* Martorell's *Tirant lo Blanc,* and finally *Don Quixote* all share this narrative feature, and with it a layering of discourses and plurality of conventional voices that set the scene and the standard for what follows. *Tirant lo Blanc,* although a prose work, retains the essential form and subject matter of medieval romance, but like its Occitan counterpart incorporates important changes in charac-ter and setting that renew the romance from within. The incongruous juxtaposition of Tirant's behavior as a courtly lover and his role as a Chris-tian knight produces a narrative dynamism that swings the reader from one extreme to the other. Familiarity once more breeds content: as notice-able as Tirant's modernity is his dialogic relationship to the past and to the tenets of French chivalric romance in particular, both those of Chrétien and the more blatantly parodic reencoding of them in works like *Jaufre.*

It is tempting to use terms such as "realism" and "naturalism" when discussing *Tirant* and *Flamenca,* and yet these are problematic concepts when we consider that they still belong to the artificial world of romance and exist at such a far remove from the nineteenth- and twentieth-century works that set the standard for the mimetic reproduction of life in art. Realism in such texts can be better measured by calibrating two narrative measurements: distance from an original model combined with proximity to a portrayal of a more verisimilar world. There are no absolutes, but a subtle and sliding scale that constructs an ambiguity that proves fruitful to later writers of romance. Just as Chrétien blends literary convention with more animated, human heroes, so Martorell uses the double paradigm of the courtly romance to create a hero who embodies both an evolved con-cept of chivalry and a modified form of courtly love, one that must match the sensual expectations of the fifteenth century while recalling the artificial refinement of earlier times. The resulting dissonance can also be termed a plastic potential of the romance, the very element that Cervantes appears to admire in *Tirant lo Blanc: Don Quixote* continues a line of parodic development that stretches back farther than *Tirant*—and as far back as Chrétien. Cervantes knew *Tirant*, Martorell knew a version of *Jaufre*, the *Jaufre* poet and the *Flamenca* poet were steeped in the works of Chrétien: these degrees of separation attest to the closeness and importance of the links between them and the part they played as the novel underwent a slow, but vital evolution of narrative fiction.

It is hardly original to suggest that parody is a part of medieval romance. However, even on as simple a level as has been laid out in this study, a reexamination of its role as a structural device in its many diverse manifestations leads to further and important consideration of the regenerative power of parody as an inbuilt form of literary criticism and source of narrative energy and not generic destruction. The double paradigm of the chivalric romance, bypassed by Bakhtin in his mapping of the history of the novel, makes an important contribution to our view of the development of fiction. Its dynamism and plurivocality have been overlooked for too long, and its valorous contribution to the history of the novel as site of confrontation and renewal should give it a more prominent place in the evolution of what became the novel. This study includes works almost all considered more or less "straight" or serious at some point in literary history: it is hard to see them that way, and there are doubtless others that would benefit from being viewed with a fresh eye. By restoring the narrative importance of the regenerative comic element to the medieval romance, we might bridge that other form of aesthetic distance—or the proclaimed alterity—that separates us from the Middle Ages, and conclude that the romance is much more than an aberrant knight in search of an outmoded form.

NOTES

Chapter 1. Rekindling the Romance: Toward and Away from the Prehistory of the Novel

1. Also discussed and translated by David H. Rosenthal in the prologue to his translation (London: Pan/Picador, 1985).

2. Ian Watt, *The Rise of the Novel,* and Michael McKeon *The Origins of the English Novel 1600–1740.* Watt's successors, Michael McKeon chief among them, have enlarged and problematized the basic model he provides by broadening the panorama of social context and focussing on the impact of cultural history on the novel: or, rather, showing that the novel is first and foremost the essential representation of cultural history. McKeon also formulates a dialectic view of the rise of the novel. Watt's playing of fantasy versus reality and universality versus individualism create useful dialectic in Watt's arguments. McKeon's Marxist dialectic chooses different and deliberate battle lines drawn along the operation of truth and virtue in key texts of the seventeenth and eighteenth centuries. McKeon delineates two particular sets of oppositions, mediated by third elements in each case. In the seventeenth century "the reigning narrative epistemology involves a dependency on received authorities and a priori traditions" (21). This he dubs "romance idealism," countered by "an empirical epistemology that derives from many sources, and this I will call 'naive empiricism'" (21). This, in turn, spawns a critical reaction he terms "extreme skepticism" (21). The first element gives way to the second, creating a conservative wave of doubt and setting the pendulum swing in motion again. This model, played out in literature, assists him in formulating questions fundamental to the search for truth in narrative, while virtue will be explored using a similar schema involving "aristocratic ideology," "progressive ideology," and "conservatism" (21).

At first appearance, McKeon's model seems a more elaborate and sociohistorically based version of Watt's, broadened to include more cultural history. McKeon critiques Watt's limited definition of formal realism and his treatment of romance, still a ubiquitous form at the time he describes, for, as he says, "even those ancient and medieval forms that define our notion of what 'romance' amounts to can be shown to reflect, critics have claimed, some major features of 'formal realism'" (3). He suggests that particularly in the literary realm explored by Watt, his patterning of development could be applied to another place and time, and that therefore his model has the potential to be ahistorical. McKeon also takes Watt to task for his reliance on the dominance of the bourgeoisie in the eighteenth century as a factor in literary production. McKeon seeks to loosen up both social and textual categorizations and reshuffle the pack into a new form. It is an enterprise fraught with danger, as Homer Obed Brown argues, for McKeon risks falling into the same trap. Of his two-fold schema, Brown writes: "These two dialectical patterns . . . are also curiously ahistorical; that is, they operate according to their own purely intellectual causality, and can be found as structural patterns of conflict in almost any particular slice of history" ("Of the Title to Things Real"). The argument that one could find the conditions ripe for the cultural changes necessary to produce the modern novel in the twelfth century is a persuasive one, and applying McKeon's schema to medieval works would be an interesting challenge. The ability to apply any fixed model of the novel at any period, with minor adjustments, makes us think again of Kundera's analysis of the novel as opposed to history rather than an agent of it: the relationship between the two seems magnetic in its attraction and simultaneous repellency.

3. "One continually wonders what exactly is the relevance for the English novel, of all the romances Baker discusses and analyses. It is hardly sufficient reason to discuss them simply because they exist. Only very seldom does Baker suggest why the romances he discusses are relevant: he adverts to 'realistic' scenes now and again" (96). He cites Baker (London: H. F. & G. Witherby, 1924), 1:111.

4. Matilda Bruckner, in *Narrative Invention,* eloquently outlines the challenges of the romance: "Romance offers a complex challenge to the person who would explore its use of convention. Readers of romance have been especially impressed by its openness, contrasting it, for example, to the closed genre of the *grand chant courtois* . . . or situating it at the origin of the modern novel. Yet as flexible as the romance narrative is, it still operates as a conventional system of repetition and variation: the great variety of materials is firmly held within the organizing force of typical patterns. Analysis must account, therefore, for the flexibility of romance convention, the expected and the unexpected" (9).

5. Lukács uses a similar opposition between the two genres, declaring in a famous formulation that "[t]he novel is the epic of a world that has been abandoned by God" (88). Lukács's concept of the novel follows the rise of individual experience and the troubled relationship of character to social context. He only briefly addresses the medieval romance: "The chivalrous novel had succumbed to the fate of every epic that wants to maintain and perpetuate a form by purely formal means after the transcendental conditions of its existence have already been condemned by the historico-philosophical dialectic" (101). The "entertainment novel" appears as the atrophied remains of a once "pure and genuine major art form, even if a problematic one: the chivalrous epic of the Middle Ages" (101).

6. Caryl Emerson and Michael Holquist explain the difference between the two terms in the glossary they append to *The Dialogic Imagination:*

> Heteroglossia. . . . The base condition governing the operation of meaning in any utterance. It is that which insures the primacy of context over text. At any given time, in any given place, there will be a set of conditions—social, historical, meteorological, physiological—that will insure that a word uttered in that place and at that time will have a meaning different than it would have under any other conditions; all utterances are heteroglot in that they are functions of a matrix of forces practically impossible to recoup, and therefore impossible to resolve. Heteroglossia is as close a conceptualization as is possible of that locus where centripetal and centrifugal forces collide; as such, it is that which a systematic linguistics must always suppress. (428)

> Polyglossia. . . . The simultaneous presence of two or more national languages interacting within a single cultural system (Bakhtin's two historical models are ancient Rome and the Renaissance). (431)

7. "What Bakhtin Left Unsaid: The Case of the Medieval Romance," in *Romance: Generic Transformation from Chrétien de Troyes to Cervantes,* ed. Kevin Brownlee and Marina Scordilis Brownlee, 23–46.

8. As an example, Segre highlights the use of such verbs as *cuidier, veoir,* and *penser* to distinguish authorial opinion from that of the characters. There are different voices, if not different languages, to be discerned in authorial asides, and in particular narrative frameworks such as the open-ended conclusion to *Le Bel Inconnu,* or in the suggestion of further episodes to be included at the listener's whim in *Jaufre.* The potential independence of creator from creation, and the uses made of the distance between the two points of view, has interesting implications, not the least of which is that what Bakhtin would consider monoglossic in literature of other periods becomes, ironically, a sign of polyglossia. Segre's most enlightening example of this is the interior monologue, so much a part of Chrétien's romances and prominent also in *Flamenca:* it is at these junctures that the authorial voice recedes most into the distance leaving the illusion of autonomy of the character.

Chapter 2. Northern Exposure:
Chivalry and Parody in the Old French Tradition

1. Cited by Erich Auerbach in *Literary Language and its Public in Late Latin Antiquity and in the Middle Ages,* chap. 4, "The Western Public and Its Language," 304, quoting the *Liber de confessione sacramentali, PL* 207, col. 1088ff.

2. This echoes St. Augustine's *Confessions,* when in bk. 1, chaps. 13–17, he describes his love of secular literature, particularly the romancelike tragic love of

Dido and Aeneas. Augustine sees his enjoyment of classical epic, drama, and poetry as distractions from the spiritual life.

3. *The Princeton Dictionary of Poetry and Poetics* (Princeton: Princeton University Press, 1965; repr. 1990). Also, on the narrowing of the term to refer to a particular kind of text, see P. Voelker, "Die Bedeutungsentwicklung des Wortes Romans."

4. Erich Auerbach succinctly characterizes the chanson de geste in his *Introduction aux études de philologie romane*: "les chansons de geste sont des oeuvres de la fin du 11e et du 12e siècle, imbues de l'eprit de la chevalerie du temps des premières croisades: esprit guerrier, féodal, fanatiquement chrétien, mélange paradoxal de christianisme et d'impérialisme agressif" [the chansons de geste are works of the end of the eleventh and beginning of the twelfth century, steeped in the chivalric spirit of the time of the first crusades: a warrior spirit, feudal, fanatically Christian, a paradoxical mixture of Christianity and imperial agression] (104). Resemblance to actual events and conditions is lacking in the roman, and yet Auerbach suggests both here and in *Mimesis* that there is a form of realism contained in the roman courtois. Everything is relative: factual history is absent from the romance—although a cursory glance at the *histoire universelle,* the first extensive and popular genre of vernacular history, reveals that it is often as much an *estoire* as are works of purely fictional intent.

5. Frye also remarks on what he sees as a fourth potential stage in some stories occurring before the recognition phase, be it tragic or comic: *sparagmos,* a tearing to pieces or disappearance. The former is best represented in the dying god myth seen in Christ's crucifixion, the fates of Osiris and Orpheus, and the story of St. George. Frye uses St. George being brought to life by a doctor in dramatic versions of his fight with the dragon as an illustration of the latter. We might add Roland and Beowulf to the list, and as an example of the translation of this motif to more comic romances the *folie* of Tristan or Yvain's disappearance into the woods as he loses his reason.

6. Allegory (14–19) is his major concern, with its subheadings of *ironia, antiphrasis, aenigma, charientismos* (saying one thing but meaning another using "kind words"), *paroemia* (a particular use of proverbs in context), *sarcasmos,* and *asteismos* (at its simplest, using polished language to deliver a harsher message). The general heading of allegory refers here to the many ways in which things can be said in a different way, either by changing the words or the tone. *Significatio* (20–23) is the other trope Haidu discusses in depth, showing how it is used variously to bring meaning to actions *per exsuperationem* (through hyperbole), *per ambiguum* (through a play on double-meanings), *per consequentiam* (through the practical conclusion to a "symbolic fact," 21), *per abscisionem* (through the statement of fact followed by no conclusion, leading the hearer to conjecture about the significance of the act), and *per similitudinem* (by analogy). Haidu asserts that these tropes, beloved of grammarians during Chrétien's time, are important interpretive keys to understanding the full implications of the romances. He finds

Cligès a particularly suitable case for study, since it is often considered the most "artificial" of Chrétien's romances, in which we are most aware of its literariness and its status as fiction. This is especially true in the prologue, in which Chrétien introduces himself as the author of other works.

7. All references to *Le Chevalier de la Charrete* are drawn from Mario Roques's edition. For the sake of brevity, I refer to Chrétien's romances by their short titles.

8. See Leslie Topsfield, *Chrétien de Troyes*, chap. 4, "Lancelot and the Quest for *Fin'Amors*," in which he remarks: "These later romances centre on a man and his lacks and failures which are symbolised in the titles, *Le Chevalier de la charrette, Le Chevalier au Lion, Le conte du Graal*. Erec and Enide, Cliges and Fenice formed complimentary social units. Lancelot, Perceval and Yvain are isolated" (105). This already suggests an authorial distance from the central character: the titles provide a rudimentary kind of irony, since the knight/cart dichotomy characterizes Lancelot, and man/beast suits Yvain. The ambiguity of *conte* and *graal* is less immediately suggestive, although the association between Perceval and an empty vessel that needs to be filled is soon apparent. On a symbolic level, the quest for the cup of life—and therefore for meaning—could be viewed as the quest of form for content, the search for the center of a decentered narrative, as Todorov would have it ("La Quête du récit," *La Poétique de la prose*).

9. I have no doubt that Joan Martorell meant to parody two of Chrétien's romances at one stroke by having his hero Tirant participate in a tournament with a helmet topped by a Grail with Carmesina's comb in it. Similarly, Carmesina sends a messenger with three hairs back to Tirant with a scolding for her lover.

10. Douglas Kelly (*Sens and Conjointure* 22–3) upholds *Lancelot*'s reputation as a romance favored rather than abandoned by its main architect when he points out that Chrétien refers to *Lancelot* on three occasions in *Yvain*.

11. In "Texte et Prétexte: *Jaufre* et *Yvain*," in *The Legacy of Chrétien de Troyes*, Tony Hunt argues that the Occitan romance *Jaufre* parallels and parodies *Yvain* on many levels. He says that *Yvain* is a "prétexte" of the later romance, as it begins with a similar false start, contains a rude herdsman, and has a similar heroine (Brunissen) and a fountain adventure.

12. John Stevens underscores the continuing "pervasiveness" of romance in *Medieval Romance: Themes and Approaches*. Italo Calvino borrows the medieval romance as a valid model in *Il Cavalliere inesistente;* he uses the form of the romance and the range of ironic tropes discussed by Haidu and Green to create an affectionate parody of the chivalric romance in particular, and of literary endeavor in general.

13. Omer Jodogne, "La parodie et la pastiche dans *Aucassin et Nicolette*," 65. All references to line numbers will be drawn from F. W. Bourdillon's edition.

14. In "Aucassin et Nicolette, Clarisse et Florent," in *Mélanges de Langue et de Littérature du Moyen-Age offerts à Jean Frappier,* Omer Jodogne makes a case for considering *Aucassin* as "la version amusante et poétique de *Clarisse et Florent*" [the amusing poetic version of *C et F*] (481). The exposé is not entirely convincing,

but the mockery of conventional love-themes and the vapid commonplaces of the romance identified by Jodogne in one particular text attest to the success of the parody in *Aucassin*.

15. See D. R. Sutherland, "The Love Meditation in Courtly Literature," in *Studies in Medieval French Literature Presented to Alfred Ewert*, where she explores one of the fundamental paradoxes of courtly literature, and the one most exploited as a source of lyric inspiration to the troubadours and of comedy to Chrétien: "Only the truly *cortes* can be *fin'aman*, yet *fin'Amors* renders its devotees incapable of observing the essential rules of *cortesia*" (153). The love that should inspire integration into courtly society leads to an inevitable phase of introspection and often self-exile for the lover. Courtly love is simultaneously a social and antisocial phenomenon, and expressed in the lyric effusions of the *pensement d'amor* "suits elegantly artificial characters like Aucassin, the Guillem of *Flamenca*, or among literary creations with more pretensions to realism, an Alexandre or a Piramus, adolescents highly trained in all the social arts, but as yet inexperienced in love" (190).

Chapter 3. Going South:
Courtliness and Comedy in the Occitan Tradition

1. *Jaufré*, ed. Clovis Brunel, 162. The date of this romance is subject to debate: Brunel (38) concurs with Gaston Paris in dating the work between 1225–28 because of their identification of the king of Aragon in the text as James I. Emmanuèle Baumgartner explores the other possibility: that the king could be Alphonse II, and that therefore the work would date from 1169–70 ("Le défi du chevalier rouge). Given the influence of Chrétien de Troyes, we are left with two hypotheses; first that the similarity of elements in *Jaufre* and *Perceval* must be because the Occitan work postdates all Chrétien's works; or alternatively that *Jaufre* influenced Chrétien.

Part of this chapter first appeared as my article "The Name of the Ruse and the Round Table: Occitan Romance and the Case for Resistance."

2. Mentioned by Martín de Riquer in "Los problemas del roman provenzal de *Jaufré*." In an even more curious setting, *Jaufre* lives on in a Tagalog version, discussed by Dean Fansler in "Metrical Romances in the Philippines," *Journal of American Folklore* 29.

3. When he meets Augier they listen to a jongleur read Marie de France's *Lai des Deux Amants* (l. 4460), in which the hero dies trying to carry the heroine up the slope of a mountain. This *épreuve* is later echoed in *Jaufre* when Mélian, the wounded lord, is forced to climb a mountain until his partially healed wounds reopen. Marie de France, as well as Chrétien, is of central importance to the intrigue of *Jaufre*.

4. Huchet's conclusions are intriguing regarding the *fée de Gibel*, her underwater kingdom, and the meaning of her inclusion. Huchet suggests that the mysterious and powerful woman has supplanted Arthur and his court as the center for

true adventure, and he says that the invention of such a female figure is a reflection of troubadour culture. She is a strong "southern" female figure in opposition to the masculine ethos of Arthur's court—but then again, so is *la Dame du Lac* in the prose Lancelot, unless she too can be seen in the same light.

5. Gauvain is preeminent among the knights as he is in Chrétien's romances. Keith Busby, in "'Moseiner Galvain l'astrucz" shows that Gauvain's narrative value as the most polished, yet ineffectual, of Arthur's knights, is maintained in *Jaufre* and elsewhere in Provençal literature. Of *Jaufre* as a whole, Busby claims: "Si l'auteur de *Jaufre* a connu toute l'oeuvre de Chrétien, ou seulement une partie, cela n'enlève rien au caractère unique de son texte. Il y a peu de romans òu l'humour, l'ironie, le burlesque, voire la parodie, s'entremêlent avec une telle énergie créatrice" [If the author of *Jaufre* knew all the works of Chrétien, or only just a part, it takes nothing from the unique character of his text. There are few romances where humor, irony, burlesque, and indeed parody, mingle with so much creative energy] (6). I can only agree with his assertion that the *matière de Bretagne* serves as a comic "arrière-plan" for Jaufré's adventures.

6. *Table des noms propres avec toutes leurs variantes*, 176. The entry runs as follows: "Talas, Tallas, Taulas, 1. aïeul d'Uterpendragon, chef du lignage du roi Artur, Lanc.pr.; var. Tailas, Talais; 2. chevalier d'Artur, Erec; Escan. 4178; Lanc.pr., var. Caulas, Etaullas, Talais, Thailais, 421, 32; Tarillas, Taulaus, Taullas, Tollas (= Talas II?); 3. chevalier de la Dame de Landemore, Meraug.; var.Caulas,-lus; 4. roi de Danemark, Claris; 5. fils de Raine, Viol.; 6.v. Tulant; 7.T. de la Deserte, chevalier, Lanc.; v.Tulas; 8. T le Grant de la Deserte, quêteur du Graal, Trist.pr.; var. Caulas; 9. T. de la Lande Reonde, un des dix Compagnons de Bretagne, Galer.; 10. T. de la Montagne, géant tué par Tristan, Trist.pr.; 11. T. de Rochemont ou de Ro(u)ge Mont, Gigl., var. Toulas; Hunb.; Ider, Meriad. 2612, var. Tala, -lac, -lais, Tallac, Toular; Perc. 16567; Perc.Cont.I; Trist.pr.; v.Aullas et Tuals; Taulat derogimon, principal adversaire de Jaufré, Jaufré; var. Taulat, Teulat; 12. T. le Roux, v. Caulas le Roux; T. le Cox (lire: le Rox), v. Aucalec le Roux; 13. Tolas, compagnon de la Table Ronde, Trist.B., = Talas 8 ou 10? (cf. picte Talarc, -lorc, -loc)."

7. Picking up on Jung's opportune statement, William Calin ("Towards a New Reading of *Jaufre*") moves on from Jung's "lecture 'folklorique et rituelle'" (435) to a Freudian reading of the romance. Nikki Kaltenbach *(Le Roman de Jaufre: A Jungian Analysis)* follows the direction of critics like Huchet who lean toward archetypal readings of the romance.

8. Walter von Wartburg, *Französisches Etymologisches Wörterbuch*, 13:14–26; Adolf Tobler and Erhard Lommatzsch, *Altfranzösisches Wörterbuch*, vol. 10, col. 815; Frédéric Godefroy, *Dictionnaire de l'ancienne langue française;* Emil Levy, *Petit dictionnaire*, 358.

9. See the discussions of Per Nykrog, *Les Fabliaux,* and Charles Muscatine, *The Old French Fabliaux,* and Howard Bloch, *The Scandal of the Fabliaux.* Nykrog views the fabliaux as inextricably bound with the courtly class, while Muscatine argues that their appeal goes beyond the boundaries of class and that their audi-

ence was much wider than previously assumed. Bloch traces issues pertaining to the body, with its *bas corporel* of members and dismemberment, and uses a sense of displacement to theorize and problematize the fabliaux and how they express the limits and transgressions of poetic representation. What he finds in the clashing of registers and language is yet another expression of modified textual dialogism:

> The ubiquitous theme of bodily dismemberment thus stands as the most manifest sign of a constant questioning of the sufficiency of poetic representation, which is also evident formally in the multiple modes of linguistic disruption to be found in the medieval comic tale—in word play; phonological, onomastic, and semantic misunderstanding; use of proverbs and extended metaphors; bilingualism. (101)

10. On the connection between fabliau and novas, see Monson, "L'Intertextualité du *Castía-Gilos.*" Also see René Lavaud and René Nelli, *Les Troubadours*, vol. 2, *Le Trésor poétique de l'Occitanie*, 186–211 and 214–35, respectively. Small fragments from a third novas are extant (Lavaud and Nelli 210–14), in which similar thematic concerns appear, as the main characters are a lord, his wife, and the young squire who loves her. Where the text breaks off, the squire is about to declare his love, setting the scene for the development of a potentially comic love triangle.

11. Ernst Gamillscheg's *Etymologisches Wörterbuch* (651) gives the use as dating from the fifteenth century. The term *novelliste*, i.e, writer of *nouvelles*, does not appear until the seventeenth century—that is, if we ignore Elias Fonsalada's vida. Tobler and Lommatzsch *(Altfranzösisches Wörterbuch)* do not show it as a literary genre, but do show it as meaning story in the singular, the equivalent of German *Rede, Geschichte*, or *Neuigkeit*. Godefroy gives no account of it as a literary term.

Chapter 4. The Uses of Literacy:
Parodic Fusion in the *Roman de Flamenca*

1. In the fabliau *La Bourgeoise d'Orléans* in Philippe Ménard's *Fabliaux Français du moyen-âge* (21–28), the heroine locks her merchant husband up when he spies on her and tests to see if she has a lover. She instructs the household servants to give a good thrashing to the cleric who is supposedly her ami. While the husband receives the pain for his trouble, the lady and her lover enjoy uninterrupted bliss, and the husband returns black and blue the following day content that he has a faithful wife.

2. Charles Grimm, *Etude sur le Roman de Flamenca* (104), quoting Aubéry's *Les Bains de Bourbon Lancy et Larchambaud*. Also, on the subject of spas in the Middle Ages, see Gérard Gouiran, "L'Odeur de soufre des eaux thermales à propos de *Flamenca* et de textes médiévaux non-littéraires." The details given about cures and baths make this passage of *Flamenca* particularly realistic, with

attention paid to the geology of the area (that permits Guillem to tunnel) as well as to the business of running the establishment, special dress required, etc. René Nelli, in *Le Roman de Flamenca: Un art d'aimer occitanien du XIIIe siècle*, reminds us that Ovid mentions baths smelling of sulphur at the infamous resort of Baiae in *Ars Amatoria*, bk. 1, 255–6. Although the bathhouse in *Flamenca* is an extraordinary setting for a courtly romance, it is a frequent image in paintings and illuminations, as Raimond Van Marle shows in *L'Iconographie de l'art profane au moyen-âge et à la Renaissance et la décoration des demeures*, 494–518. Philip Damon remarks that "medicinal baths had, in both the technical and popular literature of the Middle Ages, roughly the same status as the psychoanalysts's couch has today — part of a therapeutic process commonly associated with a somewhat basic view of the emotional life" ("Courtesy and Comedy" 610).

3. See Rita Lejeune, "Le calendrier du *Roman de Flamenca*: Contribution à l'étude de mentalités médiévales occitanes." Of these the last is most likely: allusions to the lais of Marie de France and Chrétien's works make the first date unlikely, and the influence of the first part of the *Roman de la Rose* eliminates the second from serious consideration. Ulrich Gschwind *(Le Roman de Flamenca: nouvelle occitane du XIIIe siècle)*, the most recent editor of the text, favors 1230–50 as the date of composition. In reviewing other tentative datings, Gschwind catalogues the various methods used to establish a date using internal evidence.

Grimm, writing in 1930, favors a *terminus a quo* of 1272 and a likely date of composition 1283–1300 as a result of his analysis of the heraldic blazon described toward the end of the poem: "flors jaunas sus el camp blau" [yellow flowers on a blue field] (l. 6998). According to Grimm's ingenious calculations, the arms described in the poem belonged to Robert de France and Béatrix de Bourbon, who were married in 1272, and assumed the arms in 1283 when they inherited their new lands on the death of Agnès de Bourbon, Béatrix's mother. However, a red band on the arms is missing from the poet's description, which Grimm assigns to his not being versed in heraldry. If this is the case, then perhaps the entire passage is unreliable, and Grimm's argument faulty. Rita Lejeune, using the same evidence and analyzing the tournament in detail, claims that some of the characters' names belong to historical personages of the last half of the thirteenth century. See her "Le Tournoi de Bourbon-L'Archambaud dans le *Roman de Flamenca*" and also "Flamenca: Fille fictive d'un comte de Namur." A similar analysis previously led Grimm to place the events of the text 1196–1200.

Emmanuèle Baumgartner ("Le roman aux XIIe et XIIIe siècles dans la littérature occitane") also supports a later date, seeing a definite influence of Jean de Meun on the author of *Flamenca* (635). Paul Olson, in "*Le roman de Flamenca*: History and Literary Convention," identifies Guillem as archdeacon of Nevers, c. 1190, and one of a number of clergy suspected of heresy. Thus, when Guillem becomes a Patarin, Olson treats this literally. To Olson, the story revolves around a thinly veiled set of references to Cathar heresy, but this interpretation is difficult to sustain throughout the work because of the secular nature of the tale, and because of the pervasive presence of that other heresy, the Ovidian religion of love.

4. *The Romance of Flamenca: A Provençal Poem of the Thirteenth Century,* 20. Similar conclusions are reached by J. Fabre de Morlhon, in *"Le roman de Flamenca* dans son contexte historique.*"* In addition, he tries to establish a link between the text and Arnaud or Raymond de Roquefoil as the *seners d'Alga,* and in his opening paragraph broaches the subject of the relationship of the poet to the troubled period of the Albigensian crusade.

5. A satisfactory interpretation of this passage is unavailable, and so it is not included. For discussion see Grimm, 99. The exact sense of the poetry is elusive: the different editors and translators concur on their having been a falling-out between the two named characters. See Gschwind's note to lines 1728–36 for the various interpretations made on this passage.

6. Guy Mermier, in "Ceremonial and Pageantry in an Old Provençal Romance," writes about the banquet as a sign of the general "overkill" of the work: "Even the very nature of the banquets is marred by their quality of excess: excess of food, excess of largesse, excess in expenses as well as in numbers. There is also an excess in feelings. . . . [T]he consequence of Archambaud's jealousy is a shriveling up of courtly values" (380). Mermier regards this initial excess as indicative of the perversion of courtly themes and values in the rest of the romance and as a sign of the paradoxical extremes that characterize the work.

7. There were, of course, many debate poems over who would prove the best lover, the knight or the cleric, constituting a choice between refined brawn and brain. As Charles Stebbins writes in "The Theme of the 'Clerc-Chevalier' in the 13th-Century Old Provençal Romance of *Flamenca,"* the poet provides us with a personification of the two sides of the debate. There is no conflict between the two roles: Guillem finds his success disguised as a cleric and seems set to repeat his triumph at the break-off point of the text when he performs feats of chivalry and is introduced to court by Flamenca's husband. Gérard Gouiran, taking up the theme, juxtaposes Guillem with Guilhem IX and the spirit of the first great scabrous lyrics in Occitan literature ("'Car tu es cavalliers e clercs' [*Flamenca,* v.1899]: Guilhem ou le chevalier parfait") and demonstrates the extent to which *l'habit* did not make *le moine.*

8. One thinks, for example, of "Les Fanfreluches antidotées trouvées en un monument antique" in chap. 2 of *Gargantua,* which together constitute a jumbled heap of literary remains parodying the epic. As for lists, there are, of course, the famous examples of Gargantua's games (chap. 22) and the library of St. Victor in *Pantagruel* (chap. 7), among others.

9. "Courtly Literature and the Fabliaux: Some Instances of Parody": "His audience has heard, he says, of Arthur, Perceval, Sagremor, Caradoc, Gauvain, Dodinel, Priam, Hector, Achilles, Richier, Floovant, Roland, Oliver, Turpin, Gaifier, Charlemagne, Caesar, Crescentius, and Alexander, but none is as redoutable and praiseworthy as the subject of his present poem. He causes men to behave courteously and generously, to bear arms, to sing songs, etc. As the eulogy progresses in all its detail, only the purest of medieval minds would not have grown suspicious

at the mentions of resistance at the first assault and subsequent entry into the palace, and the joke is revealed in line 28" (79).

10. As further proof that the banquet scene is a stylized scenario borrowed by the poet and used to suggest the ambience of the northern French romance, it is useful to recall Renaut de Beaujeu's *Le Bel Inconnu* (l. 2881), when Guinglain enters the palace hall of the *Cité gaste:*

> Il ne se vaut mie arester
> Tant qu'a la sale en est venus
> U les jogleors a veüs
> Sor les fenestres tos asis,
> Devant cascun un cierge espris;
> Et son estrument retenoit
> Cascuns itel con il avoit.
> L'un voit as fenestres harper,
> L'autre delés celui roter;
> L'uns estive, l'autre vïele,
> Li autres gigle et calimele
> Et cante cler comme sereine,
> Li autres la citole mainne,
> Li uns entendoit au corner
> Et l'autres au bien flahuter;
> Li un notoient lais d'amor;
> Sonnent tinbre, sonnent tabor,
> Muses, salteres et fretel,
> Et buissines et moïnel;
> Cascuns ovre de son mestier.
> (ll. 2880–99)

[He did not stop at all until he arrived in the hall, where he saw all the jongleurs seated on top of the windows, a candle lighting each one. Each held an instrument, as he would have. He saw one playing a harp at the window, another alongside plays a violin; one plays a wind instrument, another a viol, one a mandolin, another a reed pipe and sings as clearly as a siren. One plays a lute, one was playing a pipe, and another was playing the flute; some were playing *lais d'amor;* they play drums and tabors, bagpipes, psalteries and panpipes, trumpets and recorders. Each played according to his desire.]

Notable here is the reference to the siren, a foreshadowing of the mysterious kiss that reveals all shortly to be experienced by Guinglain. The passage describing this surreal accompaniment to the hero's exploration of the empty palace is worth citing in full: the *Bels Desconogutz* was known to the *Jaufre* poet (l. 108), and although Limentani's thorough comparison of French sources for *Flamenca* does not cite this particular passage, from the above description it appears that the anonymous "Bernadet" was more familiar with the details of this text than the passing reference to the hero of the title in line 679 reveals: lines 603–10 of *Flamenca* echo this passage very closely.

11. Limentani notes another similar description in *Yvain* (ll. 2340–58). In Chrétien's *Erec,* the description of the nuptials seems the grandest possible. So sumptuous is the feast that, in keeping with the modesty topos frequently employed by the author, he cannot describe it further. Chrétien's formulaic description reappears in *Jaufre* during the festivities surrounding the hero's marriage to Brunissen (ll. 9811–17).

12. Donaldson makes brief mention of an exemplary story from Gerald of Wales's late twelfth-century *Gemma Ecclesiastica* just as appropriate to *Flamenca* as to *The Miller's Tale.* Gerald tells of a priest in Worcester "who heard throughout the whole night that section of a song called a refrain. . . . It was being sung by a group of dancers outside the church. Next morning when the priest stood at the altar vested and signed with the cross, instead of the salutation, 'The Lord be with you,' he sang out in a loud voice, in English, the refrain 'Swete lamman dhin are'" (*The Jewel of the Church* 92). Gerald goes on to describe the banishment of the song by the local bishop and the shame caused to the priest.

13. See François Pirot, *Recherches sur les connaissances littéraires des troubadours* and Don Alfred Monson, *Les "Ensenhamens" Occitans.* The opening of the banquet scene in *Flamenca* when the jongleurs and tumblers give their performance recalls the third strophe of Giraut de Calanson's poem (565). Also discussed by Limentani (246).

14. "parer de son amic no.l qu[a]illa." Gschwind's note to 6277 gives a list of alternate readings, and I have opted for Nelli and Lavaud's *vueilla.*

15. The story of Floire and Blanchefleur is also echoed in the deliverance of an unwilling bride from a cruel husband (who, like Archimbaut, shows himself to be fundamentally reasonable) from a specially constructed tower. Another knightly rescue from a tower, and a possible source for *Flamenca,* is the story of the *inclusa* told by Beraus (ll. 4223–4689) in the *Roman des Sept Sages* (Misrahi 113–25). Another analogue is found in *Li Romans de Dolopathos* (Brunet, 8th story, 353–80).

16. The poet often dwells on Archimbaut's frightening appearance: Flamenca's once noble lord undergoes a transformation that makes him an archetypal ogre, giant, villain, and wild man. His barbarity is different from the emir's, but just as profound and perhaps more suggestive of the bestial side that lurks beneath a courtly exterior. Leslie Topsfield ("Intention and Ideas in *Flamenca*") points out that Archimbaut resembles the successful knight figure of Chrétien de Troyes, who has to earn the right to happiness by enduring trials and even rejection or madness.

17. Paul Rémy treats the same topic, with less importance assigned to Marcabru and more weight given to the nostalgia topos as a general feature ("Plaintes sur la déchéance des moeurs dans *Jaufre* et *Flamenca*").

18. The language game and the ritualized games of courtly love are dealt with in Tilde Sankovitch's *"The Romance of Flamenca:* The Puppeteer and the Play."

19. See Lavaud and Nelli, *Les Troubadours,* 2:794, *Li clerc si fan pastor* [The clerics are turning into shepherds] (P-C 335.31, strophe 1). Cardenal also uses the same image of women who can always find an excuse to justify taking a lover in *Las amairitz qui encolpar las vol* (P-C 335.30, 798–99).

Chapter 5. Romance into Novel: *Tirant lo Blanc*

1. The general consensus ascribes Galba much of the last quarter, dealing with Tirant's exploits in North Africa and then his homecoming and demise in the Greek Empire, perhaps ultimately because besides a few textual anomalies, these are less satisfying than the previous adventures. It is impossible to know if Martorell left any kind of plan for the conclusion, but the irony of Tirant's reunion with Carmesina and death seem more in keeping with the first three-quarters of the novel. On the composition of *Tirant* see Martín de Riquer, *Història de la Literatura Catalana: II,* 706.

2. Chapter 116, p. 368. All references to this work, subsequently noted parenthetically by chapter and followed by page, are once again taken from Martín de Riquer's edition *Tirant lo Blanc: I altres ecrits de Joanot Martorell.*

3. These have been edited by Martín de Riquer and Mario Vargas Llosa in *El Combate Imaginario: Las Cartas de Batalla de Joanot Martorell.*

4. See Rosenthal's introduction to his translation and Martín de Riquer's introduction to the Catalan edition (72–5). Roger de Flor (1280–1305), a Templar expelled from the order for blackmailing refugees from the Holy Land, was subsequently a mercenary in Sicily, Asia Minor, and Macedonia. Regarding the end of Roger's career Rosenthal writes, "Before his death he had wrested a number of concessions from the [Byzantine] imperial court: he was appointed first megaduke and then Caesar and was promised the Bulgarian tsar's daughter in marriage" (xiv). Roger's story was widely circulated in Raymond Muntaner's chronicle in the fifteenth century.

Hunyadi (1407?–56) was a successful general in holding back the Turks during the fifteenth century. Apart from his military triumph, he shares a swift and unheroic death with Tirant, dying of the plague just after a great victory. Critics also cite the similarity between the names of Tirant and Hunyadi, since his name derived from his place of origin, Wallachia: this gave the adjective *valacus* or *balachus,* which became *blac* or *vlach* as it spread into western Europe, and by popular analogy was transposed into *blanc* or *blach.* He was apparently referred to as the White Knight (Riquer 73–74).

Riquer adds a further contender to the list with the fifteenth-century Spanish knight Pedro Vásquez de Saavedra, a knight who began his colorful career in London and then went on to the court of Burgundy and then with a Burgundian contingent to help Constantinople at its hour of need (Riquer 74–5). He and Martorell were in London at about the same time, and may have met there.

Chapter 6. Conclusion: Familiarity Breeds Content

1. Miguel de Cervantes, *Don Quixote de la Mancha*, part 1, chap. 1, 78. Subsequent references to *Don Quixote* will be drawn from this edition. Long quotations in English are from Joseph R. Jones and Kenneth Douglas's edition of John Ormsby's translation; short phrases are mine unless otherwise indicated.

BIBLIOGRAPHY

Alonso, Dámaso. *Primavera temprana de la literatura europea.* Madrid: Ediciones Guadarrama, 1961.

Arthur, Ross G. *Jaufre: An Occitan Romance.* New York: Garland, 1992.

———. "The *Roman de Jaufre* and the Illusions of Romance." In *The Rusted Hauberk: Feudal Ideas of Order and Their Decline,* edited by Liam O. Purdon and Cindy L. Vitto, 245–65. Gainesville: University Press of Florida, 1994.

Asperti, Stefano. "*Flamenca* e dintorni. Considerazioni sui rapporti fra Occitania e Catalogna nel XIV secolo." *CN* 45 (1985): 59–103.

Auerbach, Erich. *Introduction aux études de philologie romane.* Frankfurt: Klostermann, 1949.

———. *Literary Language and Its Public in Late Latin Antiquity and in the Middle Ages.* Trans. Ralph Manheim. New York: Pantheon/Bollingen, 1965.

———. *Mimesis: The Representation of Reality in Western Literature.* Princeton: Princeton University Press, 1953.

Avalle-Arce, Juan Bautista. "*Tirant lo Blanc, Amadis de Gaula* y la caballeresca medieval." In *Studies in Honor of Sumner M. Greenfield,* edited by H. L. Boudreau and Luis T. Gonzalez-del-Valle, 17–32. Lincoln, Nebr.: Society of Spanish and Spanish-American Studies, 1985.

Aylward, Edward. *Martorell's "Tirant lo Blanc": A Program for Military and Social Reform in Fifteenth-Century Christendom.* Chapel Hill: North Carolina Studies in the Romance Languages and Literatures, 1985.

Bakhtin, Mikhail. *The Dialogic Imagination: Four Essays.* Trans. Caryl Emerson and Michael Holquist. Austin: University of Texas Press, 1981.

———. *Rabelais and His World.* Trans. Hélène Iswolsky. Bloomington: Indiana University Press, 1984.

Barthes, Roland. *S/Z.* Paris: Seuil, 1972.

Bartolozzi-Bustini, M. L. *La natura umana nel romanzo di un anonimo provenzale.* Milan: La Nuova Minerva, 1957.

Baumgartner, Emmanuèle. "Le défi du chevalier rouge dans *Perceval* et dans *Jaufre.*" *Le Moyen-Age* 83.2 (1977): 239–54.

————. "Le roman aux XIIe et XIIIe siècles dans la littérature occitane." In *Grundriss der romanischen Literaturen des Mittelalters: Band IV/i, Le Roman jusqu'à la fin du XIIIe siècle*, 627–44. Heidelberg: Winter, 1978.

Bec, Pierre. *Anthologie de la Prose Occitane du Moyen-Age*. 2 vols. Paris: Aubanel, 1977.

————. *Burlesque et Obscenité chez les troubadours: Pour une approche du contretexte médiéval*. Paris: Stock, 1984.

————. "Lyrique Profane et Paraphrase pieuse dans la poésie médiévale (XIIe et XIIIe siècles)." In *Jean Misrahi Memorial Volume: Studies in Medieval Literature*, edited by Hans R. Runte, 229–46. Columbia, S.C.: French Literature Publishing, 1977.

Beltran, Rafael. "*Tirant lo Blanc* i la biografia cavalleresca." In *Actes del Symposion Tirant lo Blanc*, 101–32.

Bergson, Henri. "Laughter." In *Comedy: An Essay on Comedy by George Meredith, Laughter: Henri Bergson, Appendix: The Meanings of Comedy by Wylie Sipher*, 61–192. New York: Doubleday, 1956.

Bloch, R. Howard. *The Scandal of the Fabliaux*. Chicago: University of Chicago Press, 1986.

Bond, Gerald A. *The Poetry of William VII, Count of Poitiers, IX Duke of Aquitaine*. New York: Garland, 1982.

Bourdillon, F. W., ed. *Aucassin et Nicolette*. 1919. Reprint, Manchester: Manchester University Press, 1930.

Boutière, Jean, and A. H. Schutz. *Biographies des Troubadours: Textes provençaux des XIIIe et XIVe siècles*. Paris: Nizet, 1964.

Brown, Homer Obed. "Of the Title of Things Real: Conflicting Stories." *ELH* 55.4 (1988): 917–54.

Bruckner, Matilda Tomaryn. *Interpretation, Truth, and Closure in Twelfth-Century French Fictions*. Philadelphia: University of Pennsylvania Press, 1993.

————. *Narrative Invention in Twelfth-Century Romance: The Convention of Hospitality (1160–1200)*. Lexington, Ky.: French Forum Publishers/FFM 17, 1980.

Brunel, Clovis, ed. *Jaufré: Roman Arthurien du XIIIe siècle en vers provençaux*. 2 vols. Paris: SATF, 1943.

Busby, Keith. "Courtly Literature and the Fabliaux: Some Instances of Parody." *ZRP* 102 (1986): 67–87.

————. *Gauvain in Old French Literature*. Amsterdam: Rodopi, 1980.

————. "'Moseiner Galvain l'astrucz' (*Jaufré*, v.488): Le Portrait de Gauvain d'après le roman de Jaufré et quelques troubadours de l'époque." In *Studia Occitanica*, 2:1–11.

Butturff, Douglas R. "The *Romance of Flamenca*: Spoilsport vs. Comic Hero." *KRQ* 19 (1972): 51–64.

Cacho Blecua, Juan Manuel. "El amor en el *Tirant lo Blanc*: Hipòlit y la emperadriu." In *Actes del Symposion Tirant lo Blanc*, 133–69.

Calin, William C. *The French Tradition and the Literature of Medieval England.* Toronto: University of Toronto Press, 1994.

———. "*Gui de Warewic* and the Nature of Late Anglo-Norman Romance." *Fifteenth-Century Studies* 17 (1990): 23–32.

———. "Towards a New Reading of *Jaufre*: A Dialogue with Marc-René Jung." In *Studia Occitanica,* vol.1: 13–21.

Caluwé, Jean-Michel. "*Flamenca* et l'enjeu lyrique. La méditation de Jaufre Rudel et de Peire Rogier." In *Troisième Congrès International,* 3:837–44.

Calvino, Italo. *Il Cavalliere inesistente.* Turin: Einaudi, 1966.

———. *The Uses of Literature.* Trans. Patrick Creagh. New York: Harcourt, Brace, Jovanovich, 1986.

Camproux, Charles. "Préface à Flamenca?" In *Ecrits sur les troubadours.* 2 vols. Montpellier: EDITAS/Occitania/IEU, 1984, 1:213–26.

Capellanus, Andreas. *De Amore: libri tres,* edited by E. Trojel. Munich: Eidos, 1964.

Centre d'Etudes Universitaires de l'Université de Montpellier and the S.F.A.I.E.O. *Troisième Congrès International de l'Association Internationale des Etudes Occitanes, Montpellier, 20–26 août 1990. Contacts de langues, de civilisations et intertextualité.* 3 vols. Montpellier: Université de Montpellier-III, 1992.

Cervantes, Miguel de. *Don Quixote de la Mancha.* 2 vols. Edited by Juan Bautista Avalle-Arce. Madrid: Editorial Alhambra, 1979.

———. *Don Quixote: The Ormsby Translation, Revised.* Ed. Joseph R. Jones and Kenneth Douglas. New York: W. W. Norton, 1981.

Chaucer, Geoffrey. *The Canterbury Tales.* Ed. F. N. Robinson. 1974. Reprint, Oxford: Oxford University Press, 1983.

Chevalier, Maxime. *Lectura y lectores en la Espana de los siglos XVI y XVII.* Madrid: Turner, 1976.

Chrétien de Troyes. *Le Chevalier de la charrete.* Ed. Mario Roques. Paris: Champion/CFMA 86, 1972.

———. *Yvain (Le Chevalier au Lion).* Ed. T. B. W. Reid. 1942. Reprint, Manchester: Manchester University Press, 1974.

———. *Le Conte du graal.* Geneva: Droz, 1959.

Cobby, Anne Elizabeth. *Ambivalent Conventions: Formula and Parody in Old French.* Amsterdam: Rodopi/Faux Titre 101, 1995.

Cormier, Raymond, ed. and trans. *Three Ovidian Tales of Love* (Piramus et Tisbé, Narcisus et Dané, *and* Philomena et Procné). New York: Garland, 1986.

Courcelles, Dominique de. "*Tirant lo Blanc* 'le meilleur roman du monde': Ecriture et impression d'un roman de chevalerie en Catalogne après la disparition de l'Empire chrétien d'Orient," *JMRS* 21.1 (1991): 103–28.

Dällenbach, Lucien. *Le récit spéculaire: essai sur la mise en abyme.* Paris: Seuil, 1977.

Damon, Phillip. "Courtesy and Comedy in *Le Roman de Flamenca.*" *RPhil* 17 (1963–64): 608–15.

Darrigrand, Jean-Pierre, ed. *L'Amour courtois, des troubadours à Febus: Flamenca*. Orthez: Per Noste, 1995.

Davis, Judith M. *"Audigier and the Poetics of Scatology."* In *Poetics of Love in the Middle Ages: Texts and Contexts*, edited by Moshé Lazar and Norris J. Lacy, 237–48. Fairfax, Va.: George Mason University Press, 1989.

Donaldson, E. Talbot. "Idiom of Popular Poetry in *The Miller's Tale*." In *Speaking of Chaucer*. New York: Norton, 1972.

Dragonetti, Roger. *Le gai savoir dans la rhétorique courtoise: Flamenca et Joufroi de Poitiers*. Paris: Seuil, 1982.

———. *Le Mirage des sources: l'art du faux dans le roman médiéval*. Paris: Seuil, 1987.

Dudley, Edward. *The Endless Text: Don Quixote and the Hermeneutics of Romance*. Albany: State University Press of New York, 1997.

Duran, Manuel. *"Tirant lo Blanc and some Modern Theories of the Novel."* In *Tirant lo Blanc*, edited by Solà-Solé, 39–70.

Eisenberg, Daniel. "Who Read the Romances of Chivalry?" *KRQ* 20 (1973): 209–33.

Elliott, J. H. "Self-Perception and Decline in Early Seventeenth-Century Spain." *Past and Present* 74 (1977): 41–61.

Estrada, Francisco López. "El *Tirante* castellano de 1511 y los libres de viajes." In *Actes del Symposion Tirant lo Blanc*, 441–70.

Fansler, Dean. "Metrical Romances in the Philippines." *Journal of American Folklore* 29 (1916): 203–34.

Finoli, Anna Maria. *Artes Amandi. Da Maître Elie ad Andrea Cappellano. Introduzione e testi*. Milan: Cisalpino, 1969.

Fleischman, Suzanne. "Dialectic Structures in *Flamenca*." *RF* 92.3 (1980): 223–46.

———. *"Jaufré* or Chivalry Askew: Social Overtones of Parody in Arthurian Romance." *Viator* 12 (1981): 101–29.

Flutre, Fernand. *Table des noms propres avec toutes leurs variantes figurant dans les romans du Moyen age écrits en français ou en provençal et actuellement publiés ou analysés*. Poitiers: Centre d'Etudes Supérieurs de Civilisation Médiévale, 1962.

Forster, Leonard. *The Icy Fire: Five Studies in European Petrarchism*. Cambridge: Cambridge University Press, 1969.

Frappier, Jean, ed. *La Mort le Roi Artu: Roman arthurien du XIIIe siècle*. Geneva: Droz, 1964.

Fraser, Veronica. "Humour and Satire in the Romance of *Jaufre*." *FMLS* 31.3 (1995): 223–33.

Frye, Northrop. *The Anatomy of Criticism: Four Essays*. New York: Atheneum, 1969; 1st ed. Princeton: Princeton University Press, 1957.

Gadea i Gambús, Ferran. "Joanot Martorell, Tirant lo Blanc, cavallers a la defensiva." In *Actes del Symposion Tirant lo Blanc*, 273–300.

Gamillscheg, Ernst. *Etymologisches Wörterbuch der französichen Sprache*. 2nd ed. Heidelberg: Winter 1969.

Genette, Gérard. *Palimpsestes: La littérature au second degré.* Paris: Seuil, 1982.

Gerald of Wales. *The Jewel of the Church.* Ed. and trans. John J. Hagen, O.S.A. Leiden: Brill, 1979.

Godefroy, Frédéric. *Dictionnaire de l'ancienne langue française.* 1889. Reprint, Nendeln, Liechtenstein: Kraus, 1969.

Goldin, Frederick. *Lyrics of the Troubadours and Trouvères.* New York: Anchor, 1973.

Gouiran, Gérard. "'Car tu es cavalliers e clercs' (*Flamenca*, v.1899): Guilhem ou le chevalier parfait." In *Le Clerc au Moyen-âge,* 197–214. Aix-en-Provence: Publications du CUERMA/Sénéfiance 37, 1995.

———. "L'Odeur de soufre des eaux thermales à propos de *Flamenca* et de textes médiévaux non-littéraires." In *L'Eau au Moyen-Age,* 173–84. Aix-en-Provence: Publications du CUERMA/Sénéfiance 15, 1983.

Graves, Rolande. *Flamenca: Variations sur les thèmes de l'amour courtois.* Vol. 5. New York: Peter Lang/American University Series 2, 1983.

Green, Dennis H. *Irony in the Medieval Romance.* Cambridge: Cambridge University Press, 1979.

Griffin, David A. "The Author of *Jaufre:* A Biographical Note on an Anonymous Poet." In *Studia Occitanica,* 2:309–17.

Grifoll, Isabel. "Per a una cosmètica del llibertí: Trufes literàries al cap. CLXXXIX del *Tirant lo Blanc.*" In *Actes del Symposion Tirant lo Blanc,* 317–59.

Grimm, Charles. *Etude sur le Roman de Flamenca: Poème provençal du XIIIe siècle.* Paris: Droz, 1930.

Gschwind, Ulrich. *Le Roman de Flamenca: nouvelle occitane du XIIIe siècle.* 2 vols. Berne: Francke, 1976.

Haidu, Peter. *Aesthetic Distance in Chrétien de Troyes: Irony and Comedy in "Cligès" and "Perceval."* Geneva: Droz, 1968.

———. "Making It (New) in the Middle Ages: Towards a Poetics of Alterity." *Diacritics* (Summer 1974): 1–11.

Harrison, Ann Tukey. "Arthurian Women in *Jaufre.*" In *Studia Occitanica,* 2:65–74.

Harrison, Ruth. "The Spirited Lady Through Nicolete to Rosalind." Diss. University of Oregon, 1974.

Hart, Thomas R. *Cervantes and Ariosto: Renewing Fiction.* Princeton: Princeton University Press, 1989.

———. "Comedy and Chivalry in *Tirant lo Blanc.*" In *The Age of the Catholic Monarchs, 1474–1516: Literary Studies in Memory of Keith Whinnom,* edited by Alan Deyermond and Ian Macpherson, 64–70. Liverpool: Liverpool University Press, 1989.

———. "*Tirant lo Blanc:* Between Romance and Epic." In *Letters and Society in Fifteenth-Century Spain: Studies Presented to P. E. Russell on his Eightieth Birthday,* edited by Alan D. Deyermond and Jeremy Lawrence. Llangrannog: Dolphin, 1993.

Hill, R. T., and Thomas G. Bergin, eds. *Anthology of the Provençal Troubadours.* 2 vols. 2nd ed. 1973. Reprint, New Haven: Yale University Press, 1975.

Hubert, M. J., and Marion E. Porter, eds. *The Romance of Flamenca*. Princeton: Princeton University Press, 1962.

Huchet, Jean-Charles. "De *Dilexi quoniam* à *Ailas! Que plans?* de la citation à l'intertexte dans *Flamenca*." In *Troisième Congrès International*, 3:957–66.

———. *L'Etreinte des Mots: Flamenca, entre poésie et roman*. Caen: Paradigme, 1993.

———. "*Jaufre* et *Flamenca*: Novas ou romans?" *RLR* 96.2 (1992): 275–300.

———. "*Jaufre* et le Graal." *Vox Romanica* 53 (1994): 156–74.

———. "Le Roman à nu: *Jaufré*." *Littérature* 74 (1989): 91–99.

———. *Le Roman occitan médiéval*. Paris: PUF, 1991.

———. "'Trouver' contre le livre." *RLR* 92 (1988): 19–40.

Huizinga, Johan. *The Autumn of the Middle Ages*. 1919. Reprint, Chicago: University of Chicago Press, 1996.

Hunt, Tony. "La parodie médiévale: le cas d'*Aucassin et Nicolette*." *Rom* 100 (1979): 341–81.

———. "Texte et Prétexte: Jaufre et Yvain." In *The Legacy of Chrétien de Troyes*, edited by Norris J. Lacy, Douglas Kelly, and Keith Busby, 125–42. Amsterdam: Rodopi, 1988.

Huot, Sylvia. *From Song to Book: The Poetics of Writing in Old French Lyric and Lyrical Narrative Poetry*. Ithaca: Cornell University Press, 1987.

Jauss, Hans-Robert. "The Alterity and Modernity of Medieval Literature." *NLH* 10.2 (1979): 181–227.

———. "Le sens de l'aventure dans le roman de *Jaufré*." In *Actes et Mémoires du Premier Congrès International de la Langue et Littérature du Midi de la France*, 28–33. Avignon: Palais du Roure, 1957.

Jewers, Caroline. "The Name of the Ruse and the Round Table: Occitan Romance and the Case for Cultural Resistance." *Neophilologus* 81 (1997): 187–200.

———. "Sentimental Education: The *Roman de Flamenca* and the Renaissance of the Ovidian Hero." In *Proceedings of the Medieval Association of the Mid-West*, edited by Mel Storm, 2:58–70. Emporia, Kans.: Emporia State University, 1993.

Jodogne, Omer. "Aucassin et Nicolette, Clarisse et Florent." In *Mélanges de Langue et de Littérature du Moyen-Age offerts à Jean Frappier*, 453–81. Geneva: Droz, 1970.

———. "La parodie et la pastiche dans *Aucassin et Nicolette*." *Cahiers de l'Association Internationale des Etudes Françaises* 12 (1960): 53–65.

Jung, Marc-René. "Lecture de *Jaufre*." In *Mélanges de langues et de littatures romanes offerts à Carl Theodor Gossen*, edited by Germán Colón and Robert Kopp, 1:427–51. Bern and Liège: Franke/Marche Romane, 1976.

Kaltenbach, Nikki L. *Le Roman de Jaufre: A Jungian Analysis*. New York: Peter Lang/Studies in the Humanities, Literature-Politics-Society 30, 1998.

Kay, Sarah. "*Flamenca* et le problème du déjà-dit." *RLR* 92.1 (1988): 41–60.

Keller, Hans Erich. *Studia Occitanica in Memoriam Paul Rémy*. 2 vols. Kalamazoo, Mich.: Medieval Institute Publications/WMU, 1986.

Kelly, Douglas. *The Art of Medieval French Romance.* Madison: University of Wisconsin Press, 1992.

———. *Sens and Conjointure in the* Chevalier de la charrette. The Hague: Mouton, 1966.

Ker, W. P. *Epic and Romance: Essays on Medieval Literature.* 1908. Reprint, New York: Dover, 1957.

Krueger, Roberta L. *Women Readers and the Ideology of Gender in Old French Verse Romance.* Cambridge: Cambridge University Press/Cambridge Studies in French 43, 1993.

Kundera, Milan. "The Depreciated Legacy of Cervantes." In *The Art of the Novel.* Paris: 1986. New York: Grove, 1988.

———. "Le jour où Panurge ne fera plus rire." Spec. issue of *L'Infini* 39 (1992).

Lacy, Norris J. "Courtliness and Comedy in *Aucassin et Nicolette.*" In *Essays in Early French Literature Presented to Barbara M. Craig,* 65–72. York, S.C: French Literature Publications, 1982.

———. "The Fabliaux and Comic Logic." *EsCr* 16.1 (1976): 39–45.

Lavaud, René, and René Nelli, eds. *Les Troubadours: Jaufre, Flamenca, Barlaam et Josaphat.* Vol. 1. Paris: Desclée de Brouwer, 1960.

———. *Les Troubadours: Le Trésor poétique de l'Occitanie.* Vol. 2. Paris: Desclée de Brouwer, 1966.

Leclanche, Jean-Luc, ed. *Le Conte de Floire et de Blanchefleur.* Paris: Champion, 1980.

Lejeune, Rita. "Flamenca: Fille fictive d'un comte de Namur." In *Littérature et société occitane au Moyen-Age,* 341–53. Liège: Marche Romane, 1979.

———. "La date du *Roman de Jaufré.* A propos d'une édition récente." *Le Moyen Age* 4 (1948): 257–99.

———. "Le calandrier du *Roman de Flamenca:* Contribution à l'étude de mentalités médiévales occitanes." In *Mélanges d'histoire littéraire, de linguistique et de philologie romanes offerts à Charles Rostaing,* edited by Jacques de Caluwé, Jean-Marie D'Heur, and René Dumas, 586–617. Liège: Marche Romane, 1974.

———. "Le Tournoi de Bourbon-L'Archambaud dans le *Roman de Flamenca:* Essai de datation de l'oeuvre." In *Mélanges de Philologie romane offerts à Charles Camproux,* 129–47. Montpellier: Centre d'Etudes Occitanes de l'Université Paul-Valéry, 1978.

Levin, Harry. *Contexts of Criticism.* Cambridge, Mass.: Harvard University Press, 1957.

Levy, Emile. *Petit Dictionnaire Provençal-Français.* Raphèle-lès-Arles: Marcel Petit, 1980.

Lewent, Kurt. *Bruchstücke des provenzalischen Versromans Flamenca.* Halle: Niemeyer, 1926.

Lewis, C. S. *The Allegory of Love.* Oxford: Clarendon Press, 1936.

———. *The Discarded Image.* Cambridge: Cambridge University Press, 1964.

Liborio, Mariantonia. "*Aucassin et Nicolette:* I limiti di una parodia." *CN* 30 (1970): 156–71.

Limentani, Alberto. *L'Eccezione narrativa: La Provenza medievale e l'arte del racconto*. Turin: Einaudi, 1977.

Lodge, David. *Small World*. London: Secker & Warburg, 1984.

Lorain, Marie-Thérèse. "Humeurs, Bains et Tisanes: L'Eau dans la médecine médiévale." In *L'Eau au Moyen-Age*, 261–73.

Luce-Dudemaine, Marie-Dominique. "Un nouvel art d'aimer, la contestation des valeurs courtoises dans *Flamenca*." *RLR* 92 (1988): 61–76.

Lukács, Georg. *The Theory of the Novel: A Historico-Philosophical Essay on the Forms of Great Epic Literature*. Trans. Anna Bostock. Berlin: Cassirer, 1920; Cambridge, Mass.: The MIT Press, 1977.

Maddox, Donald. "Generic Intertextuality in Arthurian Literature: The Specular Encounter." In *Text and Intertext in Medieval Arthurian Literature*. New York: Garland, 1996.

Marshall, J. H., ed. *The "Razos de Trobar" of Raimon Vidal and Associated Texts*. London: Oxford University Press, 1972.

Martin, June Hall. *Love's Fools: Aucassin, Troilus, Calisto and the Parody of the Courtly Lover*. London: Tamesis, 1972.

Martorell, Joanot, and Martí Joan de Galba. *Tirant lo Blanc*. Trans. David H. Rosenthal. London: Pan/Picador, 1985.

McDermott, Hubert. *Novel and Romance: The Odyssey to Tom Jones*. Totowa, N.J.: Barnes and Noble, 1989.

McKeon, Michael. *The Origins of the English Novel 1600–1740*. Baltimore: Johns Hopkins, 1987.

Ménard, Philippe, ed. *Fabliaux Français du moyen-âge*. 2 vols. Geneva: Droz, 1979.

———. *Le Rire et le sourire dans le roman courtois en France au Moyen-Age (1150–1250)*. Geneva: Droz, 1969.

Mermier, Guy. "Ceremonial and Pageantry in an Old Provençal Romance." *Michigan Academician* 15.3 (1983): 369–81.

Merrill, Charles J. "Reading *Tirant lo Blanc* as Medieval Romance." In *Tirant lo Blanc*, edited by Solà-Solé, 165–80.

Micha, Alexandre. "Le Roman en vers en France au XIIe siècle: Chrétien de Troyes." In *Grundriss Band IV/i*, 231–64.

Miralles, Carles. "La dona és el món." In *Actes del Symposion Tirant lo Blanc*, 485–540.

Misrahi, Jean, ed. *Le Roman des Sept Sages*. 1933. Reprint, Geneva: Slatkine, 1975.

Monson, Don Alfred. *Les "Ensenhamens" Occitans: Essai de délimitation du genre*. Paris: Klincksieck, 1981.

———. "L'Intertextualité du *Castía-Gilos*." *RLR* 96.2 (1992): 310–26.

Moore, Arthur. "Sir Thopas as Criticism of Fourteenth-Century Minstrelsy." *JEGP* 53 (1954): 532–45.

Morlhon, J. Fabre de. "*Le roman de Flamenca* dans son contexte historique." In *Mélanges . . . Charles Camproux*, 85–91.

Muscatine, Charles. *Chaucer and the French Tradition: A Study in Style and Meaning.* 1957. Berkeley: University of California Press, 1964.

———. *The Old French Fabliaux.* New Haven: Yale University Press, 1986.

Nelli, René, ed. *Ecrivains anti-conformistes du moyen-age occitan: La Femme et l'Amour.* Vol. 1. Paris: Phébus, 1977.

———. *Le Roman de Flamenca: Un art d'aimer occitanien du XIIIe siècle.* Carcassonne: Institut d'Estudis Occitans, 1989.

Nelli, René, and René Lavaud. "Examen du *roman de Flamenca.*" *CdS* 44.339 (Feb. 1957): 192–214.

Nykrog, Per. *Les Fabliaux.* Geneva: Droz, 1973.

Ollier, Marie-Louise. "Le récit bref au Moyen-Age: Les *Lais* de Marie de France ou le recueil comme forme." In *La Nouvelle: Genèse, codification, et rayonnement d'un genre médiéval. Actes du Colloque international de Montréal (McGill University, 14–16 octobre 1982),* edited by Michelangelo Picone, Giuseppe Di Stefano, and Pamela D. Stewart, 64–79. Montréal: Plato Academic Press, 1983.

Olson, Elder. *The Theory of Comedy.* Bloomington: Indiana University Press, 1968.

Olson, Paul. "*Le Roman de Flamenca:* History and Literary Convention." *SP* 55 (1958): 7–23.

Ovidius, Naso Publius. *The Art of Love and Other Poems.* Trans. J. H. Mozley. Cambridge, Mass.: Harvard University Press, 1962.

Paterson, Linda. *The World of the Troubadours: Medieval Occitan Society, c. 1100–c. 1300.* Cambridge, U.K.: Cambridge University Press, 1993.

Pearsall, Derek. *The Canterbury Tales.* London: Allen & Unwin, 1985.

Pelan, Margaret M., ed. *Floire et Blancheflor: Second Version.* Paris: Ophrys, 1975.

Pierce, Frank. "The Role of Sex in *Tirant lo Blanc.*" *Estudis Romànics* 10 (1962): 291–300.

Pigman, G. W. "Versions of Imitation in the Renaissance." *RQ* 33 (1980): 1–32.

Pillet, Alfred, and Henry Carstens. *Bibliographie der Troubadours.* Halle: Max Niemeyer Verlag, 1933.

Pirot, François. *Recherches sur les connaissances littéraires des troubadours occitans et catalans des XIIe et XIIIe siècles: Les "sirventes-ensenhamens" de Guerau de Cabrera, Giraut de Calanson et Bertrand de Paris.* Barcelona: Real Academía de Buenas Letras, 1972.

Preminger, Alex, Frank J. Warnke, and O. B. Hardison Jr., eds. *The Princeton Dictionary of Poetry and Poetics.* Princeton: Princeton University Press, 1974.

Rabelais, François. *Oeuvres Complètes.* Ed. Guy Demerson. Paris: Seuil, 1973.

Ramos, Rafael. "*Tirant lo Blanc, Lancelot du Lac,* y el *Libre de l'ordre de cavalleria.*" *La Corónica* 23.2 (1995): 74–87.

Raupach, Manfred. "Elias Fonsalada Kritische Ausgabe." *ZRP* 90 (1974): 141–73.

Rémy, Paul. "Plaintes sur la déchéance des moeurs dans *Jaufré* et *Flamenca. Rom Gand* 16 (1976): 175–93.

Richmond, Velma Bourgeois. *The Legend of Guy of Warwick.* New York: Garland/Garland Studies in Medieval Literature 14, 1996.

Ricks, Christopher. "Laurence Sterne." In *The Novelist As Innovator,* 16–33, 24–5. London: British Broadcasting Corporation, 1965.

Riley, E. C. *Cervantes's Theory of the Novel,* Oxford: Clarendon Press, 1962.

Riquer, Martín de. "Cervantes y la caballeresca." In *Suma cervantina,* edited by J. B. Avalle-Arce and E. C. Riley, 273–92. London: Tamesis, 1973.

———. *Història de la Literatura Catalana: II.* 3 vols. Barcelona: Ariel, 1964.

———. "Los problemas del roman provenzal de *Jaufré.* Recuil de travaux offert à M. Clovis Brunel, membre de l'Institut, directeur honnoraire de l'Ecole des Chartes, 1: 435–61. Paris: Société de l'Ecole des Chartes, 1955.

———, ed. *Los Trovadores.* 3 vols. Barcelona: Planeta, 1976.

———, ed. *Tirant lo Blanc I altres escrits de Joanot Martorell.* 2nd ed. Barcelona: Clàssics Catalans Ariel 1, 1982.

Riquer, Martín de, and Mario Vargas Llosa, eds. *El Combate Imaginario: Las Cartas de Batalla de Joanot Martorell.* Barcelona: Barral, 1972.

Rose, Margaret A. *Parody: Ancient, Modern, and Post-Modern.* Cambridge: Cambridge University Press, 1993.

Roubaud, Sylvia. "Chevalier contre chien: L'étrange duel du 'Tirant lo Blanc.'" In *Mélanges de la Casa de Velázquez,* 131–54. New ed. Madrid: Casa de Velázquez, 1970.

Sankovitch, Tilde. "*The Romance of Flamenca*: The Puppeteer and the Play." *Neophil* 60.1 (1976): 8–19.

Sansone, Giuseppe. "*Tirant lo Blanc* et le vie del romanzo." In *Actes del Symposion Tirant lo Blanc,* 557–72.

Sargent, Barbara Nelson. "Parody in *Aucassin et Nicolette:* Some Further Considerations." *FR* 43 (1970): 597–605.

Scholes, Robert, and Robert Kellogg. *The Nature of Narrative.* New York: Oxford University Press, 1966.

Segre, Cesare. "La communicación indirecta en *Tirant lo Blanc.*" In *Actes del Symposion Tirant lo Blanc,* 573–86.

———. "What Bakhtin Left Unsaid: The Case of the Medieval Romance." In *Romance: Generic Transformation from Chrétien de Troyes to Cervantes,* edited by Kevin Brownlee and Marina Scordilis Brownlee, 23–46. Hanover, N.H.: University Press of New England, 1985.

Shedd, Gordon M. "*Flamenca:* A Medieval Satire on Courtly Love." *ChauRev* 2.1 (1967): 43–65.

Smith, Nathaniel B. "*Aucassin et Nicolette* as Stylistic Comedy." *KRQ* 26 (1979): 479–90.

Solà-Solé, Josep, ed. *Tirant lo Blanc: Text and Context. Proceedings of the Second Catalan Symposium (Volume in Memory of Pere Masdevall).* New York: Peter Lang/Catalan Studies: Translations and Criticism 11, 1993.

Solterer, Helen. "*Sermo* and *juglar:* Language Games in *Flamenca.*" In *The Spirit of the Court: Selected Proceedings of the Fourth Congress of the International Courtly Literature Society (Toronto, 1983),* edited by Glyn S. Burgess and Robert A. Taylor, 330–38. Cambridge: Brewer, 1985.

Spraycar, Rudy S. "Genre and Convention in *Aucassin et Nicolette.*" *RR* 76 (1983): 94–115.

Stebbins, Charles E. "L'Inspiration possible de Marcabru relativement aux thèmes du bon vieux temps et de la déchéance morale du monde dans *Flamenca.*" *RLR* 82 (1976): 185–97.

———. "Religious and Erotic Elements in *Flamenca:* The Uneasy Alliance." *RPhil* 35.1 (1981): 217–23.

———. "The Theme of the 'Clerc-Chevalier' in the 13th-Century Old Provençal Romance of *Flamenca.*" *RLV* 44.2 (1978): 508–16.

Stevens, John. *Medieval Romance: Themes and Approaches.* London: Hutchinson, 1973.

Sutherland, D. R. "The Love Meditation in Courtly Literature." In *Studies in Medieval French Literature Presented to Alfred Ewert,* 165–93. Oxford: Oxford University Press, 1961.

Symposion Tirant lo Blanc. *Actes del Symposion Tirant lo Blanc.* Barcelona: Quaderns Crema, 1993.

Tattersall, Jill. "Shifting Perspectives and the Illusion of Reality in *Aucassin et Nicolette.*" *FS* 38 (1984): 257–67.

———. "Social Observation and Comment in *Aucassin et Nicolette.*" *NeuMitt* 86 (1985): 551–65.

Terry, Arthur. "Character and Role in *Tirant lo Blanc.*" In *Essays in Narrative Fiction in the Iberian Peninsula in Honour of Frank Pierce,* 177–95. Oxford: Dolphin, 1982.

———. *A Literary History of Spain: Catalan Literature.* London: Ernest Benn, 1977.

Tobler, Adolf, and Erhard Lommatzsch. *Altfranzösisches Wörterbuch.* Wiesbaden: Franz Steiner, 1976.

Topsfield, Leslie T. *Chrétien de Troyes: A Study of the Arthurian Romances.* Cambridge: Cambridge University Press, 1981.

———. "Intention and Ideas in *Flamenca.*" *MAe* 35.1 (1966): 119–23.

Torres-Alcalà, Antonio. "Satirical Tradition in Courtly Narrative." In *Josep Maria Solà-Solé: Homage, Homenaje, Homenatge (Miscelánea de estudios de amigos y discípulos),* edited by Antonio Torres-Alcalà, Victorio Agüera, and Nathaniel B. Smith. Barcelona: Puvill, 1984.

———. "*Tirant lo Blanc:* Between the Spirit and the Flesh." In *Tirant lo Blanc,* edited by Solà-Solé, 203–12.

Trojel, E., ed. *Ovid: De Amore.* Munich: Eidos, 1964.

van Beysterveldt, Antony. "*Jaufré* y la *Crónica de Tablante de Ricamonte.*" In *Studia Occitanica,* 2:203-9.

Vance, Eugene. "*Aucassin et Nicolette* as a Medieval Comedy of Signification and Exchange." In *The Nature of Medieval Narrative,* edited by Minnette Grunmann-Gaudet and Robin F. Jones, 57–76. Lexington, Ky.: French Forum Publishing, 1980.

Van der Horst, C. H. M., ed. *Blandin de Cornouaille.* The Hague: Mouton, 1974.

Van Marle, Raimond. *L'Iconographie de l'art profane au moyen-âge et à la Renaissance et la décoration des demeures: La Vie quotidienne.* Vol. 1. 1931. Reprint, New York: Hacker, 1971.

Vargas Llosa, Mario. "Carta de batalla por Tirant lo Blanc." *Revista de Occidente* 70 (1969): 1–21.

———. *Carta de batalla por Tirant lo Blanc.* Barcelona: Seix Barral, 1991.

Villalmanzo, Jesus. *Joanot Martorell: Biografía ilustrada y diplomatario.* Valencia: Ajuntament de Valencia, 1995.

Vitz, Evelyn Birge. *Orality and Performance in Early French Romance.* Woodbridge, Suffolk, U.K.: D. S. Brewer, 1999.

Voelker, P. "Die Bedeutungsentwicklung des Wortes Romans." *ZRP* 10 (1886): 485–525.

Wartburg, Walther von. *Französisches Etymologisches Wörterbuch.* Tübingen: Photomechanischer Neudruck, 1948.

Watt, Ian. *The Rise of the Novel.* Berkeley: University of California Press, 1965.

Weigand, Hermann J. "*Flamenca*: A Post-Arthurian Romance of Courtly Love." *Euphorion* 58.2 (1964): 129–52.

Wicks, Ulrich. *Picaresque Narrative, Picaresque Fictions: A Theory and Research Guide.* New York: Greenwood, 1989.

Williamson, Edwin. *The Half-Way House of Fiction: Don Quixote and Arthurian Romance.* Oxford: Clarendon Press, 1984.

Yates, Alan. "*Tirant lo Blanc*: The Ambiguous Hero." In *Hispanic Studies in Honour of Frank Pierce,* edited by John England, 181–98. Sheffield: Department of Hispanic Studies, 1980.

Zak, Nancy C. *The Portrayal of the Heroine in Chrétien de Troyes's* Erec et Enide, Gottfried von Strassburg's *Tristan, and* Flamenca. Göppingen: Kümmerle Verlag, 1983.

Zumthor, Paul. *Essai de Poétique médiévale.* Paris: Seuil, 1972.

———. "Genèse et évolution du genre." In *Grundriss Band IV/i,* 60–122.

INDEX

Caroline Jewers is an associate professor of French at the University of Kansas in Lawrence. She has published articles on the troubadours and *trobairitz*, French and Occitan romances, medievalism, and film.